Shojo Beat

Ultra Maniac™

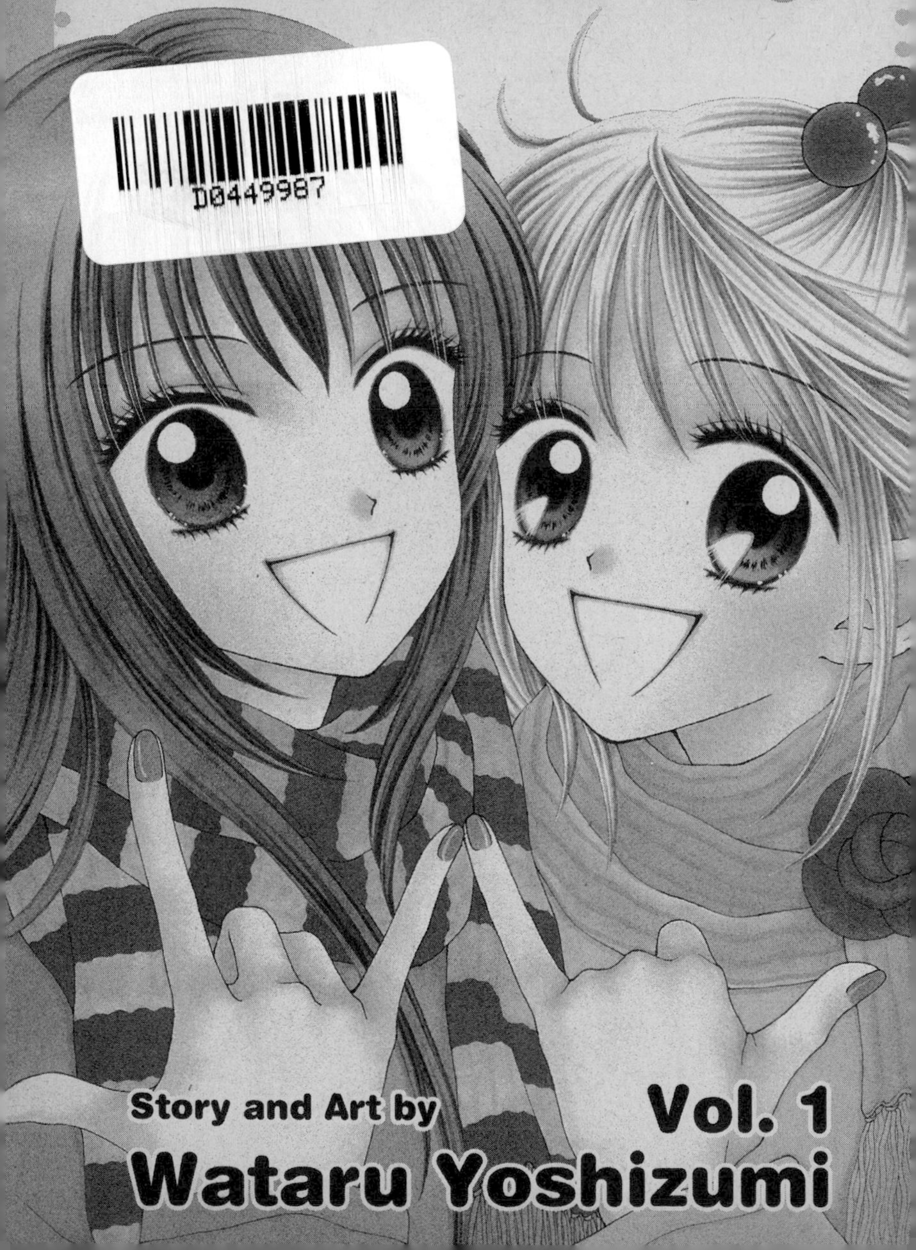

Vol. 1

Story and Art by
Wataru Yoshizumi

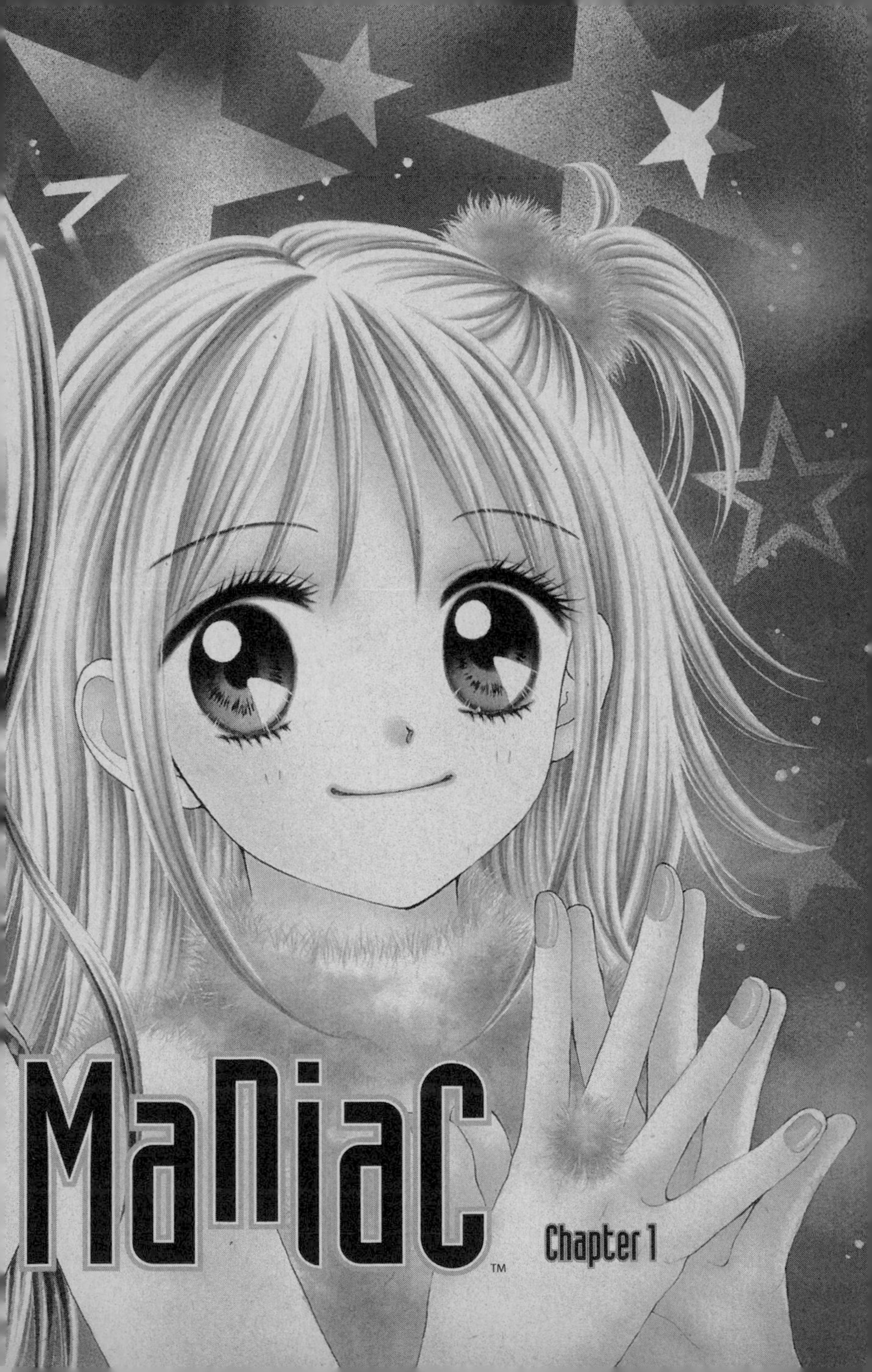
ManiaC™
Chapter 1

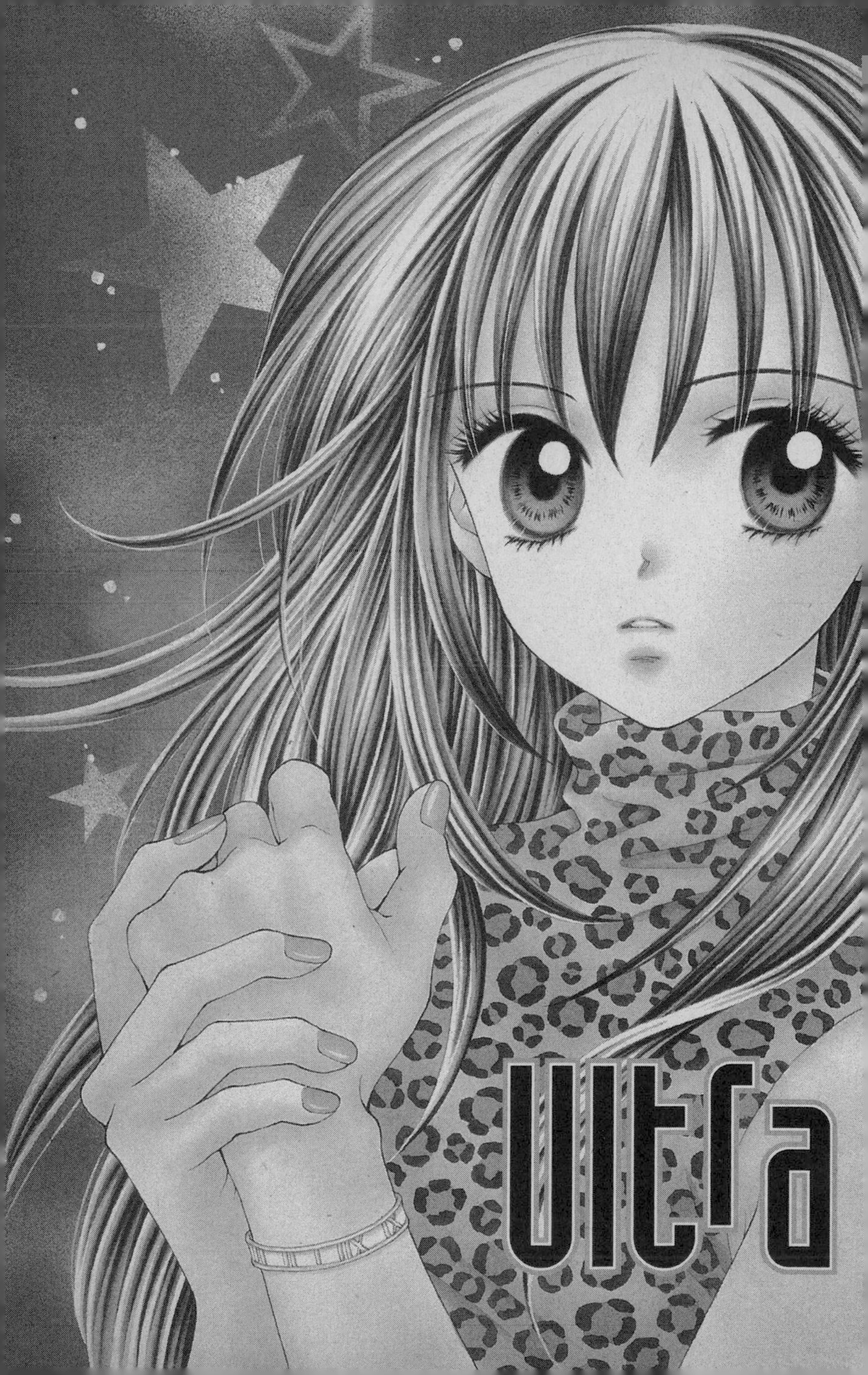
Ultra

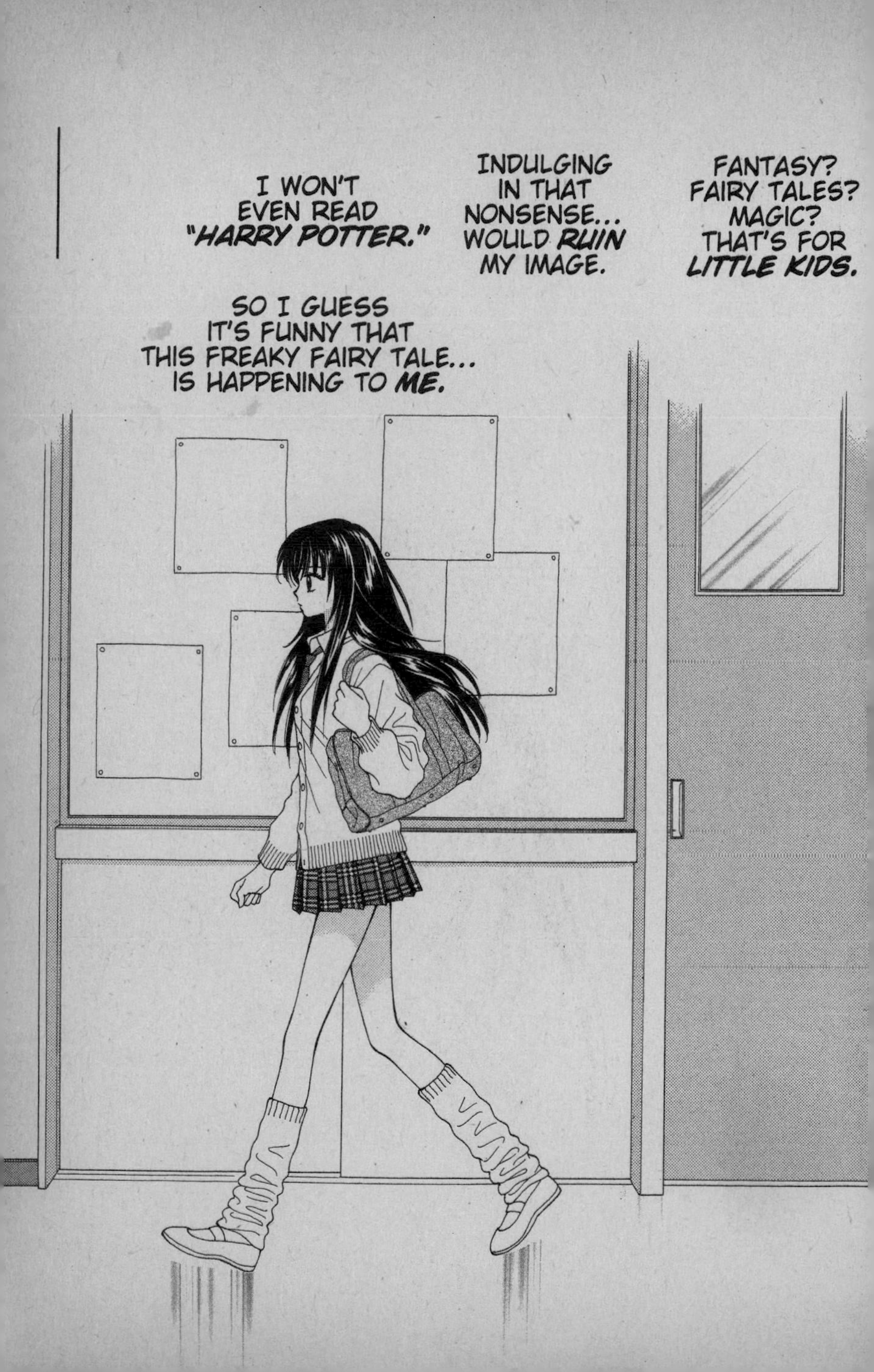
FANTASY? FAIRY TALES? MAGIC? THAT'S FOR *LITTLE KIDS.*
INDULGING IN THAT NONSENSE... WOULD *RUIN* MY IMAGE.
I WON'T EVEN READ *"HARRY POTTER."*
SO I GUESS IT'S FUNNY THAT THIS FREAKY FAIRY TALE... IS HAPPENING TO *ME.*

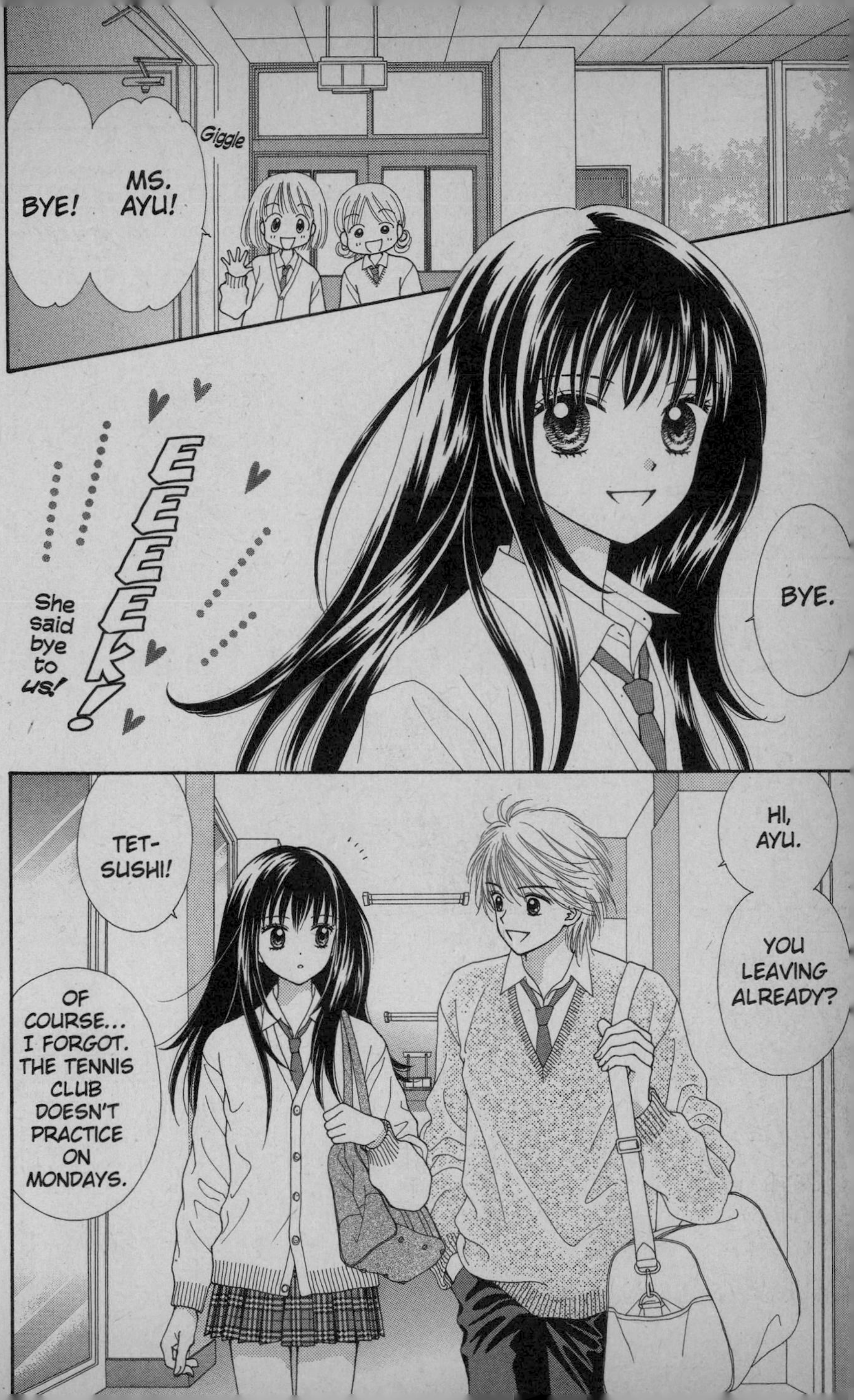
Giggle
MS. AYU!
BYE!
BYE.
EEEEEK!
She said bye to us!
HI, AYU.
YOU LEAVING ALREADY?
TET-SUSHI!
OF COURSE... I FORGOT. THE TENNIS CLUB DOESN'T PRACTICE ON MONDAYS.

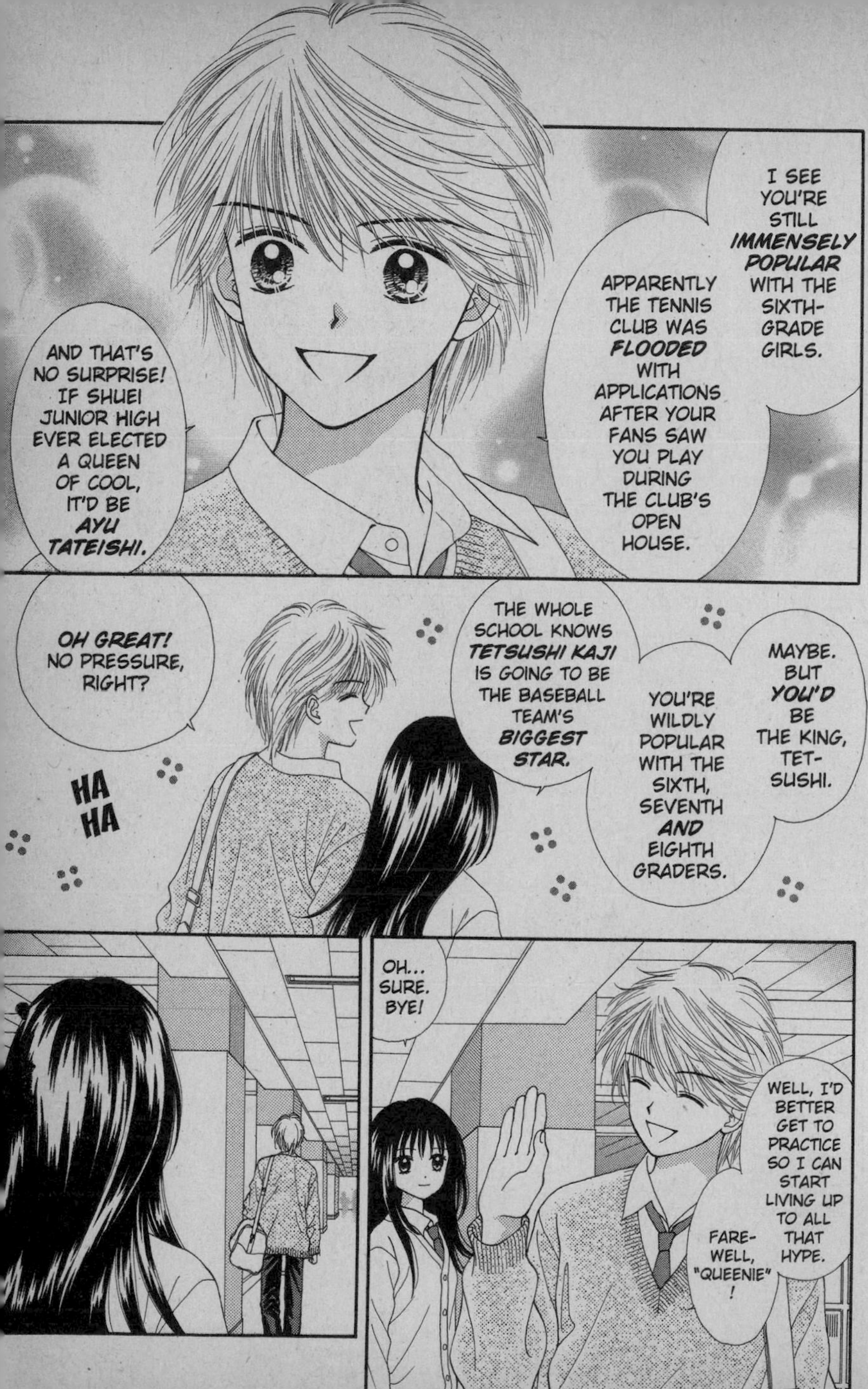
I SEE YOU'RE STILL IMMENSELY POPULAR WITH THE SIXTH-GRADE GIRLS.
APPARENTLY THE TENNIS CLUB WAS FLOODED WITH APPLICATIONS AFTER YOUR FANS SAW YOU PLAY DURING THE CLUB'S OPEN HOUSE.
AND THAT'S NO SURPRISE! IF SHUEI JUNIOR HIGH EVER ELECTED A QUEEN OF COOL, IT'D BE AYU TATEISHI.
MAYBE. BUT YOU'D BE THE KING, TET-SUSHI.
YOU'RE WILDLY POPULAR WITH THE SIXTH, SEVENTH AND EIGHTH GRADERS.
THE WHOLE SCHOOL KNOWS TETSUSHI KAJI IS GOING TO BE THE BASEBALL TEAM'S BIGGEST STAR.
OH GREAT! NO PRESSURE, RIGHT?
HA HA
WELL, I'D BETTER GET TO PRACTICE SO I CAN START LIVING UP TO ALL THAT HYPE.
FAREWELL, "QUEENIE"!
OH... SURE. BYE!

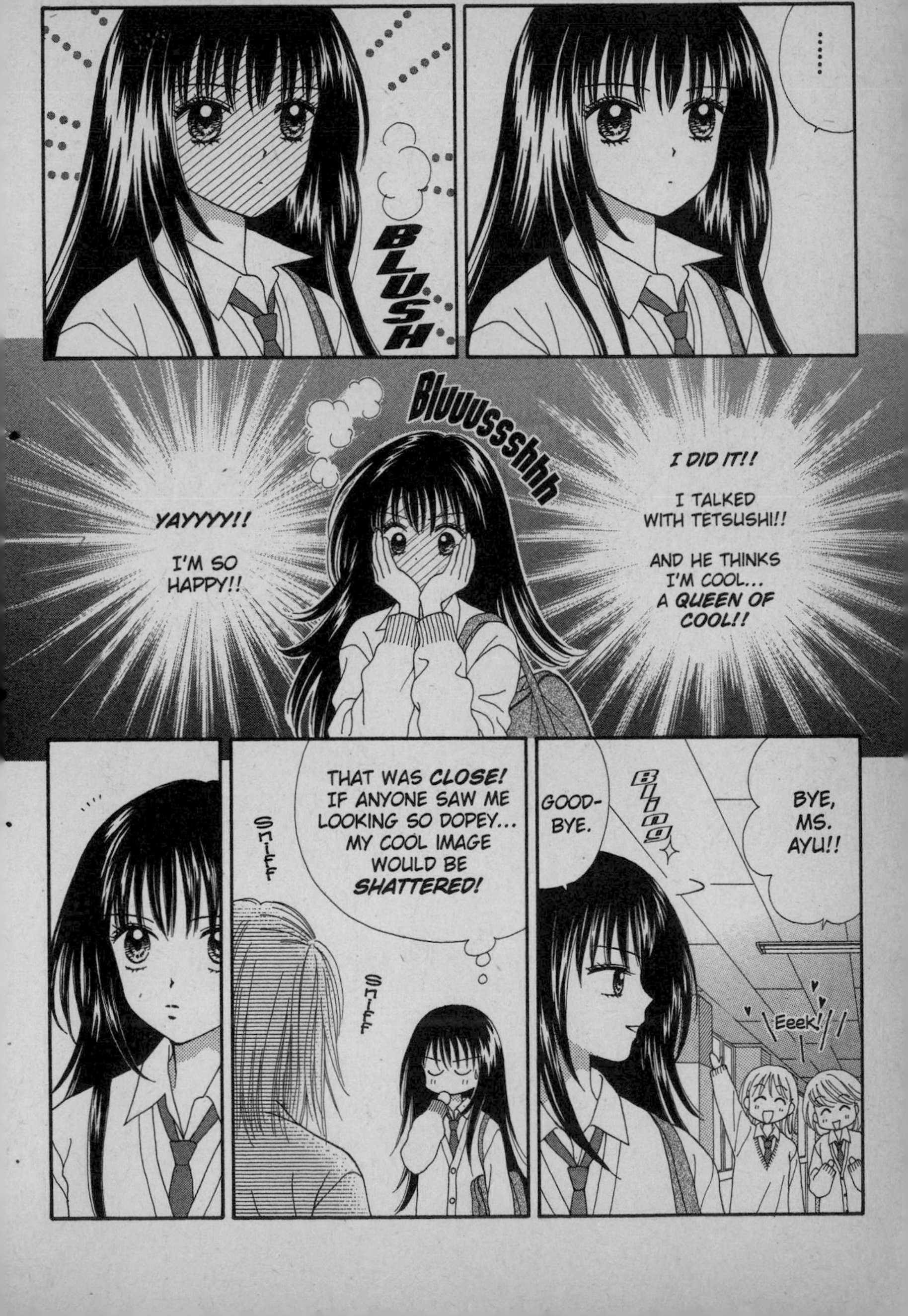
……
BLUSH
Bluuussshhh
I DID IT!!
I TALKED WITH TETSUSHI!!
AND HE THINKS I'M COOL… A QUEEN OF COOL!!
YAYYYY!!
I'M SO HAPPY!!
BYE, MS. AYU!!
Bling
GOOD-BYE.
Eeek!
THAT WAS CLOSE! IF ANYONE SAW ME LOOKING SO DOPEY… MY COOL IMAGE WOULD BE SHATTERED!
SNIFF
SNIFF

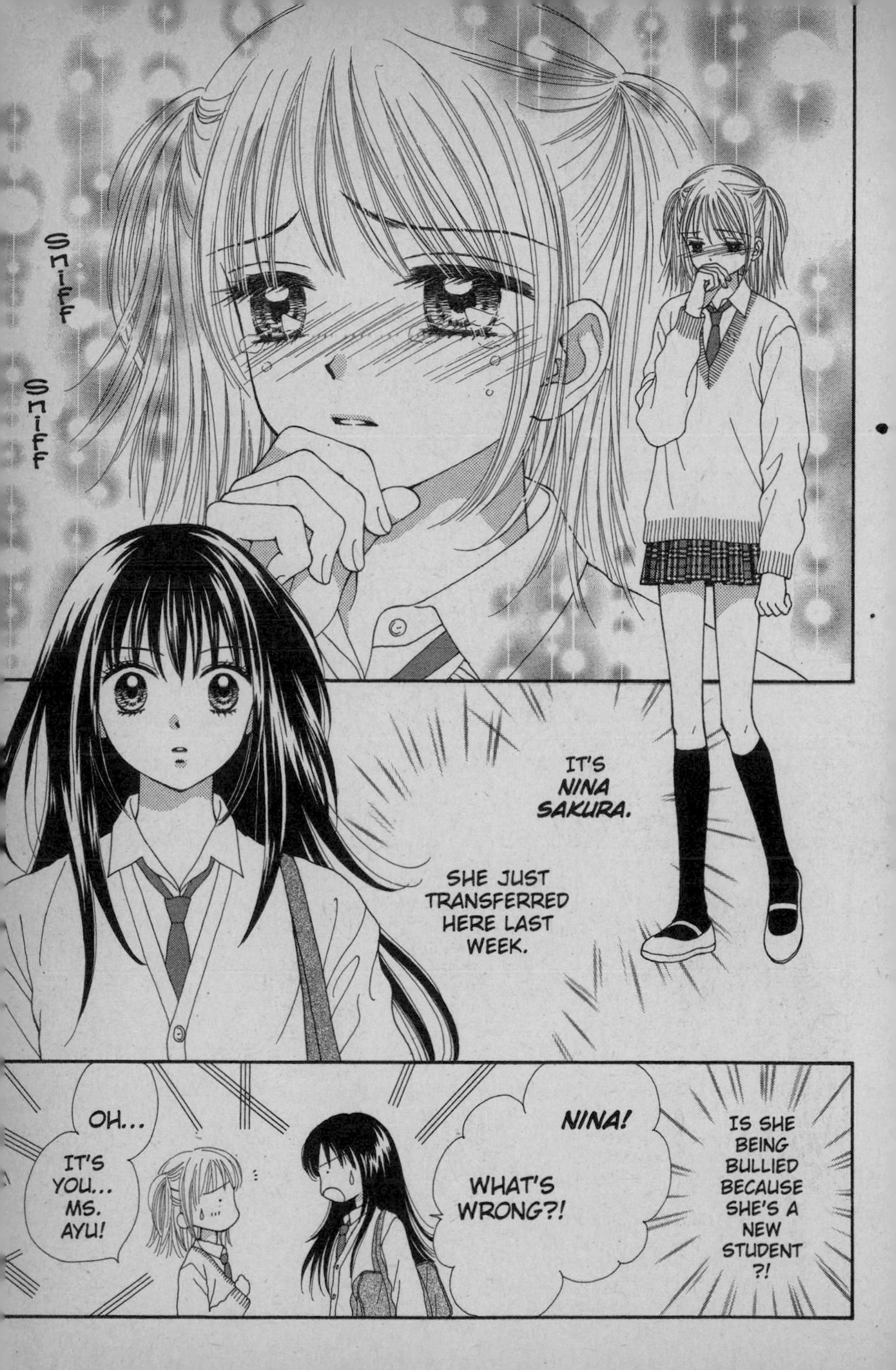
SNIFF
SNIFF
IT'S NINA SAKURA.
SHE JUST TRANSFERRED HERE LAST WEEK.
IS SHE BEING BULLIED BECAUSE SHE'S A NEW STUDENT?!
NINA!
WHAT'S WRONG?!
OH...
IT'S YOU... MS. AYU!

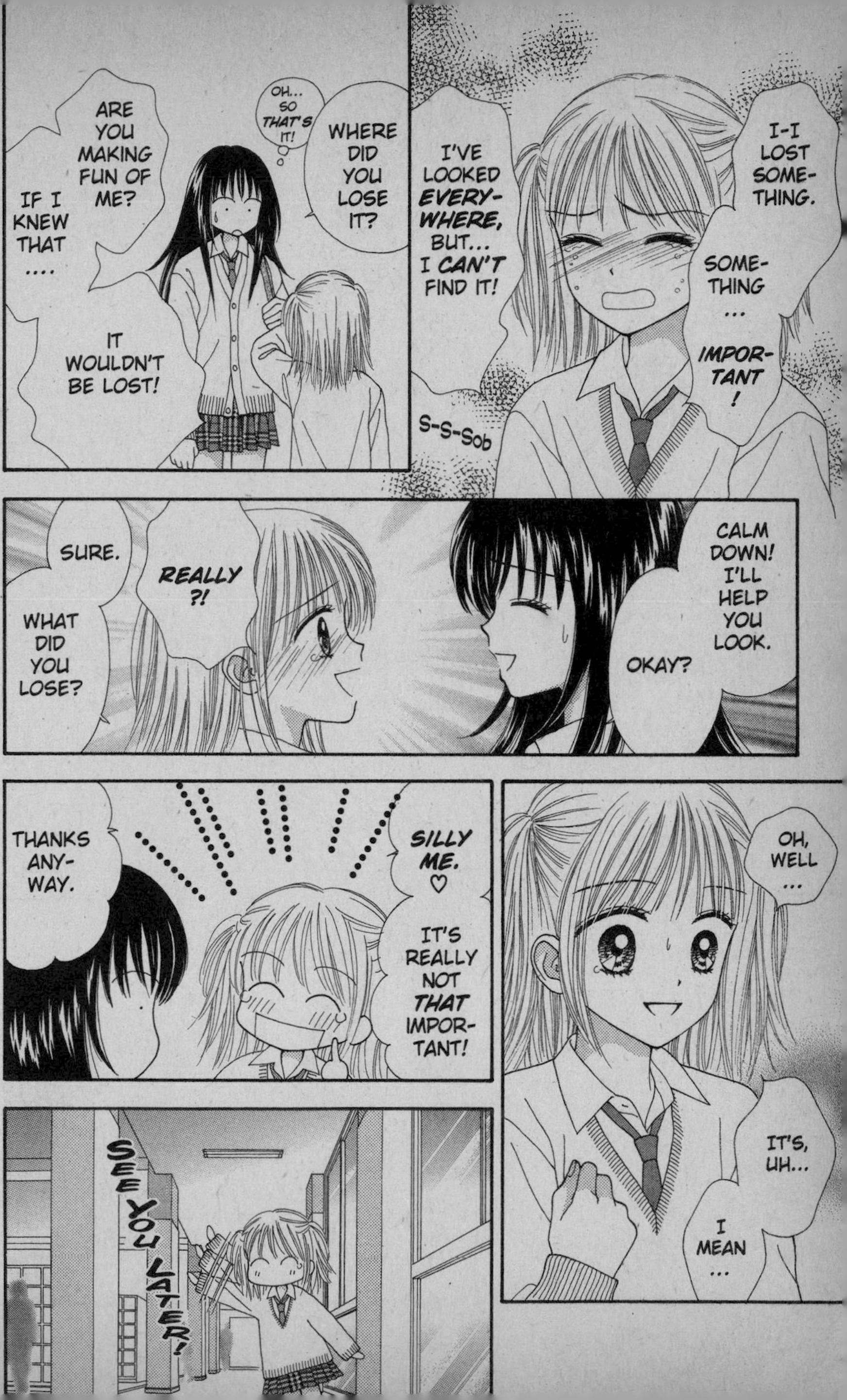
I-I LOST SOMETHING.
SOMETHING... IMPORTANT!
I'VE LOOKED EVERYWHERE, BUT... I CAN'T FIND IT!
S-S-Sob
WHERE DID YOU LOSE IT?
OH... SO THAT'S IT!
ARE YOU MAKING FUN OF ME?
IF I KNEW THAT ....
IT WOULDN'T BE LOST!
CALM DOWN! I'LL HELP YOU LOOK.
OKAY?
REALLY?!
SURE.
WHAT DID YOU LOSE?
OH, WELL...
IT'S, UH...
I MEAN...
SILLY ME. ♡
IT'S REALLY NOT THAT IMPORTANT!
THANKS ANYWAY.
SEE YOU LATER!

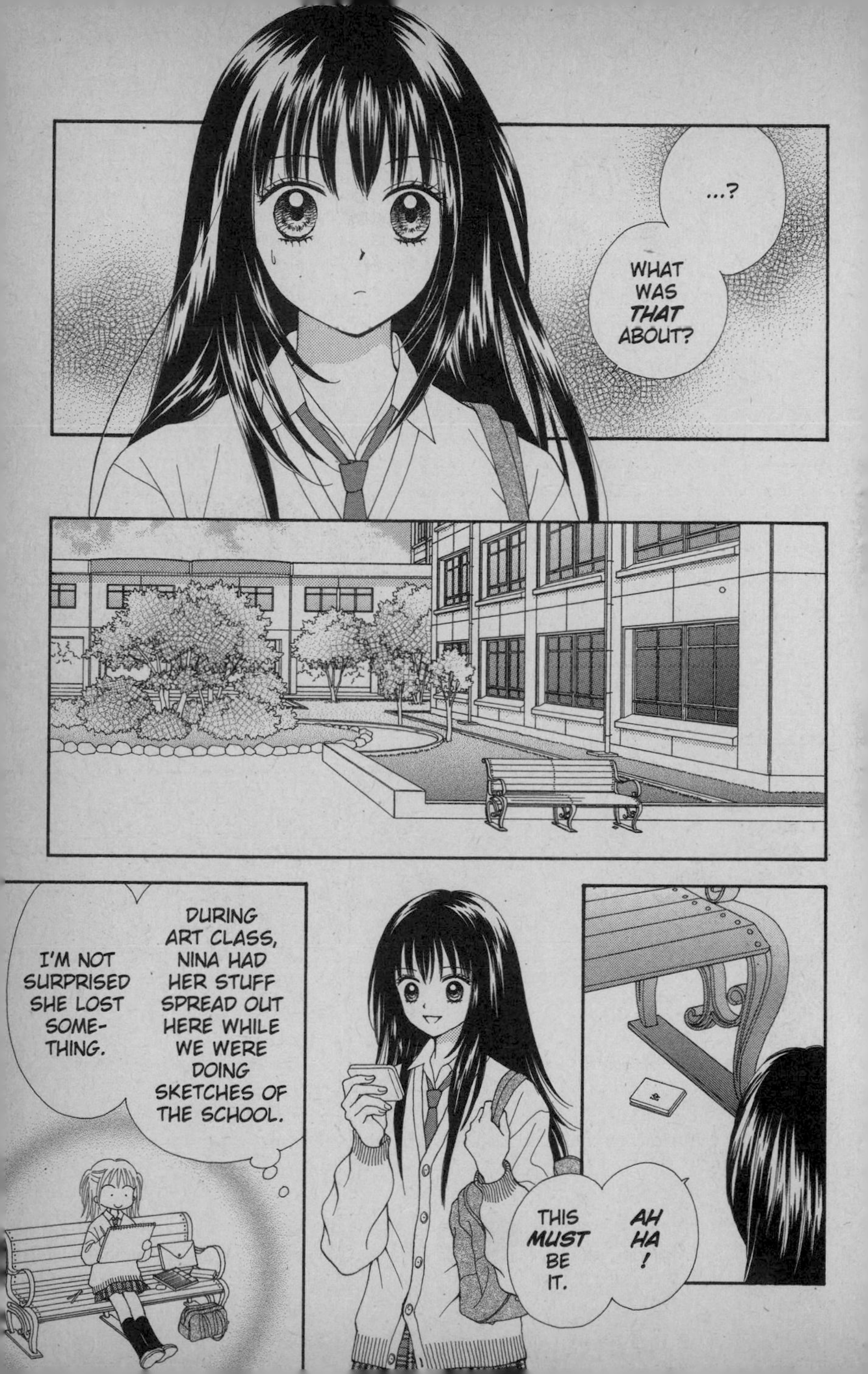
...?
WHAT WAS *THAT* ABOUT?
AH HA!
THIS *MUST* BE IT.
DURING ART CLASS, NINA HAD HER STUFF SPREAD OUT HERE WHILE WE WERE DOING SKETCHES OF THE SCHOOL.
I'M NOT SURPRISED SHE LOST SOME-THING.

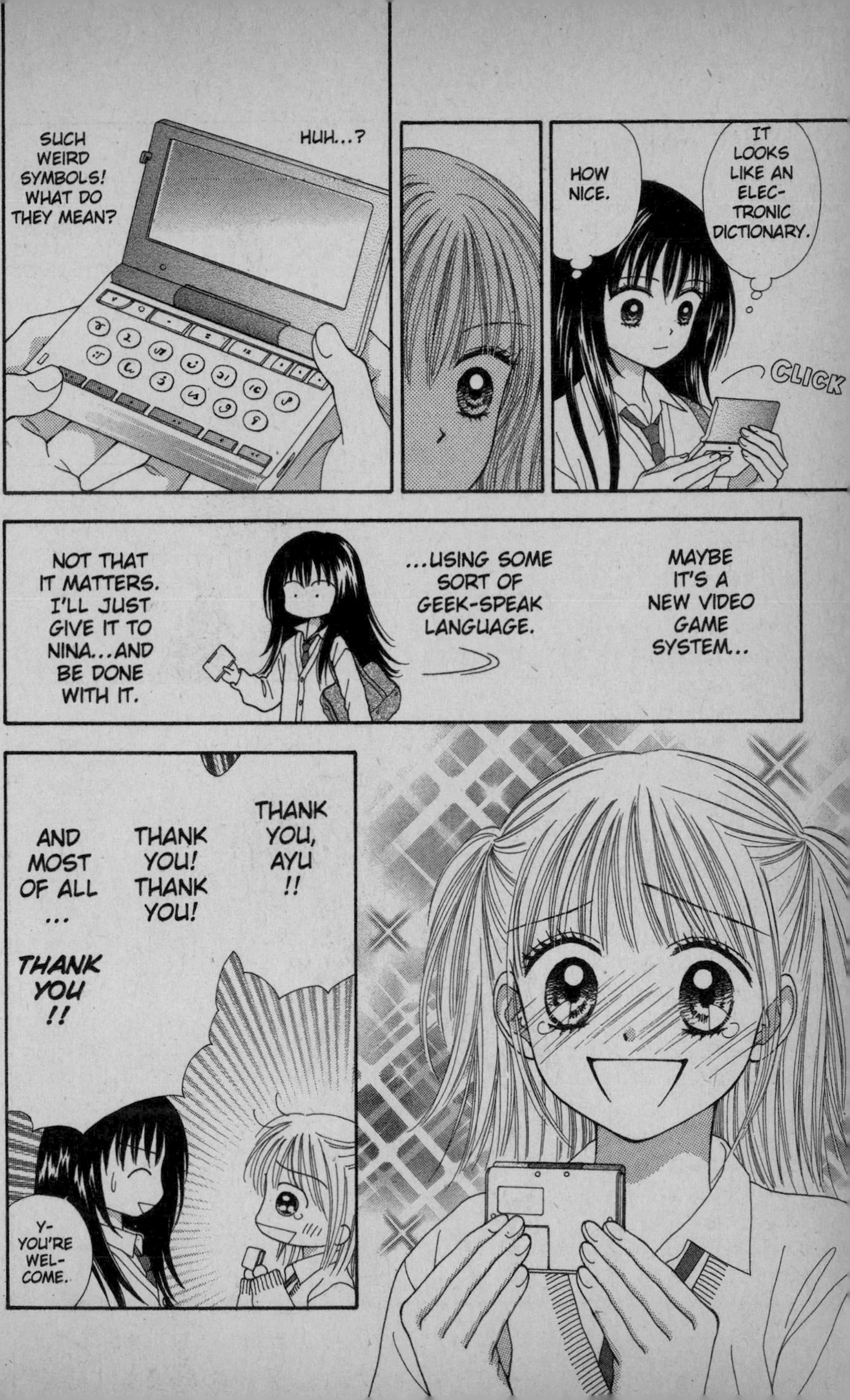
IT LOOKS LIKE AN ELEC-TRONIC DICTIONARY.
HOW NICE.
CLICK
HUH...?
SUCH WEIRD SYMBOLS! WHAT DO THEY MEAN?
MAYBE IT'S A NEW VIDEO GAME SYSTEM...
...USING SOME SORT OF GEEK-SPEAK LANGUAGE.
NOT THAT IT MATTERS. I'LL JUST GIVE IT TO NINA...AND BE DONE WITH IT.
THANK YOU, AYU !!
THANK YOU! THANK YOU!
AND MOST OF ALL ...
THANK YOU !!
Y-YOU'RE WEL-COME.

FREE TALK 1

Hi! I'm Wataru Yoshizumi. Thanks so much for reading my thirtieth comic, "Ultra Maniac."

This is a big deal for me because it's my first (!!) fantasy series. (Of course, I did write a short comic once that had a sci-fi flavor to it. It was called "Anaza Dei". . . oops, I mean "Another Day.")

Another reason I'm excited about "Ultra Maniac" is that it features another first for me. For the first time (!!), I'm doing a comic in which two girls are the main characters!

Whenever I begin production, I always take to heart that "I'm going to create something that's different from what I've written before." But, I feel, the fantasy genre is really more of a direct challenge to me.

Unlike my character, Ayu, I've never deliberately shunned fantasy. Still, doing a fantasy series is going to be a challenge for me. . . and, I hope, fun for you!

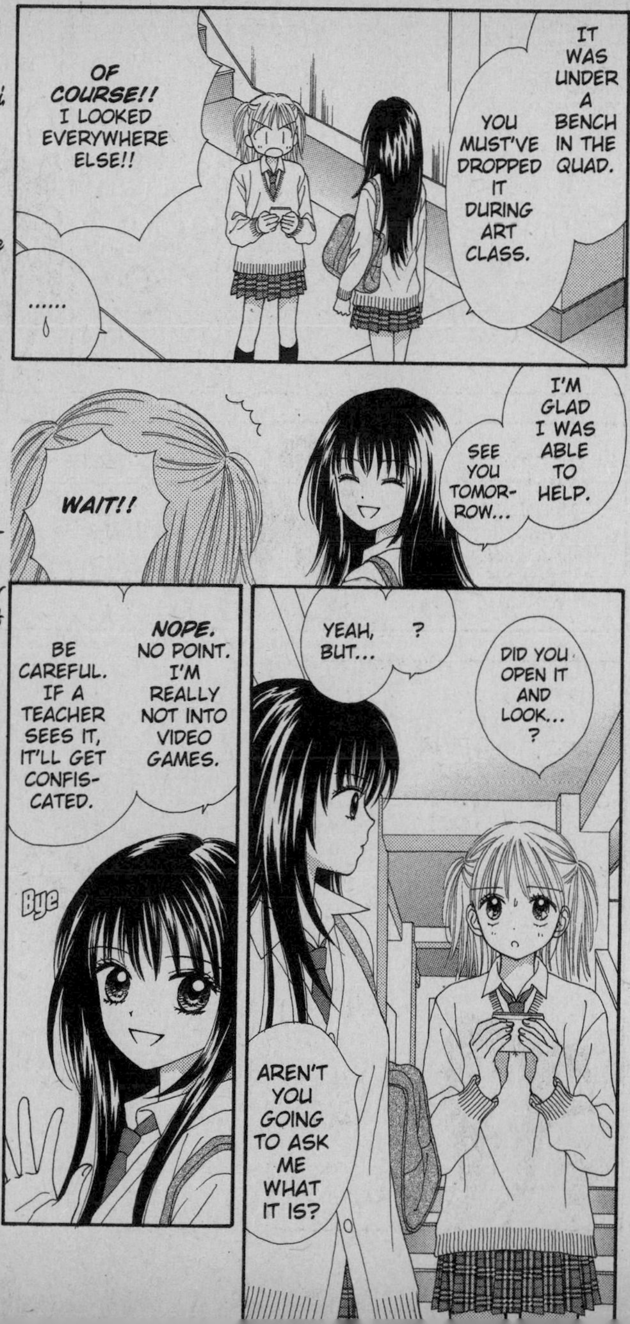
IT WAS UNDER A BENCH IN THE QUAD.
YOU MUST'VE DROPPED IT DURING ART CLASS.
OF COURSE!! I LOOKED EVERYWHERE ELSE!!
......
I'M GLAD I WAS ABLE TO HELP.
SEE YOU TOMORROW...
WAIT!!
DID YOU OPEN IT AND LOOK...?
?
YEAH, BUT...
AREN'T YOU GOING TO ASK ME WHAT IT IS?
NOPE. NO POINT. I'M REALLY NOT INTO VIDEO GAMES.
BE CAREFUL. IF A TEACHER SEES IT, IT'LL GET CONFISCATED.
Bye

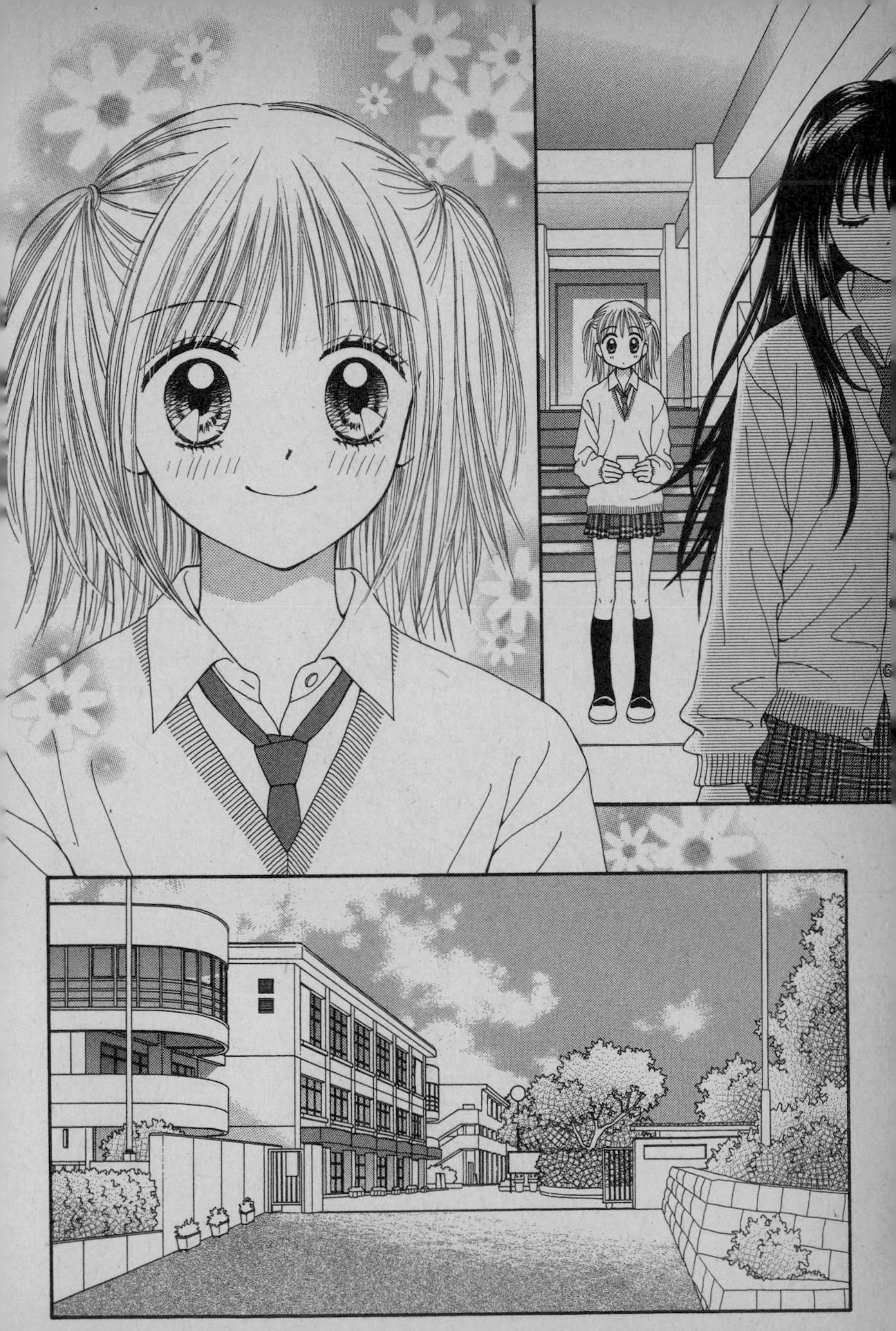

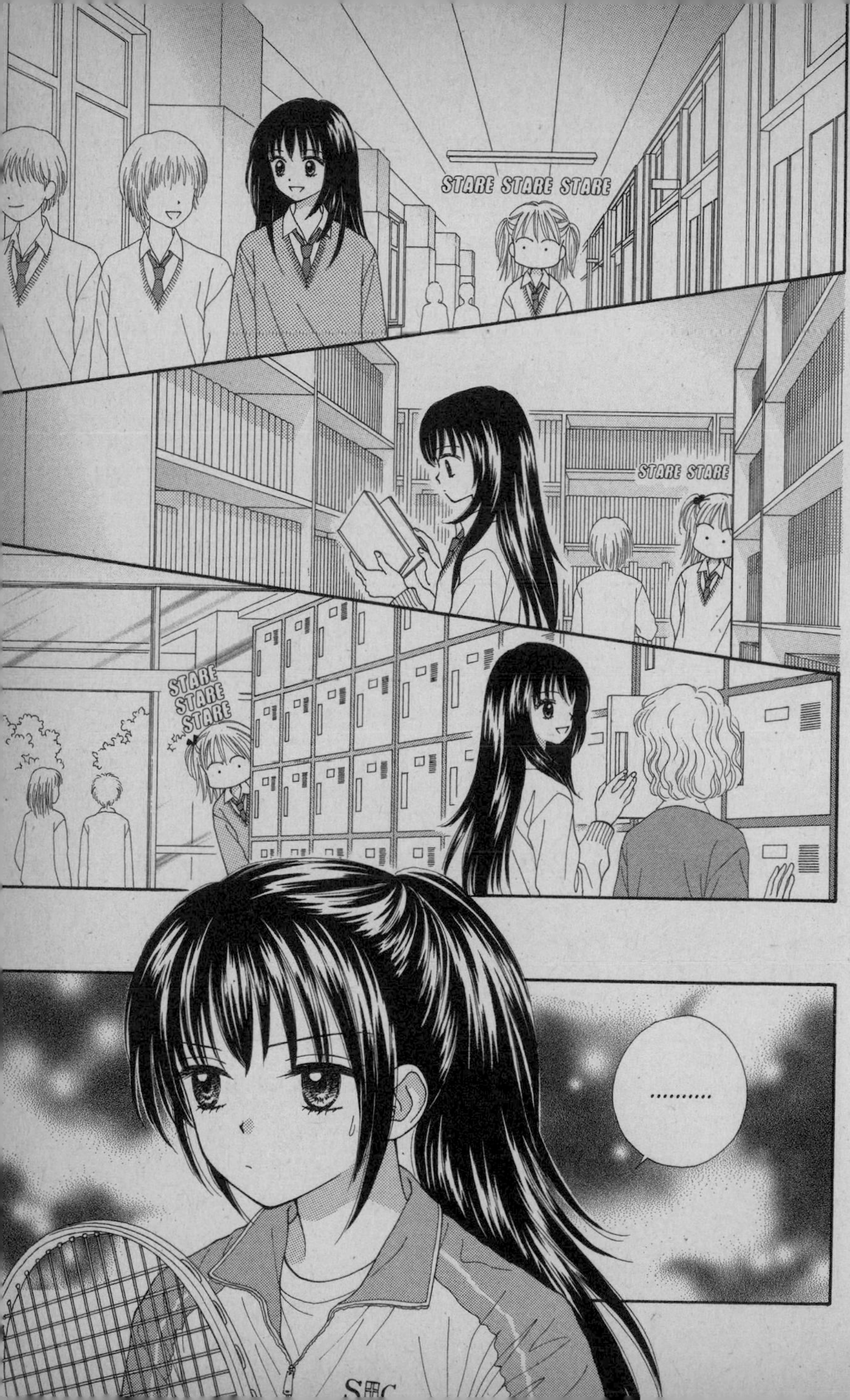
STARE STARE STARE
STARE STARE
STARE STARE STARE
....

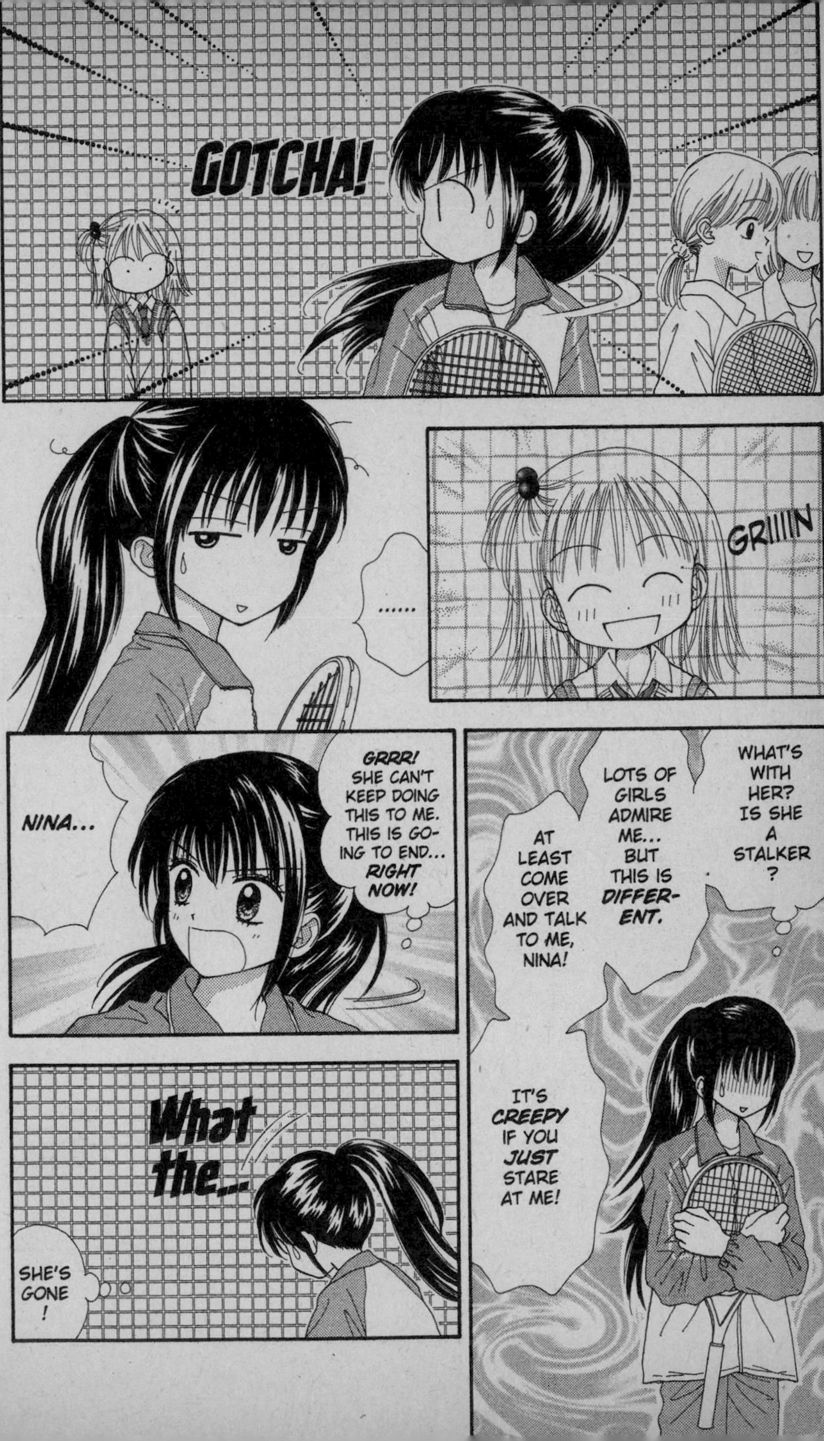
GOTCHA!
GRIIIIN
......
WHAT'S WITH HER? IS SHE A STALKER?
LOTS OF GIRLS ADMIRE ME... BUT THIS IS DIFFERENT.
AT LEAST COME OVER AND TALK TO ME, NINA!
IT'S CREEPY IF YOU JUST STARE AT ME!
GRRR! SHE CAN'T KEEP DOING THIS TO ME. THIS IS GOING TO END... RIGHT NOW!
NINA...
What the...
SHE'S GONE!

FREE TALK 2

If you mention **Ribon Comics**, most people think of fantasy stories. That's probably because one of **Ribon's** most famous comics is "Tokimeki Tonight." It's a series with a very strong fantasy image.

And that image was very much on my mind when I started this series. As a **Ribon** author, I wanted to challenge myself--**at least once**--in this genre. But I've never had the confidence to actually do it. So I kept postponing it. . .until now.

I thought, "If I just do it, I might be surprised. It might be easier than it looks!

"And, because I don't know a lot about traditional fantasy stories, I'll probably do it differently than every-one else. And that might make my series new and original!"

At least that's my hope. Ha! Ha!

It's hard, but I guess it's just part of my evolution as a manga creator! And it's good for me to study and learn, isn't it?

I have to admit, that after having done so much manga, the idea of studying seems like a luxury. . .and a little pretentious.

Despite that, I'm sucking it up and tackling the job!

By the way, in a previous comic's Free Talk, I wrote about "fantasy storylines I wanted to write." But that story and this work are a little different. I changed my mind. I do that sometimes. Ha! Ha!

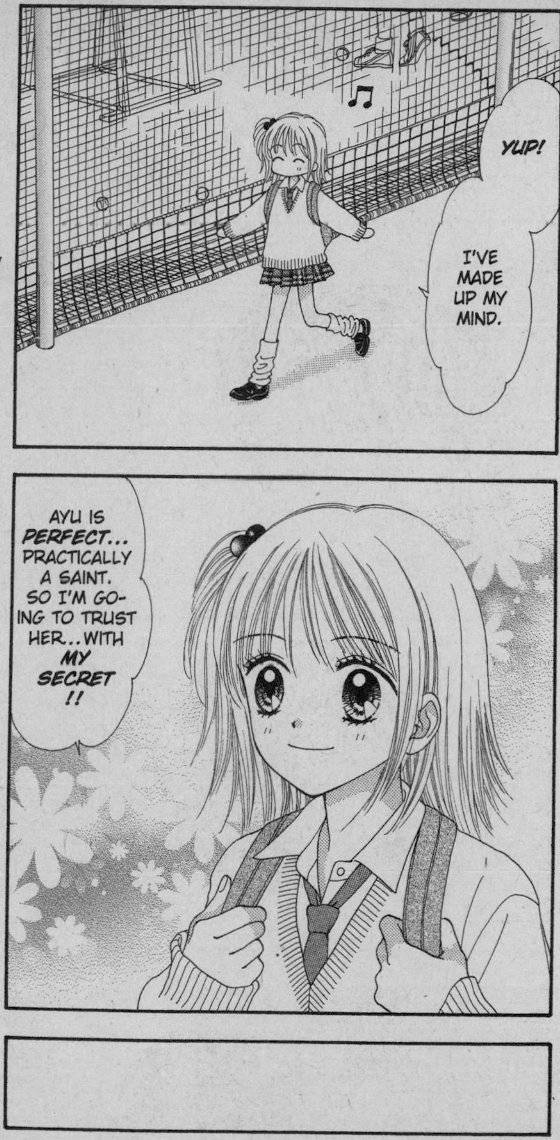
YUP!
I'VE MADE UP MY MIND.
AYU IS PERFECT... PRACTICALLY A SAINT. SO I'M GO-ING TO TRUST HER...WITH MY SECRET !!

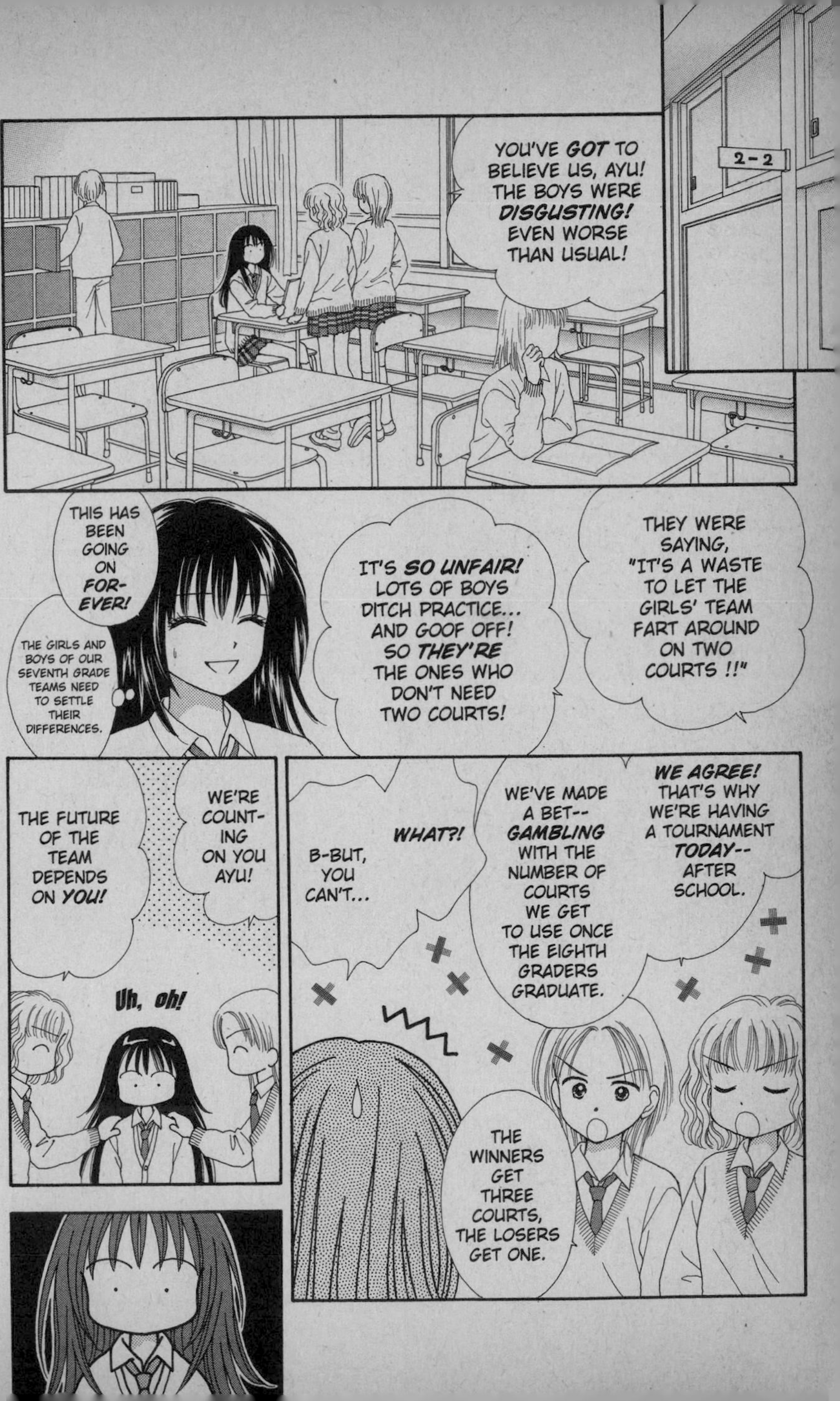
2-2
YOU'VE *GOT* TO BELIEVE US, AYU! THE BOYS WERE ***DISGUSTING!*** EVEN WORSE THAN USUAL!
THEY WERE SAYING, "IT'S A WASTE TO LET THE GIRLS' TEAM FART AROUND ON TWO COURTS !!"
IT'S ***SO UNFAIR!*** LOTS OF BOYS DITCH PRACTICE... AND GOOF OFF! SO ***THEY'RE*** THE ONES WHO DON'T NEED TWO COURTS!
THIS HAS BEEN GOING ON ***FOR-EVER!***
THE GIRLS AND BOYS OF OUR SEVENTH GRADE TEAMS NEED TO SETTLE THEIR DIFFERENCES.
WE AGREE! THAT'S WHY WE'RE HAVING A TOURNAMENT ***TODAY***-- AFTER SCHOOL.
WE'VE MADE A BET-- ***GAMBLING*** WITH THE NUMBER OF COURTS WE GET TO USE ONCE THE EIGHTH GRADERS GRADUATE.
WHAT?!
B-BUT, YOU CAN'T...
THE WINNERS GET THREE COURTS, THE LOSERS GET ONE.
WE'RE COUNTING ON YOU AYU!
THE FUTURE OF THE TEAM DEPENDS ON ***YOU!***
Uh, oh!

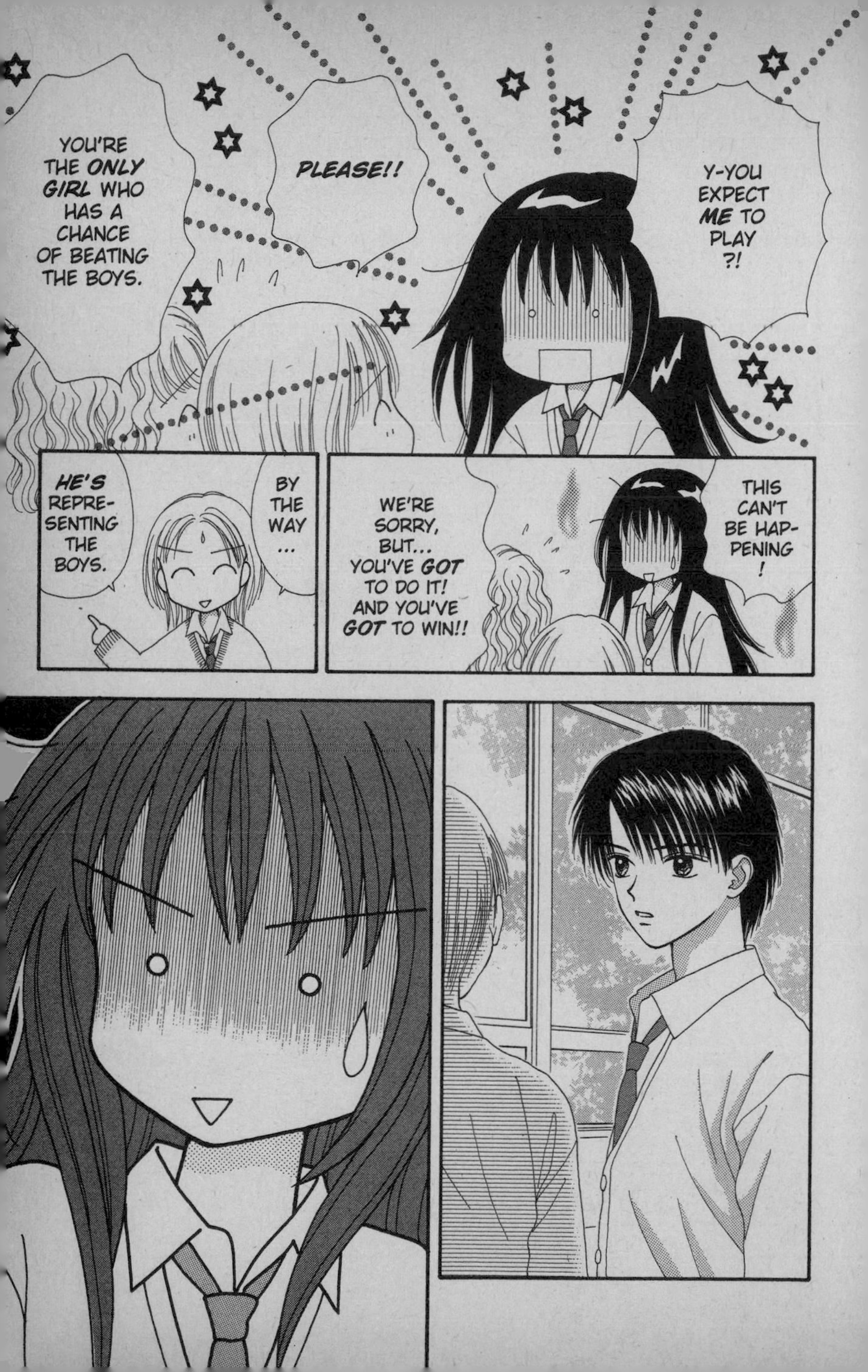
Y-YOU EXPECT ME TO PLAY ?!
PLEASE!!
YOU'RE THE ONLY GIRL WHO HAS A CHANCE OF BEATING THE BOYS.
THIS CAN'T BE HAPPENING!
WE'RE SORRY, BUT... YOU'VE GOT TO DO IT! AND YOU'VE GOT TO WIN!!
BY THE WAY ...
HE'S REPRESENTING THE BOYS.

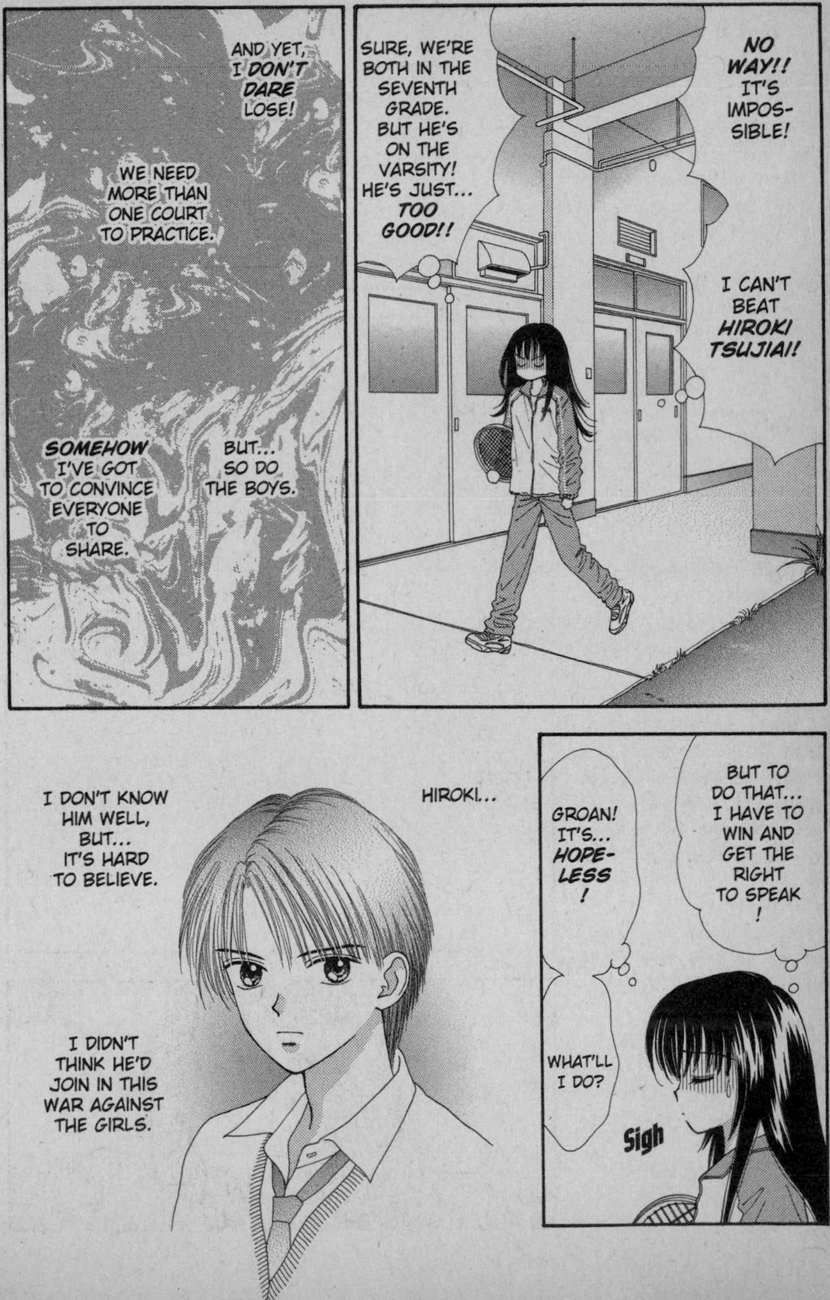
NO WAY!! IT'S IMPOSSIBLE!
SURE, WE'RE BOTH IN THE SEVENTH GRADE. BUT HE'S ON THE VARSITY! HE'S JUST... TOO GOOD!!
I CAN'T BEAT HIROKI TSUJIAI!
AND YET, I DON'T DARE LOSE!
WE NEED MORE THAN ONE COURT TO PRACTICE.
BUT... SO DO THE BOYS.
SOMEHOW I'VE GOT TO CONVINCE EVERYONE TO SHARE.
BUT TO DO THAT... I HAVE TO WIN AND GET THE RIGHT TO SPEAK!
GROAN! IT'S... HOPELESS!
WHAT'LL I DO?
Sigh
HIROKI...
I DON'T KNOW HIM WELL, BUT... IT'S HARD TO BELIEVE.
I DIDN'T THINK HE'D JOIN IN THIS WAR AGAINST THE GIRLS.

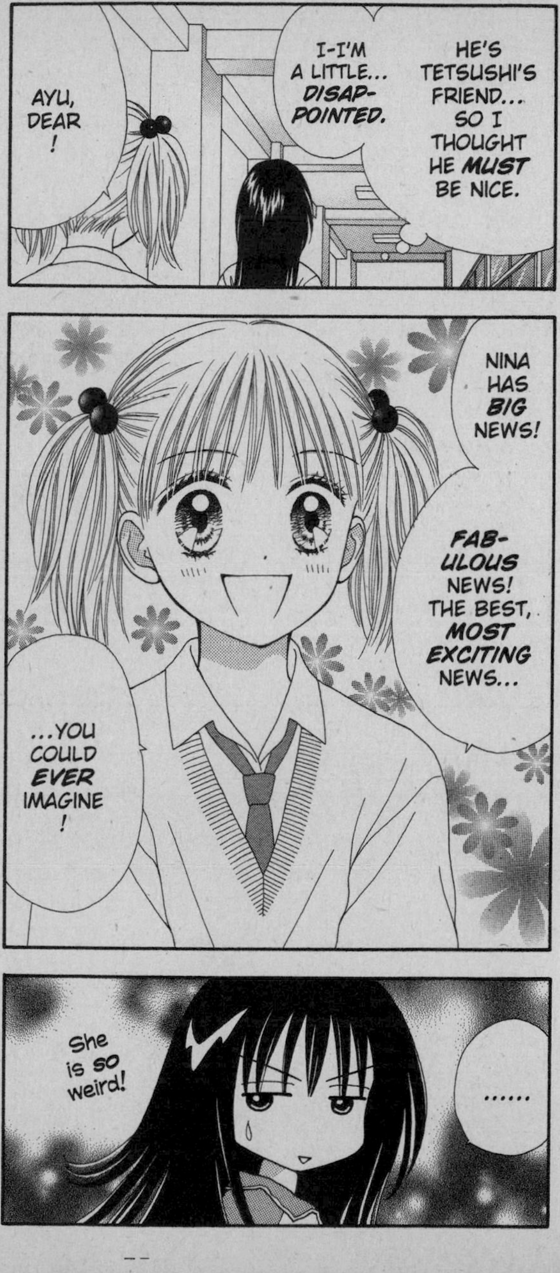
HE'S TETSUSHI'S FRIEND... SO I THOUGHT HE MUST BE NICE.
I-I'M A LITTLE... DISAP-POINTED.
AYU, DEAR!
NINA HAS BIG NEWS!
FAB-ULOUS NEWS! THE BEST, MOST EXCITING NEWS...
...YOU COULD EVER IMAGINE!
......
She is so weird!

FREE TALK 3

For a long time, I'd been thinking of doing a story about a devil boy who transferred to a school. He and the main character, a girl, both fall in love at first sight and become a couple. I was sure they'd be a very funny couple.

However, I changed my mind because I thought it would be boring if the couple got together right away.

Plus, a friend suggested that I take two of my "beautiful females--who are normally supporting characters--and make them main characters."

I thought, "Hey, that might be good, too."

And so, Ayu and Nina were instantly created.

I originally wanted to use the name "Ayu" for the main character of my series "Random Walk." But, about that time, there was a singer--Ms. Ayumi Hamazaki--who became famous. So I nixed that.

But enough time has passed now that I figured it would be okay to use the name in "Ultra Maniac."

As for Nina. . .that's simple. I thought Nina would be a name that could be used in both an alien and Japanese context.

I hope you enjoy both girls!!

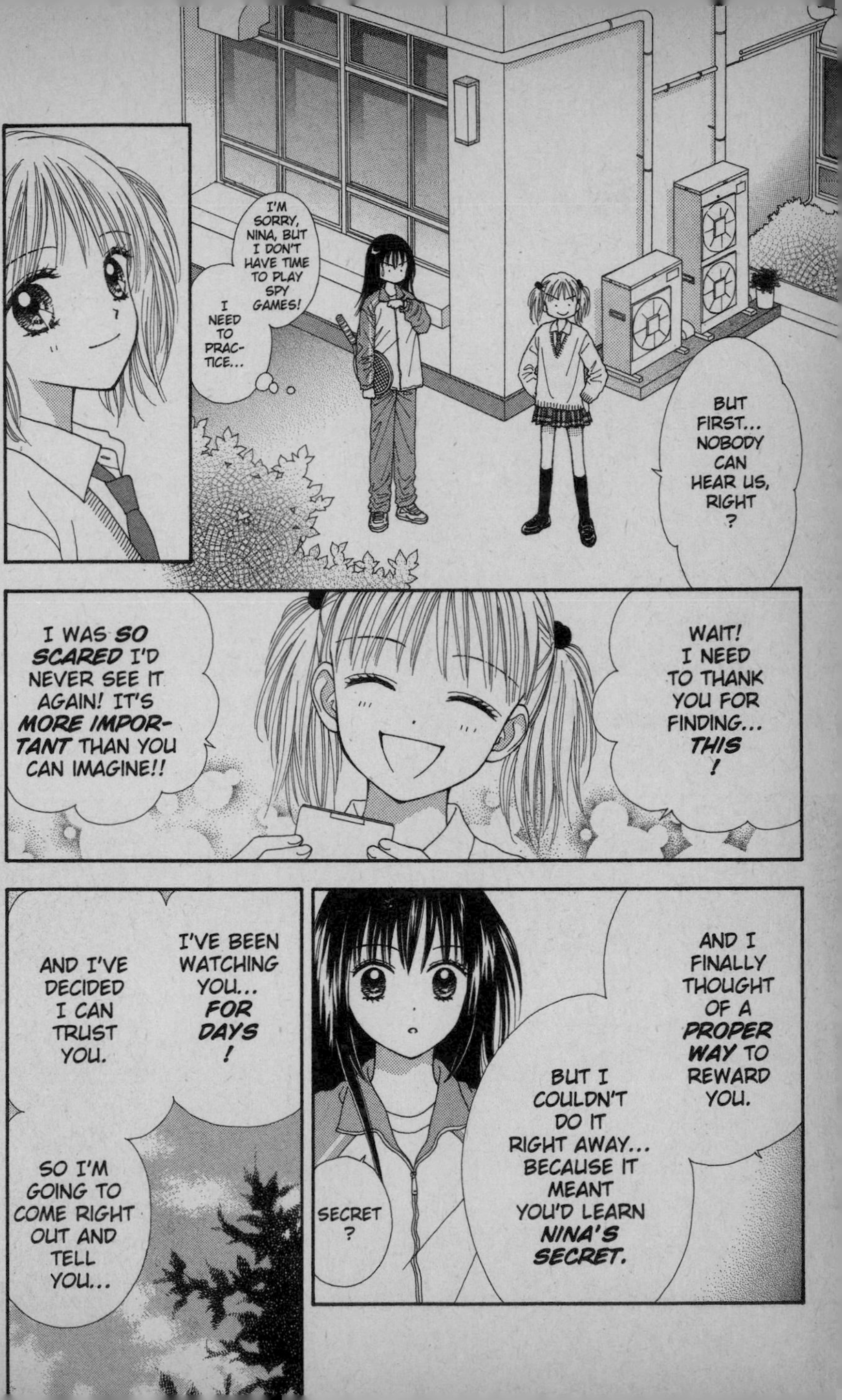

BUT FIRST... NOBODY CAN HEAR US, RIGHT?
I'M SORRY, NINA, BUT I DON'T HAVE TIME TO PLAY SPY GAMES!
I NEED TO PRAC-TICE...
WAIT! I NEED TO THANK YOU FOR FINDING... THIS!
I WAS SO SCARED I'D NEVER SEE IT AGAIN! IT'S MORE IMPOR-TANT THAN YOU CAN IMAGINE!!
AND I FINALLY THOUGHT OF A PROPER WAY TO REWARD YOU.
BUT I COULDN'T DO IT RIGHT AWAY... BECAUSE IT MEANT YOU'D LEARN NINA'S SECRET.
SECRET?
I'VE BEEN WATCHING YOU... FOR DAYS!
AND I'VE DECIDED I CAN TRUST YOU.
SO I'M GOING TO COME RIGHT OUT AND TELL YOU...

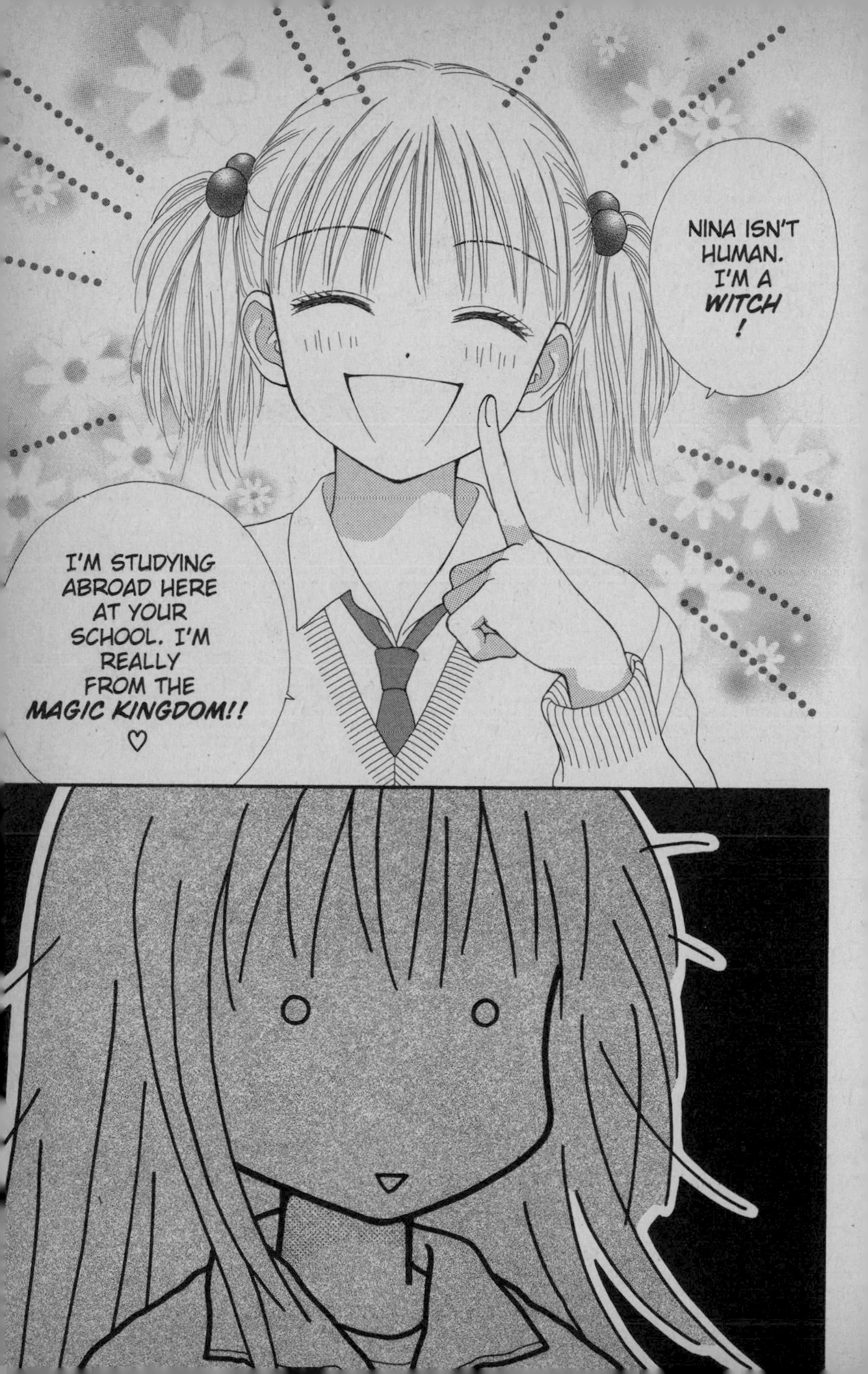
NINA ISN'T HUMAN. I'M A *WITCH*!
I'M STUDYING ABROAD HERE AT YOUR SCHOOL. I'M REALLY FROM THE *MAGIC KINGDOM!!* ♡

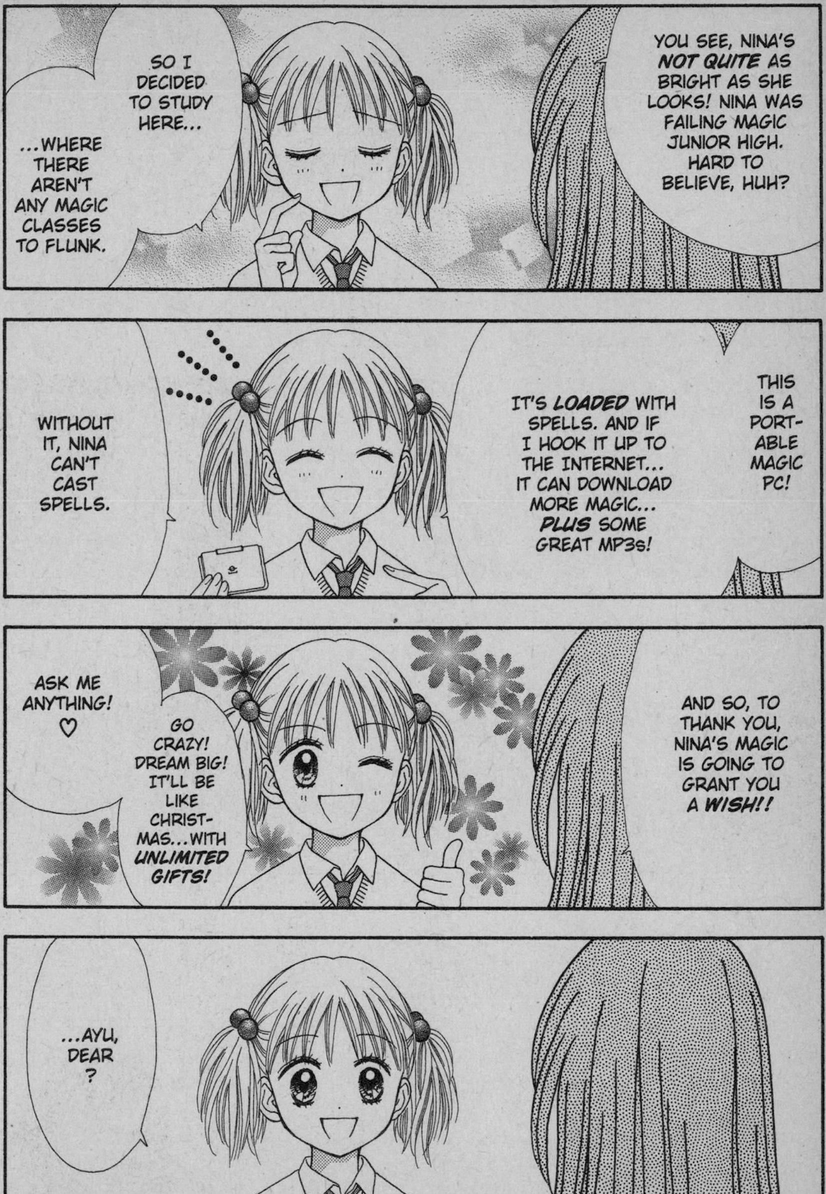
YOU SEE, NINA'S **NOT QUITE** AS BRIGHT AS SHE LOOKS! NINA WAS FAILING MAGIC JUNIOR HIGH. HARD TO BELIEVE, HUH?
SO I DECIDED TO STUDY HERE...
...WHERE THERE AREN'T ANY MAGIC CLASSES TO FLUNK.
THIS IS A PORT-ABLE MAGIC PC!
IT'S **LOADED** WITH SPELLS. AND IF I HOOK IT UP TO THE INTERNET... IT CAN DOWNLOAD MORE MAGIC... **PLUS** SOME GREAT MP3s!
WITHOUT IT, NINA CAN'T CAST SPELLS.
AND SO, TO THANK YOU, NINA'S MAGIC IS GOING TO GRANT YOU A **WISH!!**
GO CRAZY! DREAM BIG! IT'LL BE LIKE CHRIST-MAS...WITH **UNLIMITED GIFTS!**
ASK ME ANYTHING! ♡
...AYU, DEAR ?

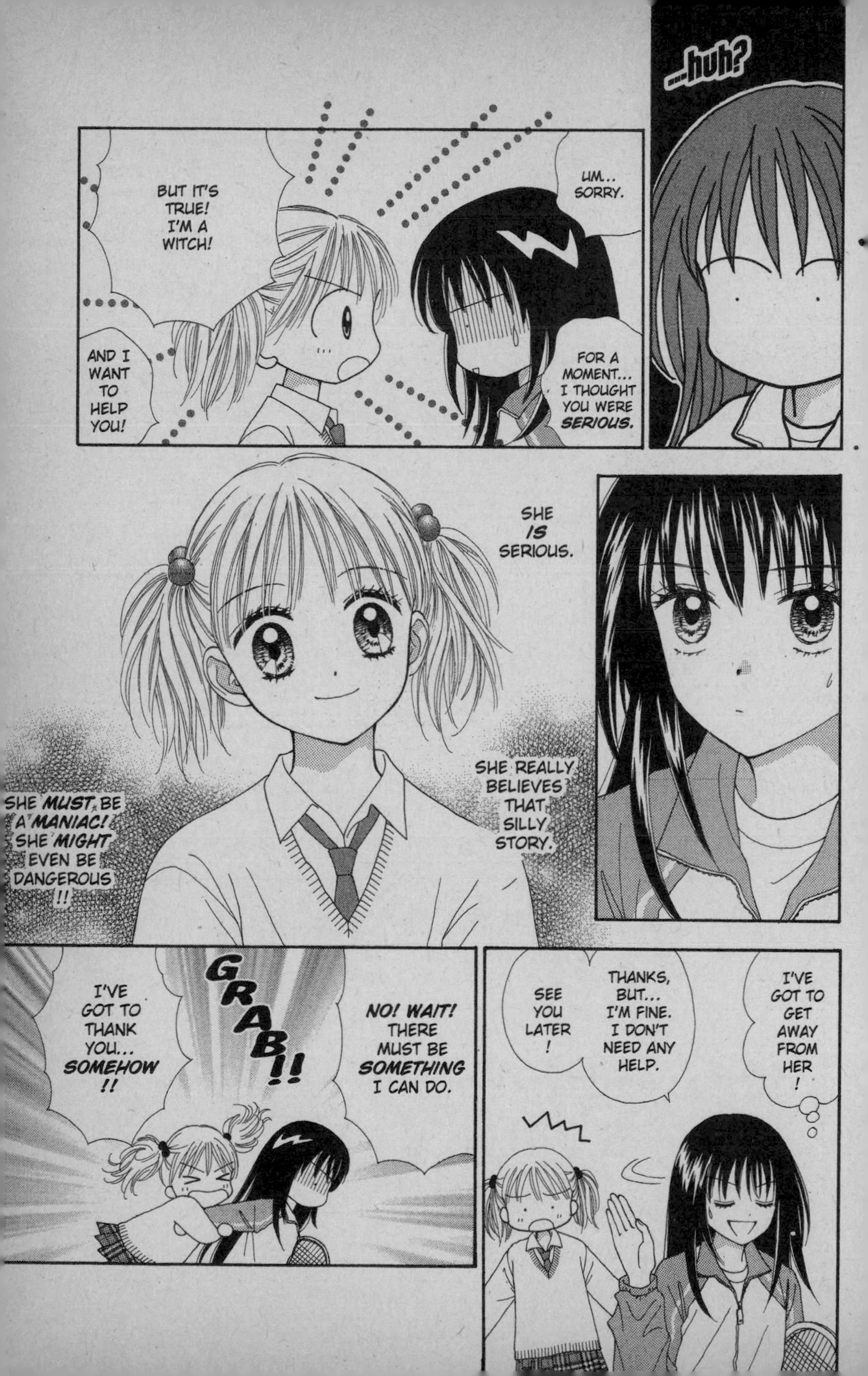
...huh?
UM... SORRY.
FOR A MOMENT... I THOUGHT YOU WERE SERIOUS.
BUT IT'S TRUE! I'M A WITCH!
AND I WANT TO HELP YOU!
SHE IS SERIOUS.
SHE REALLY BELIEVES THAT SILLY STORY.
SHE MUST BE A MANIAC! SHE MIGHT EVEN BE DANGEROUS!!
I'VE GOT TO GET AWAY FROM HER!
THANKS, BUT... I'M FINE. I DON'T NEED ANY HELP.
SEE YOU LATER!
NO! WAIT! THERE MUST BE SOMETHING I CAN DO.
GRAB!!
I'VE GOT TO THANK YOU... SOMEHOW!!

OH, ALL RIGHT. CAST A SPELL!
MAKE ME STRONG ENOUGH AND FAST ENOUGH...
TO BEAT HIROKI TSUJIAI IN A TENNIS MATCH!
THAT'LL TAKE REAL MAGIC... MAYBE EVEN A MIRACLE!
A MIRACLE?
NO PROBLEM!
I JUST HAVE TO FIND THE RIGHT SPELL IN MY COMPUTER!
blip blip blip blip blip blip blip blip blip blip
......
THIS IS CRAZY! EVEN I KNOW THAT SPELLS ARE CAST WITH MAGIC WANDS! AND USE ICKY INGREDIENTS...
LIKE TOAD WARTS, SPIDER WHISKERS AND...
OH, THE SILLY IDEAS YOU HUMANS HAVE!
NOBODY USES SMELLY OLD POTIONS ANYMORE. COMPUTERS ARE SO MUCH MORE CONVENIENT!
THAT'S WHY WE WITCHES INVENTED 'EM. AND THE INTERNET! THAT WAS OURS TOO!
......
OOOH!
I FOUND A GREAT SPELL! ♡

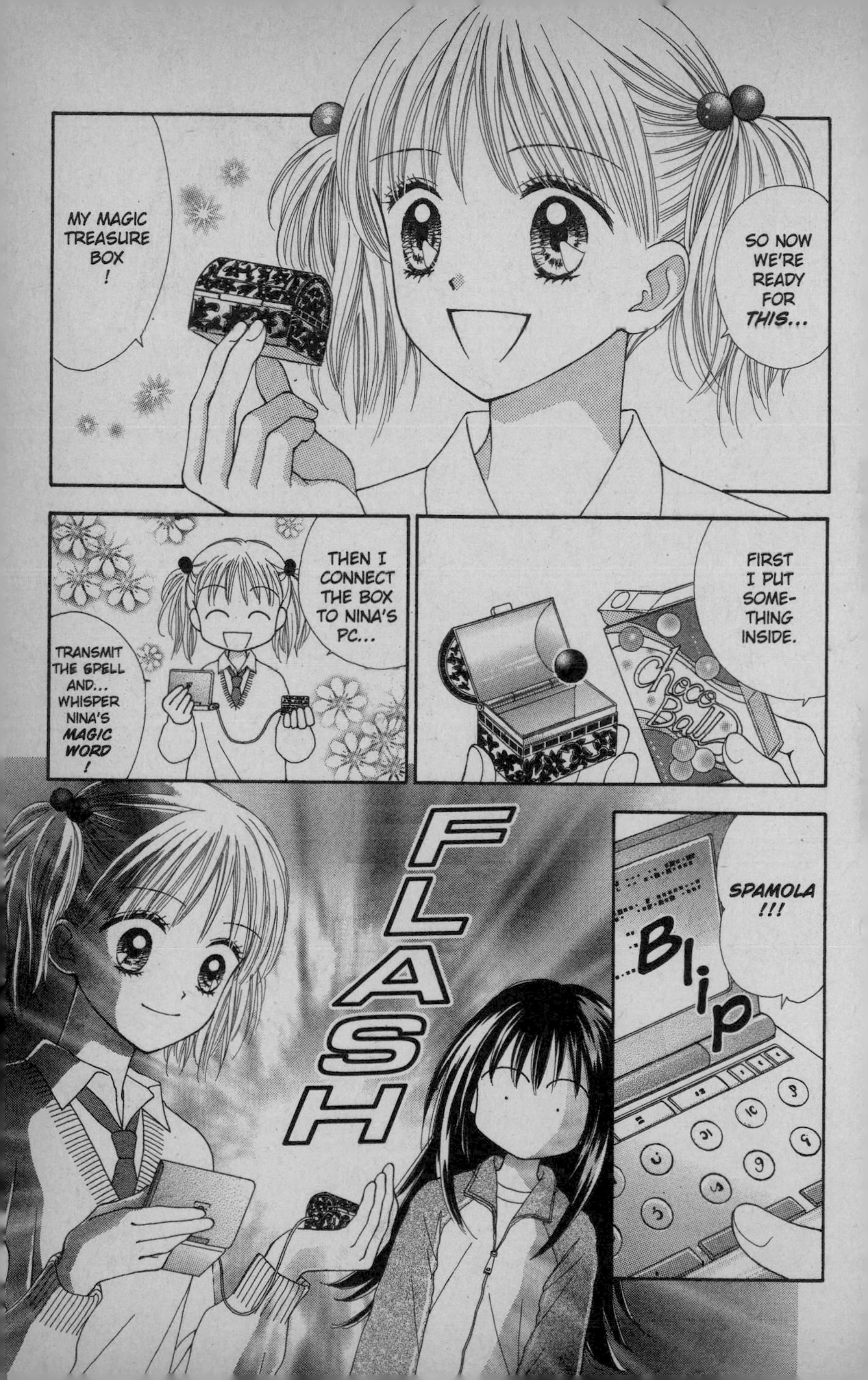
SO NOW WE'RE READY FOR *THIS*...
MY MAGIC TREASURE BOX !
FIRST I PUT SOME-THING INSIDE.
Choco Ball
THEN I CONNECT THE BOX TO NINA'S PC...
TRANSMIT THE SPELL AND... WHISPER NINA'S *MAGIC WORD* !
SPAMOLA !!!
Blip
FLASH

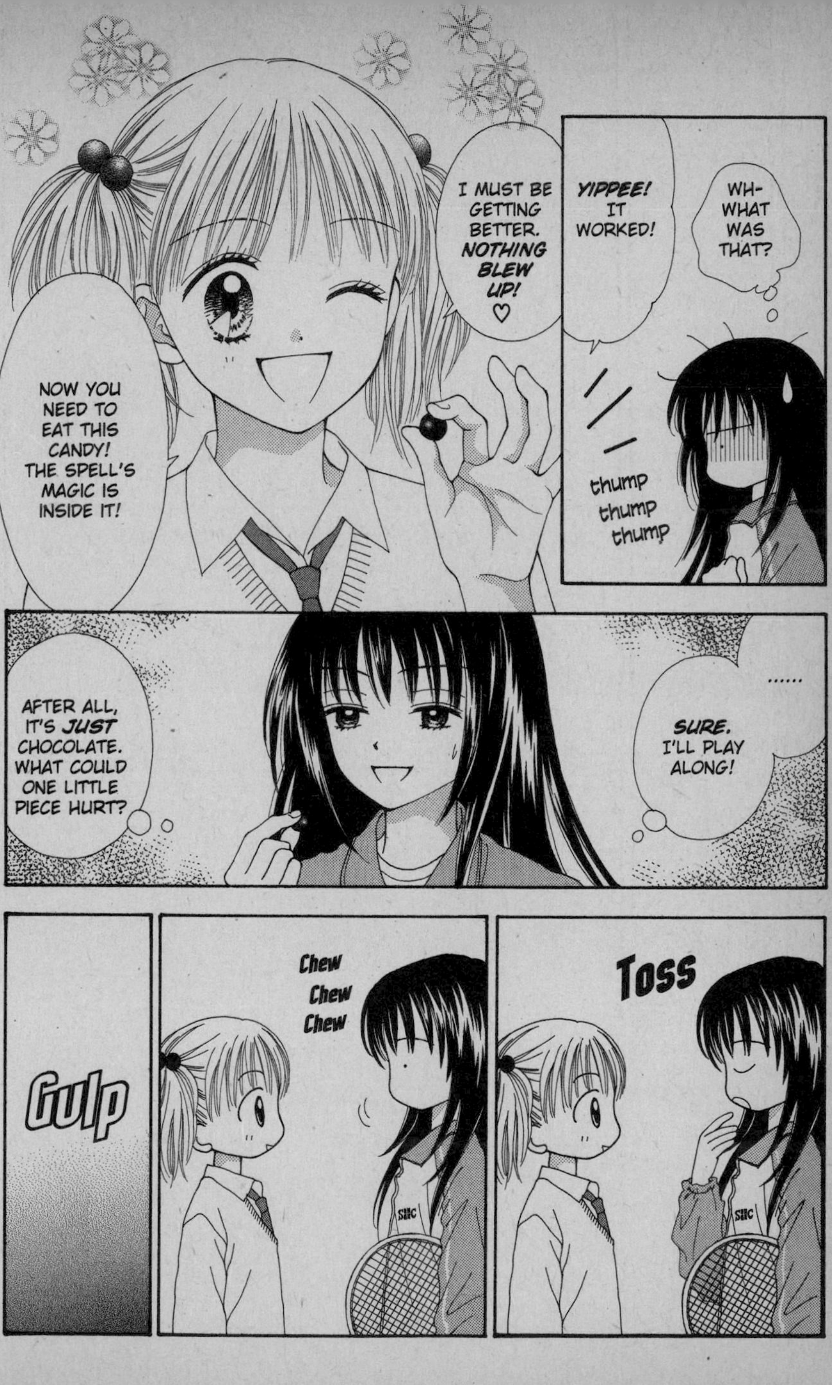
WH- WHAT WAS THAT?
YIPPEE! IT WORKED!
thump thump thump
I MUST BE GETTING BETTER. NOTHING BLEW UP! ♡
NOW YOU NEED TO EAT THIS CANDY! THE SPELL'S MAGIC IS INSIDE IT!
......
SURE. I'LL PLAY ALONG!
AFTER ALL, IT'S JUST CHOCOLATE. WHAT COULD ONE LITTLE PIECE HURT?
Toss
Chew Chew Chew
Gulp

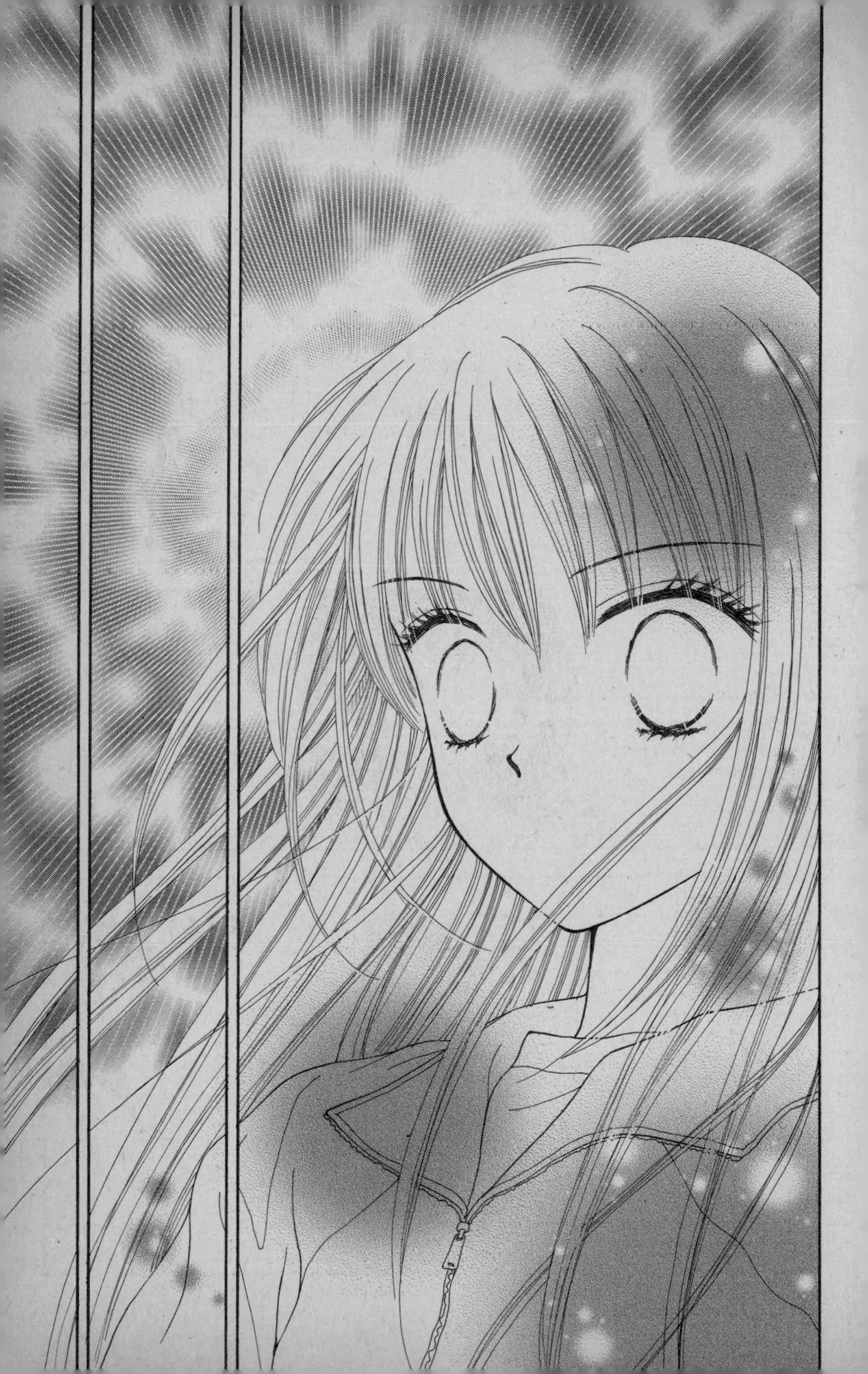

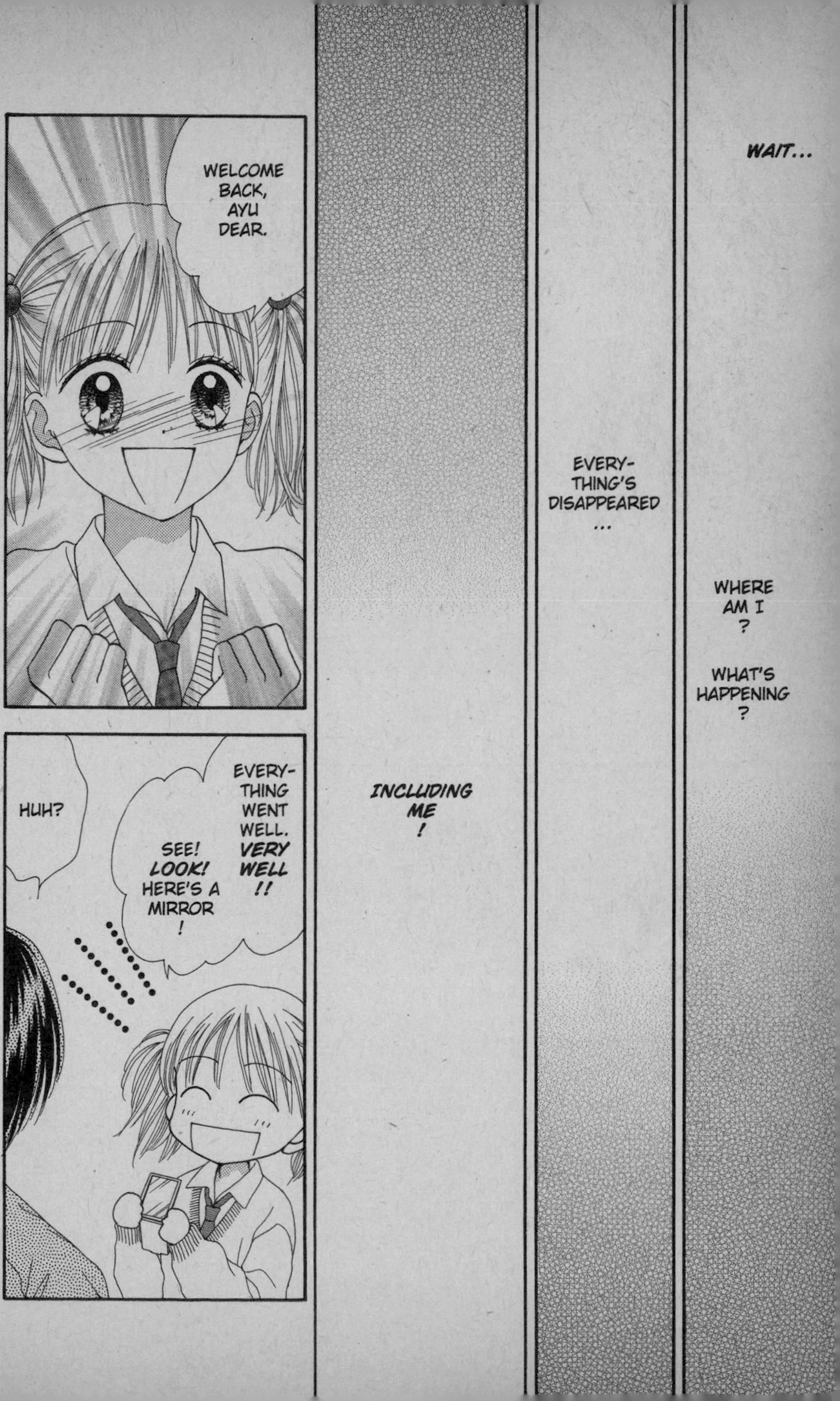
WAIT...
WHERE AM I?
WHAT'S HAPPENING?
EVERYTHING'S DISAPPEARED...
INCLUDING ME!
WELCOME BACK, AYU DEAR.
EVERYTHING WENT WELL. VERY WELL!!
SEE! LOOK! HERE'S A MIRROR!
HUH?

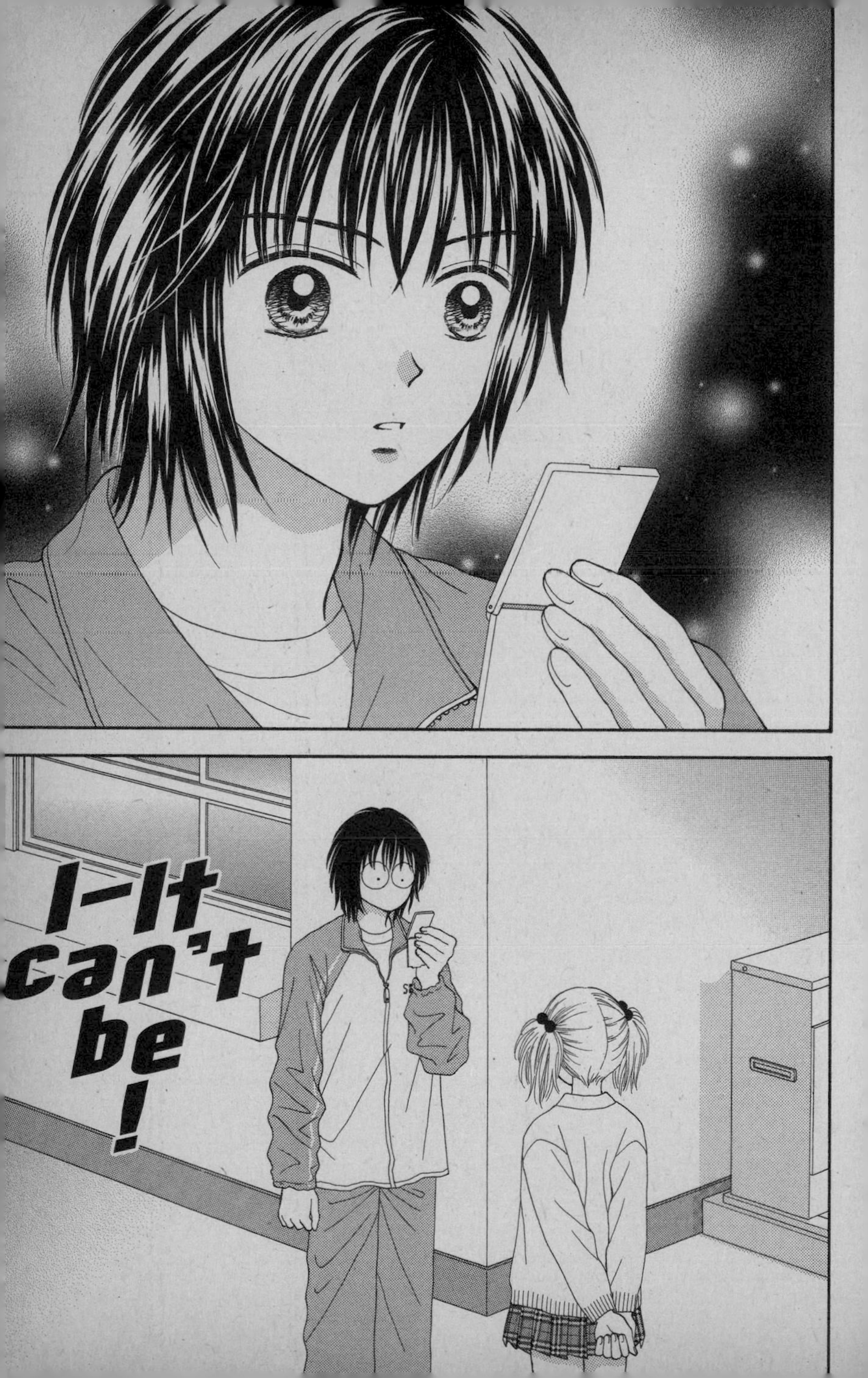
I-It can't be!

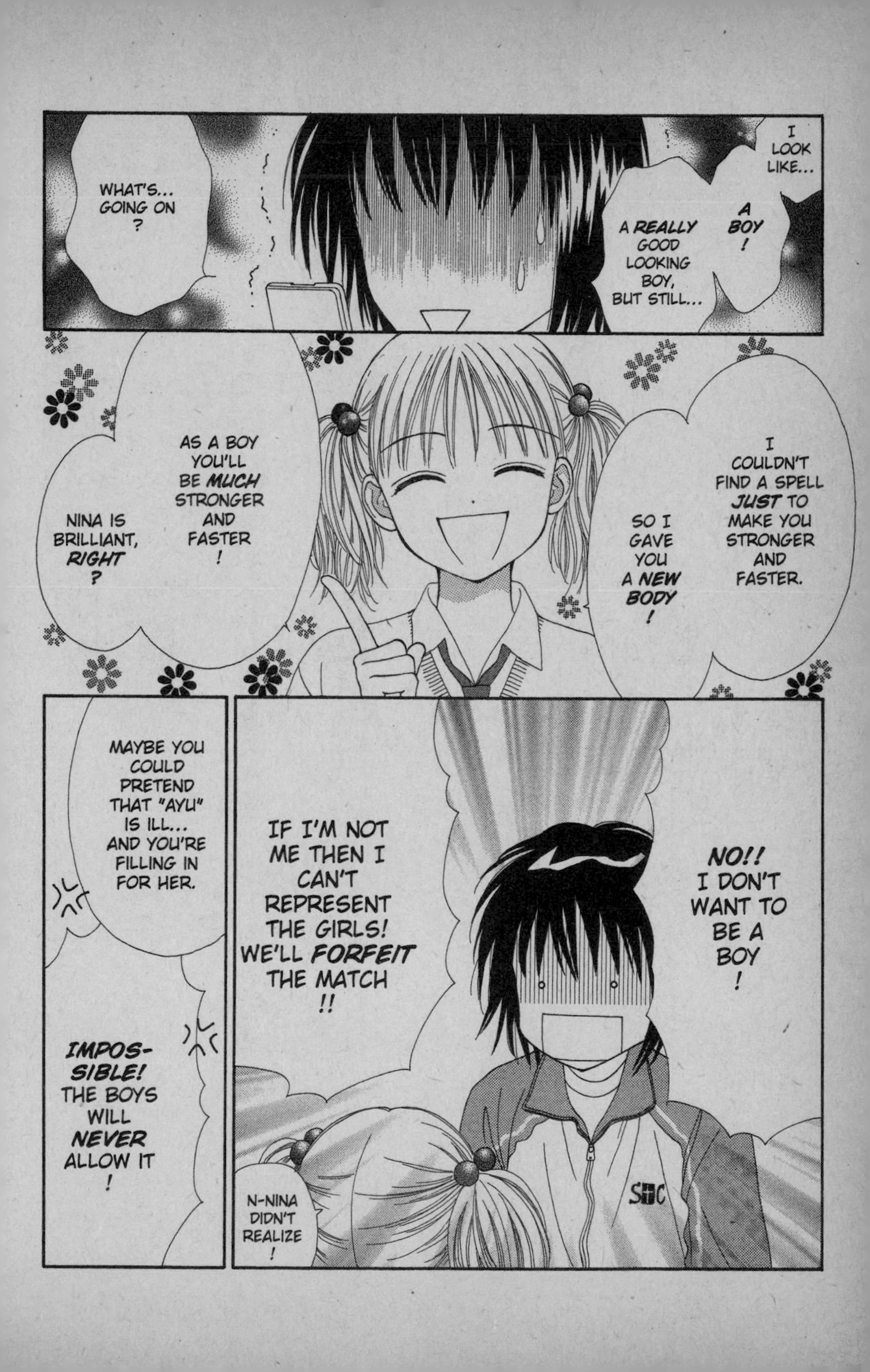
I LOOK LIKE... A BOY!
A REALLY GOOD LOOKING BOY, BUT STILL...
WHAT'S... GOING ON?
I COULDN'T FIND A SPELL JUST TO MAKE YOU STRONGER AND FASTER.
SO I GAVE YOU A NEW BODY!
AS A BOY YOU'LL BE MUCH STRONGER AND FASTER!
NINA IS BRILLIANT, RIGHT?
NO!! I DON'T WANT TO BE A BOY!
IF I'M NOT ME THEN I CAN'T REPRESENT THE GIRLS! WE'LL FORFEIT THE MATCH!!
N-NINA DIDN'T REALIZE!
MAYBE YOU COULD PRETEND THAT "AYU" IS ILL... AND YOU'RE FILLING IN FOR HER.
IMPOSSIBLE! THE BOYS WILL NEVER ALLOW IT!

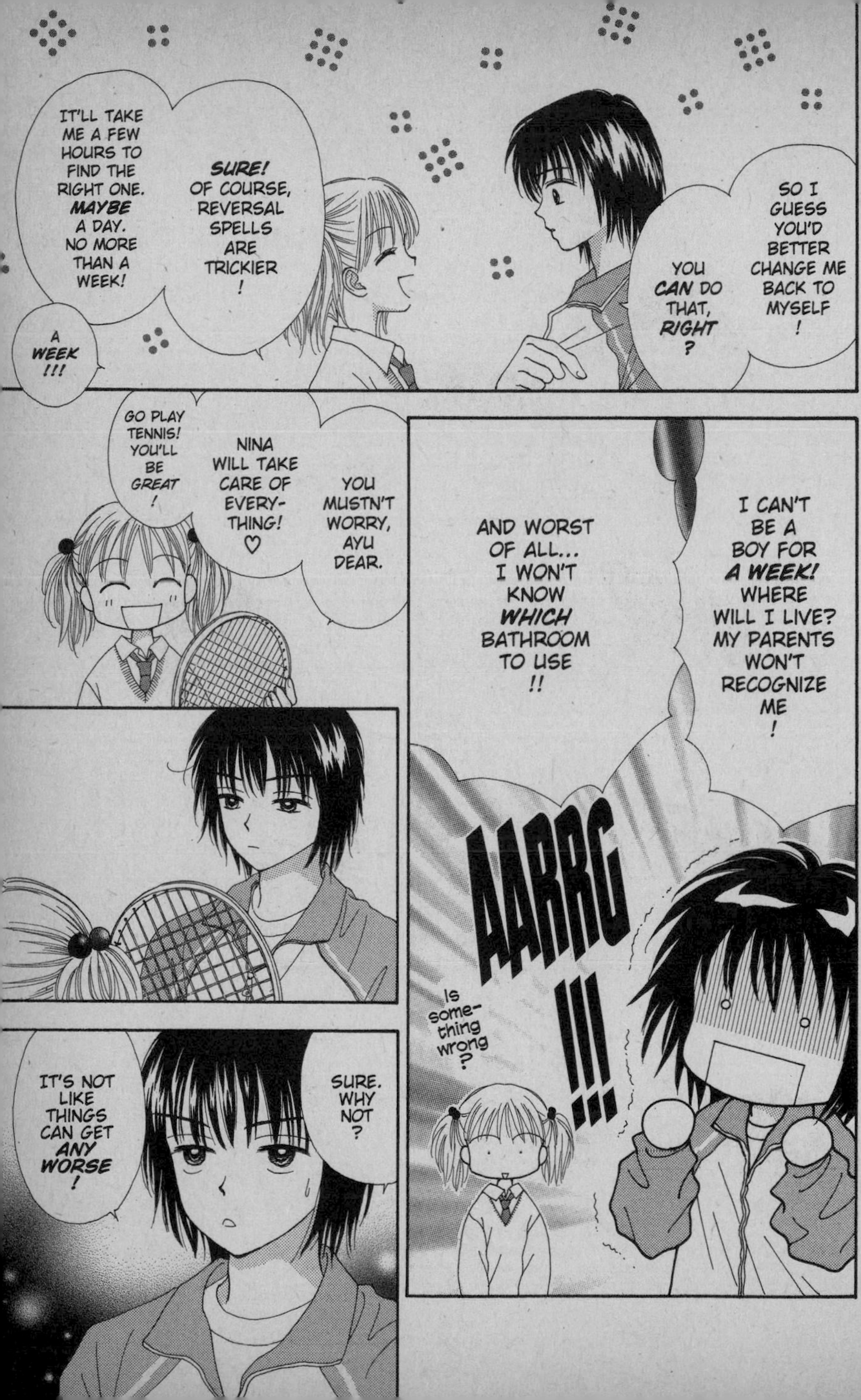
SO I GUESS YOU'D BETTER CHANGE ME BACK TO MYSELF!
YOU *CAN* DO THAT, *RIGHT*?
SURE! OF COURSE, REVERSAL SPELLS ARE TRICKIER!
IT'LL TAKE ME A FEW HOURS TO FIND THE RIGHT ONE. *MAYBE* A DAY. NO MORE THAN A WEEK!
A *WEEK*!!!
I CAN'T BE A BOY FOR *A WEEK!* WHERE WILL I LIVE? MY PARENTS WON'T RECOGNIZE ME!
AND WORST OF ALL... I WON'T KNOW *WHICH* BATHROOM TO USE!!
AARRG!!!
Is something wrong?
YOU MUSTN'T WORRY, AYU DEAR.
NINA WILL TAKE CARE OF EVERYTHING! ♡
GO PLAY TENNIS! YOU'LL BE *GREAT*!
SURE. WHY NOT?
IT'S NOT LIKE THINGS CAN GET *ANY WORSE*!

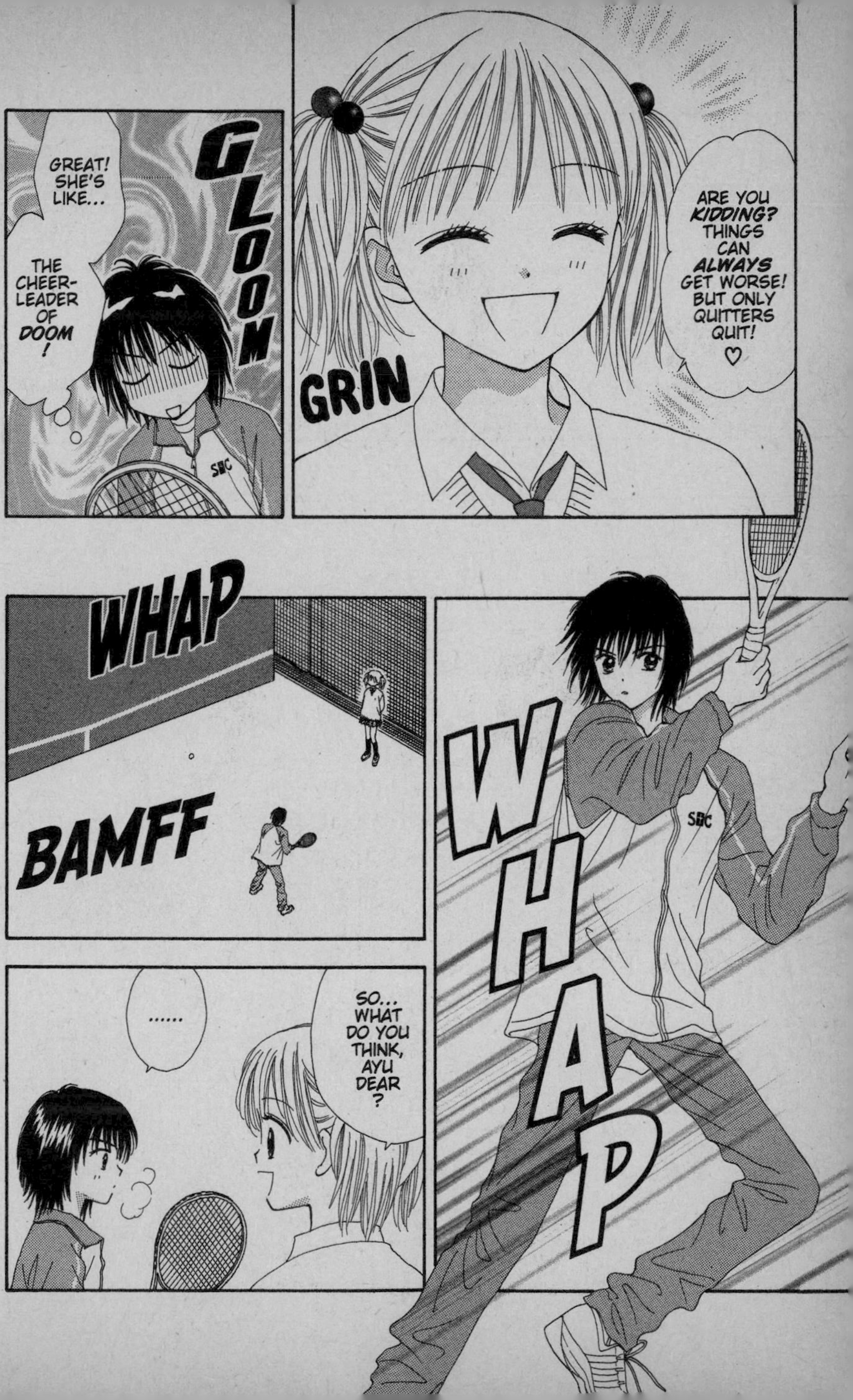
ARE YOU *KIDDING?* THINGS CAN *ALWAYS* GET WORSE! BUT ONLY QUITTERS QUIT! ♡
GRIN
GLOOM
GREAT! SHE'S LIKE...
THE CHEERLEADER OF *DOOM*!
WHAP
WHAP
BAMFF
SO... WHAT DO YOU THINK, AYU DEAR?
......

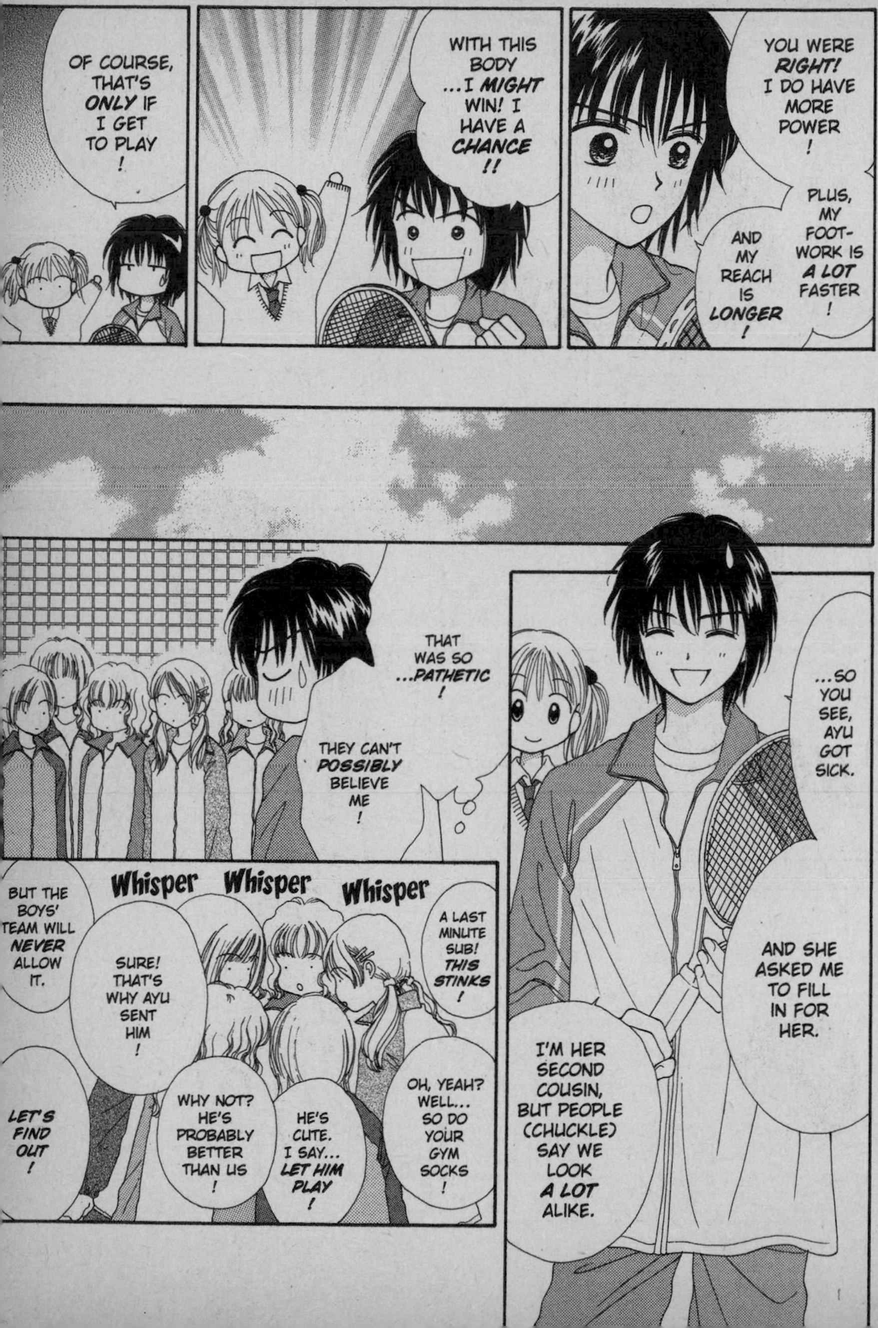
YOU WERE RIGHT! I DO HAVE MORE POWER!
PLUS, MY FOOTWORK IS A LOT FASTER!
AND MY REACH IS LONGER!
WITH THIS BODY ...I MIGHT WIN! I HAVE A CHANCE!!
OF COURSE, THAT'S ONLY IF I GET TO PLAY!
...SO YOU SEE, AYU GOT SICK.
AND SHE ASKED ME TO FILL IN FOR HER.
I'M HER SECOND COUSIN, BUT PEOPLE (CHUCKLE) SAY WE LOOK A LOT ALIKE.
THAT WAS SO ...PATHETIC!
THEY CAN'T POSSIBLY BELIEVE ME!
Whisper
Whisper
Whisper
A LAST MINUTE SUB! THIS STINKS!
SURE! THAT'S WHY AYU SENT HIM!
BUT THE BOYS' TEAM WILL NEVER ALLOW IT.
OH, YEAH? WELL... SO DO YOUR GYM SOCKS!
HE'S CUTE. I SAY... LET HIM PLAY!
WHY NOT? HE'S PROBABLY BETTER THAN US!
LET'S FIND OUT!

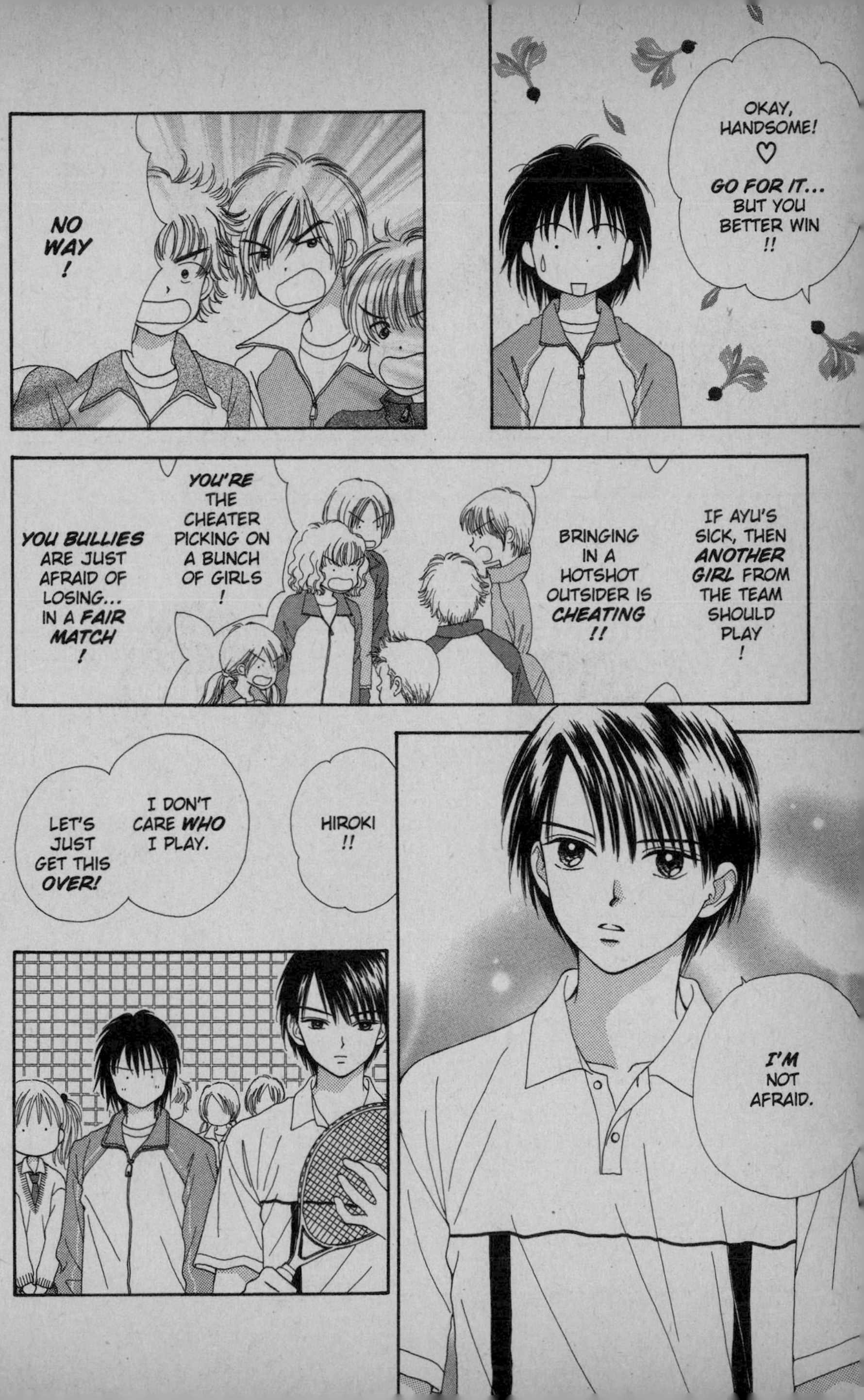
OKAY, HANDSOME! ♡ GO FOR IT... BUT YOU BETTER WIN !!
NO WAY !
IF AYU'S SICK, THEN ANOTHER GIRL FROM THE TEAM SHOULD PLAY !
BRINGING IN A HOTSHOT OUTSIDER IS CHEATING !!
YOU'RE THE CHEATER PICKING ON A BUNCH OF GIRLS !
YOU BULLIES ARE JUST AFRAID OF LOSING... IN A FAIR MATCH !
I'M NOT AFRAID.
HIROKI !!
I DON'T CARE WHO I PLAY.
LET'S JUST GET THIS OVER!

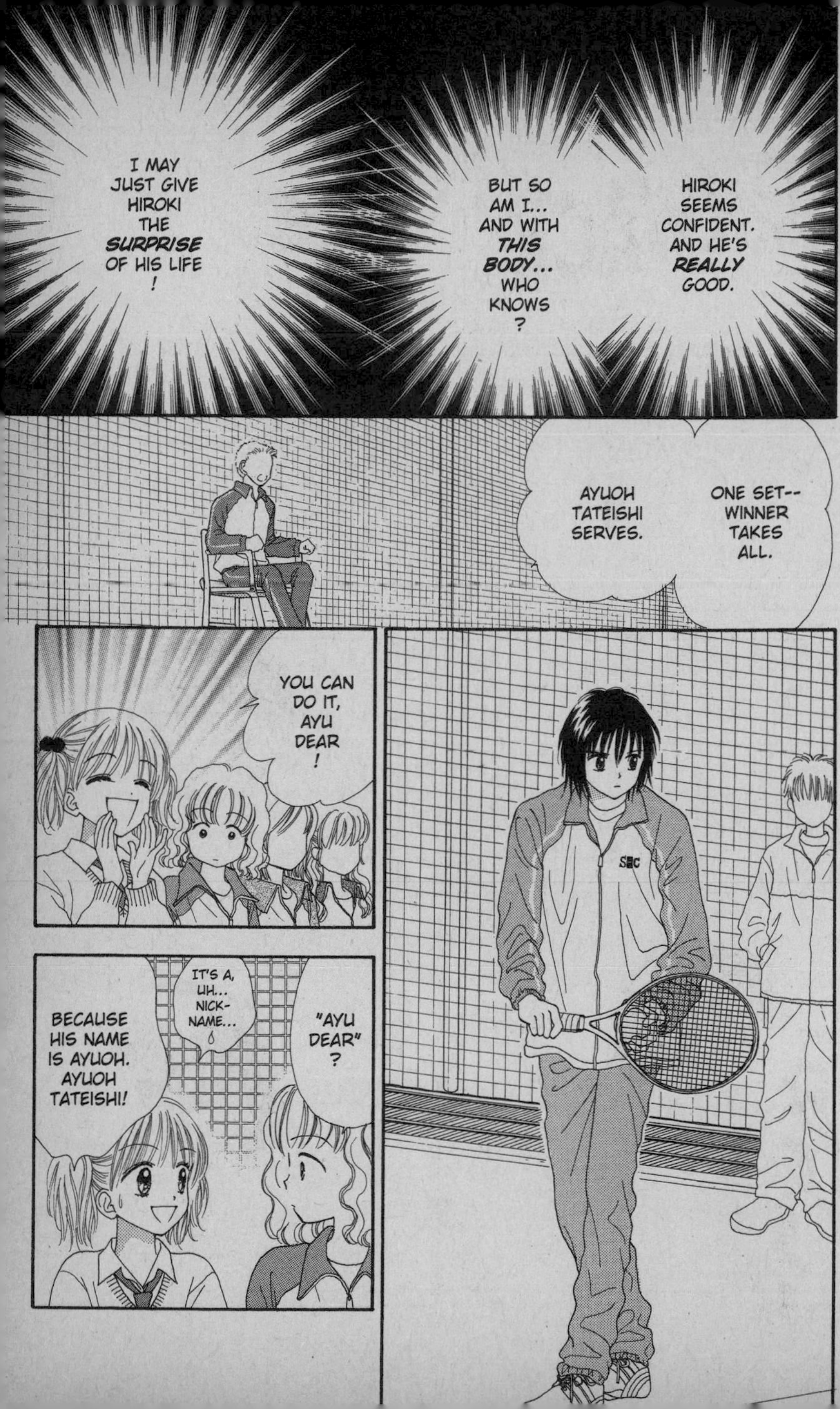
HIROKI SEEMS CONFIDENT. AND HE'S REALLY GOOD.
BUT SO AM I... AND WITH THIS BODY... WHO KNOWS?
I MAY JUST GIVE HIROKI THE SURPRISE OF HIS LIFE!
ONE SET-- WINNER TAKES ALL.
AYUOH TATEISHI SERVES.
YOU CAN DO IT, AYU DEAR!
"AYU DEAR"?
IT'S A, UH... NICK-NAME...
BECAUSE HIS NAME IS AYUOH. AYUOH TATEISHI!

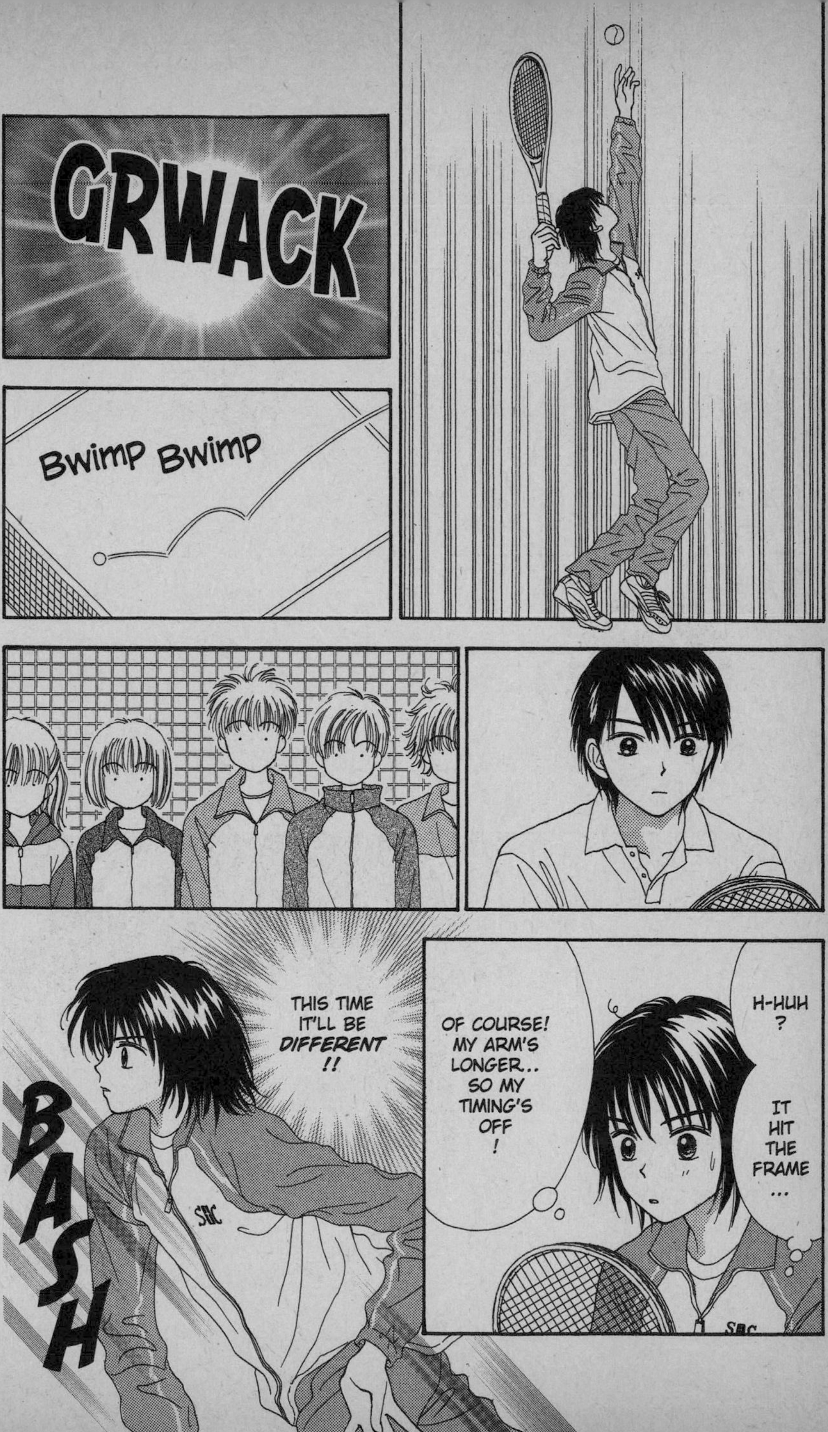
GRWACK
Bwimp Bwimp
H-HUH?
IT HIT THE FRAME...
OF COURSE! MY ARM'S LONGER... SO MY TIMING'S OFF!
THIS TIME IT'LL BE DIFFERENT!!
BASH

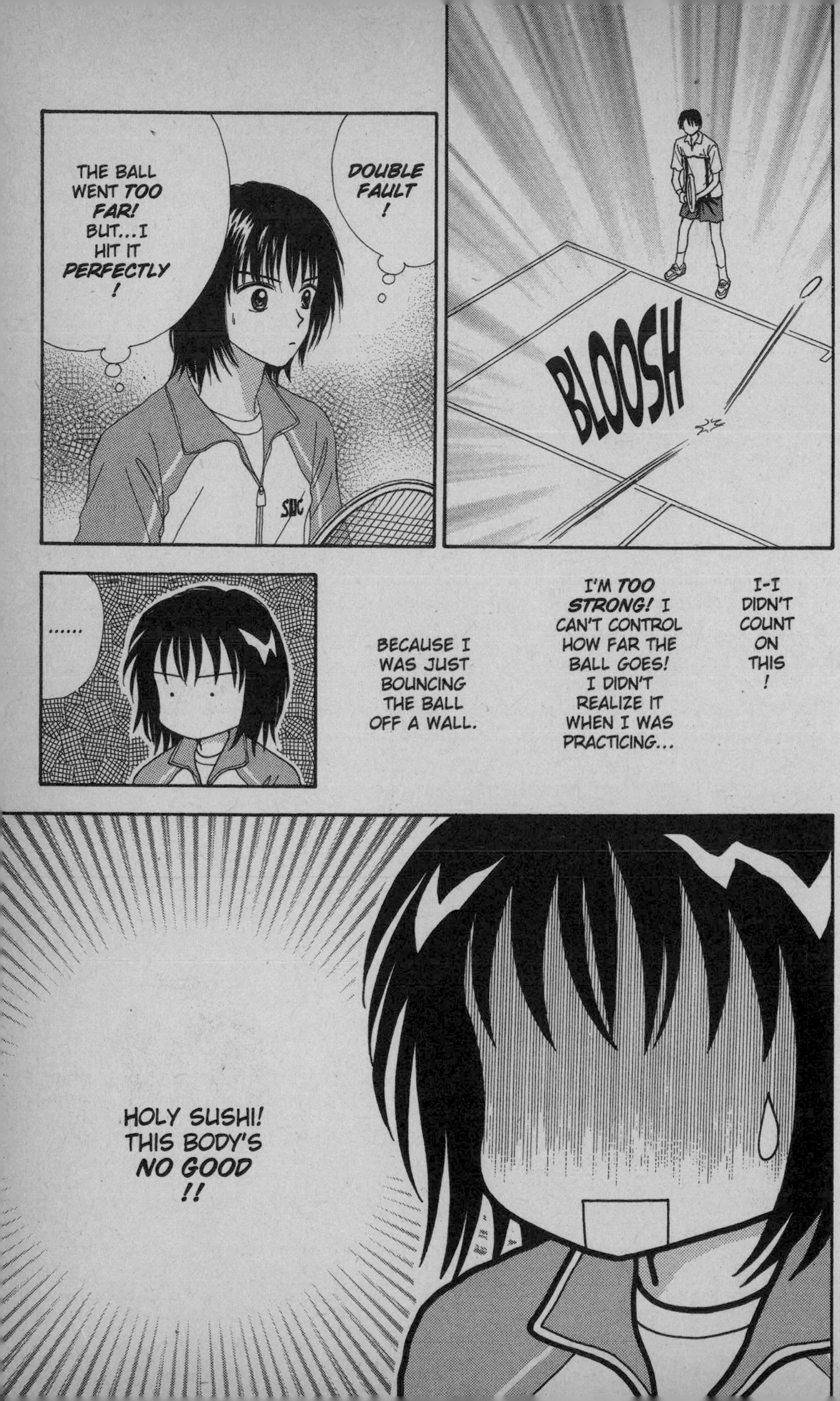
BLOOSH
DOUBLE FAULT!
THE BALL WENT TOO FAR! BUT...I HIT IT PERFECTLY!
I-I DIDN'T COUNT ON THIS!
I'M TOO STRONG! I CAN'T CONTROL HOW FAR THE BALL GOES! I DIDN'T REALIZE IT WHEN I WAS PRACTICING...
BECAUSE I WAS JUST BOUNCING THE BALL OFF A WALL.
......
HOLY SUSHI! THIS BODY'S NO GOOD!!

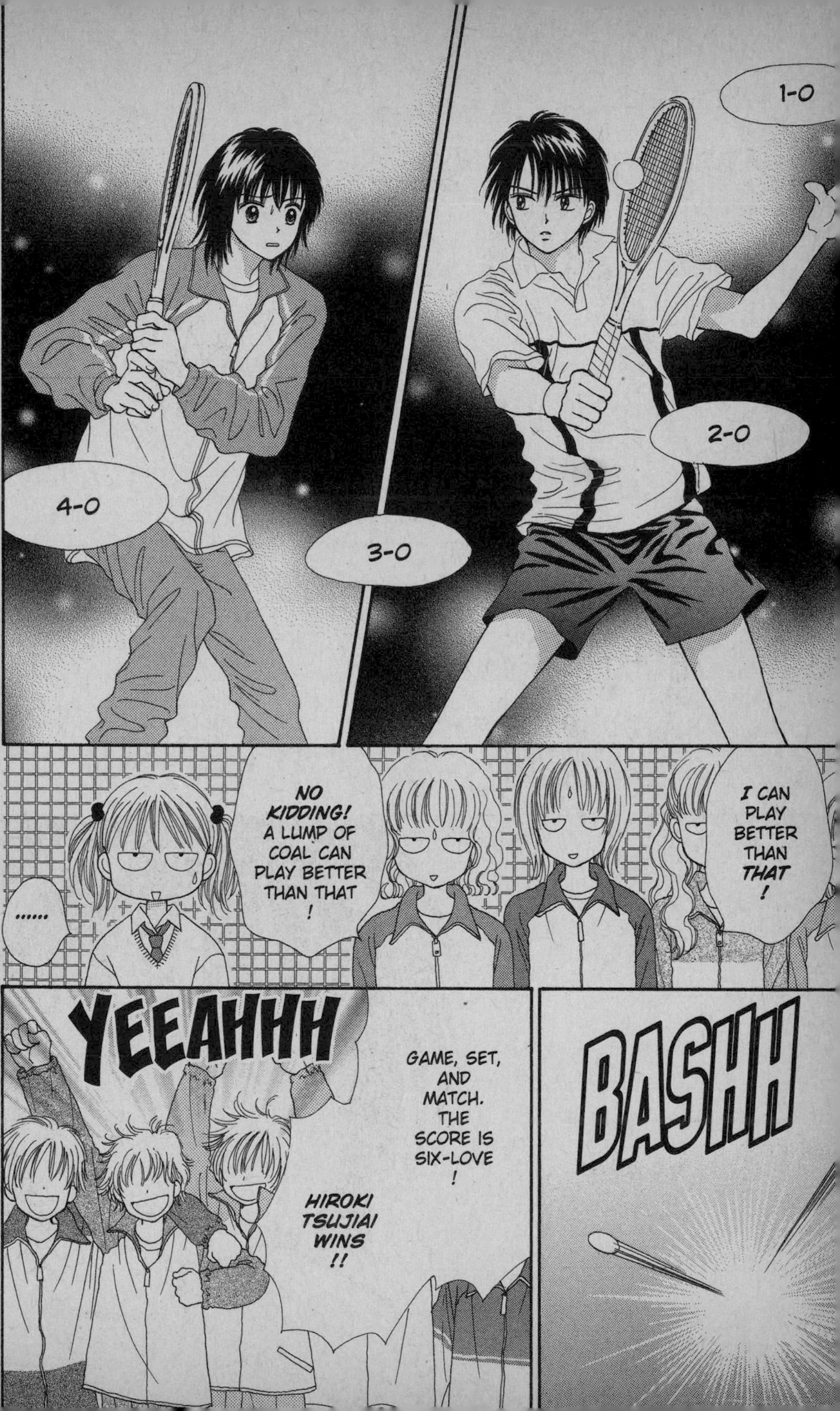
1-0
2-0
3-0
4-0
I CAN PLAY BETTER THAN THAT!
NO KIDDING! A LUMP OF COAL CAN PLAY BETTER THAN THAT!
......
BASHH
GAME, SET, AND MATCH. THE SCORE IS SIX-LOVE!
HIROKI TSUJIAI WINS!!
YEEAHHH

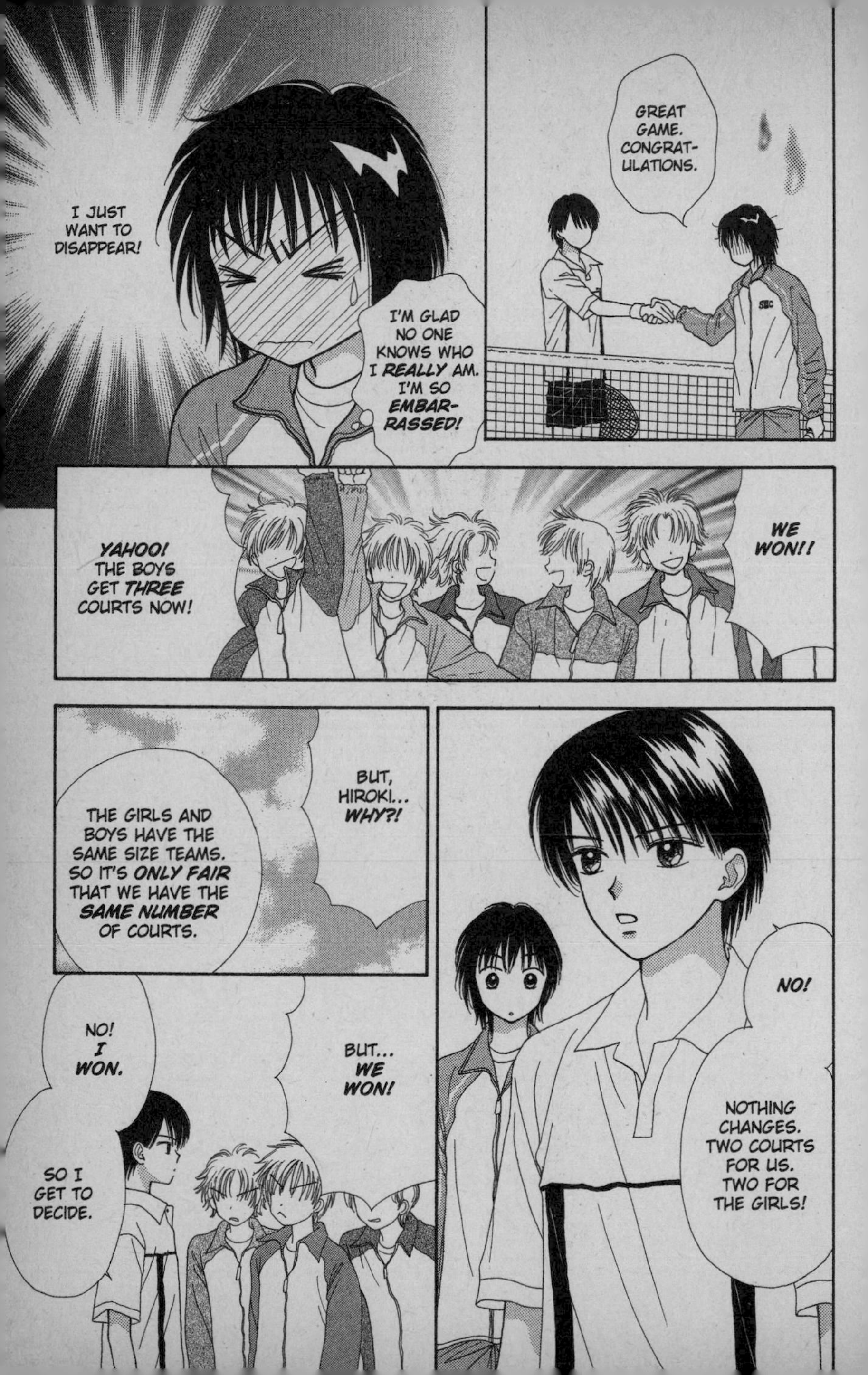
GREAT GAME. CONGRATULATIONS.
I'M GLAD NO ONE KNOWS WHO I REALLY AM. I'M SO EMBARRASSED!
I JUST WANT TO DISAPPEAR!
WE WON!!
YAHOO! THE BOYS GET THREE COURTS NOW!
NO!
NOTHING CHANGES. TWO COURTS FOR US. TWO FOR THE GIRLS!
BUT, HIROKI... WHY?!
THE GIRLS AND BOYS HAVE THE SAME SIZE TEAMS. SO IT'S ONLY FAIR THAT WE HAVE THE SAME NUMBER OF COURTS.
BUT... WE WON!
NO! I WON.
SO I GET TO DECIDE.

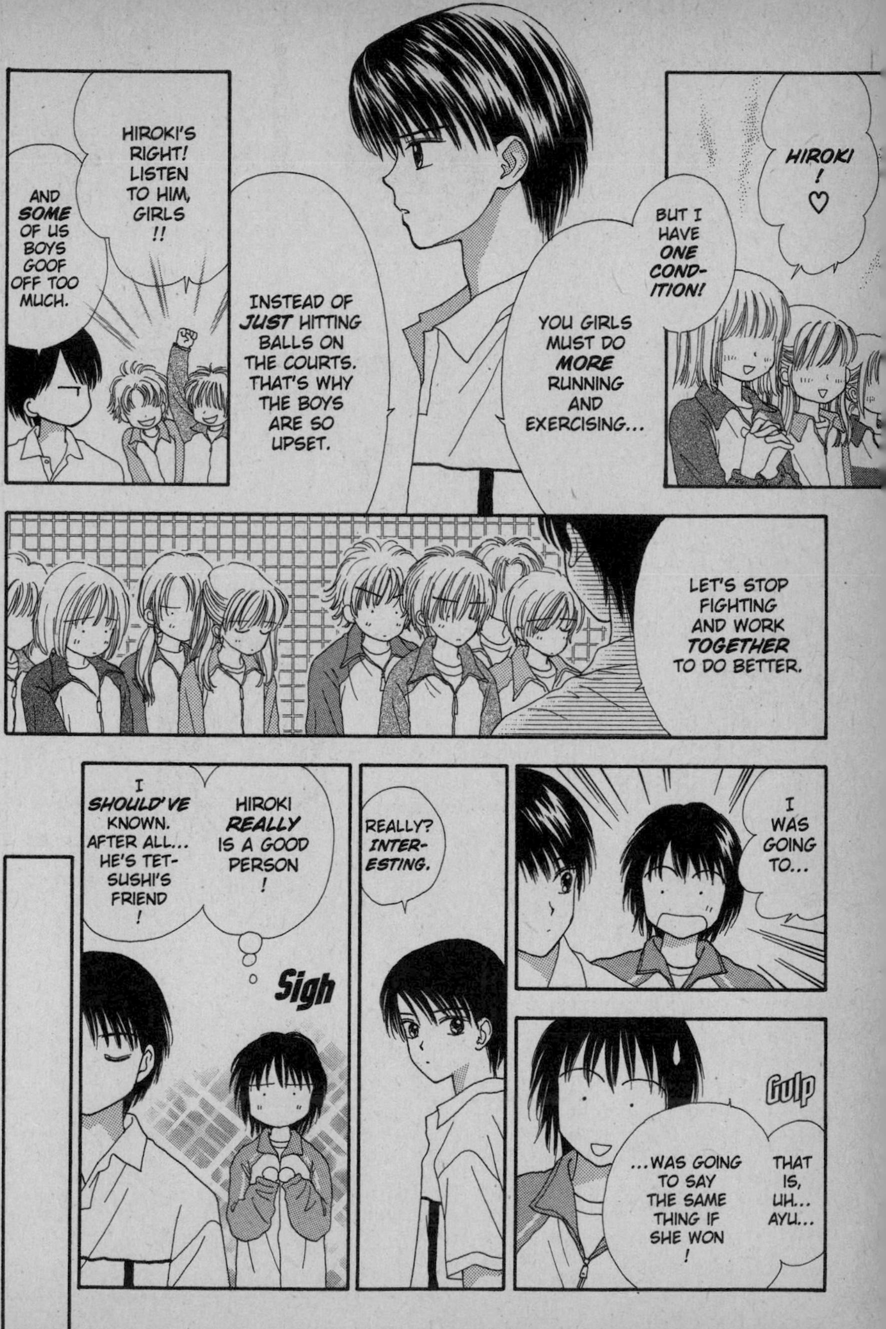
HIROKI! ♡
BUT I HAVE ONE CONDITION!
YOU GIRLS MUST DO MORE RUNNING AND EXERCISING...
INSTEAD OF JUST HITTING BALLS ON THE COURTS. THAT'S WHY THE BOYS ARE SO UPSET.
HIROKI'S RIGHT! LISTEN TO HIM, GIRLS!!
AND SOME OF US BOYS GOOF OFF TOO MUCH.
LET'S STOP FIGHTING AND WORK TOGETHER TO DO BETTER.
I WAS GOING TO...
THAT IS, UH... AYU...
...WAS GOING TO SAY THE SAME THING IF SHE WON!
Gulp
REALLY? INTERESTING.
HIROKI REALLY IS A GOOD PERSON!
I SHOULD'VE KNOWN. AFTER ALL... HE'S TETSUSHI'S FRIEND!
Sigh

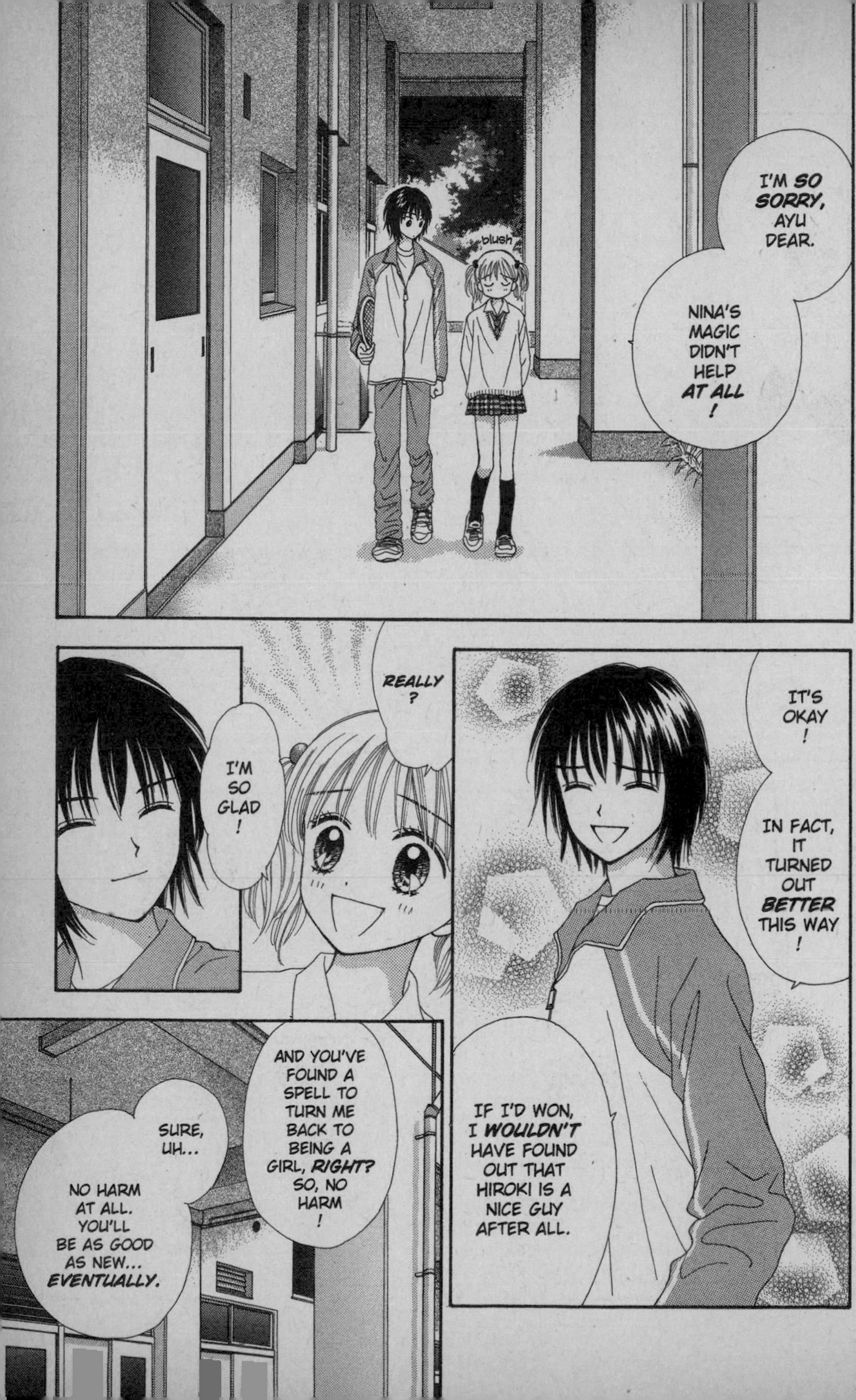
I'M SO SORRY, AYU DEAR.
NINA'S MAGIC DIDN'T HELP AT ALL!
blush
IT'S OKAY!
IN FACT, IT TURNED OUT BETTER THIS WAY!
IF I'D WON, I WOULDN'T HAVE FOUND OUT THAT HIROKI IS A NICE GUY AFTER ALL.
REALLY?
I'M SO GLAD!
AND YOU'VE FOUND A SPELL TO TURN ME BACK TO BEING A GIRL, RIGHT? SO, NO HARM!
SURE, UH...
NO HARM AT ALL. YOU'LL BE AS GOOD AS NEW... EVENTUALLY.

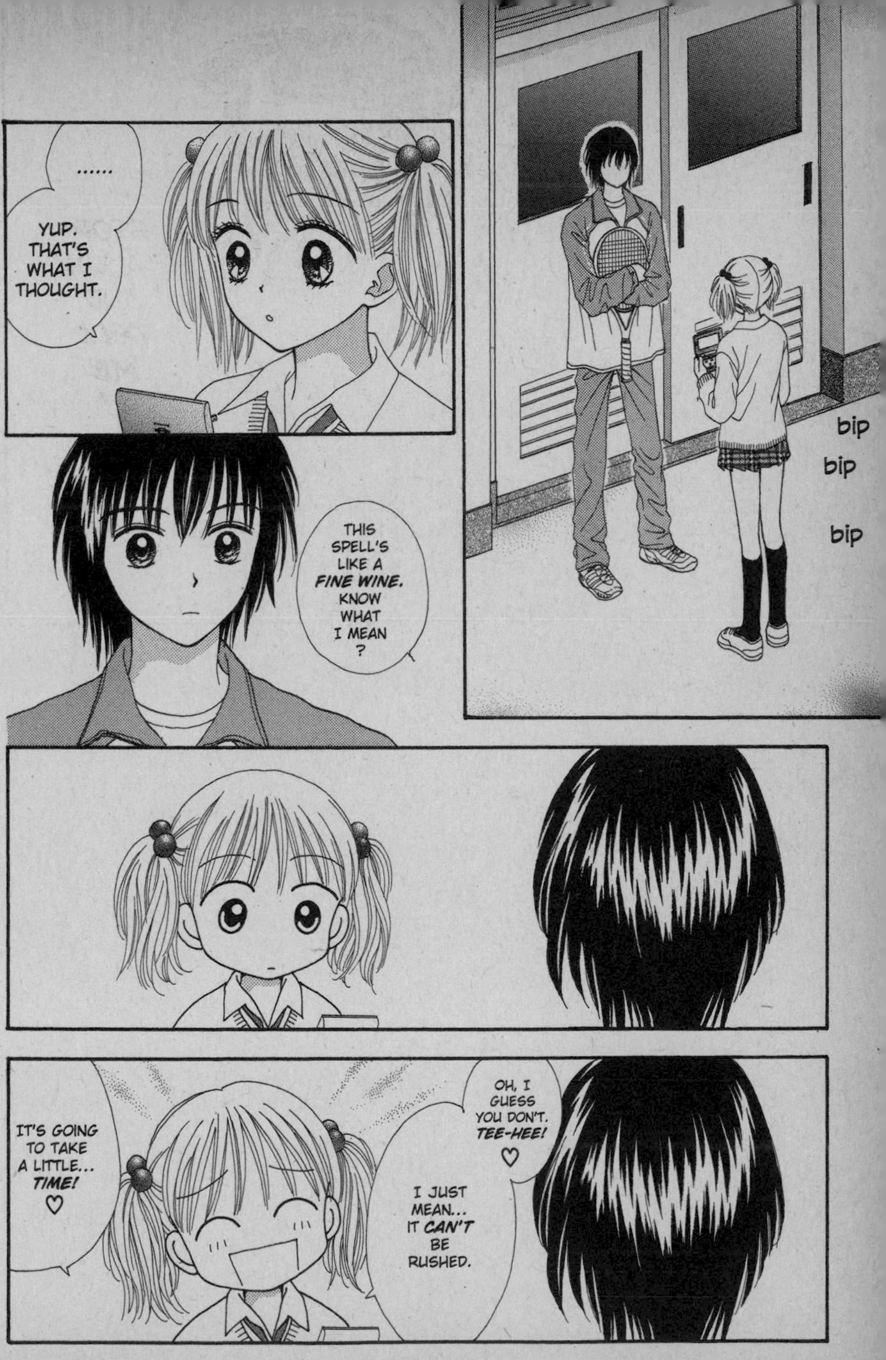
bip
bip
bip
......
YUP. THAT'S WHAT I THOUGHT.
THIS SPELL'S LIKE A FINE WINE. KNOW WHAT I MEAN?
OH, I GUESS YOU DON'T. TEE-HEE! ♡
I JUST MEAN... IT CAN'T BE RUSHED.
IT'S GOING TO TAKE A LITTLE... TIME! ♡

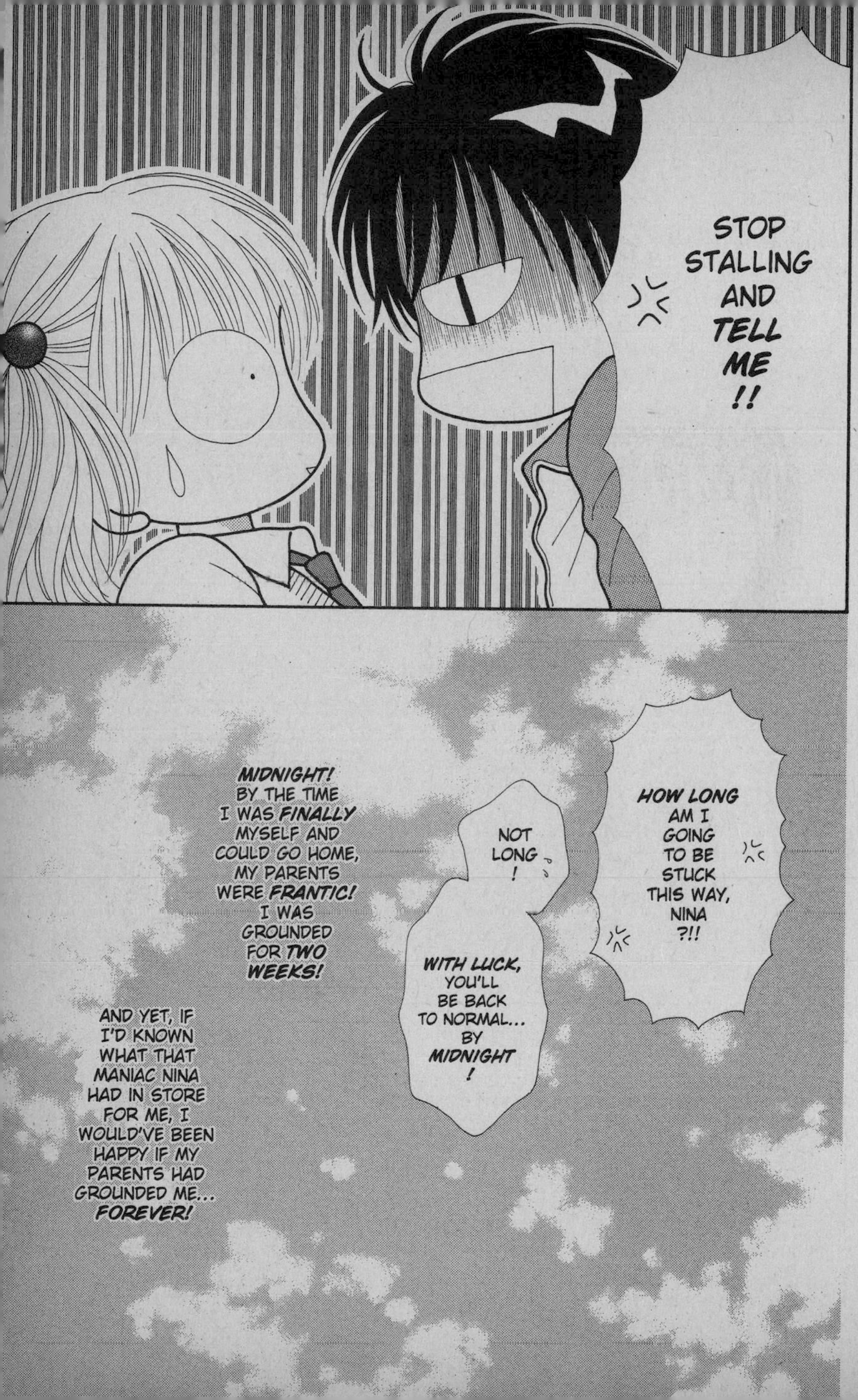
STOP STALLING AND TELL ME!!
HOW LONG AM I GOING TO BE STUCK THIS WAY, NINA?!!
NOT LONG!
WITH LUCK, YOU'LL BE BACK TO NORMAL... BY MIDNIGHT!
MIDNIGHT! BY THE TIME I WAS FINALLY MYSELF AND COULD GO HOME, MY PARENTS WERE FRANTIC! I WAS GROUNDED FOR TWO WEEKS!
AND YET, IF I'D KNOWN WHAT THAT MANIAC NINA HAD IN STORE FOR ME, I WOULD'VE BEEN HAPPY IF MY PARENTS HAD GROUNDED ME... FOREVER!

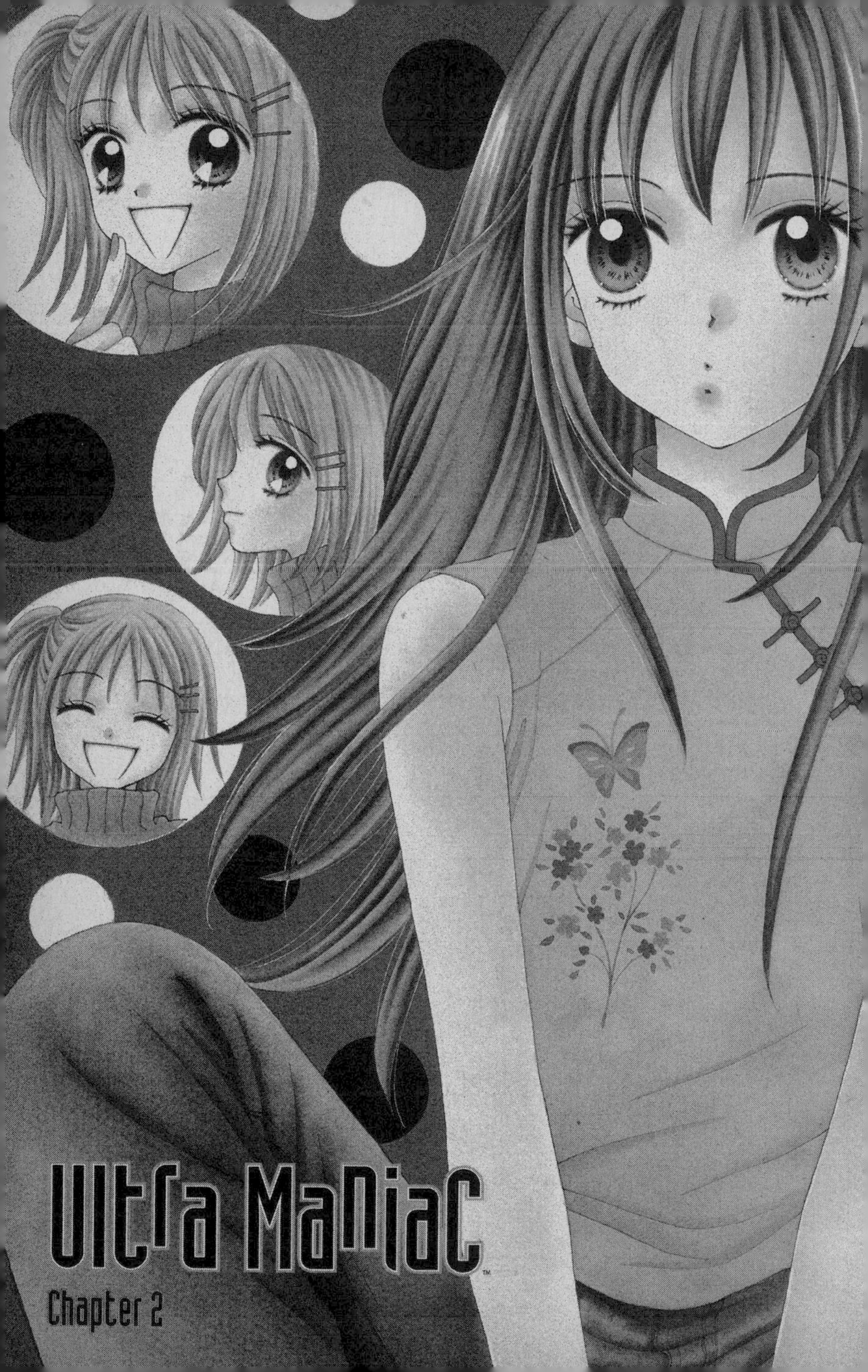
Ultra Maniac™
Chapter 2

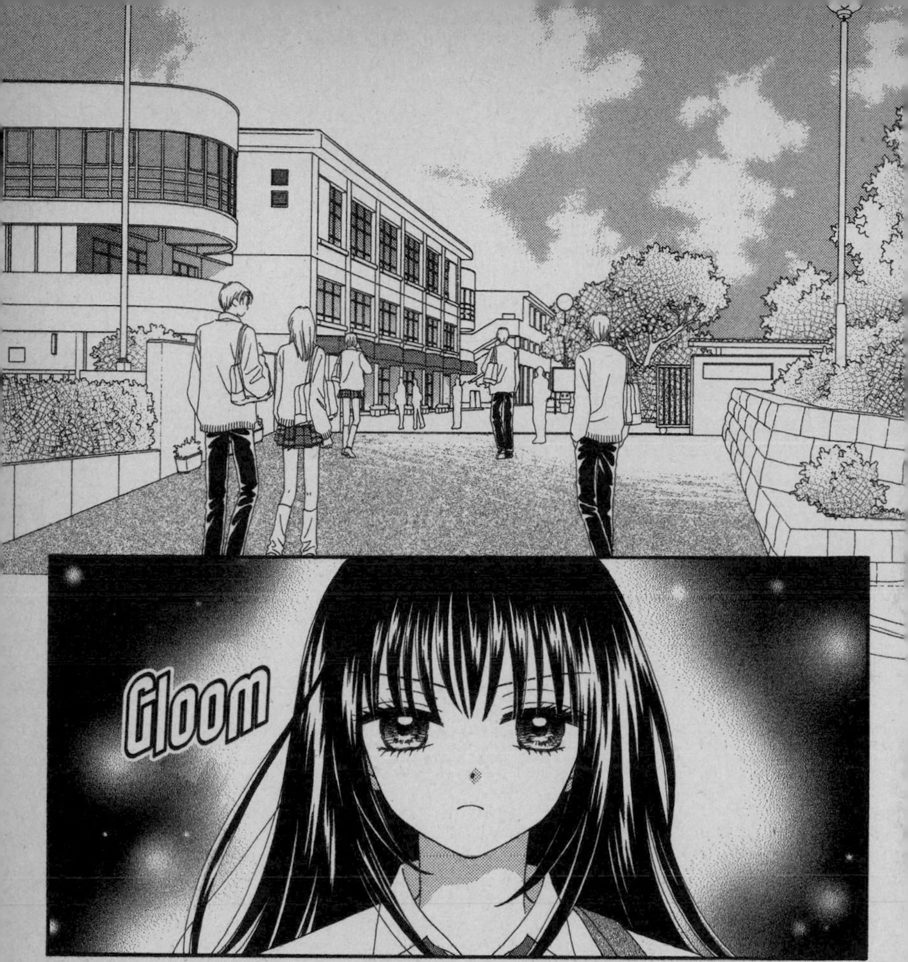
Gloom

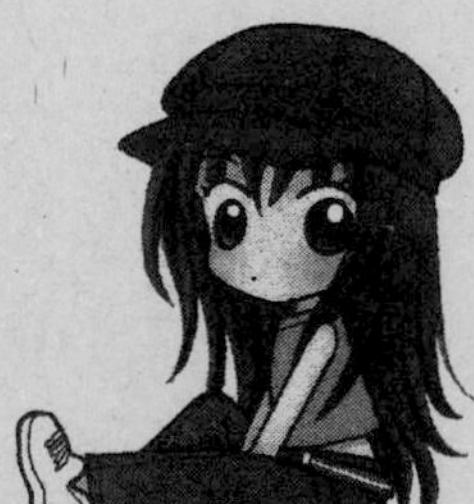

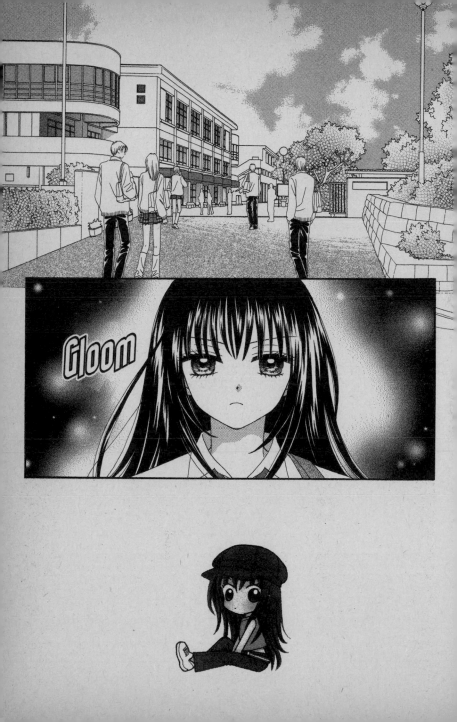

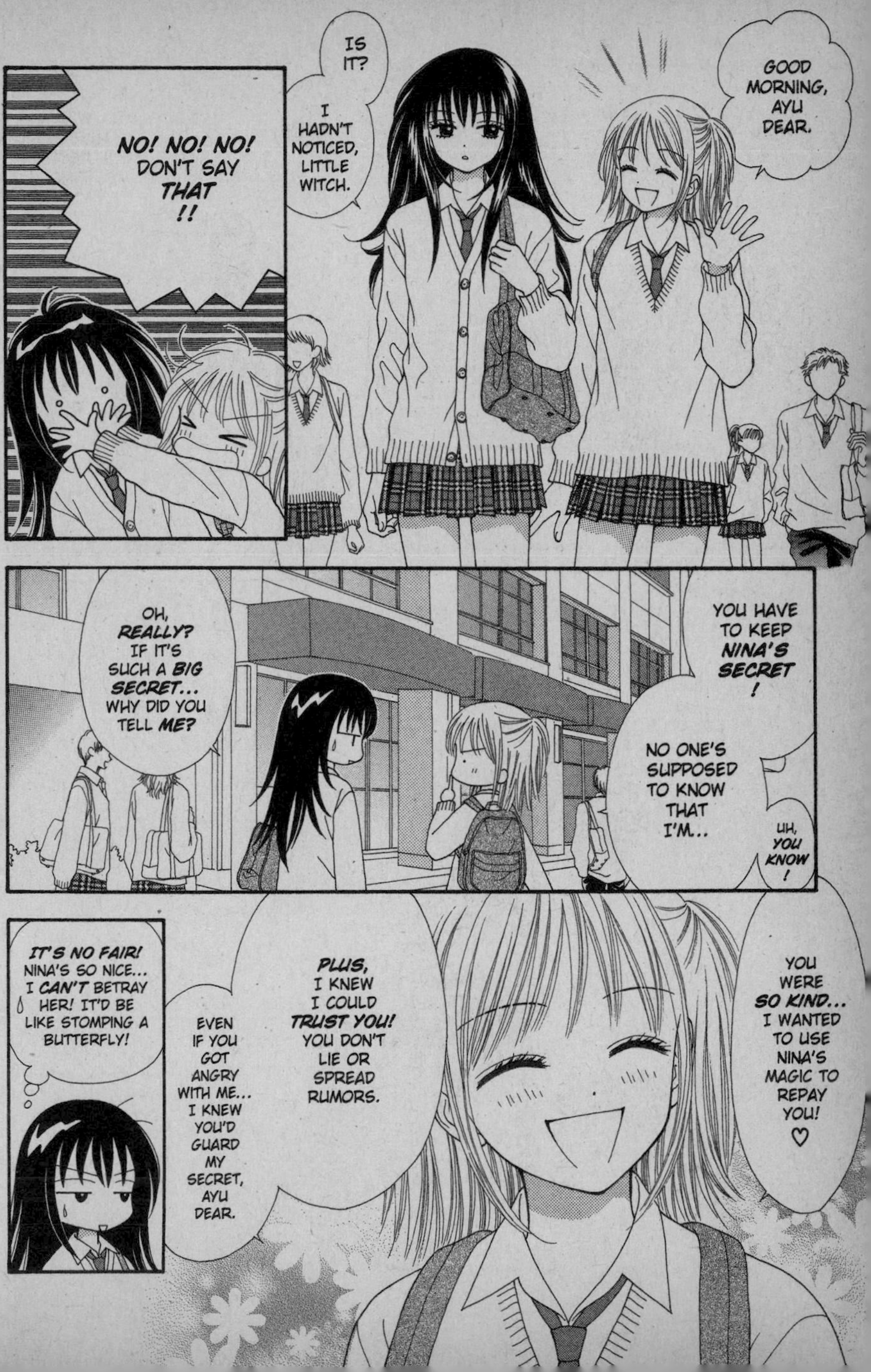
GOOD MORNING, AYU DEAR.
IS IT?
I HADN'T NOTICED, LITTLE WITCH.
NO! NO! NO! DON'T SAY THAT!!
YOU HAVE TO KEEP NINA'S SECRET!
NO ONE'S SUPPOSED TO KNOW THAT I'M...
UH, YOU KNOW!
OH, REALLY? IF IT'S SUCH A BIG SECRET... WHY DID YOU TELL ME?
YOU WERE SO KIND... I WANTED TO USE NINA'S MAGIC TO REPAY YOU! ♡
PLUS, I KNEW I COULD TRUST YOU! YOU DON'T LIE OR SPREAD RUMORS.
EVEN IF YOU GOT ANGRY WITH ME... I KNEW YOU'D GUARD MY SECRET, AYU DEAR.
IT'S NO FAIR! NINA'S SO NICE... I CAN'T BETRAY HER! IT'D BE LIKE STOMPING A BUTTERFLY!

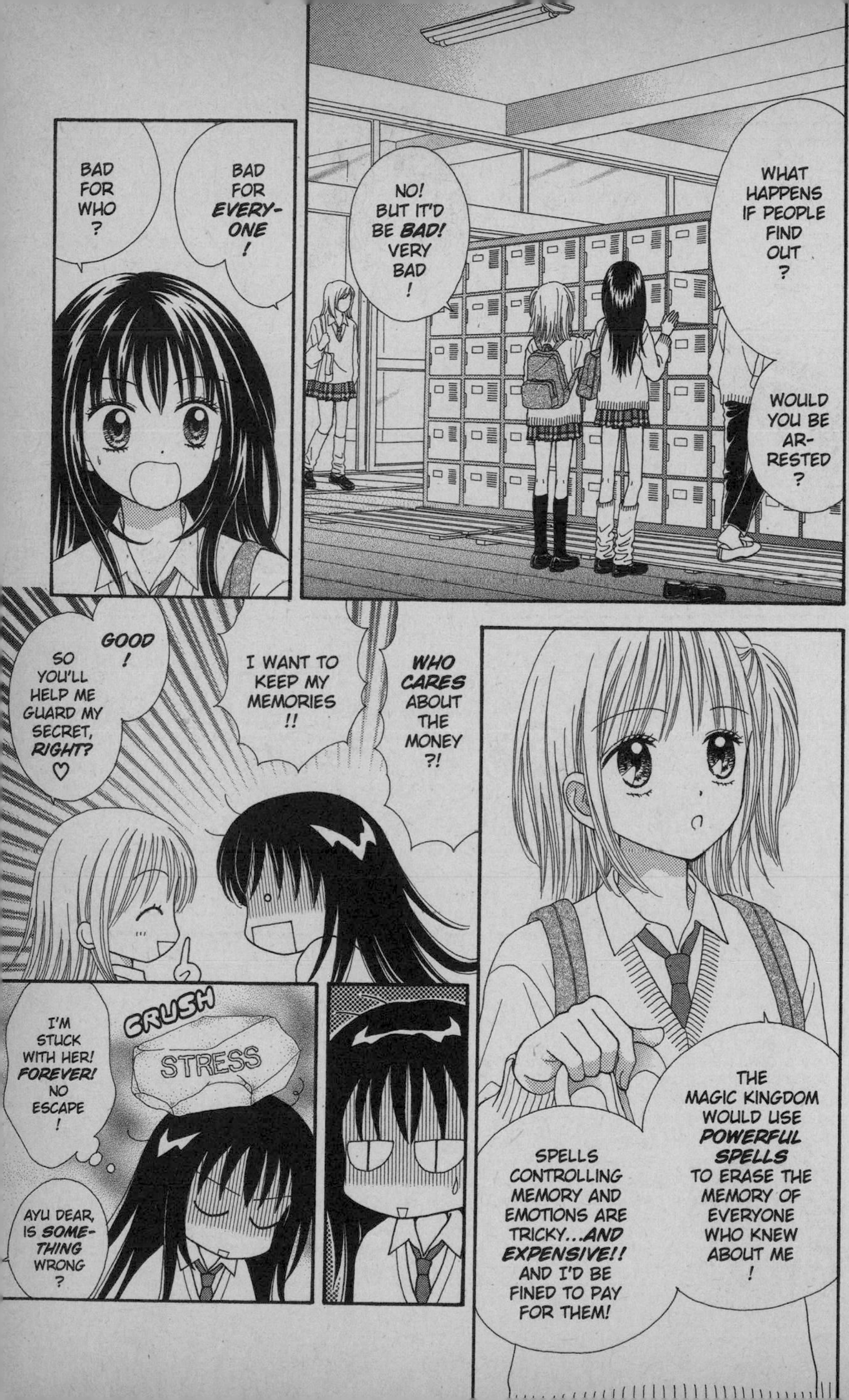
WHAT HAPPENS IF PEOPLE FIND OUT?
WOULD YOU BE AR-RESTED?
NO! BUT IT'D BE BAD! VERY BAD!
BAD FOR EVERY-ONE!
BAD FOR WHO?
THE MAGIC KINGDOM WOULD USE POWERFUL SPELLS TO ERASE THE MEMORY OF EVERYONE WHO KNEW ABOUT ME!
SPELLS CONTROLLING MEMORY AND EMOTIONS ARE TRICKY...AND EXPENSIVE!! AND I'D BE FINED TO PAY FOR THEM!
WHO CARES ABOUT THE MONEY?!
I WANT TO KEEP MY MEMORIES!!
GOOD!
SO YOU'LL HELP ME GUARD MY SECRET, RIGHT? ♡
CRUSH
STRESS
I'M STUCK WITH HER! FOREVER! NO ESCAPE!
AYU DEAR, IS SOME-THING WRONG?

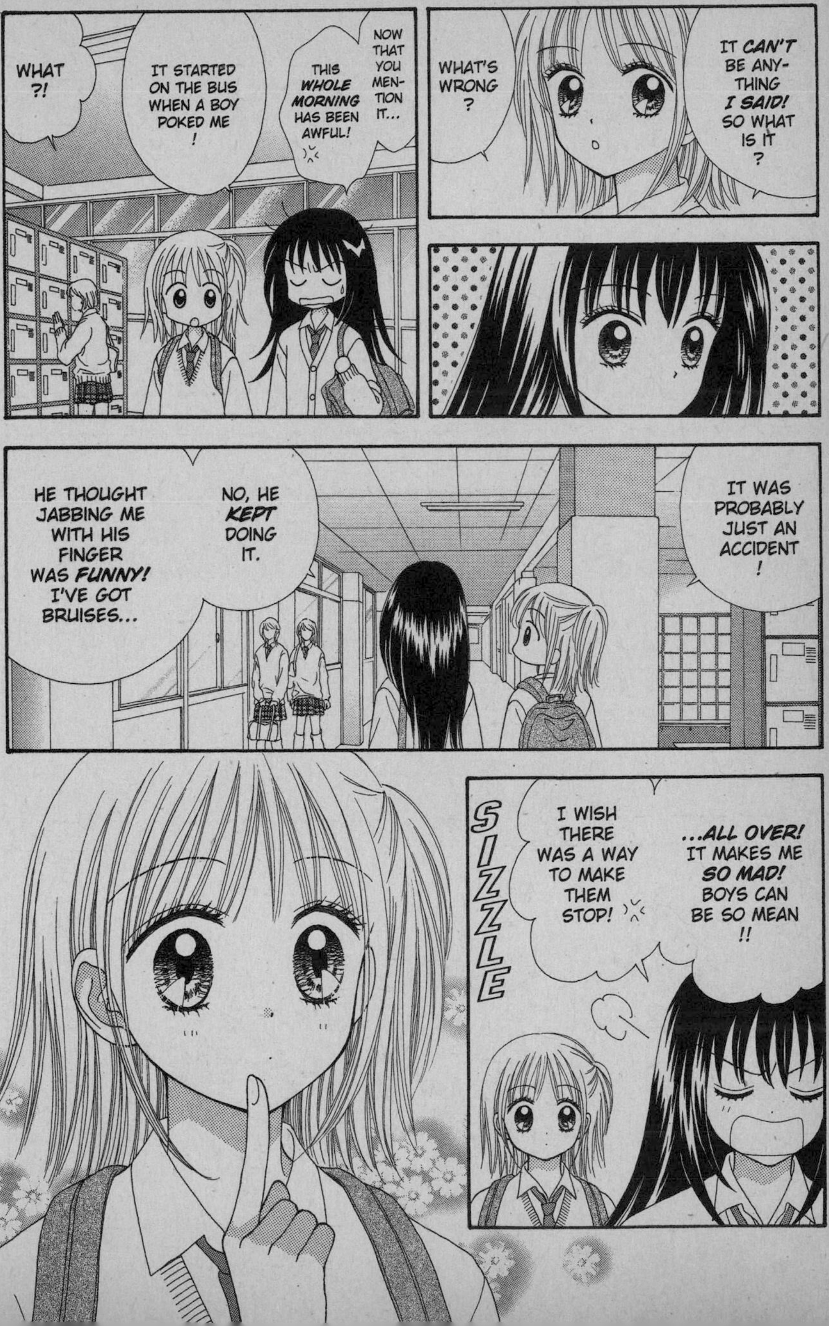
IT CAN'T BE ANYTHING I SAID! SO WHAT IS IT?
WHAT'S WRONG?
NOW THAT YOU MENTION IT...
THIS WHOLE MORNING HAS BEEN AWFUL!
IT STARTED ON THE BUS WHEN A BOY POKED ME!
WHAT?!
IT WAS PROBABLY JUST AN ACCIDENT!
NO, HE KEPT DOING IT.
HE THOUGHT JABBING ME WITH HIS FINGER WAS FUNNY! I'VE GOT BRUISES...
...ALL OVER! IT MAKES ME SO MAD! BOYS CAN BE SO MEAN!!
I WISH THERE WAS A WAY TO MAKE THEM STOP!
SIZZLE

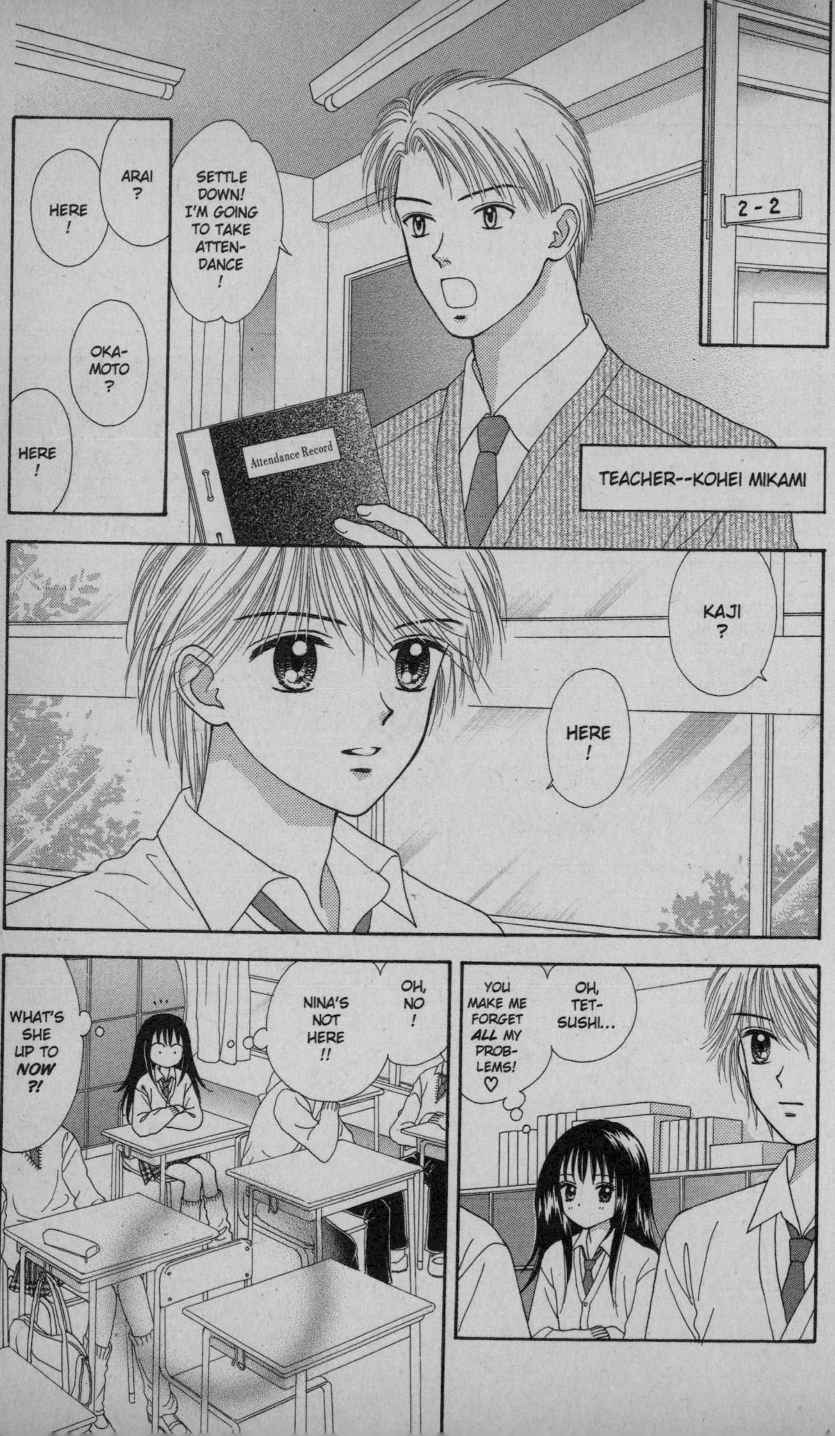
2-2
TEACHER--KOHEI MIKAMI
SETTLE DOWN! I'M GOING TO TAKE ATTEN-DANCE!
ARAI?
HERE!
OKA-MOTO?
HERE!
KAJI?
HERE!
OH, TET-SUSHI...
YOU MAKE ME FORGET *ALL* MY PROB-LEMS! ♡
OH, NO!
NINA'S NOT HERE!!
...
WHAT'S SHE UP TO *NOW*?!

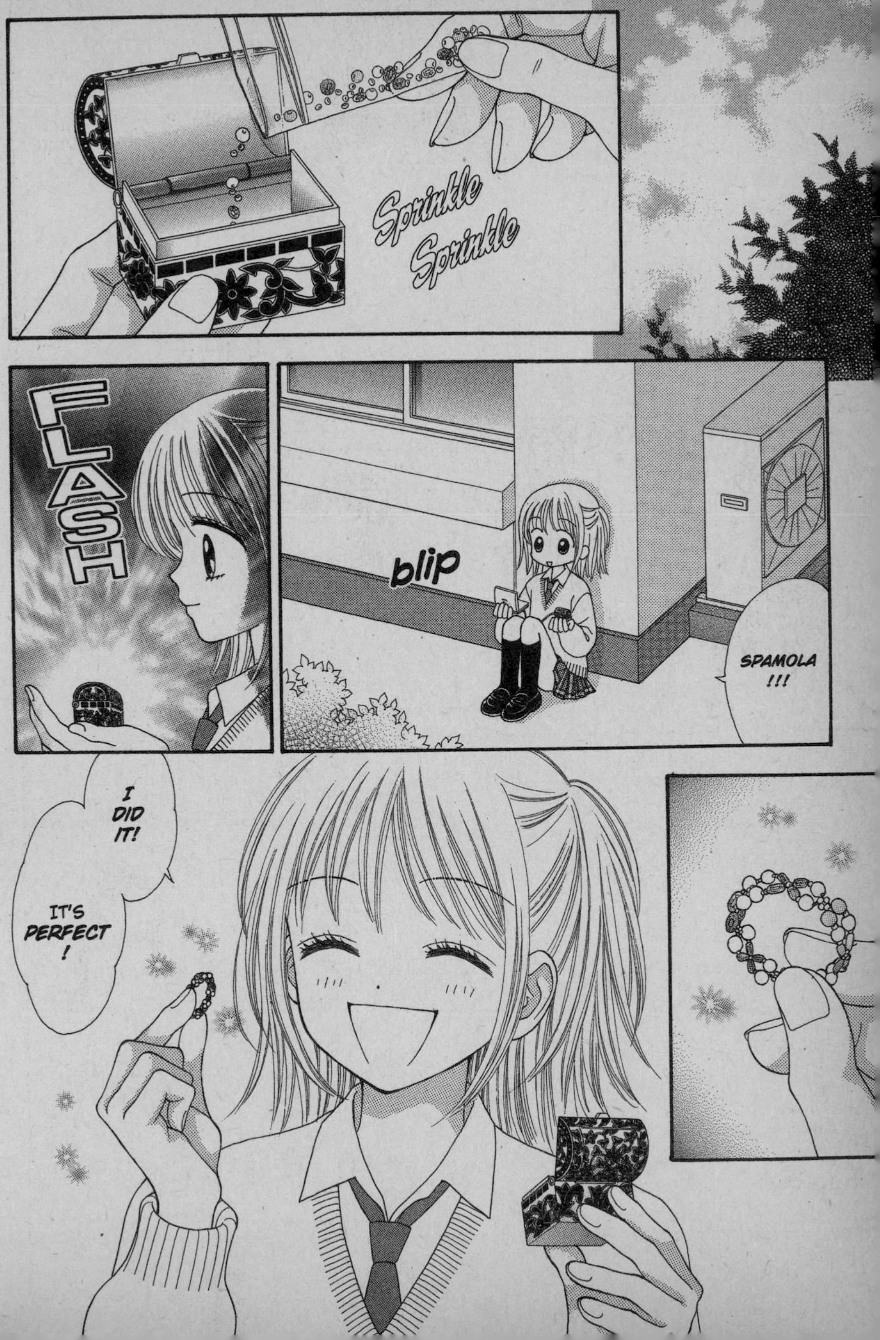
Sprinkle
Sprinkle
SPAMOLA !!!
blip
FLASH
I DID IT!
IT'S PERFECT !

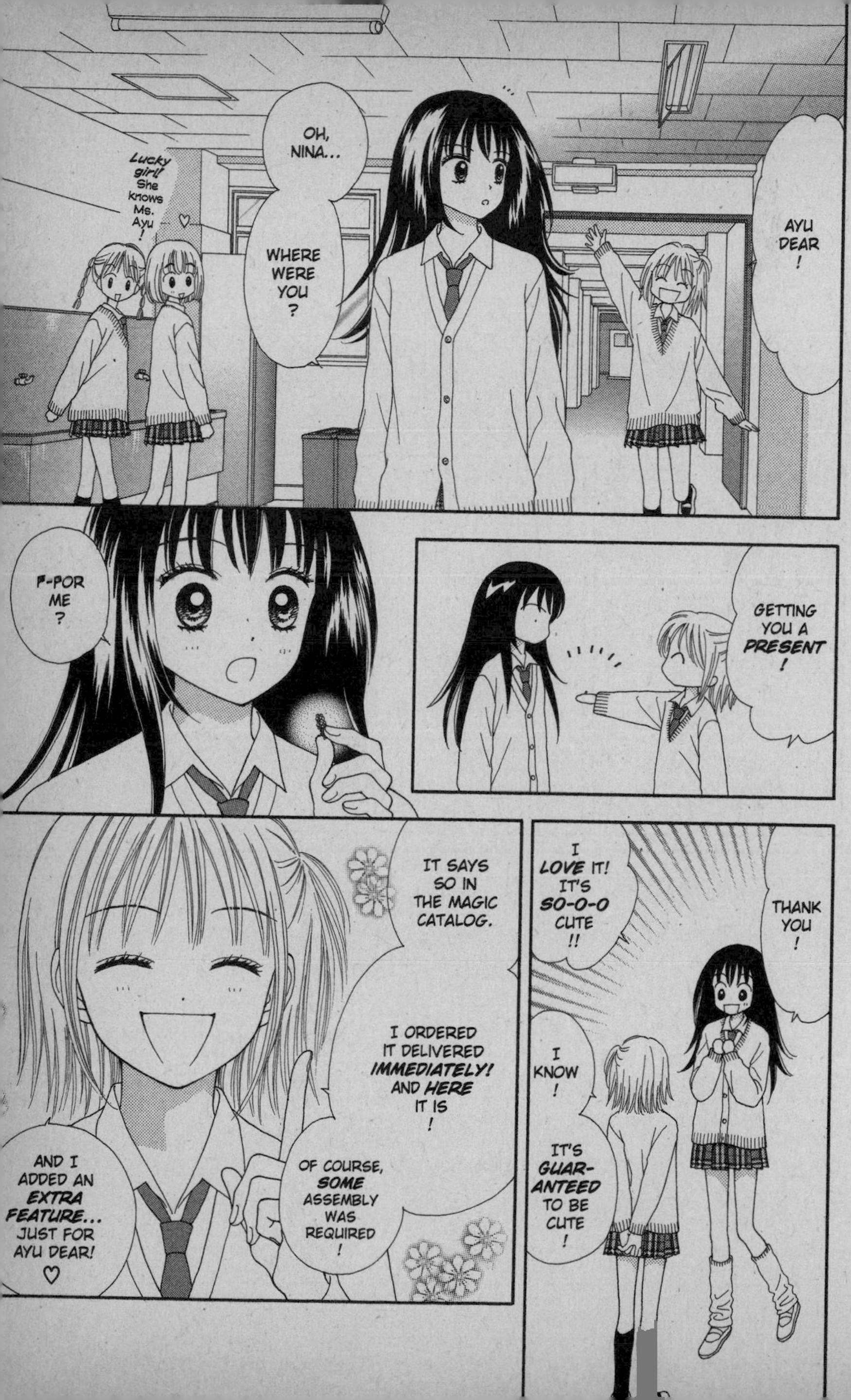
AYU DEAR!
OH, NINA...
WHERE WERE YOU?
Lucky girl! She knows Ms. Ayu! ♡
GETTING YOU A PRESENT!
F-FOR ME?
THANK YOU!
I LOVE IT! IT'S SO-O-O CUTE!!
I KNOW!
IT'S GUARANTEED TO BE CUTE!
IT SAYS SO IN THE MAGIC CATALOG.
I ORDERED IT DELIVERED IMMEDIATELY! AND HERE IT IS!
OF COURSE, SOME ASSEMBLY WAS REQUIRED!
AND I ADDED AN EXTRA FEATURE... JUST FOR AYU DEAR! ♡

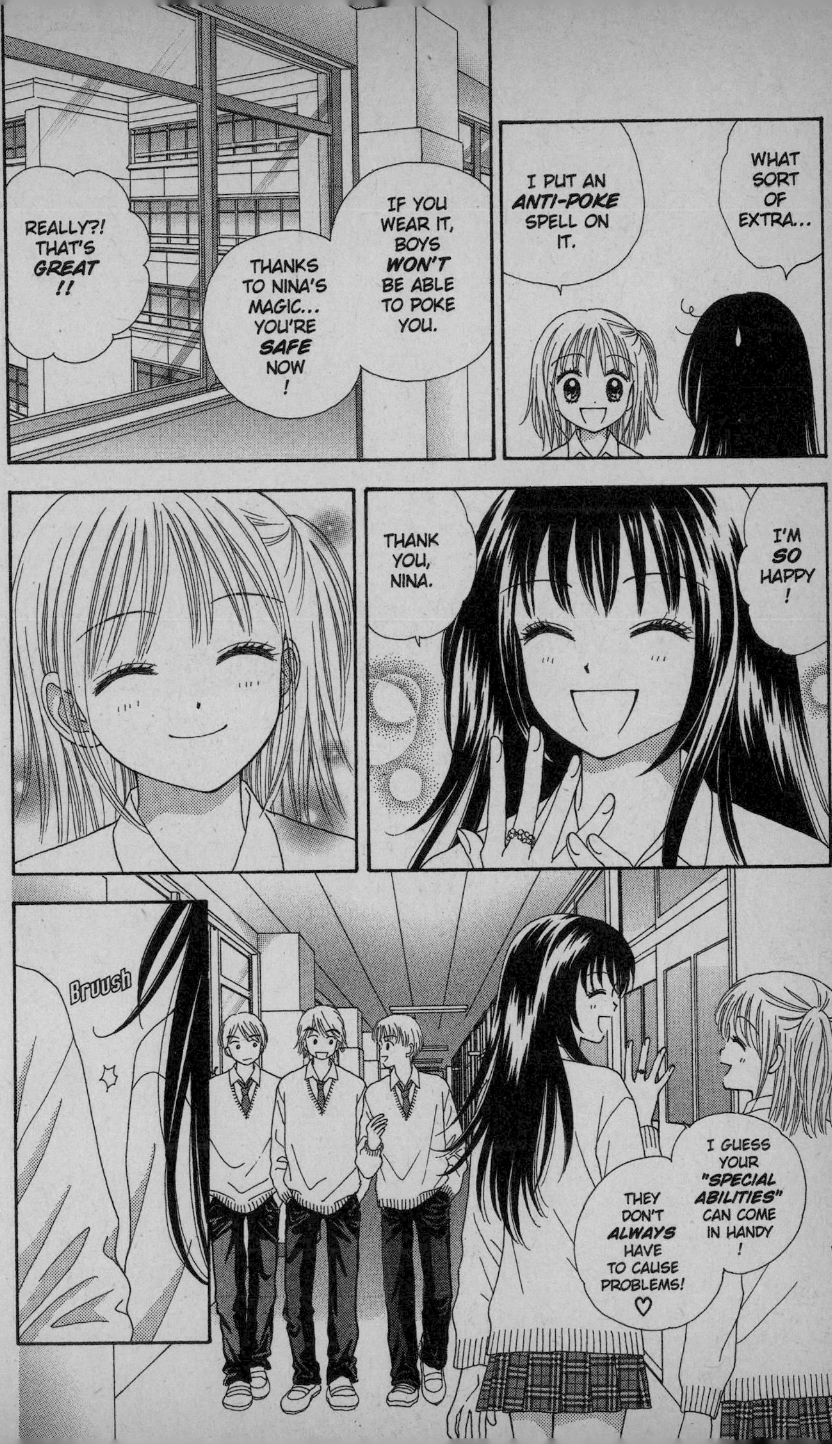

WHAT SORT OF EXTRA...
I PUT AN ANTI-POKE SPELL ON IT.
IF YOU WEAR IT, BOYS WON'T BE ABLE TO POKE YOU.
THANKS TO NINA'S MAGIC... YOU'RE SAFE NOW!
REALLY?! THAT'S GREAT!!
I'M SO HAPPY!
THANK YOU, NINA.
I GUESS YOUR "SPECIAL ABILITIES" CAN COME IN HANDY!
THEY DON'T ALWAYS HAVE TO CAUSE PROBLEMS! ♡
Bruush

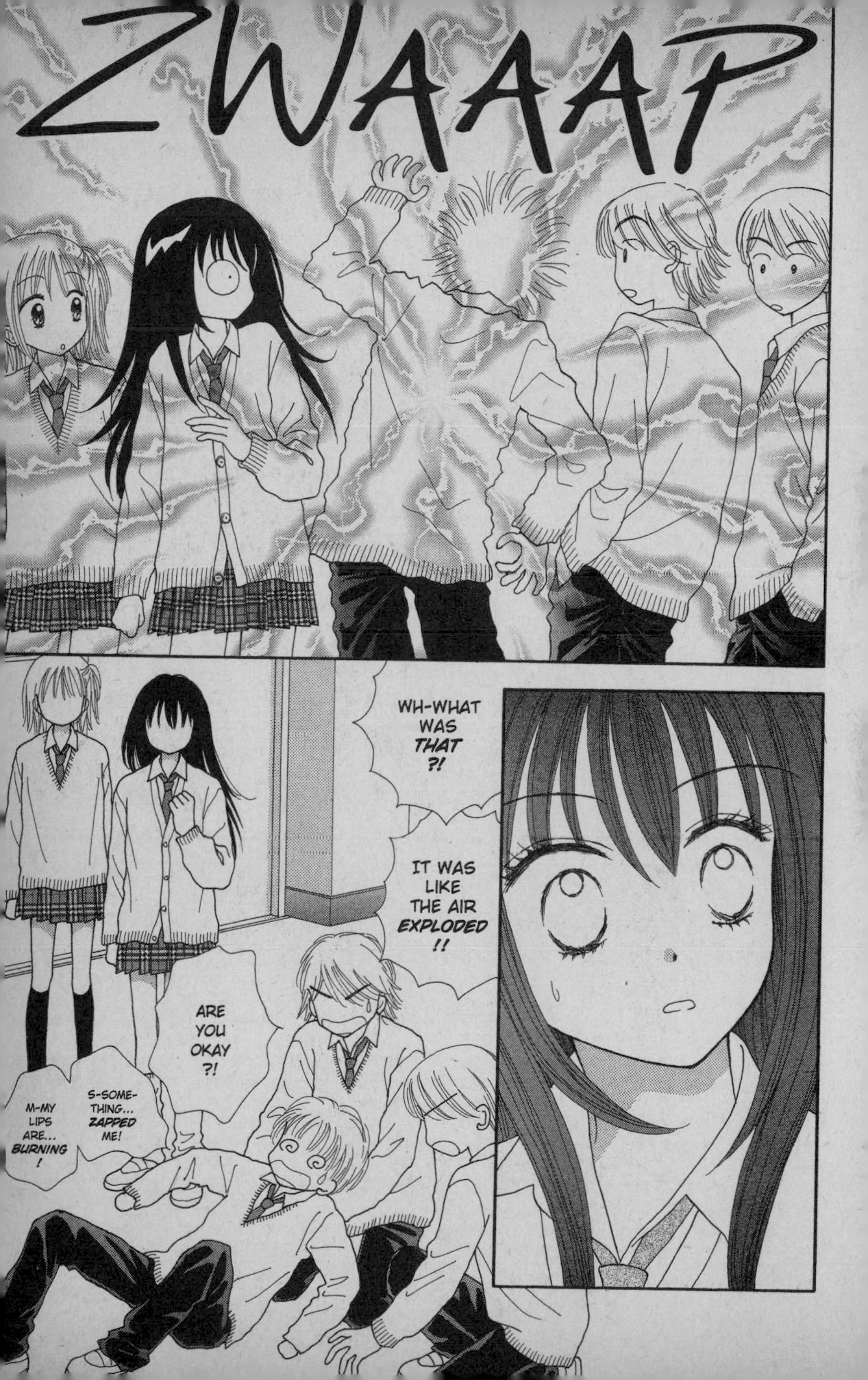
ZWAAAP
WH-WHAT WAS THAT?!
IT WAS LIKE THE AIR EXPLODED!!
ARE YOU OKAY?!
S-SOMETHING... ZAPPED ME!
M-MY LIPS ARE... BURNING!

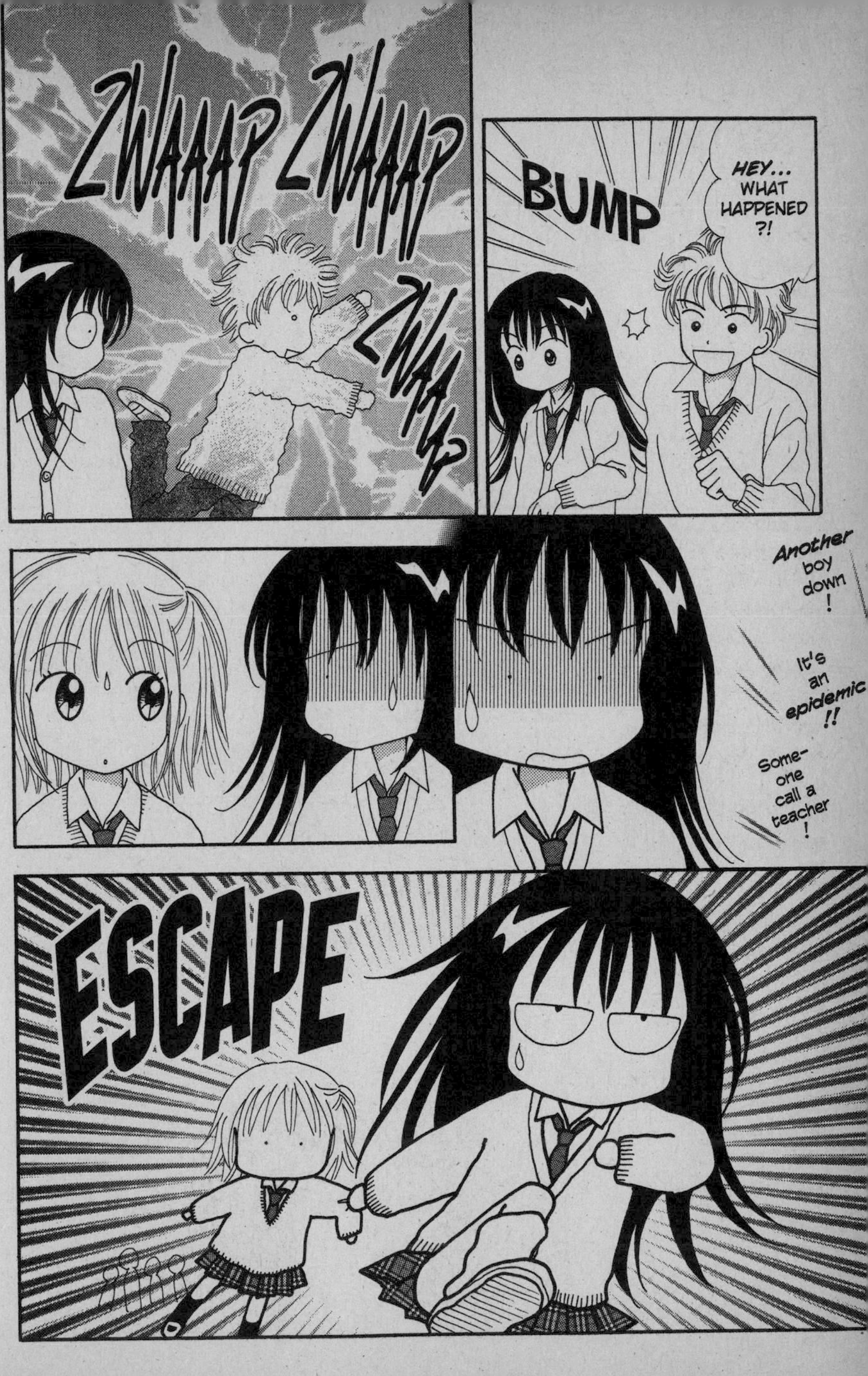
BUMP
HEY... WHAT HAPPENED ?!
ZWAAAP ZWAAAP
ZWAAAP
Another boy down!
It's an epidemic!!
Some-one call a teacher!
ESCAPE

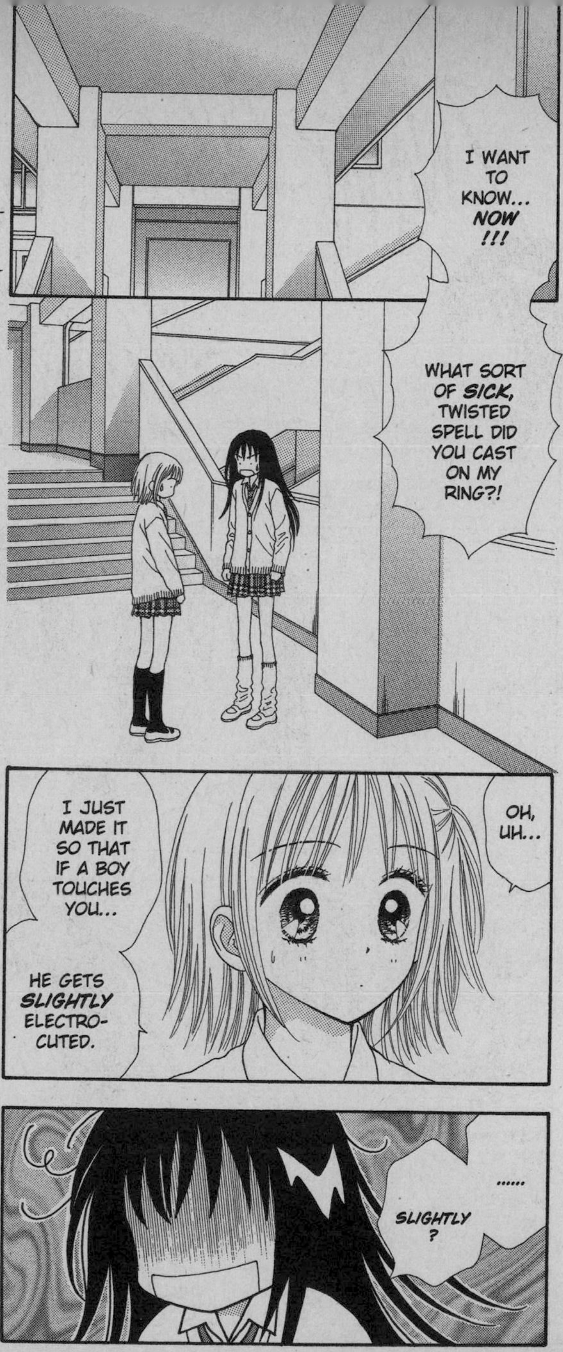
I WANT TO KNOW... NOW !!!
WHAT SORT OF SICK, TWISTED SPELL DID YOU CAST ON MY RING?!
OH, UH...
I JUST MADE IT SO THAT IF A BOY TOUCHES YOU...
HE GETS SLIGHTLY ELECTROCUTED.
......
SLIGHTLY ?

FREE TALK 4

In the past, most of my main characters have been high school students. Since magic is an important part of "Ultra Maniac," it seemed appropriate to make the characters younger. So I put them in junior high.

My series, "We're in Mint Condition"("Minton a Bokura"), was also about junior high students. But in that series I took a different approach to the art. I made the characters look like adolescents and by the time I finished I was really tired of that look. So, this time around, I decided to draw the characters as if they were older, but make them behave more like junior high kids.

I think the thing that has changed the most about my art is that I'm drawing a lot more eyelashes.

Why? Well, I think wearing mascara is becoming more popular with students. But also. . . I just like drawing eyelashes.

Most of the time, I draw eyelashes and mascara as if I'm putting mascara on myself. (Ha. Ha.) As a result, sometimes the characters end up with too much.

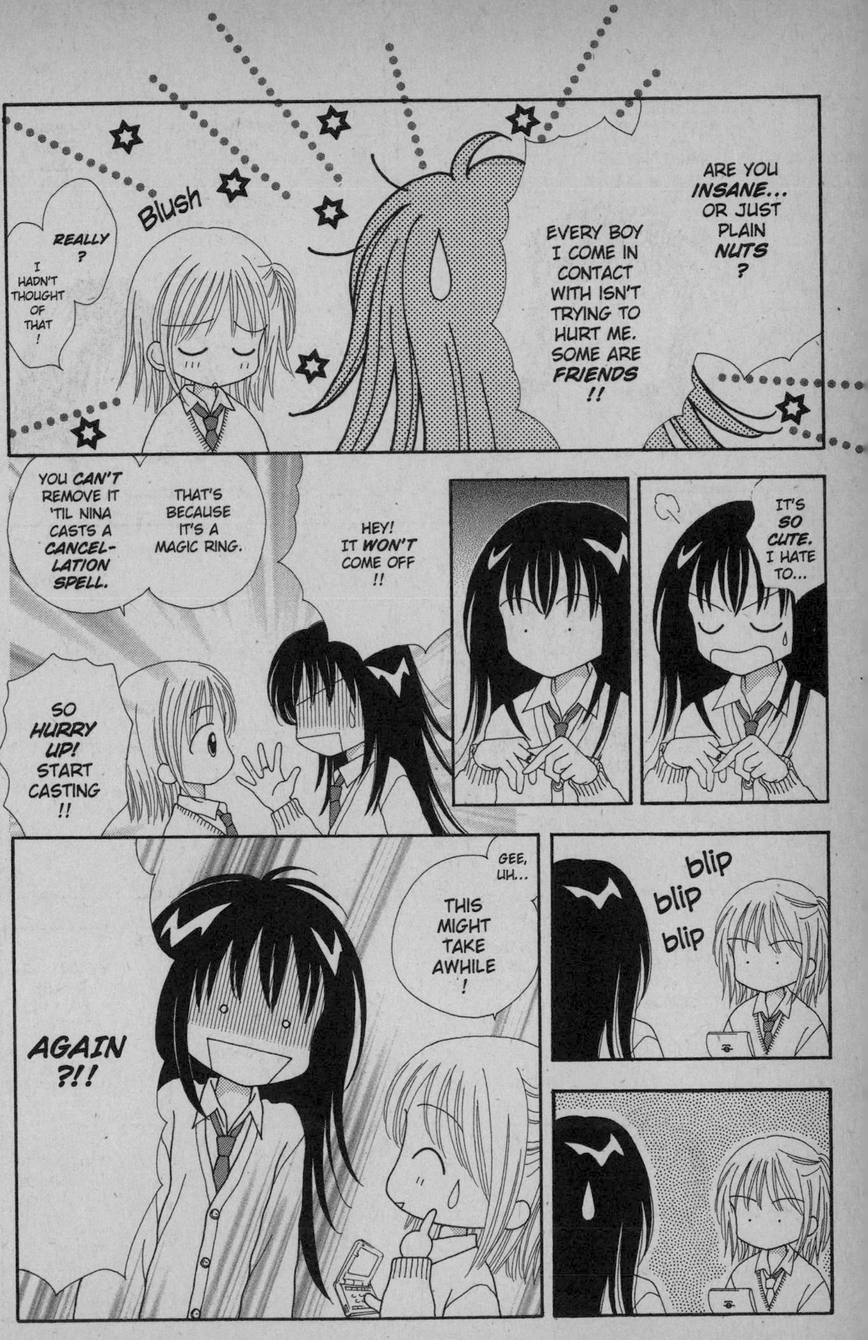
ARE YOU INSANE... OR JUST PLAIN NUTS?
EVERY BOY I COME IN CONTACT WITH ISN'T TRYING TO HURT ME. SOME ARE FRIENDS!!
Blush
REALLY? I HADN'T THOUGHT OF THAT!
IT'S SO CUTE. I HATE TO...
HEY! IT WON'T COME OFF!!
THAT'S BECAUSE IT'S A MAGIC RING.
YOU CAN'T REMOVE IT 'TIL NINA CASTS A CANCEL-LATION SPELL.
SO HURRY UP! START CASTING!!
blip
blip
blip
GEE, UH...
THIS MIGHT TAKE AWHILE!
AGAIN?!!

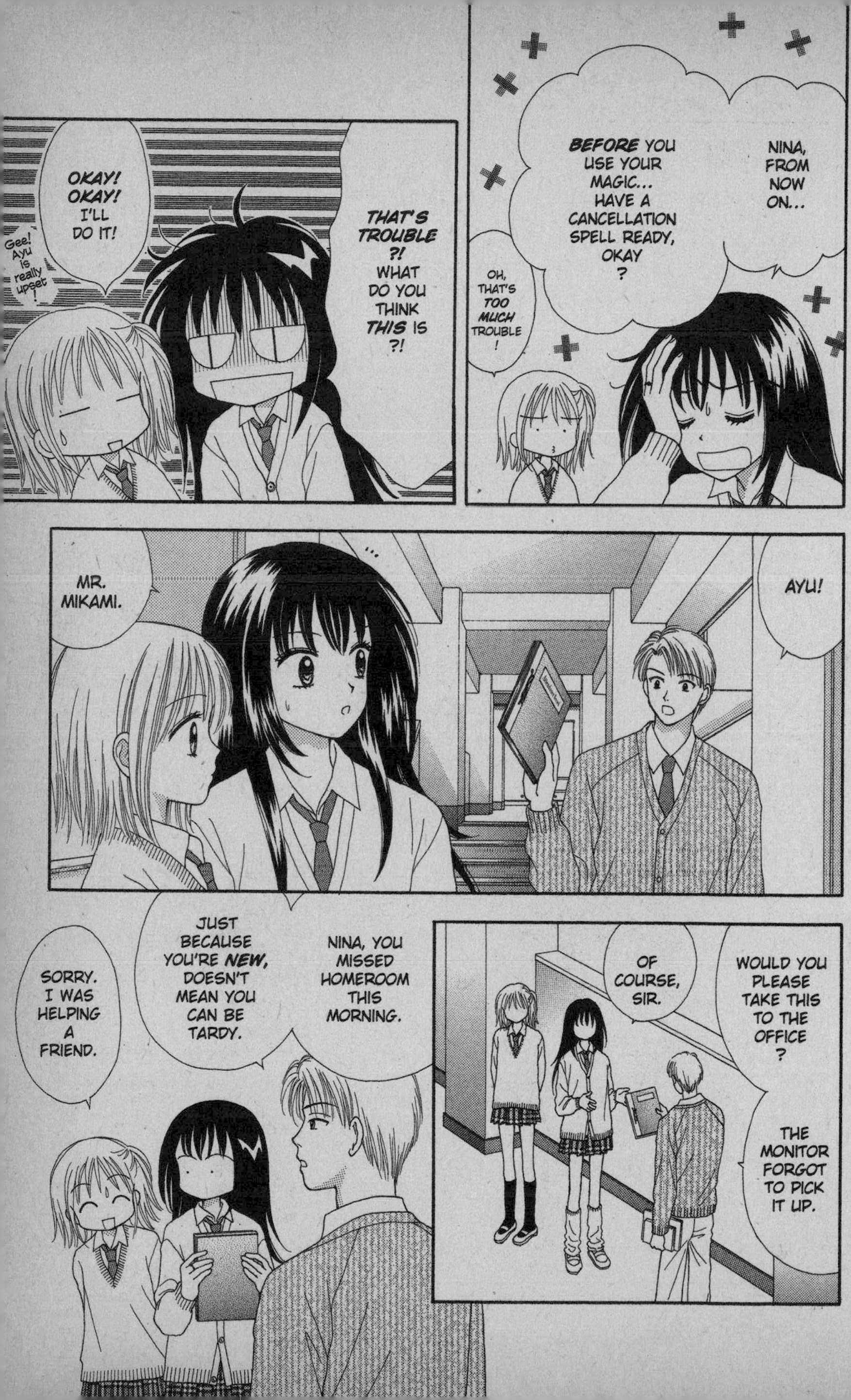
NINA, FROM NOW ON...
BEFORE YOU USE YOUR MAGIC... HAVE A CANCELLATION SPELL READY, OKAY?
OH, THAT'S TOO MUCH TROUBLE!
THAT'S TROUBLE?! WHAT DO YOU THINK THIS IS?!
OKAY! OKAY! I'LL DO IT!
Gee! Ayu is really upset!
AYU!
...
MR. MIKAMI.
WOULD YOU PLEASE TAKE THIS TO THE OFFICE?
THE MONITOR FORGOT TO PICK IT UP.
OF COURSE, SIR.
NINA, YOU MISSED HOMEROOM THIS MORNING.
JUST BECAUSE YOU'RE NEW, DOESN'T MEAN YOU CAN BE TARDY.
SORRY. I WAS HELPING A FRIEND.

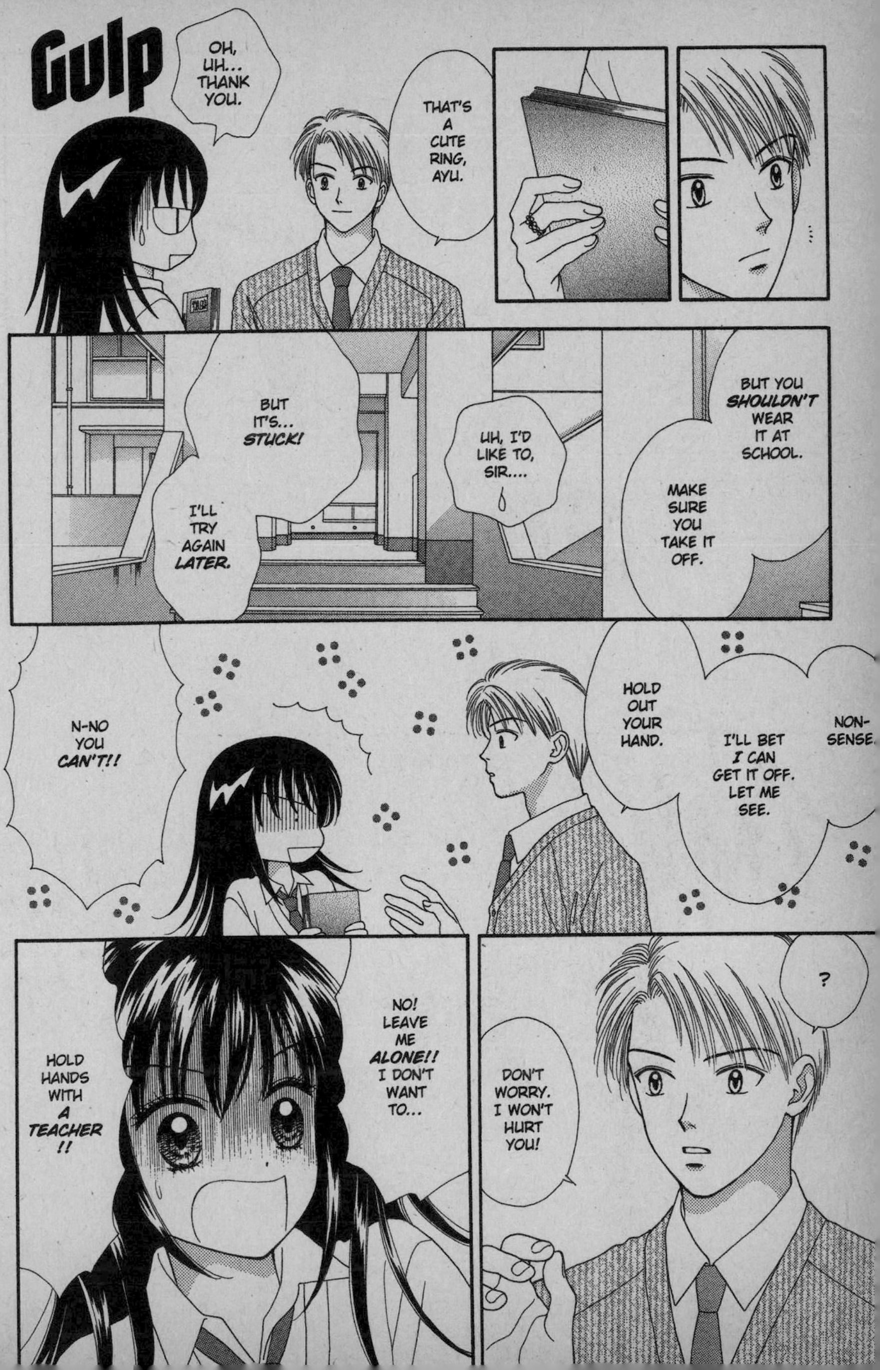
...
THAT'S A CUTE RING, AYU.
OH, UH... THANK YOU.
Gulp
BUT YOU SHOULDN'T WEAR IT AT SCHOOL.
MAKE SURE YOU TAKE IT OFF.
UH, I'D LIKE TO, SIR....
BUT IT'S... STUCK!
I'LL TRY AGAIN LATER.
NON-SENSE.
I'LL BET I CAN GET IT OFF. LET ME SEE.
HOLD OUT YOUR HAND.
N-NO YOU CAN'T!!
?
DON'T WORRY. I WON'T HURT YOU!
NO! LEAVE ME ALONE!! I DON'T WANT TO...
HOLD HANDS WITH A TEACHER!!

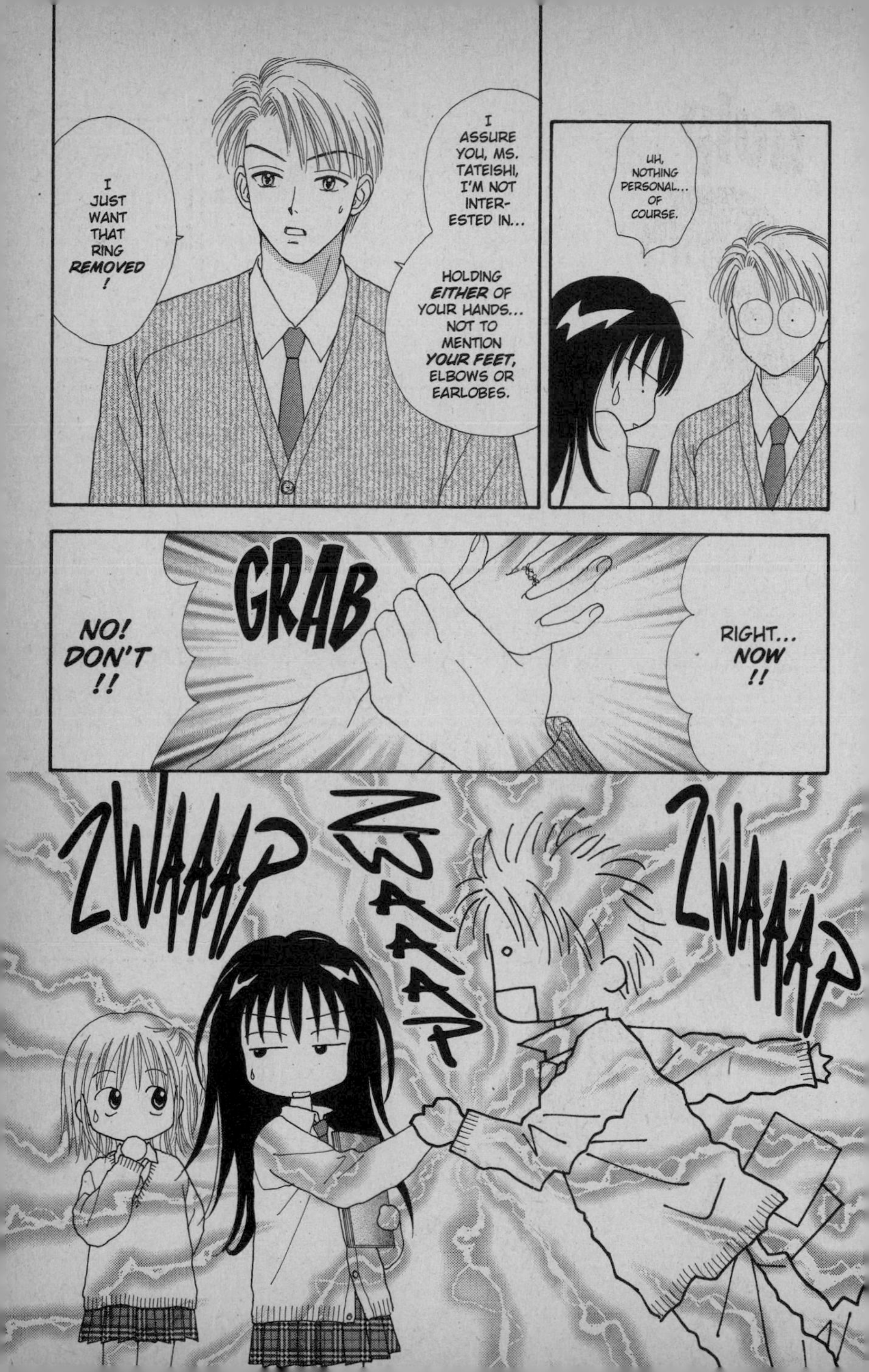
UH, NOTHING PERSONAL... OF COURSE.
I ASSURE YOU, MS. TATEISHI, I'M NOT INTER-ESTED IN...
HOLDING *EITHER* OF YOUR HANDS... NOT TO MENTION *YOUR FEET*, ELBOWS OR EARLOBES.
I JUST WANT THAT RING *REMOVED*!
RIGHT... *NOW*!!
GRAB
NO! DON'T!!
ZWAAAP
ZWAAAP
ZWAAAP

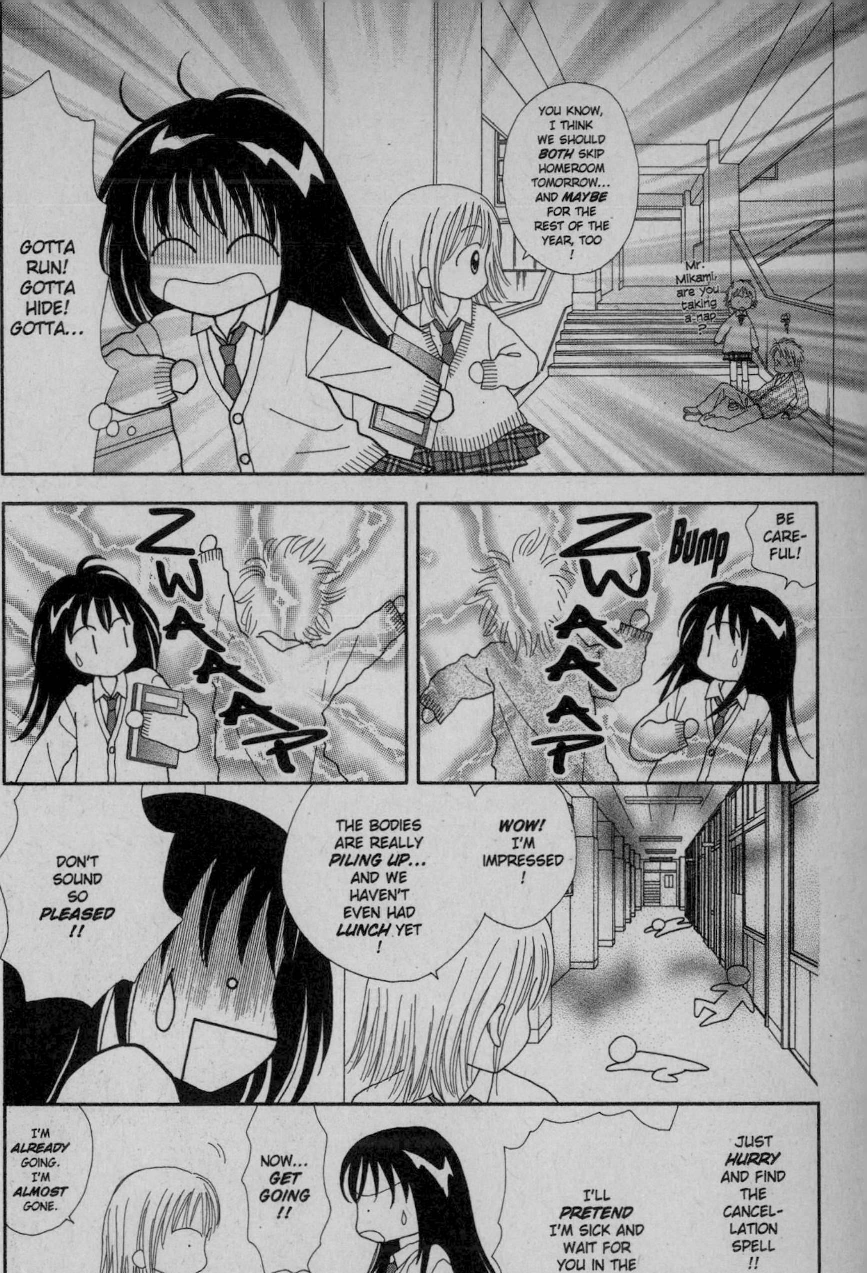
YOU KNOW, I THINK WE SHOULD BOTH SKIP HOMEROOM TOMORROW... AND MAYBE FOR THE REST OF THE YEAR, TOO!
Mr. Mikami, are you taking a nap?
GOTTA RUN! GOTTA HIDE! GOTTA...
BE CAREFUL!
Bump
ZWAAAAP
ZWAAAAP
WOW! I'M IMPRESSED!
THE BODIES ARE REALLY PILING UP... AND WE HAVEN'T EVEN HAD LUNCH YET!
DON'T SOUND SO PLEASED!!
JUST HURRY AND FIND THE CANCELLATION SPELL!!
I'LL PRETEND I'M SICK AND WAIT FOR YOU IN THE INFIRMARY.
NOW... GET GOING!!
I'M ALREADY GOING. I'M ALMOST GONE.

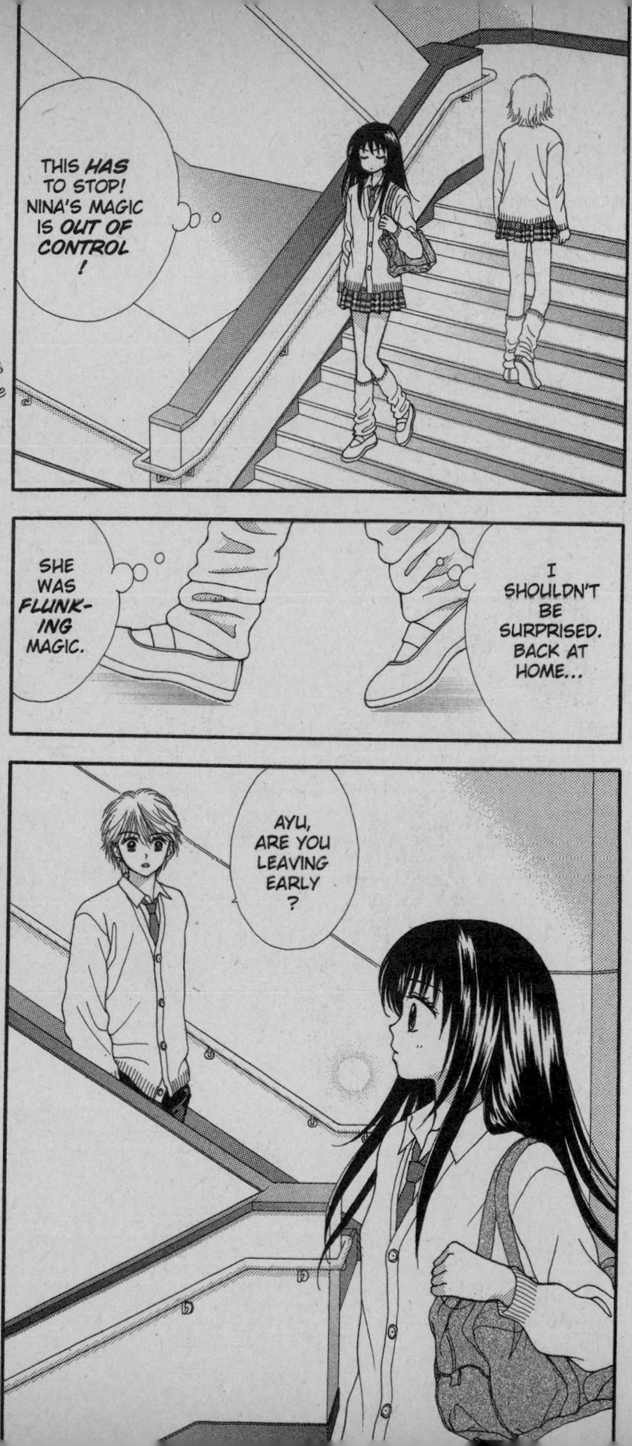
THIS *HAS* TO STOP! NINA'S MAGIC IS *OUT OF CONTROL*!
I SHOULDN'T BE SURPRISED. BACK AT HOME...
SHE WAS *FLUNKING* MAGIC.
AYU, ARE YOU LEAVING EARLY?

FREE TALK 5

Around the time "Ultra Maniac" started, the first "Harry Potter" movie was in theaters and was a huge hit.

Even before that, of course, I'd heard about "Harry." The book was a best seller and I knew it was supposed to be a lot of fun. So I really wanted to read it.

The hardback, however, was so big and heavy . . . I decided to wait for the paperback. I waited and waited . . . and the paperback still wasn't published. Since I was doing a fantasy series, I really felt I should read "Harry" for reference! So I finally bought a copy of the hardback and lugged this mammoth tome home.

Unfortunately . . . I got so busy working that I never got around to reading "Harry." So, here it sits unread and I'm already seven months into this series!

Of course, I haven't seen the movie yet either. At this rate, I probably won't read any of the books until the entire "Harry Potter" series is finished!

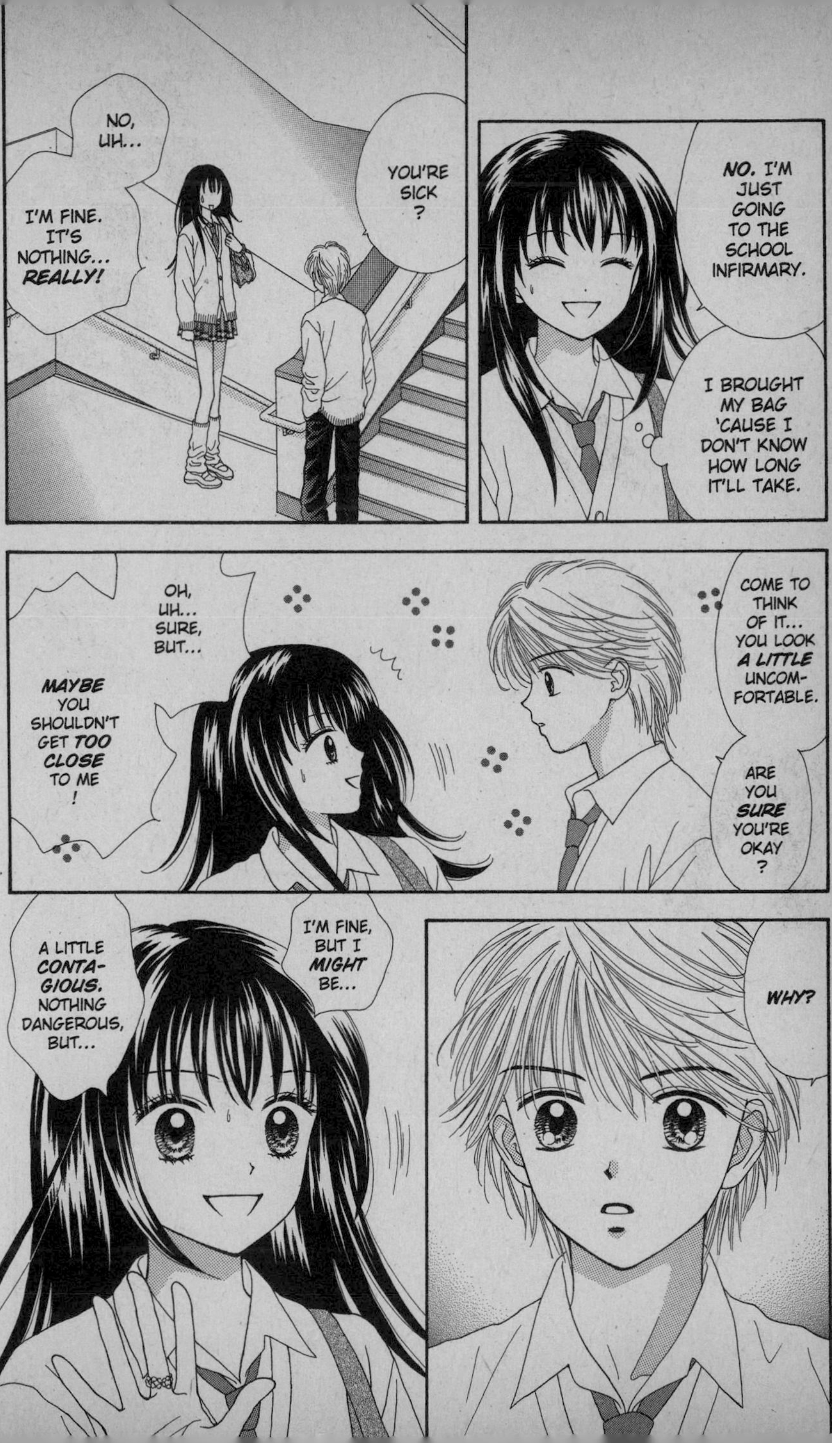
NO. I'M JUST GOING TO THE SCHOOL INFIRMARY.
I BROUGHT MY BAG 'CAUSE I DON'T KNOW HOW LONG IT'LL TAKE.
YOU'RE SICK?
NO, UH...
I'M FINE. IT'S NOTHING... REALLY!
COME TO THINK OF IT... YOU LOOK A LITTLE UNCOMFORTABLE.
ARE YOU SURE YOU'RE OKAY?
OH, UH... SURE, BUT...
MAYBE YOU SHOULDN'T GET TOO CLOSE TO ME!
WHY?
I'M FINE, BUT I MIGHT BE...
A LITTLE CONTAGIOUS. NOTHING DANGEROUS, BUT...

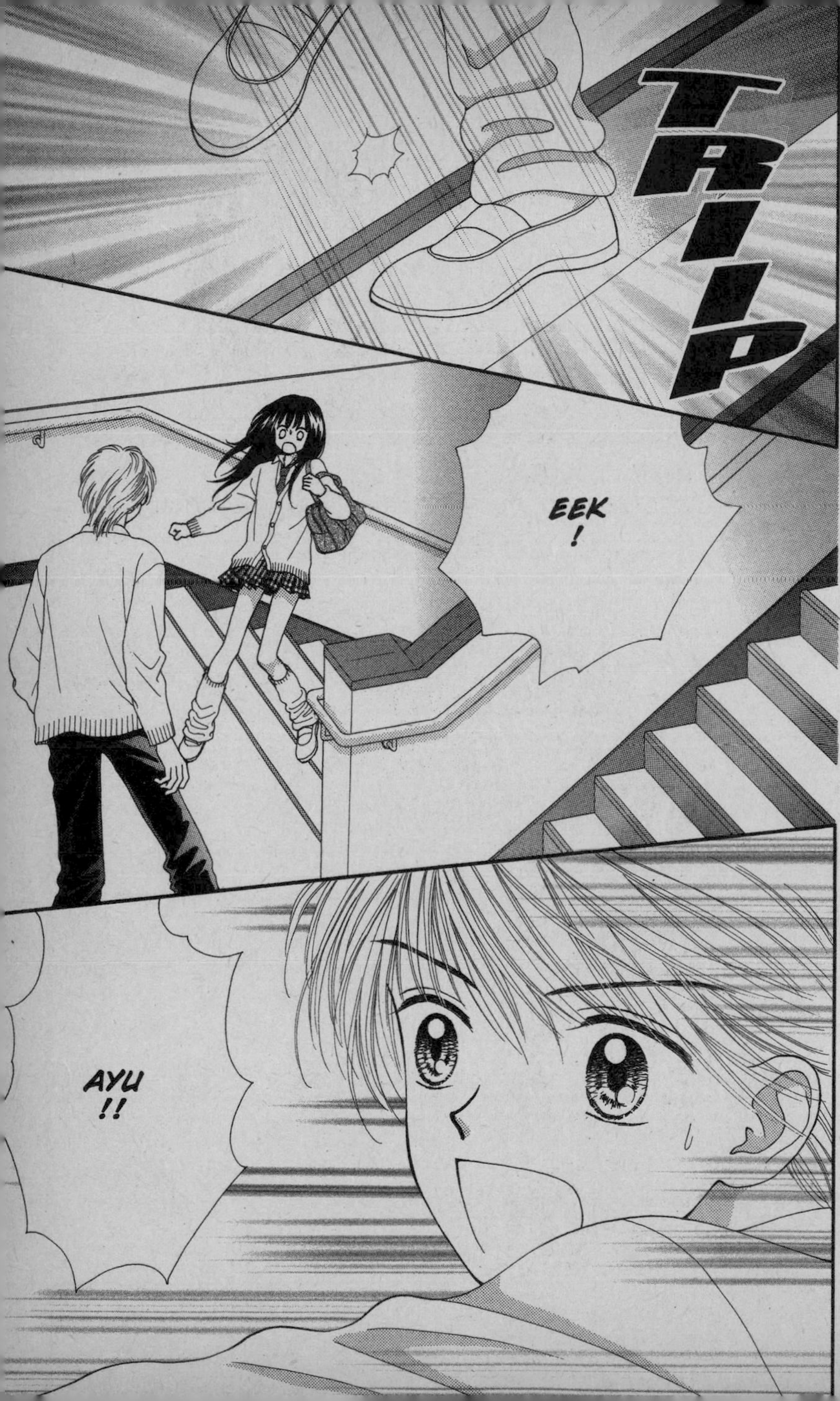
TRIP
EEK!
AYU!!

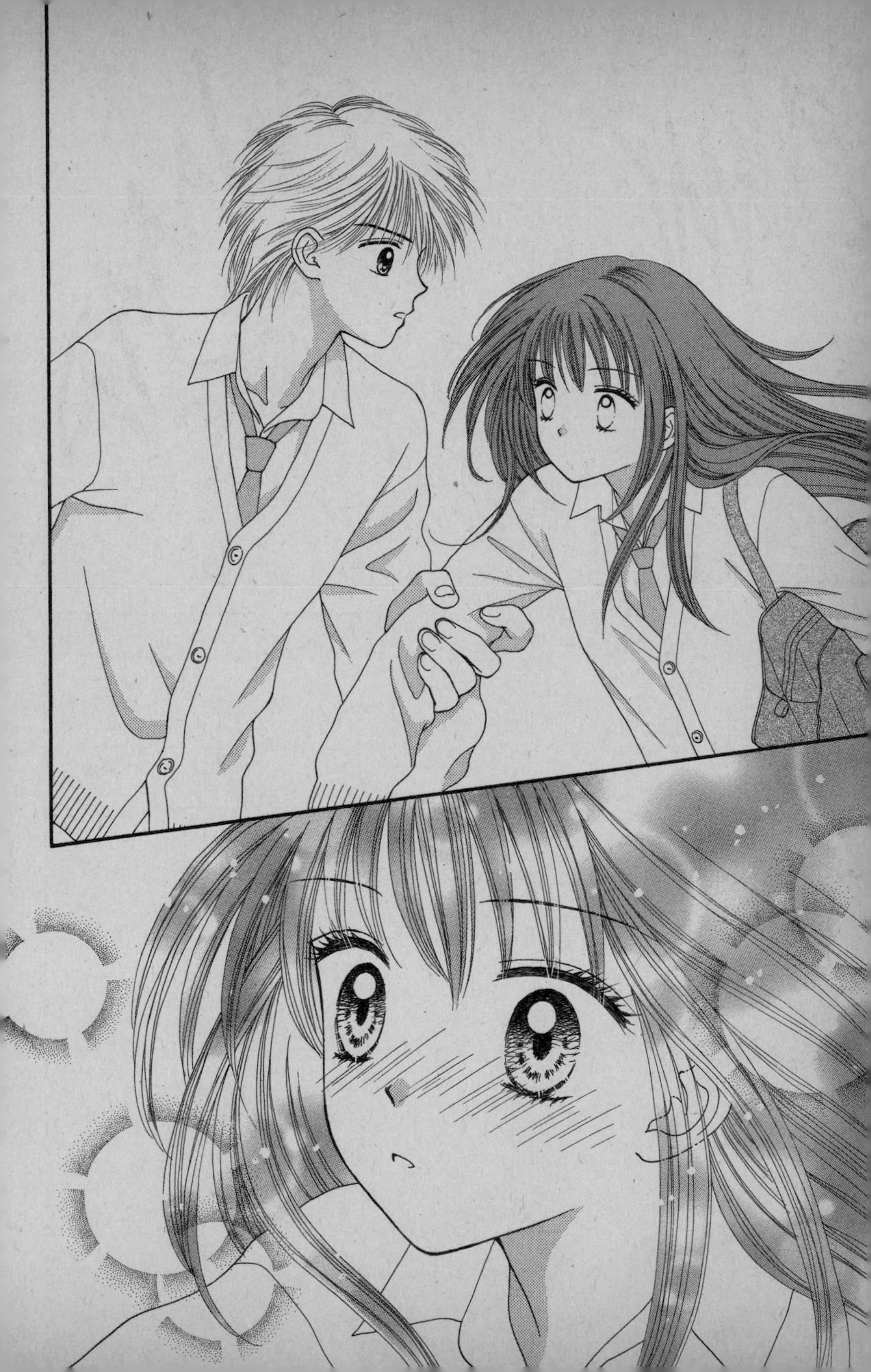

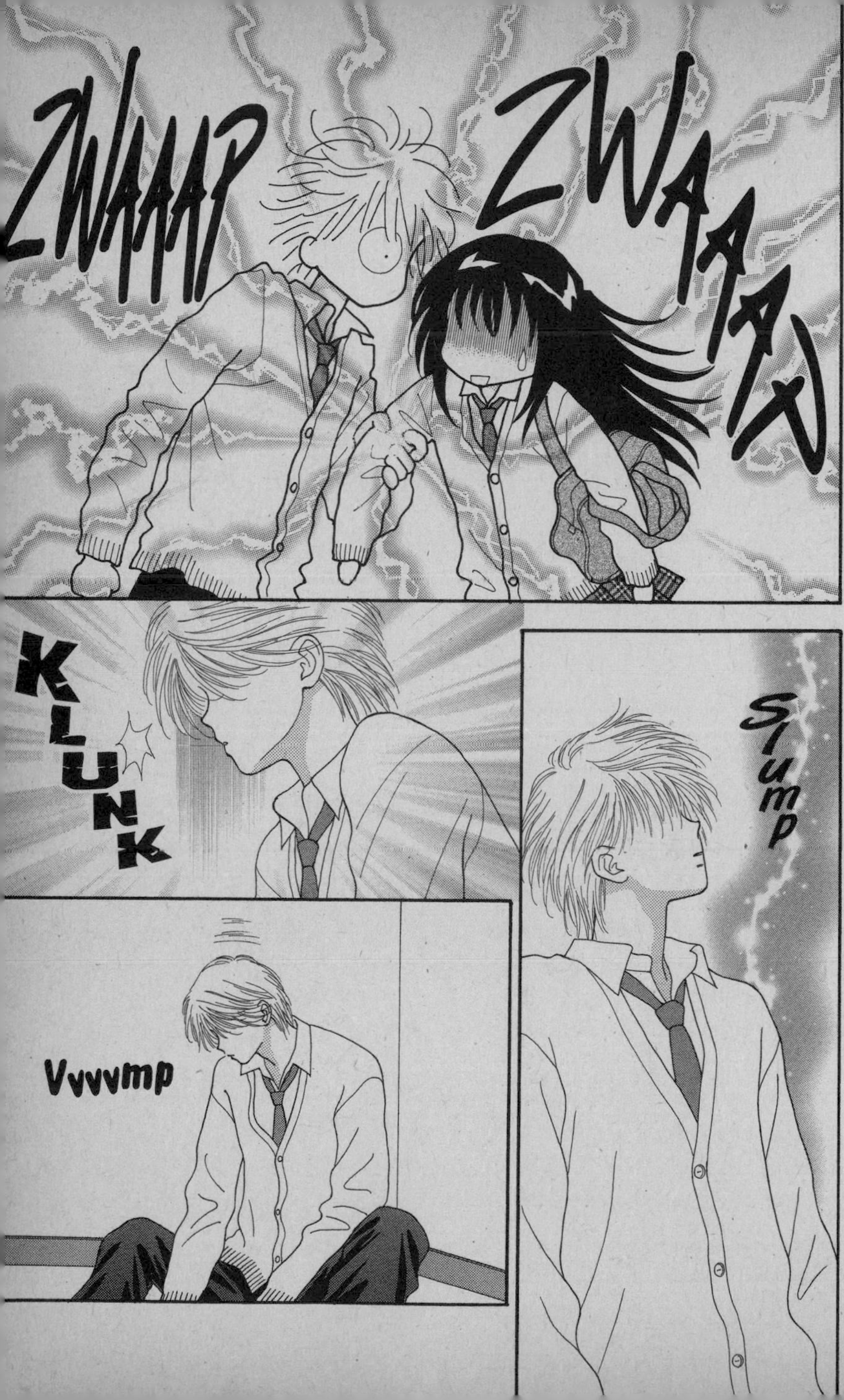
ZWAAAP
ZWAAAP
Slump
KLUNK
Vvvvmp

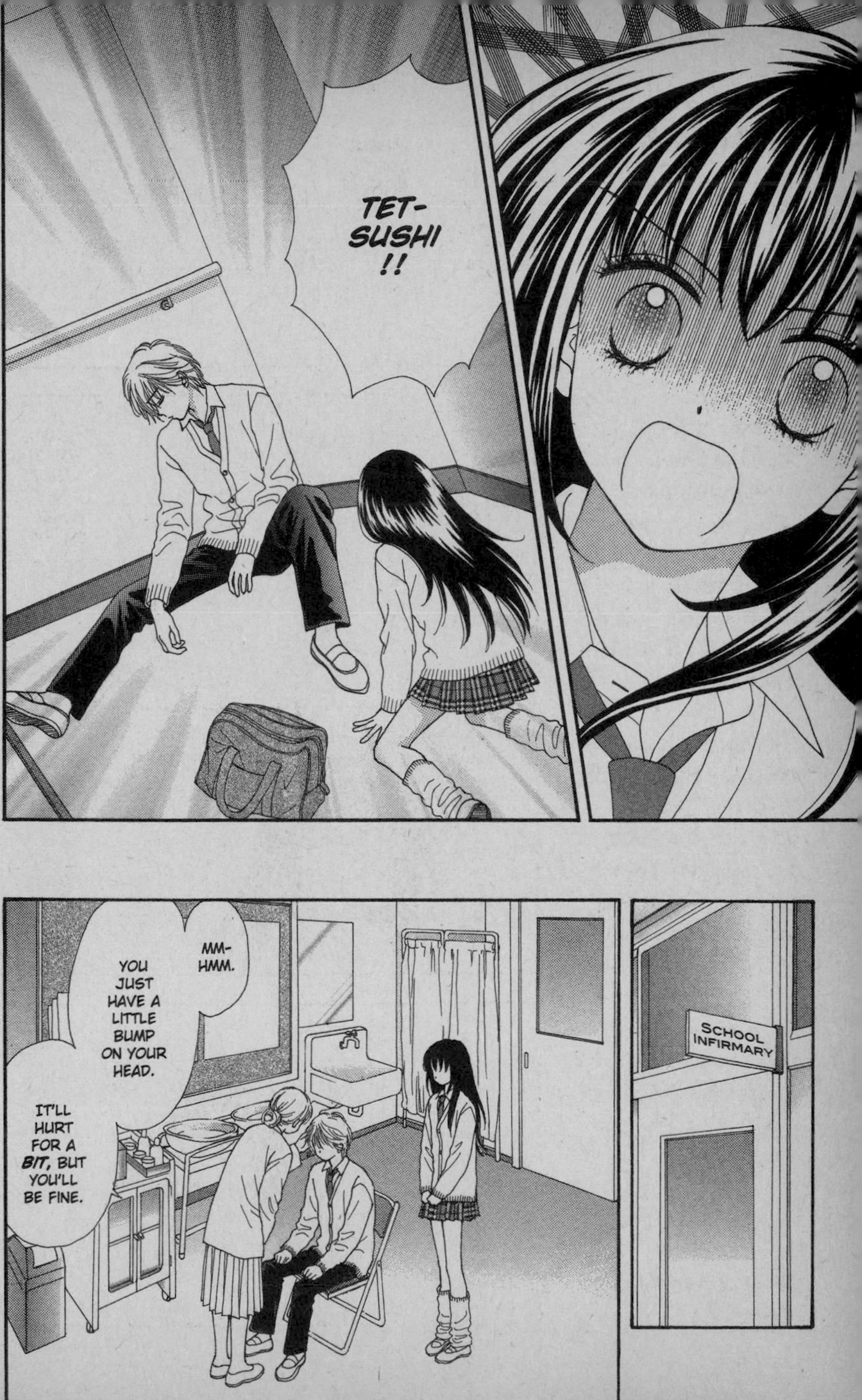
TET-SUSHI !!
SCHOOL INFIRMARY
MM-HMM.
YOU JUST HAVE A LITTLE BUMP ON YOUR HEAD.
IT'LL HURT FOR A BIT, BUT YOU'LL BE FINE.

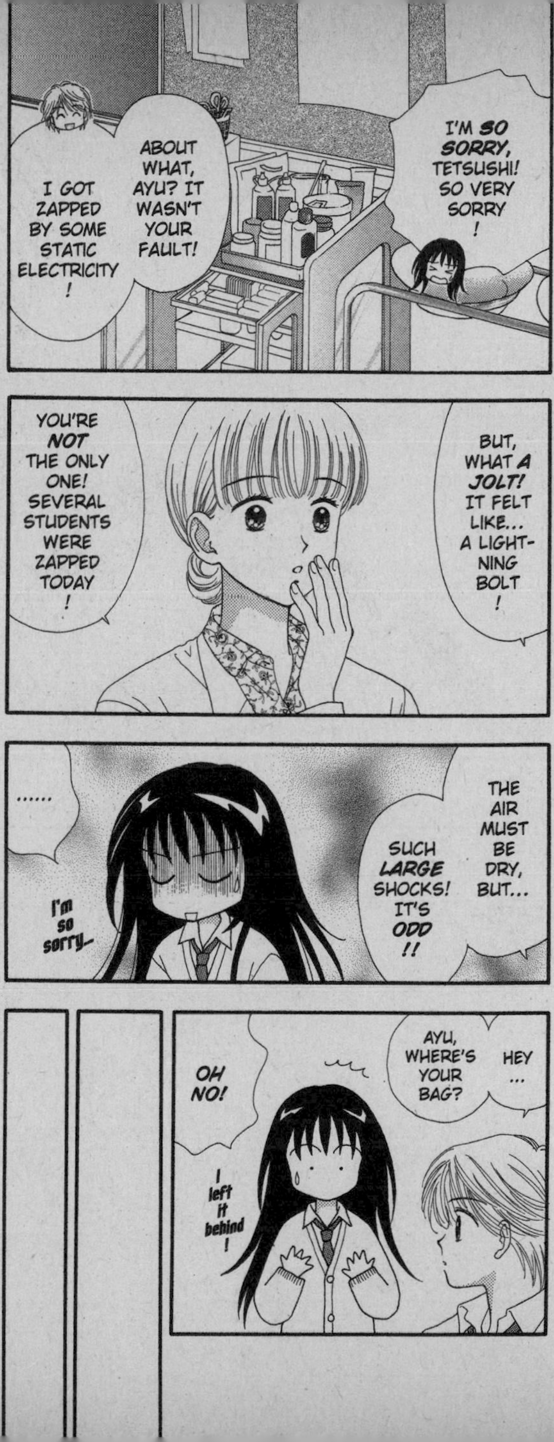
I'M SO SORRY, TETSUSHI! SO VERY SORRY!
ABOUT WHAT, AYU? IT WASN'T YOUR FAULT!
I GOT ZAPPED BY SOME STATIC ELECTRICITY!
BUT, WHAT A JOLT! IT FELT LIKE... A LIGHT-NING BOLT!
YOU'RE NOT THE ONLY ONE! SEVERAL STUDENTS WERE ZAPPED TODAY!
THE AIR MUST BE DRY, BUT...
SUCH LARGE SHOCKS! IT'S ODD!!
I'm so sorry
......
HEY...
AYU, WHERE'S YOUR BAG?
OH NO!
I left it behind!

FREE TALK 6

I modeled the Magic Treasure Box after a silver pill case I got at a souvenir shop in Dubai. This shop was selling all sorts of cute silver items like pill cases with mosaics of camels and palaces (the ones where the roofs looks like onions) on them. So I bought a bunch for my friends as gifts.

I'll admit that the flower pattern of the Magic Treasure Box is a little bit on the Arabian side.

The Magic PC is modeled after an electronic dictionary I found while browsing around a Bic Camera store. I found one I really liked. This was the first time I ever bought an electronic dictionary and I'm glad I got it. It's really handy!!

Like when I'm writing up the script, and I'm not sure about the right kanji symbol, I can verify it. It's a priceless treasure to me.

By the way, I can look up English words too. I look them up phonetically using katakana.

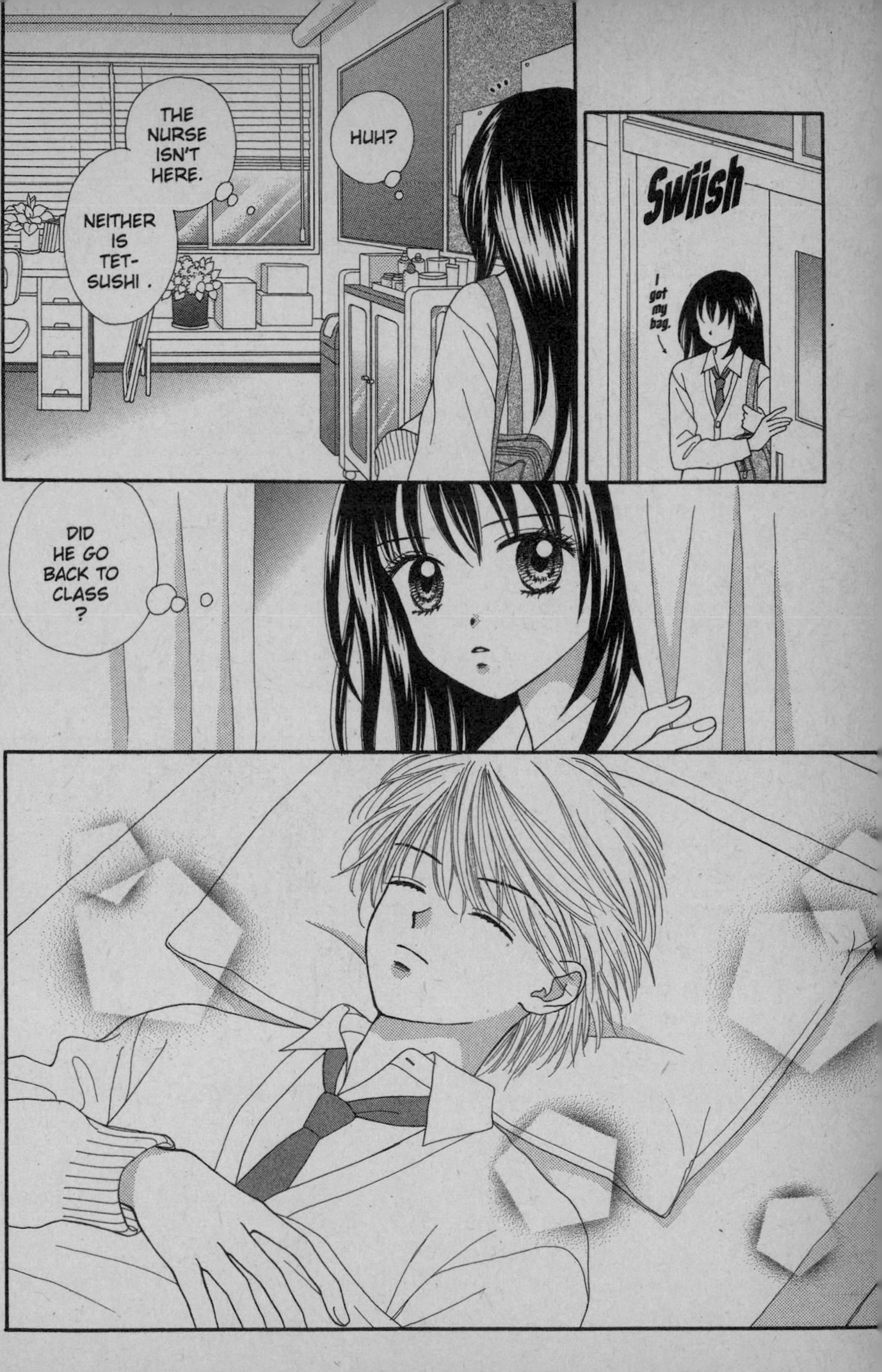
Swiish
I got my bag.
HUH?
THE NURSE ISN'T HERE.
NEITHER IS TET-SUSHI.
DID HE GO BACK TO CLASS?

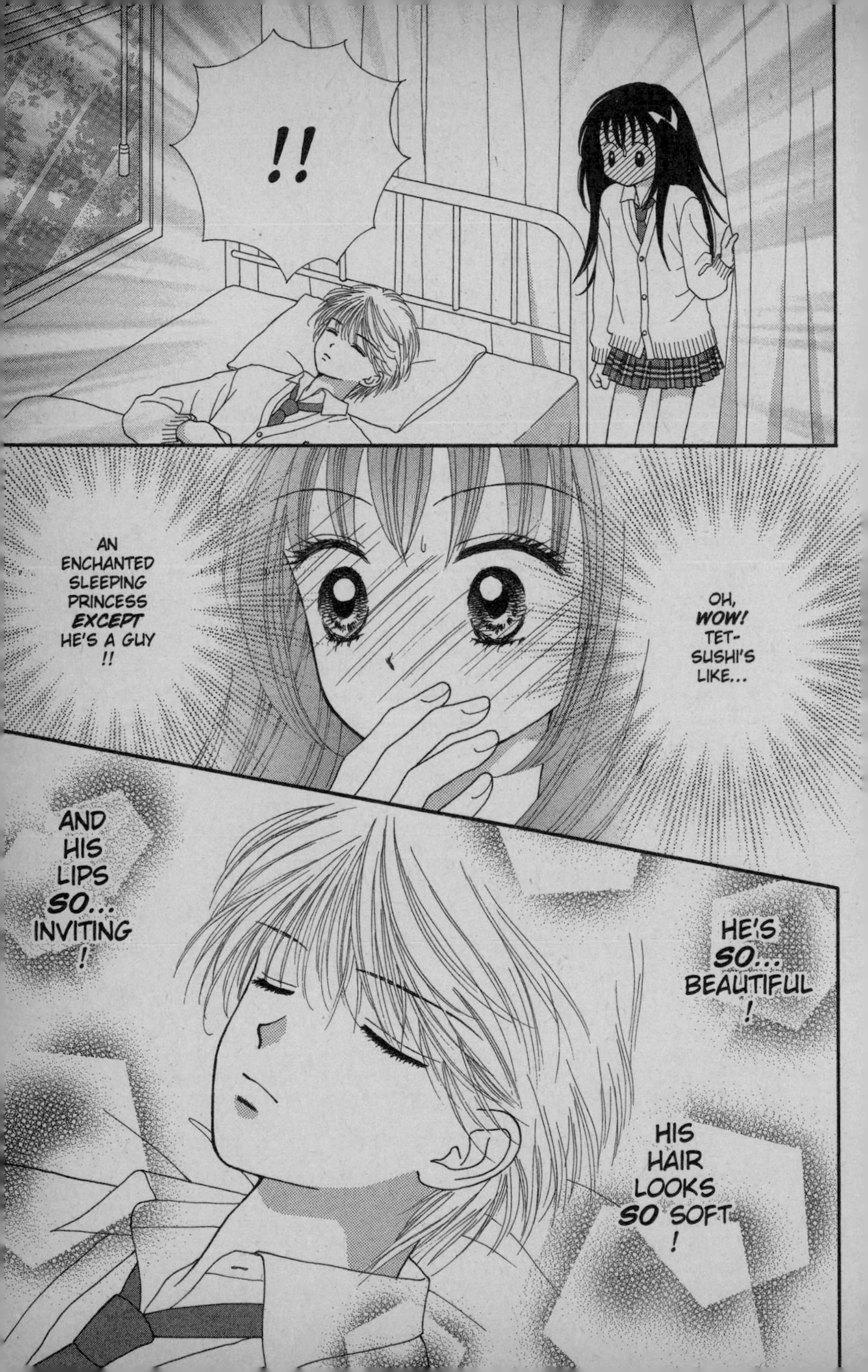
!!
OH, WOW! TET-SUSHI'S LIKE...
AN ENCHANTED SLEEPING PRINCESS EXCEPT HE'S A GUY!!
HE'S SO... BEAUTIFUL!
HIS HAIR LOOKS SO SOFT!
AND HIS LIPS SO... INVITING!

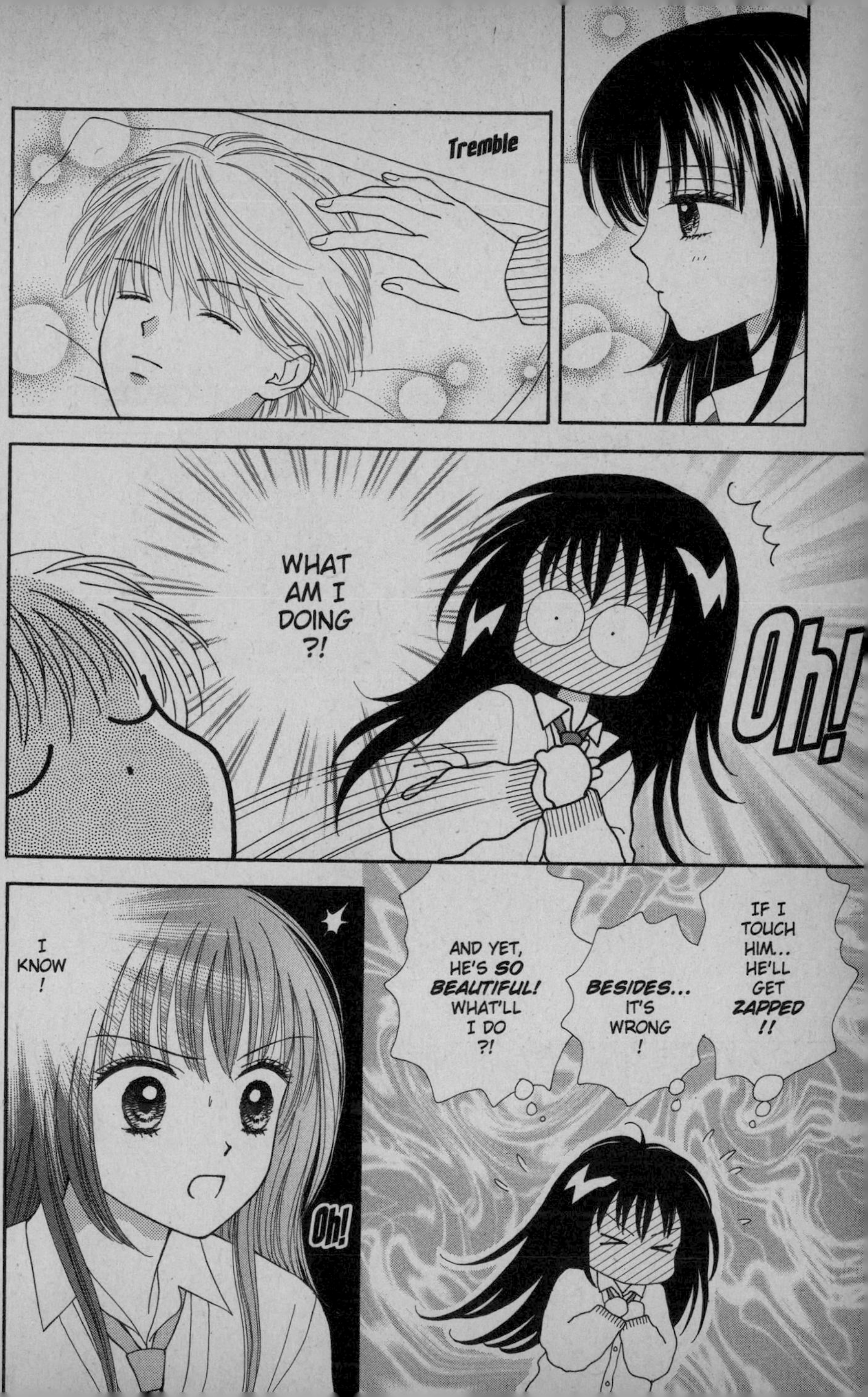
Tremble
Oh!
WHAT AM I DOING ?!
IF I TOUCH HIM... HE'LL GET ZAPPED !!
BESIDES... IT'S WRONG !
AND YET, HE'S SO BEAUTIFUL! WHAT'LL I DO ?!
Oh!
I KNOW !

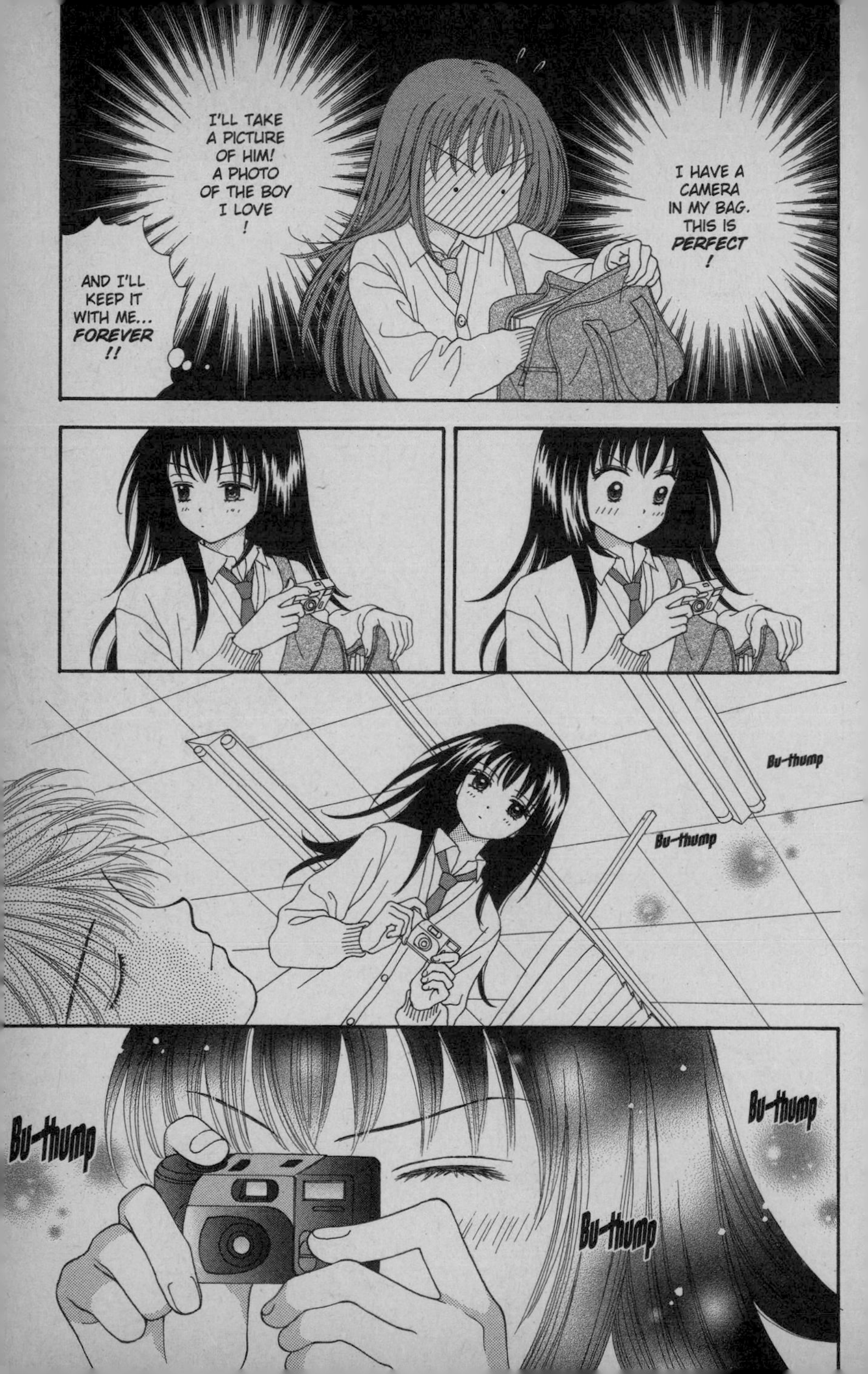
I HAVE A CAMERA IN MY BAG. THIS IS *PERFECT*!
I'LL TAKE A PICTURE OF HIM! A PHOTO OF THE BOY I LOVE!
AND I'LL KEEP IT WITH ME... *FOREVER*!!
Bu-thump
Bu-thump
Bu-thump
Bu-thump
Bu-thump

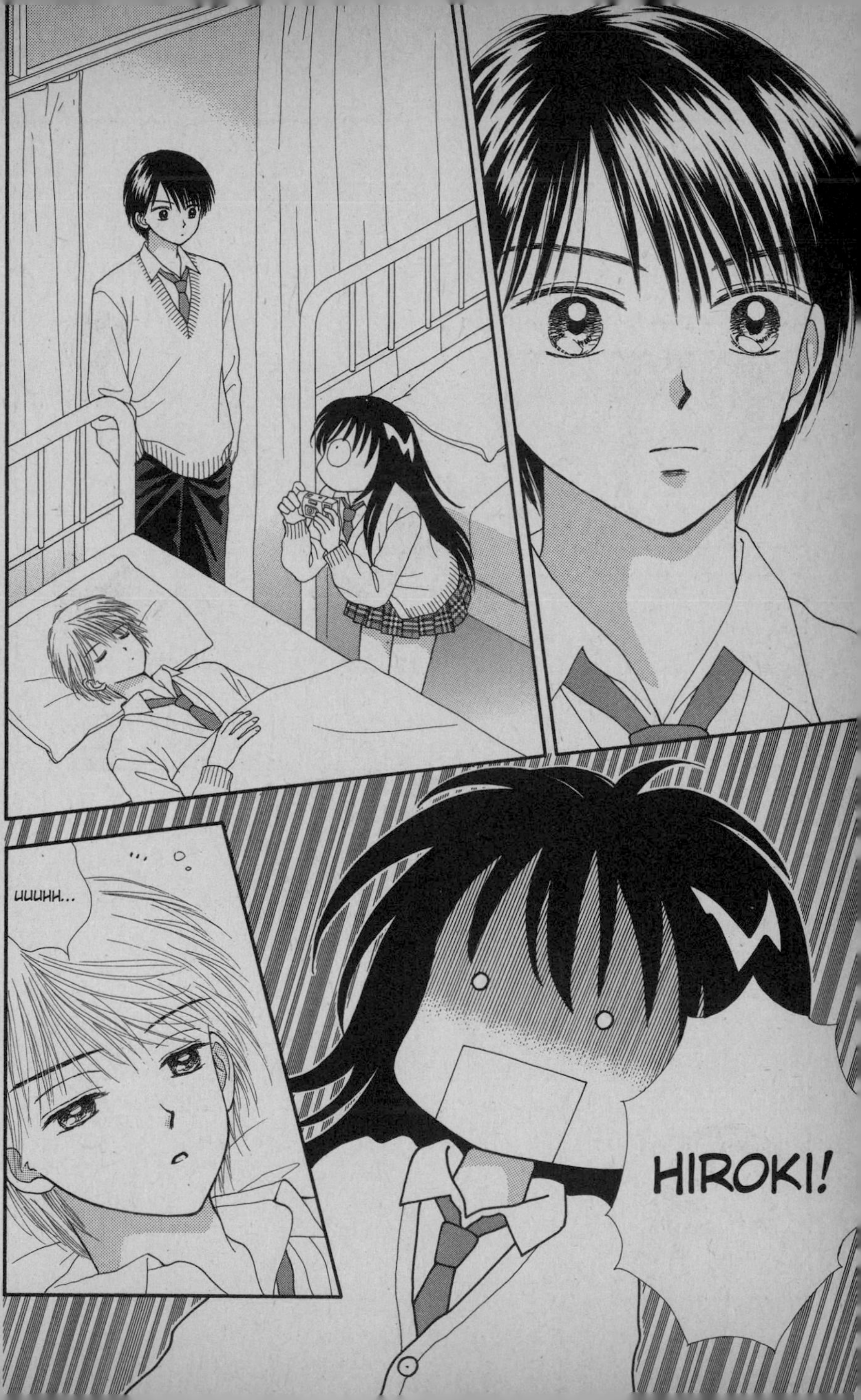
HIROKI!
...
UUUHH...

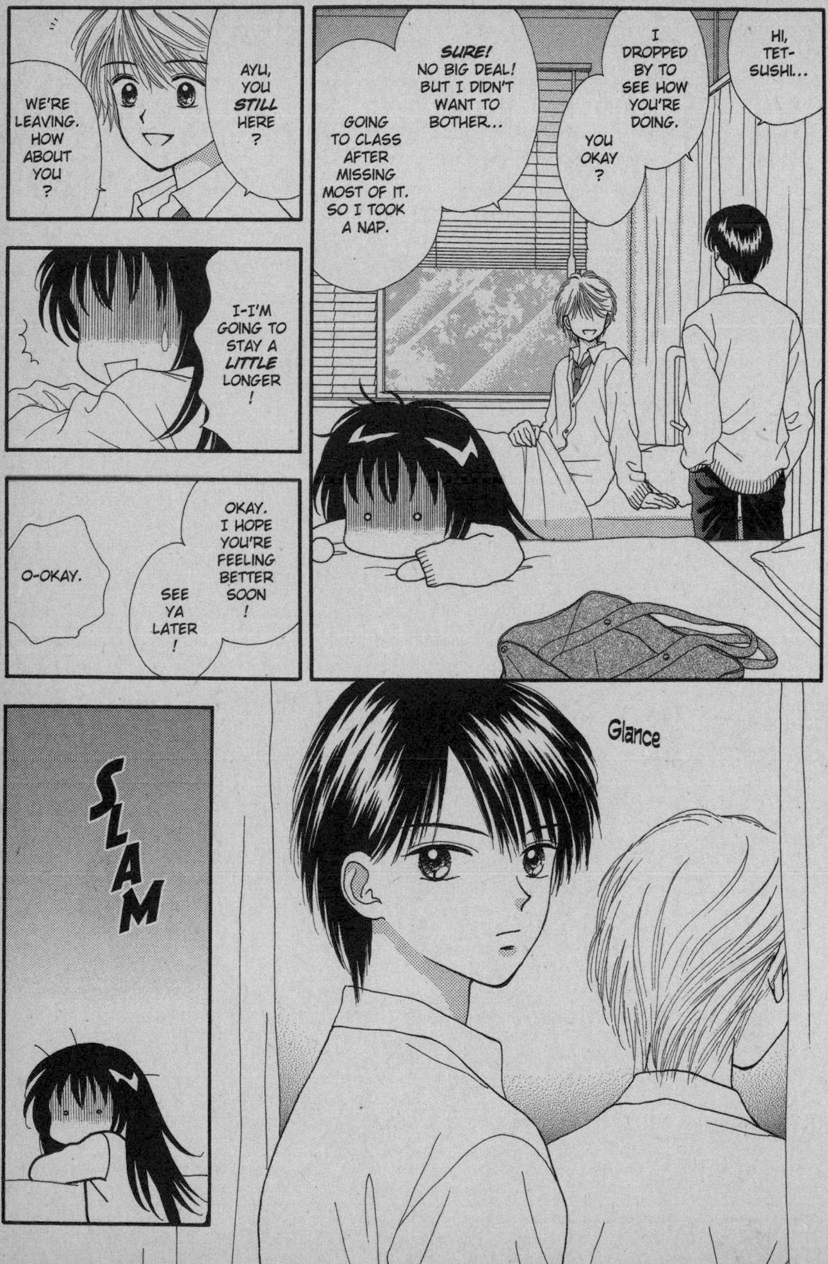
HI, TET-SUSHI...
I DROPPED BY TO SEE HOW YOU'RE DOING.
YOU OKAY?
SURE! NO BIG DEAL! BUT I DIDN'T WANT TO BOTHER...
GOING TO CLASS AFTER MISSING MOST OF IT. SO I TOOK A NAP.
AYU, YOU STILL HERE?
WE'RE LEAVING. HOW ABOUT YOU?
I-I'M GOING TO STAY A LITTLE LONGER!
OKAY. I HOPE YOU'RE FEELING BETTER SOON!
SEE YA LATER!
O-OKAY.
Glance
SLAM

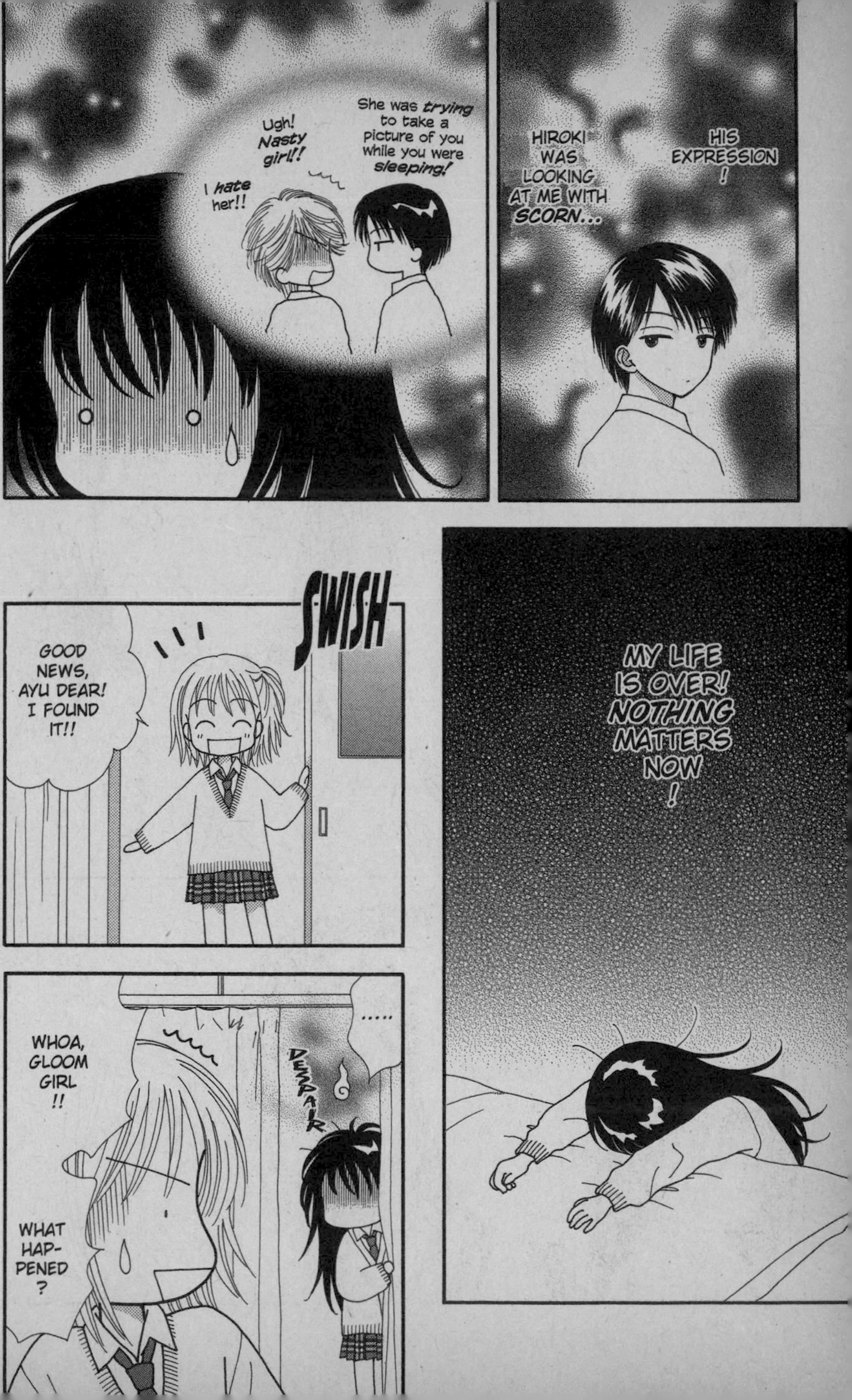
HIS EXPRESSION!
HIROKI WAS LOOKING AT ME WITH SCORN...
She was *trying* to take a picture of you while you were *sleeping!*
Ugh! *Nasty girl!!*
I *hate* her!!
MY LIFE IS OVER! NOTHING MATTERS NOW!
SWISH
GOOD NEWS, AYU DEAR! I FOUND IT!!
.....
DESPAIR
WHOA, GLOOM GIRL!!
WHAT HAP-PENED?

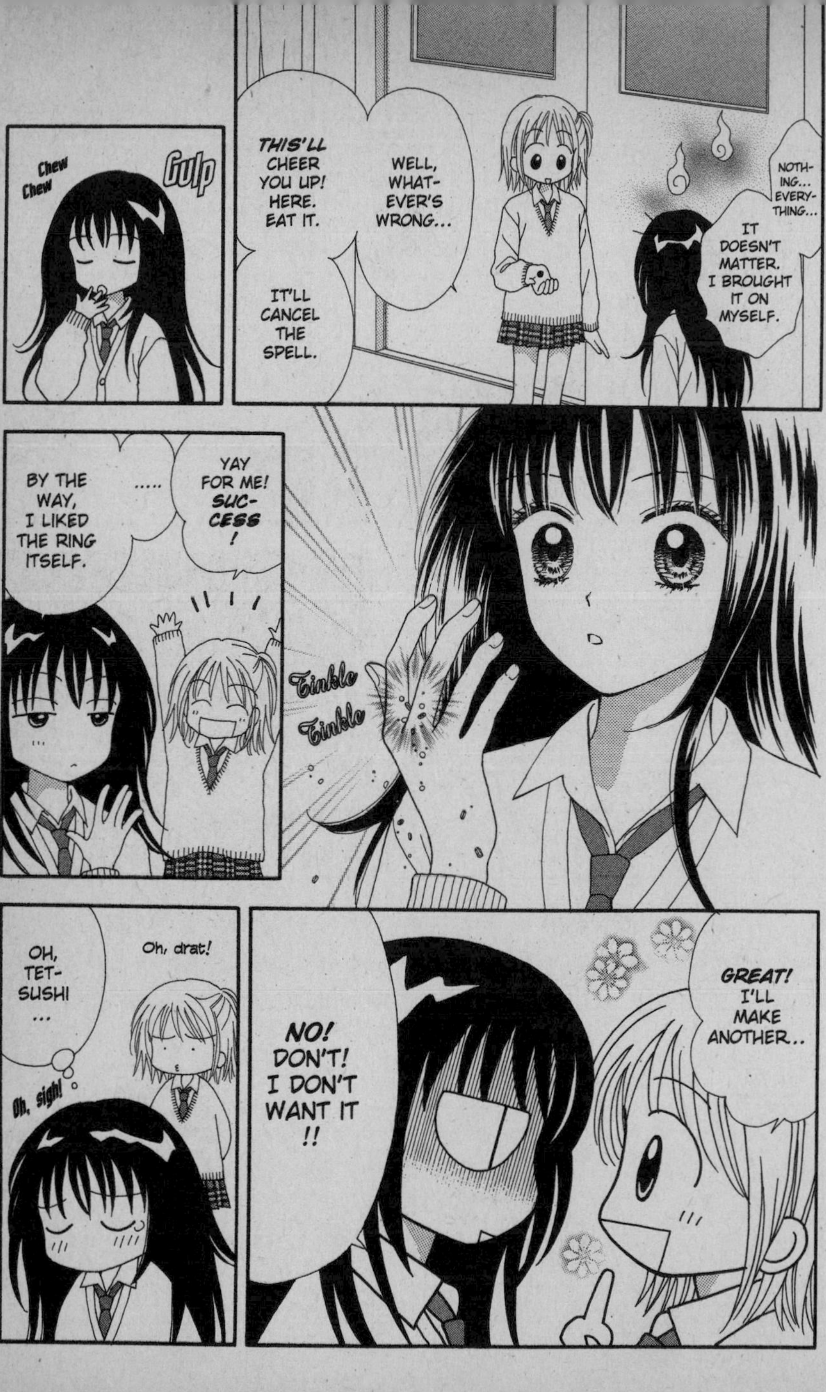
NOTHING... EVERYTHING...
IT DOESN'T MATTER. I BROUGHT IT ON MYSELF.
WELL, WHATEVER'S WRONG...
THIS'LL CHEER YOU UP! HERE. EAT IT.
IT'LL CANCEL THE SPELL.
Gulp
Chew Chew
Tinkle Tinkle
YAY FOR ME! SUCCESS!
.....
BY THE WAY, I LIKED THE RING ITSELF.
GREAT! I'LL MAKE ANOTHER...
NO! DON'T! I DON'T WANT IT!!
Oh, drat!
OH, TETSUSHI...
Oh, sigh!

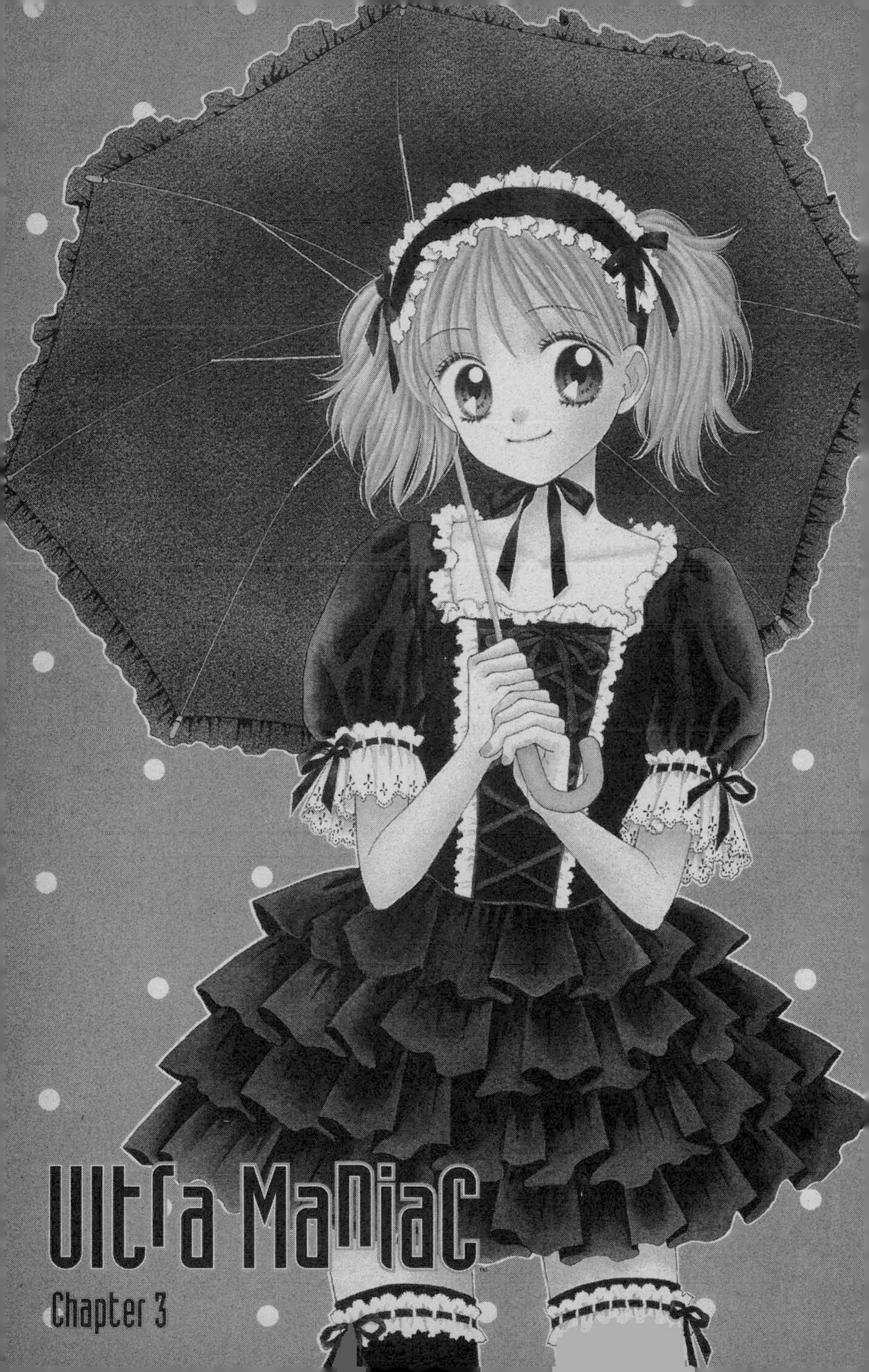
Ultra Maniac
Chapter 3

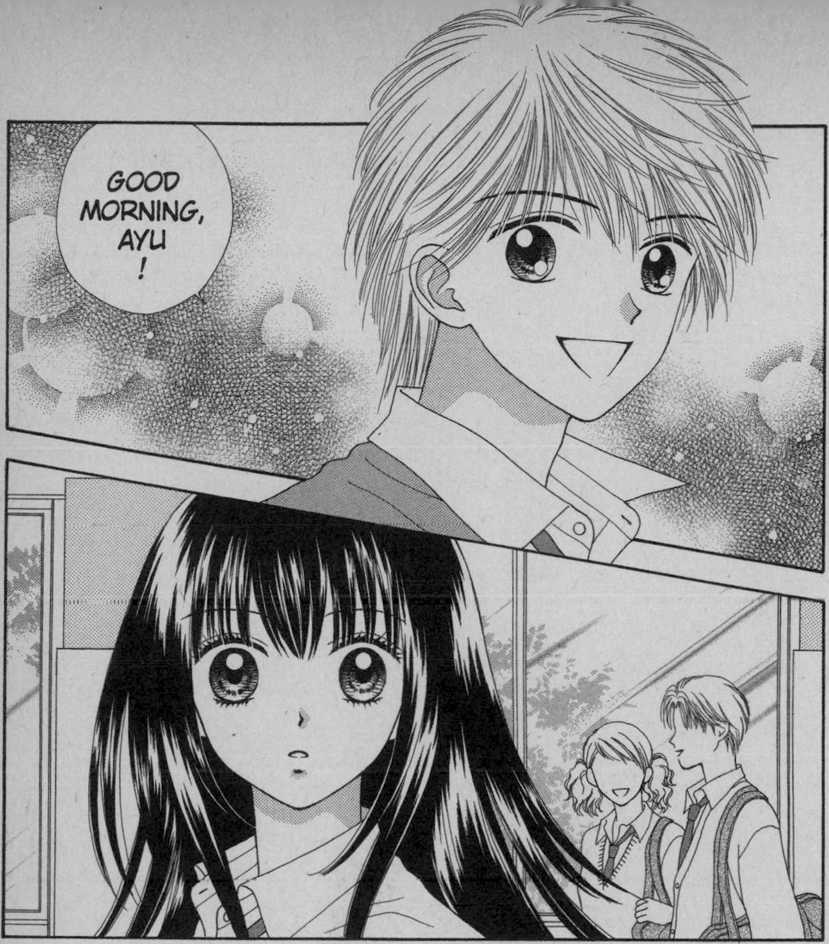
GOOD MORNING, AYU!
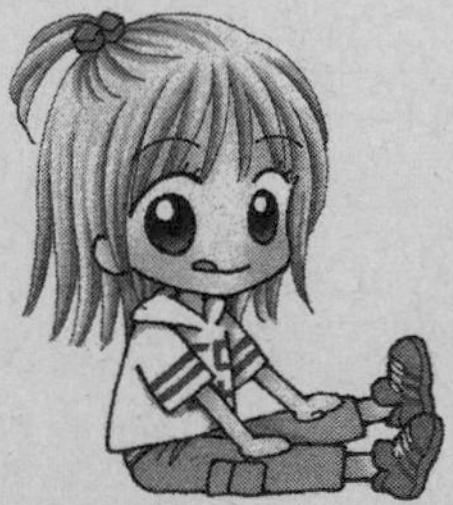

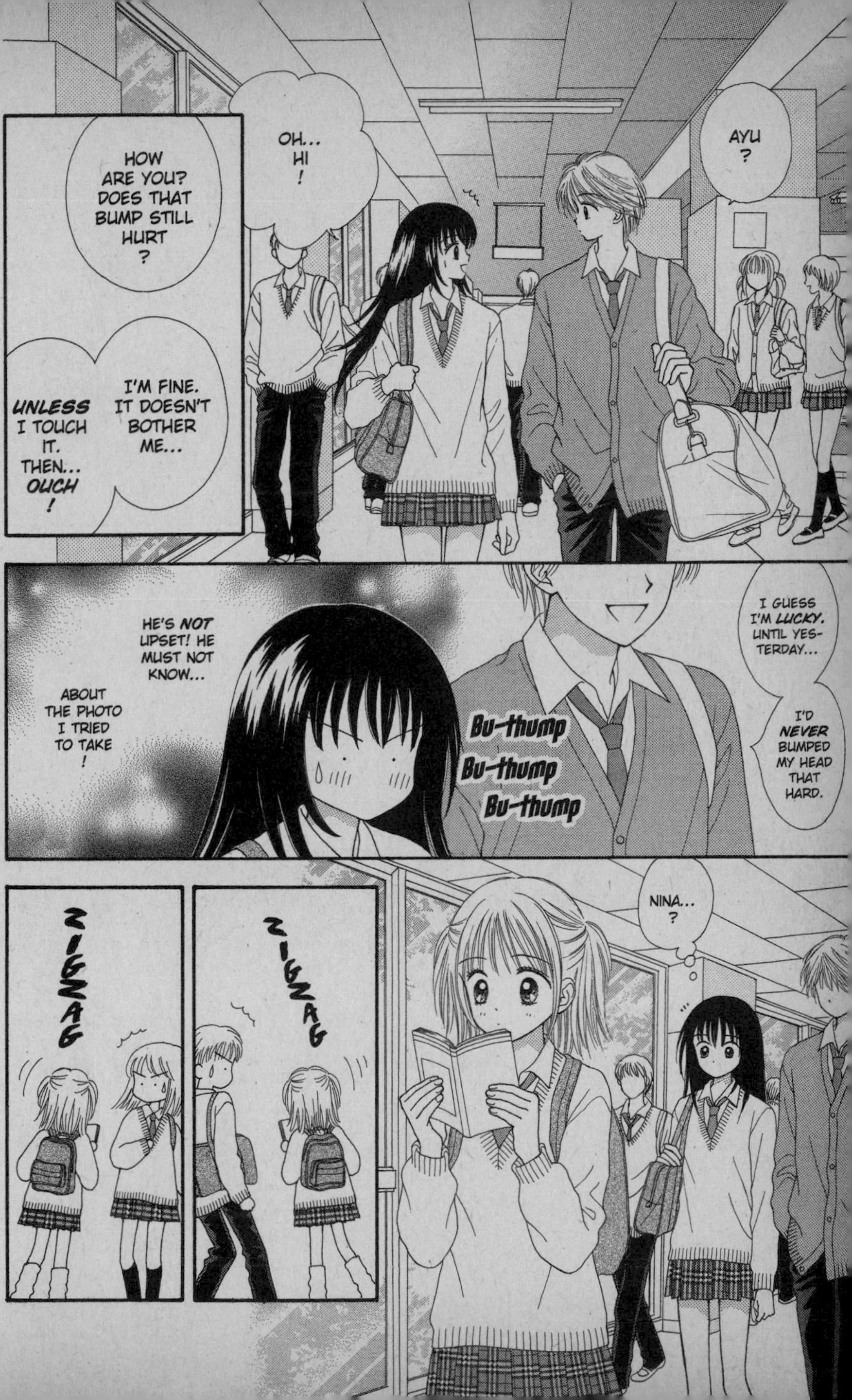
AYU?
OH... HI!
HOW ARE YOU? DOES THAT BUMP STILL HURT?
I'M FINE. IT DOESN'T BOTHER ME...
UNLESS I TOUCH IT. THEN... OUCH!
I GUESS I'M LUCKY. UNTIL YESTERDAY...
I'D NEVER BUMPED MY HEAD THAT HARD.
Bu-thump
Bu-thump
Bu-thump
HE'S NOT UPSET! HE MUST NOT KNOW...
ABOUT THE PHOTO I TRIED TO TAKE!
NINA...?
ZIGZAG
ZIGZAG

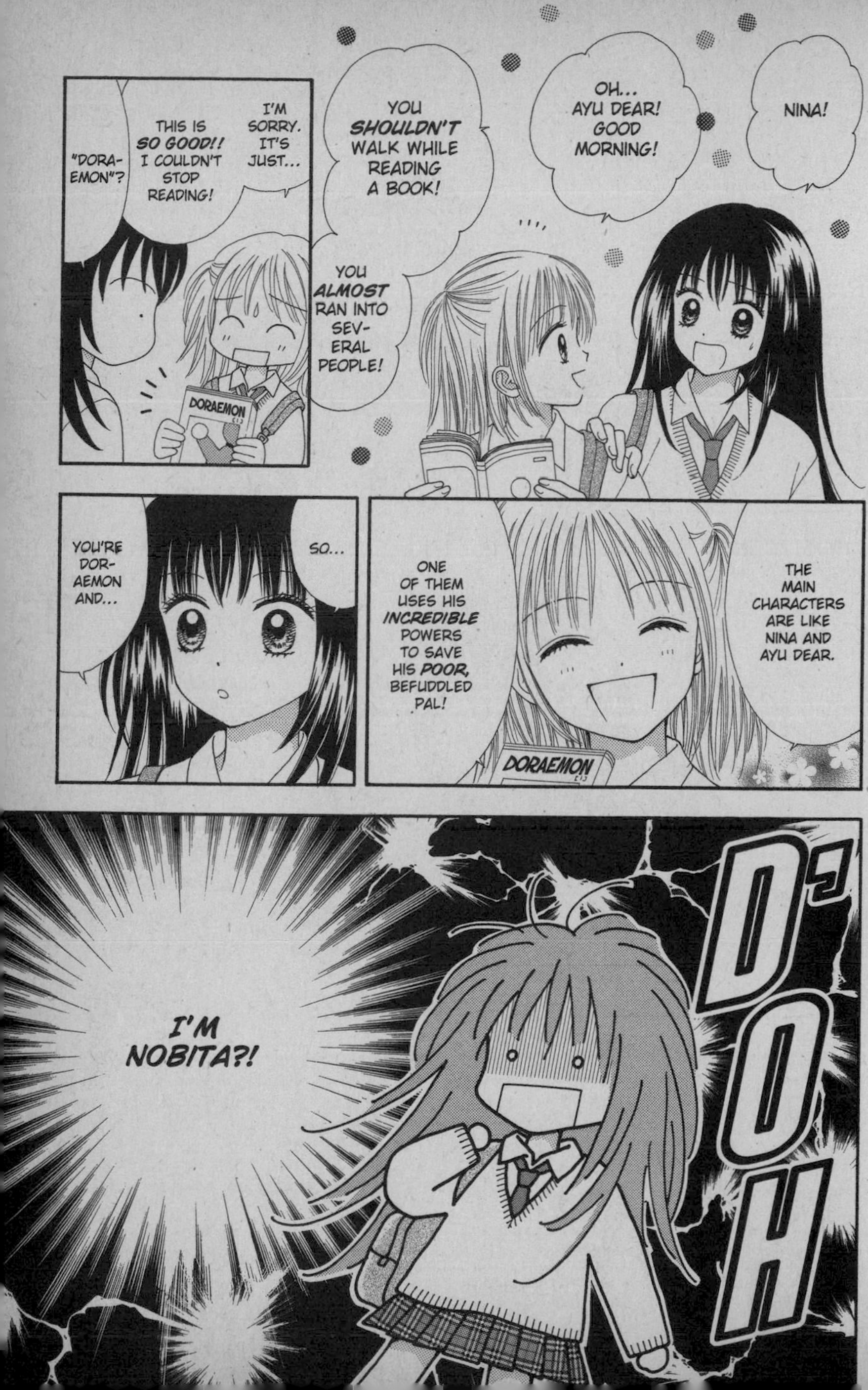
NINA!
OH... AYU DEAR! GOOD MORNING!
YOU *SHOULDN'T* WALK WHILE READING A BOOK!
YOU *ALMOST* RAN INTO SEV-ERAL PEOPLE!
I'M SORRY. IT'S JUST...
THIS IS *SO GOOD!!* I COULDN'T STOP READING!
"DORA-EMON"?
DORAEMON
THE MAIN CHARACTERS ARE LIKE NINA AND AYU DEAR.
ONE OF THEM USES HIS *INCREDIBLE* POWERS TO SAVE HIS *POOR,* BEFUDDLED PAL!
DORAEMON
SO...
YOU'RE DOR-AEMON AND...
DOOH
I'M NOBITA?!

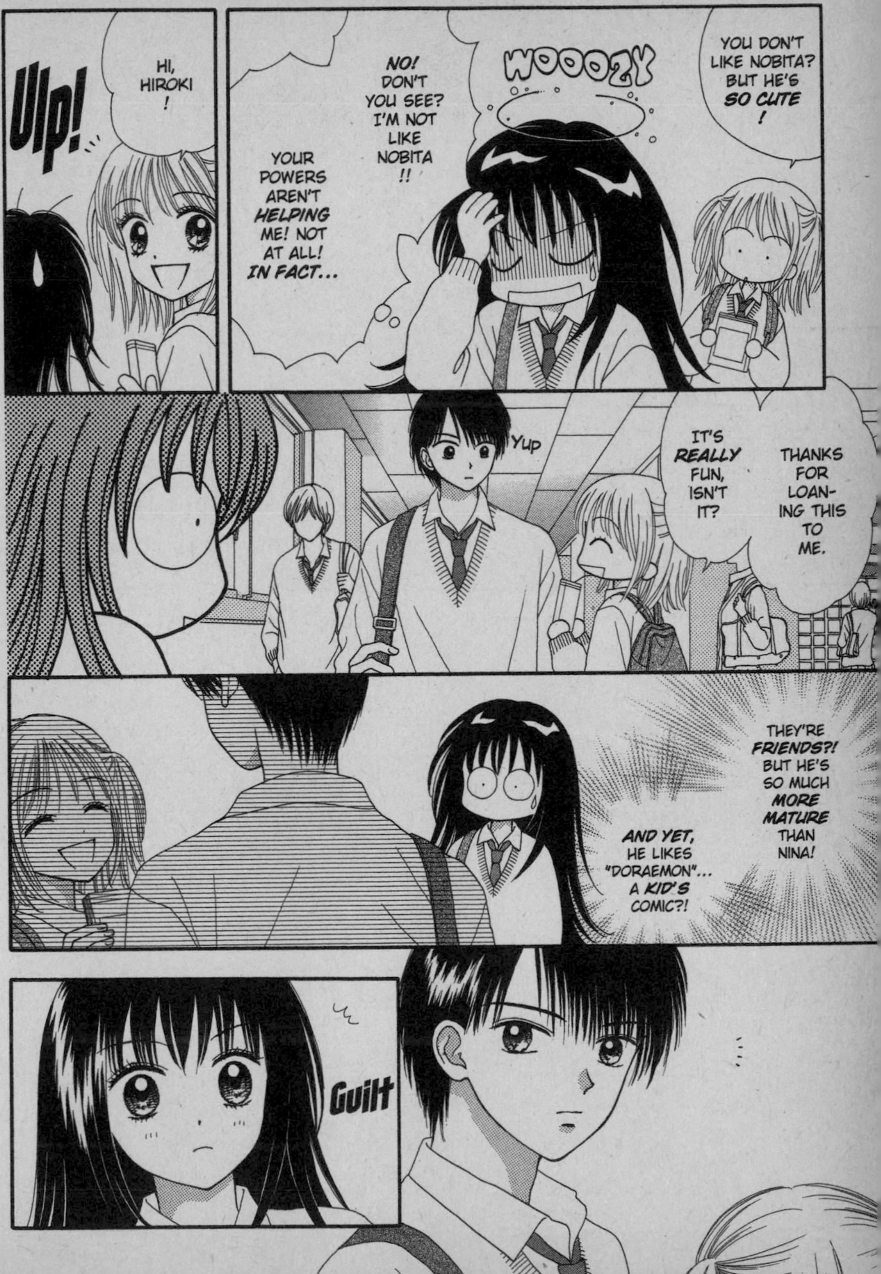
YOU DON'T LIKE NOBITA? BUT HE'S SO CUTE!
WOOOZY
NO! DON'T YOU SEE? I'M NOT LIKE NOBITA!!
YOUR POWERS AREN'T HELPING ME! NOT AT ALL! IN FACT...
HI, HIROKI!
Ulp!
THANKS FOR LOAN-ING THIS TO ME.
IT'S REALLY FUN, ISN'T IT?
Yup
THEY'RE FRIENDS?! BUT HE'S SO MUCH MORE MATURE THAN NINA!
AND YET, HE LIKES "DORAEMON"... A KID'S COMIC?!
...
Guilt

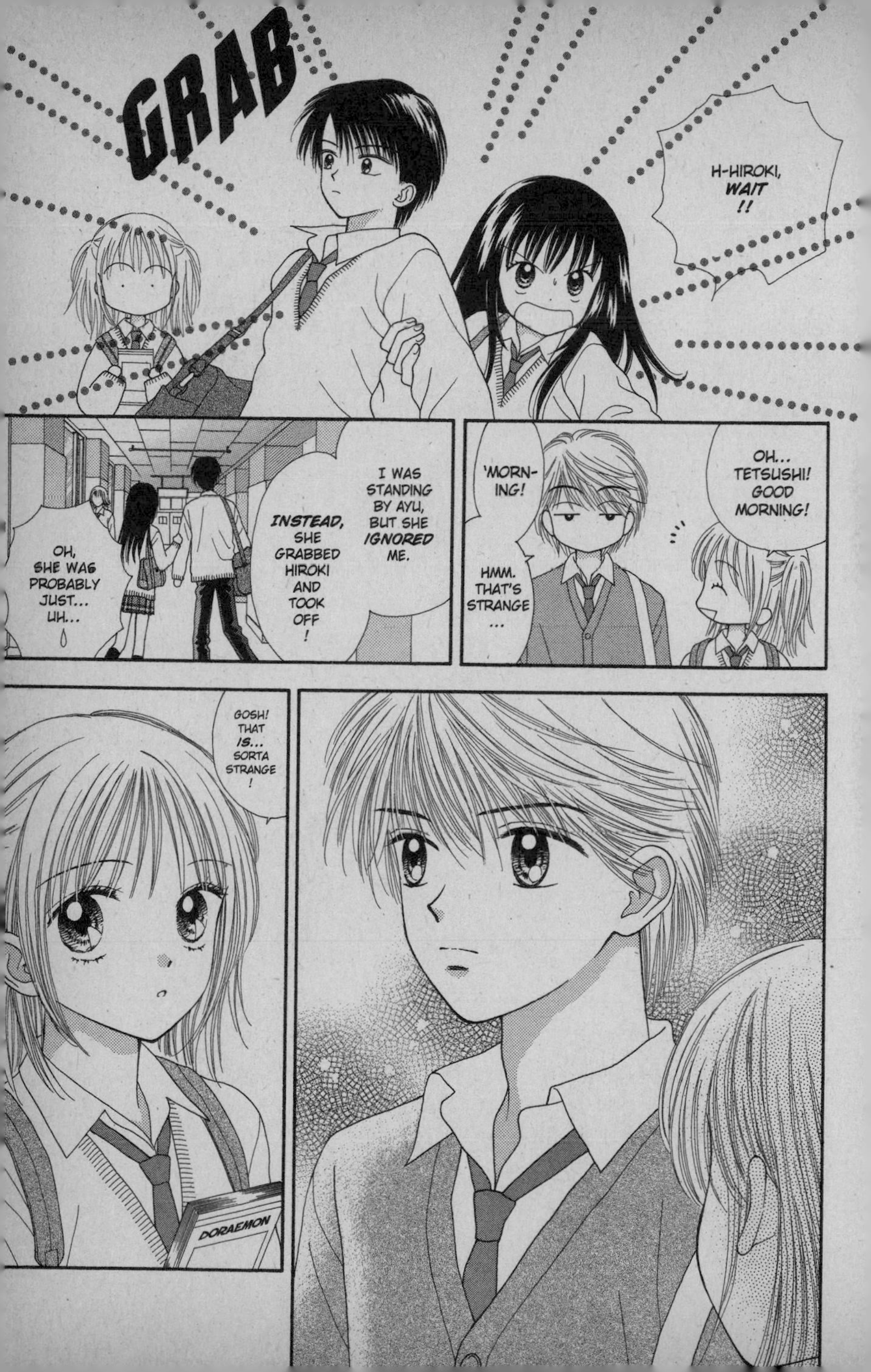
H-HIROKI, WAIT !!
GRAB
OH... TETSUSHI! GOOD MORNING!
'MORNING!
HMM. THAT'S STRANGE...
I WAS STANDING BY AYU, BUT SHE IGNORED ME.
INSTEAD, SHE GRABBED HIROKI AND TOOK OFF!
OH, SHE WAS PROBABLY JUST... UH...
GOSH! THAT IS... SORTA STRANGE!
DORAEMON

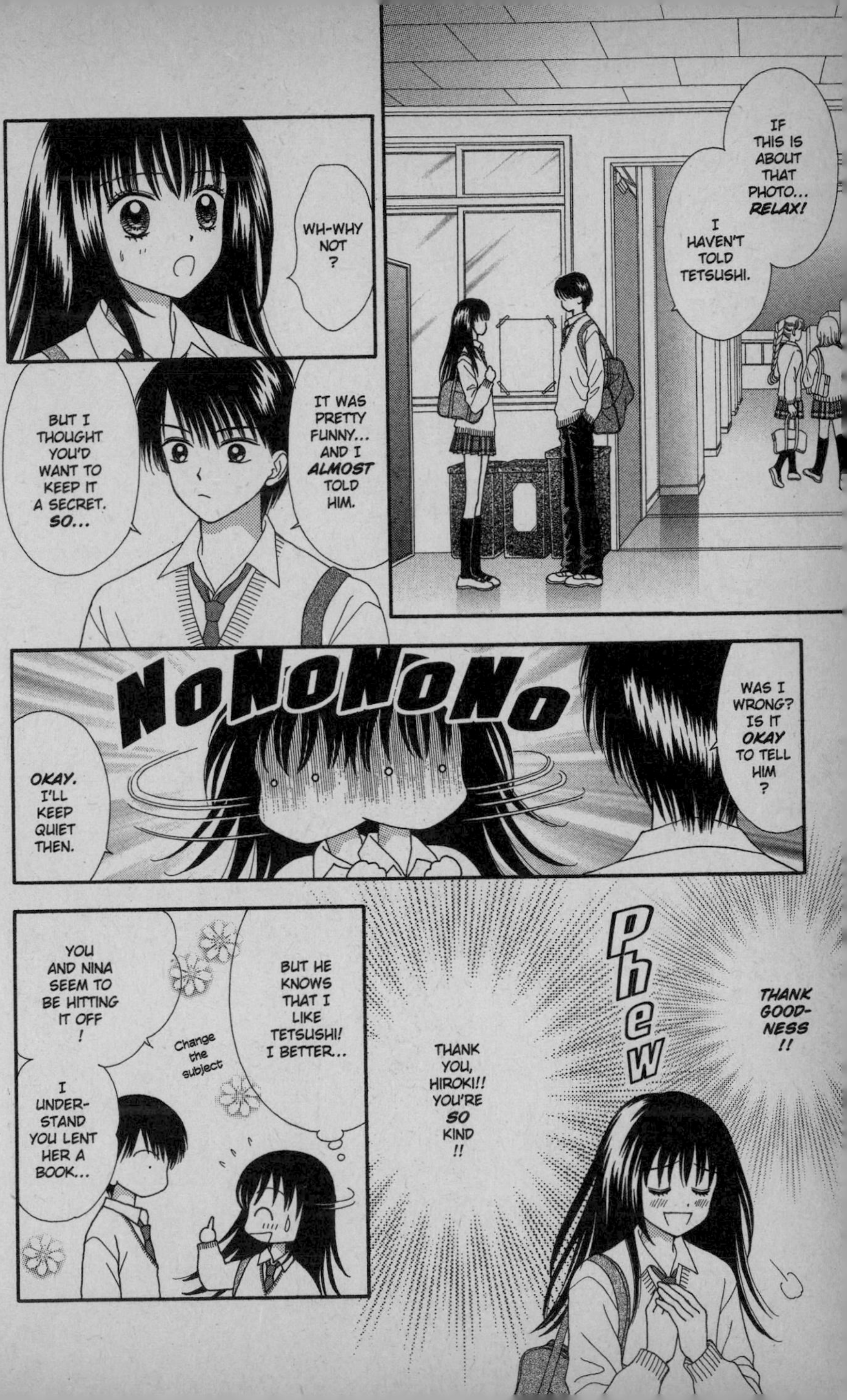
IF THIS IS ABOUT THAT PHOTO... RELAX!
I HAVEN'T TOLD TETSUSHI.
WH-WHY NOT?
IT WAS PRETTY FUNNY... AND I ALMOST TOLD HIM.
BUT I THOUGHT YOU'D WANT TO KEEP IT A SECRET. SO...
WAS I WRONG? IS IT OKAY TO TELL HIM?
NONONONONO
OKAY. I'LL KEEP QUIET THEN.
Phew
THANK GOODNESS!!
THANK YOU, HIROKI!! YOU'RE SO KIND!!
BUT HE KNOWS THAT I LIKE TETSUSHI! I BETTER...
Change the subject
YOU AND NINA SEEM TO BE HITTING IT OFF!
I UNDERSTAND YOU LENT HER A BOOK...

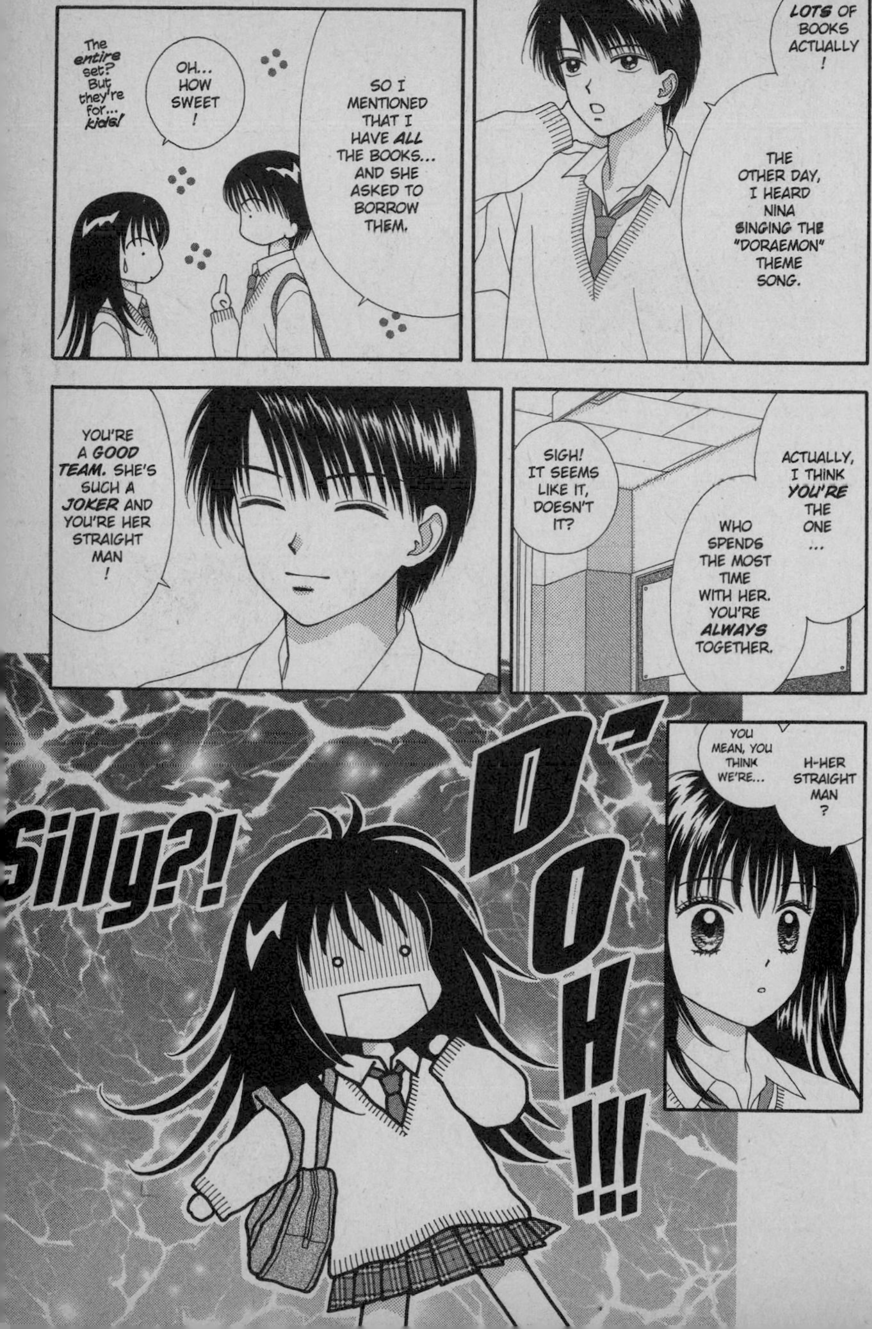
LOTS OF BOOKS ACTUALLY!
THE OTHER DAY, I HEARD NINA SINGING THE "DORAEMON" THEME SONG.
SO I MENTIONED THAT I HAVE ALL THE BOOKS... AND SHE ASKED TO BORROW THEM.
OH... HOW SWEET!
The entire set? But they're for... kids!
ACTUALLY, I THINK YOU'RE THE ONE...
WHO SPENDS THE MOST TIME WITH HER. YOU'RE ALWAYS TOGETHER.
SIGH! IT SEEMS LIKE IT, DOESN'T IT?
YOU'RE A GOOD TEAM. SHE'S SUCH A JOKER AND YOU'RE HER STRAIGHT MAN!
YOU MEAN, YOU THINK WE'RE...
H-HER STRAIGHT MAN?
D'OH!!!
Silly?!

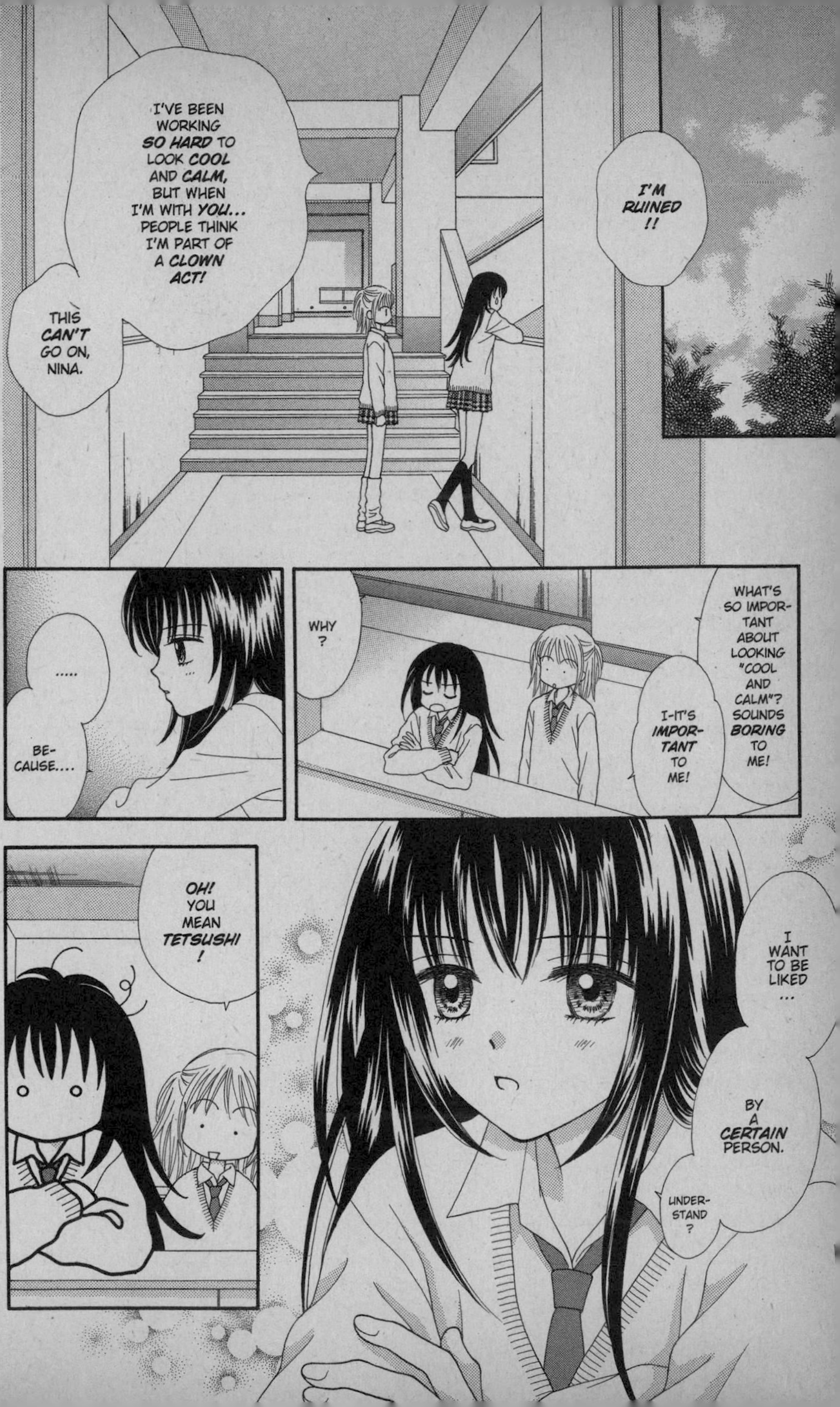
I'M RUINED!!
I'VE BEEN WORKING SO HARD TO LOOK COOL AND CALM, BUT WHEN I'M WITH YOU... PEOPLE THINK I'M PART OF A CLOWN ACT!
THIS CAN'T GO ON, NINA.
WHAT'S SO IMPORTANT ABOUT LOOKING "COOL AND CALM"? SOUNDS BORING TO ME!
I-IT'S IMPORTANT TO ME!
WHY?
.....
BE-CAUSE....
I WANT TO BE LIKED...
BY A CERTAIN PERSON.
UNDER-STAND?
OH! YOU MEAN TETSUSHI!

FREE TALK 7

The bead ring that showed up in Chapter 2 was something that I actually owned. In fact, I made it myself. But it's gone now. I dropped it and lost it somewhere.

You see, my hands are rather small, so the ring was pretty loose. (I used a design for the ring, but the size was set and I couldn't change it.) Even so, I wasn't too worried. I figured that since the ring was touching me, I'd quickly realize if it fell off. . . or so I thought. I guess I was naive. By the time I realized it was gone, it was too late. I had no idea where I dropped it.

I only wore it once. . . and lost it within the first few hours. According to Ms. Ai Yazawa, when your hand's moving—such as when you're taking something out of a purse—it's easy for a ring to get caught on something and get pulled off. But because your finger is touching something else. . . your sense of touch is concentrated on that. And so, you don't notice the ring slipping off.

Since I lost it so easily, I don't wear loose rings anymore. I'm too scared of losing them.

Sometimes I wonder where my bead ring is now. . . and whether someone else is wearing it. If so, I hope she has bigger hands than mine!

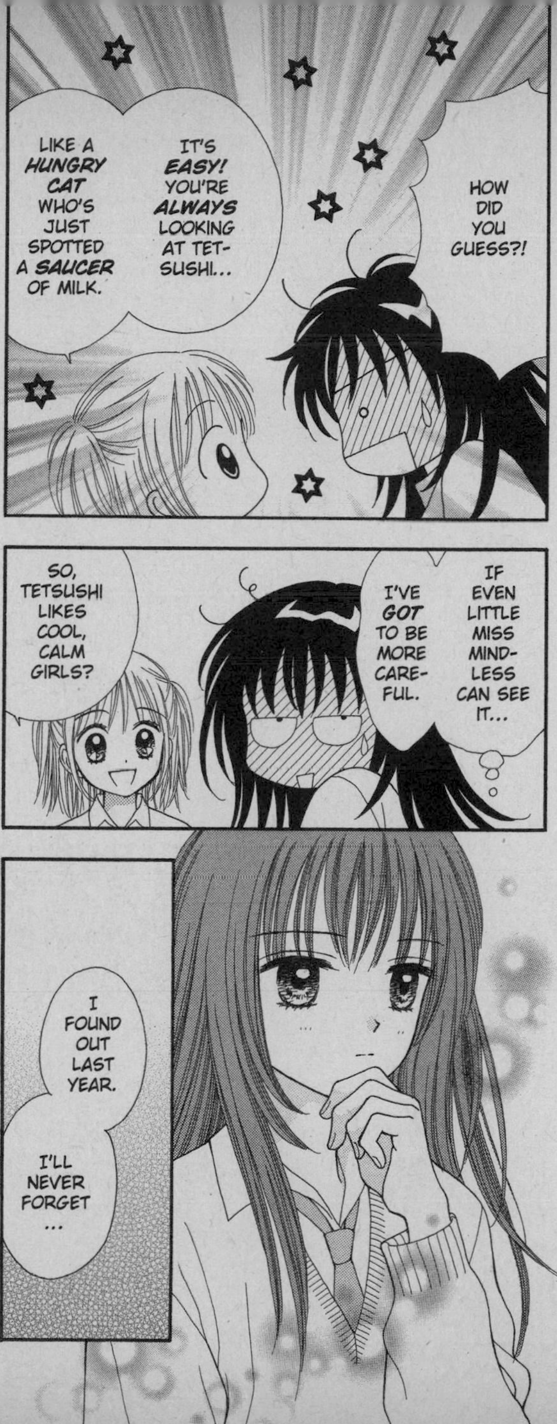
HOW DID YOU GUESS?!
IT'S EASY! YOU'RE ALWAYS LOOKING AT TETSUSHI...
LIKE A HUNGRY CAT WHO'S JUST SPOTTED A SAUCER OF MILK.
IF EVEN LITTLE MISS MINDLESS CAN SEE IT...
I'VE GOT TO BE MORE CAREFUL.
SO, TETSUSHI LIKES COOL, CALM GIRLS?
I FOUND OUT LAST YEAR.
I'LL NEVER FORGET ...

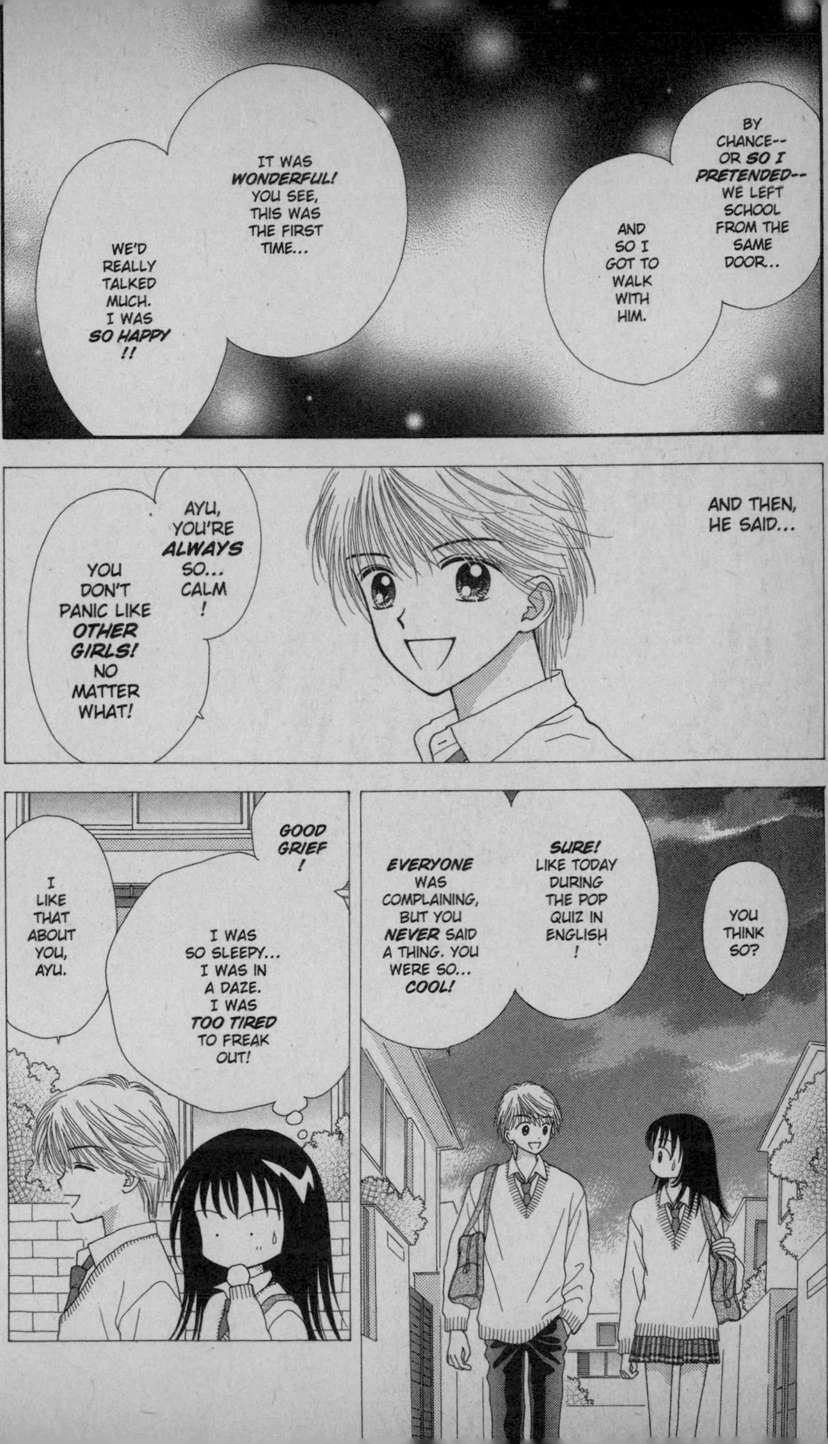
BY CHANCE-- OR SO I PRETENDED-- WE LEFT SCHOOL FROM THE SAME DOOR...
AND SO I GOT TO WALK WITH HIM.
IT WAS WONDERFUL! YOU SEE, THIS WAS THE FIRST TIME...
WE'D REALLY TALKED MUCH. I WAS SO HAPPY!!
AND THEN, HE SAID...
AYU, YOU'RE ALWAYS SO... CALM!
YOU DON'T PANIC LIKE OTHER GIRLS! NO MATTER WHAT!
YOU THINK SO?
SURE! LIKE TODAY DURING THE POP QUIZ IN ENGLISH!
EVERYONE WAS COMPLAINING, BUT YOU NEVER SAID A THING. YOU WERE SO... COOL!
GOOD GRIEF!
I WAS SO SLEEPY... I WAS IN A DAZE. I WAS TOO TIRED TO FREAK OUT!
I LIKE THAT ABOUT YOU, AYU.

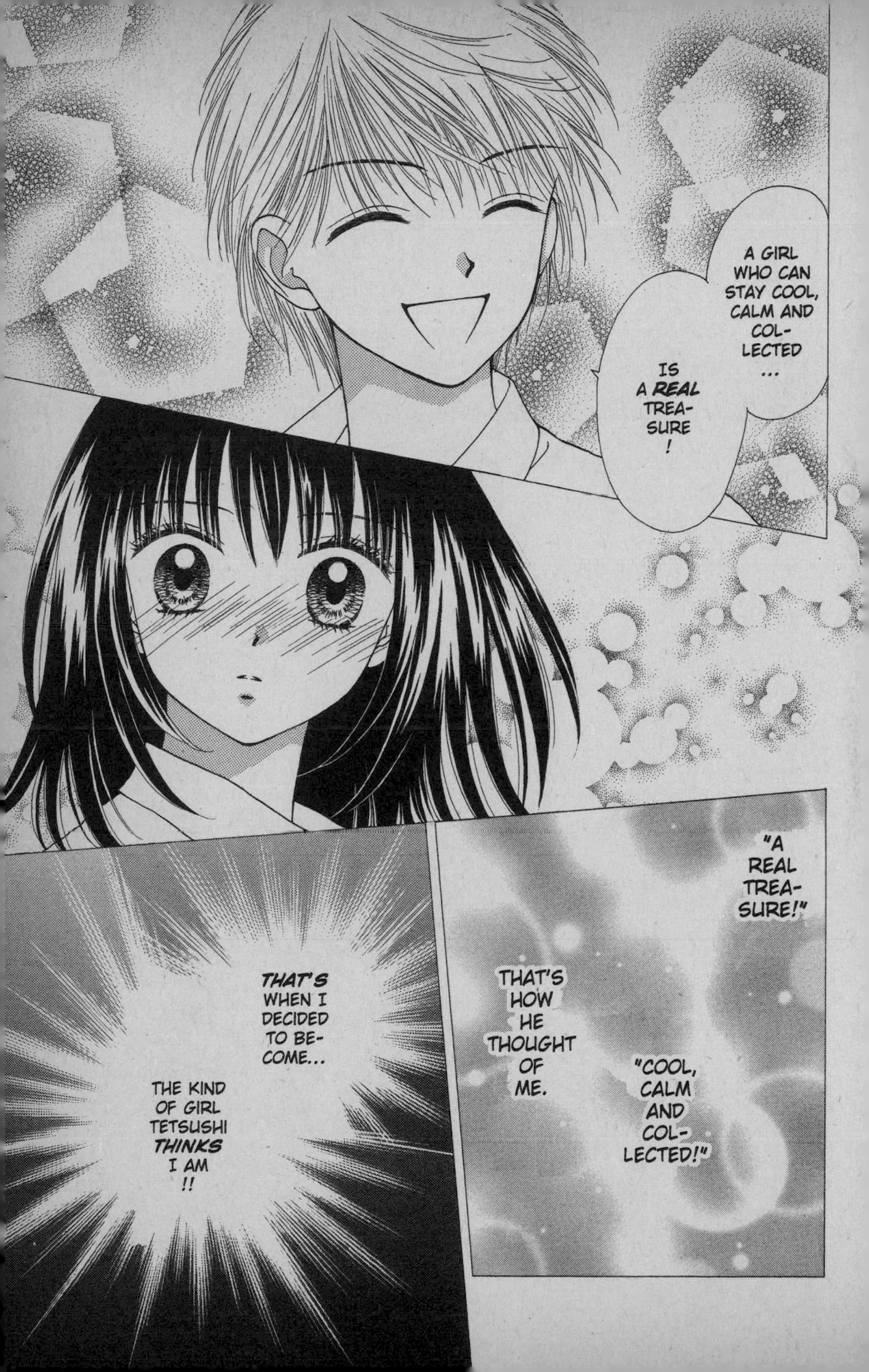
A GIRL WHO CAN STAY COOL, CALM AND COL-LECTED...
IS A *REAL* TREA-SURE!
"A REAL TREA-SURE!"
"COOL, CALM AND COL-LECTED!"
THAT'S HOW HE THOUGHT OF ME.
THAT'S WHEN I DECIDED TO BE-COME...
THE KIND OF GIRL TETSUSHI *THINKS* I AM!!

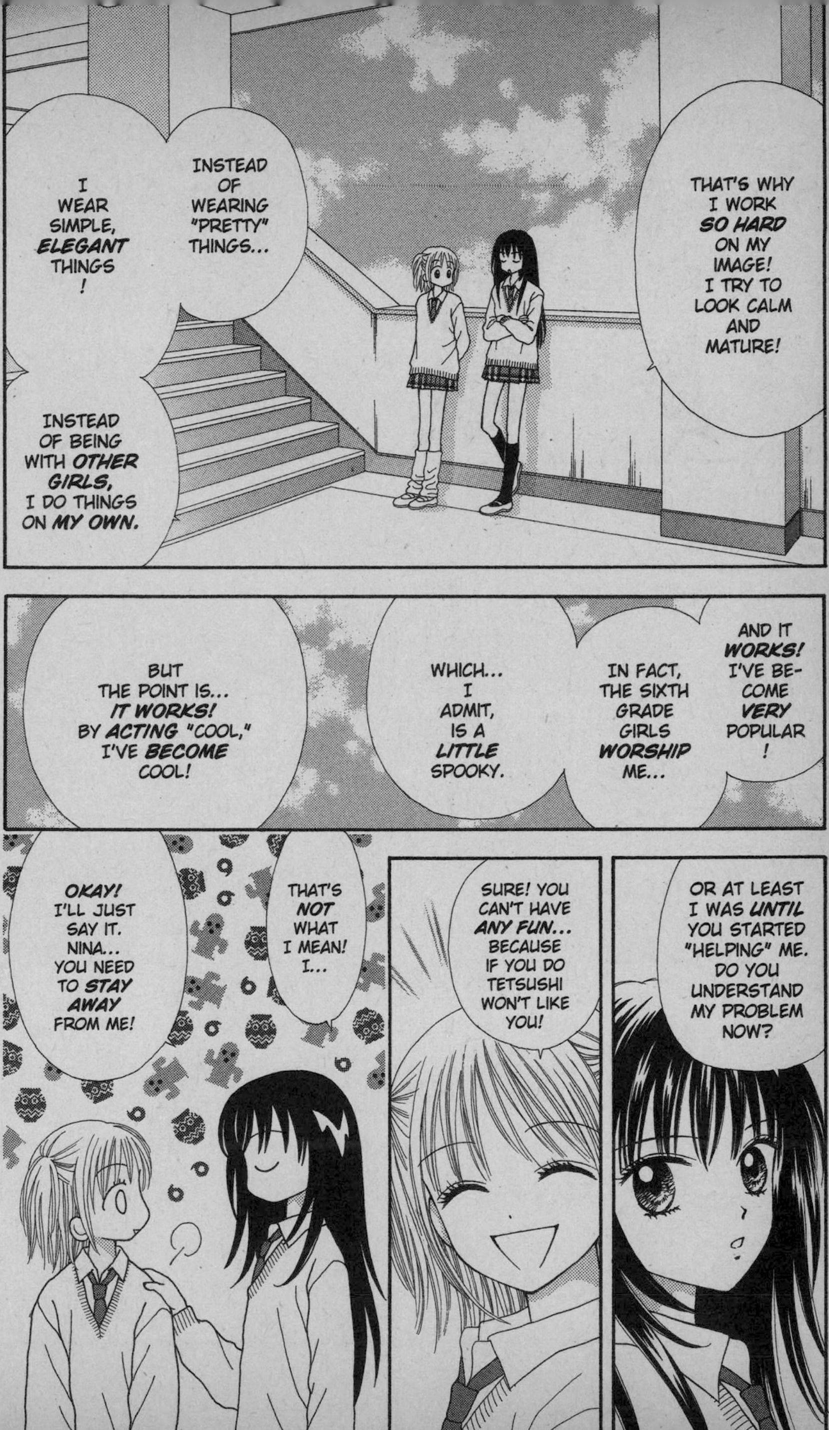
THAT'S WHY I WORK SO HARD ON MY IMAGE! I TRY TO LOOK CALM AND MATURE!
INSTEAD OF WEARING "PRETTY" THINGS...
I WEAR SIMPLE, ELEGANT THINGS!
INSTEAD OF BEING WITH OTHER GIRLS, I DO THINGS ON MY OWN.
AND IT WORKS! I'VE BE-COME VERY POPULAR!
IN FACT, THE SIXTH GRADE GIRLS WORSHIP ME...
WHICH... I ADMIT, IS A LITTLE SPOOKY.
BUT THE POINT IS... IT WORKS! BY ACTING "COOL," I'VE BECOME COOL!
OR AT LEAST I WAS UNTIL YOU STARTED "HELPING" ME. DO YOU UNDERSTAND MY PROBLEM NOW?
SURE! YOU CAN'T HAVE ANY FUN... BECAUSE IF YOU DO TETSUSHI WON'T LIKE YOU!
THAT'S NOT WHAT I MEAN! I...
OKAY! I'LL JUST SAY IT. NINA... YOU NEED TO STAY AWAY FROM ME!

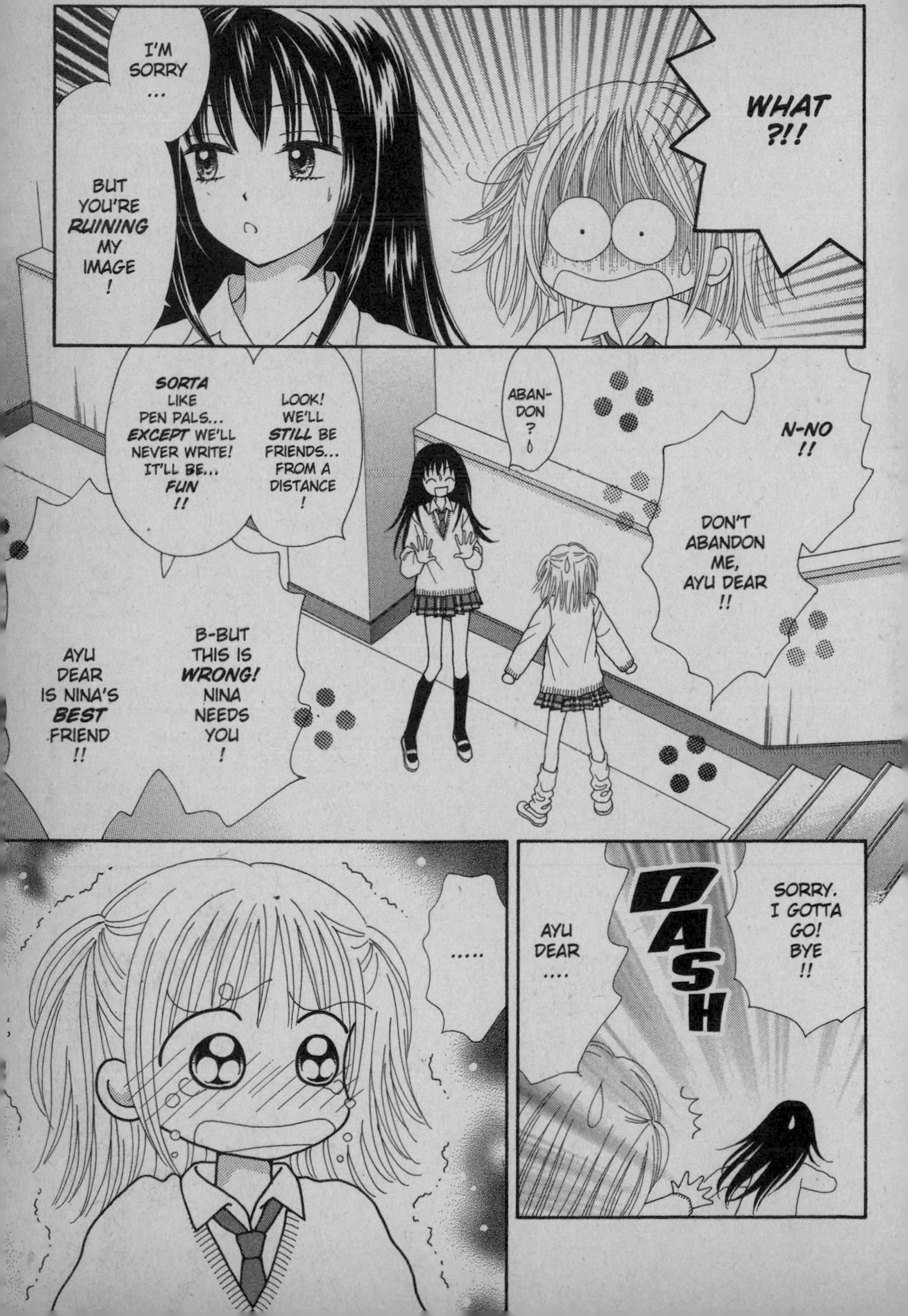
WHAT ?!!
I'M SORRY ...
BUT YOU'RE RUINING MY IMAGE !
ABAN-DON ?
N-NO !!
DON'T ABANDON ME, AYU DEAR !!
LOOK! WE'LL STILL BE FRIENDS... FROM A DISTANCE !
SORTA LIKE PEN PALS... EXCEPT WE'LL NEVER WRITE! IT'LL BE... FUN !!
B-BUT THIS IS WRONG! NINA NEEDS YOU !
AYU DEAR IS NINA'S BEST FRIEND !!
SORRY. I GOTTA GO! BYE !!
DASH
AYU DEAR ....
.....

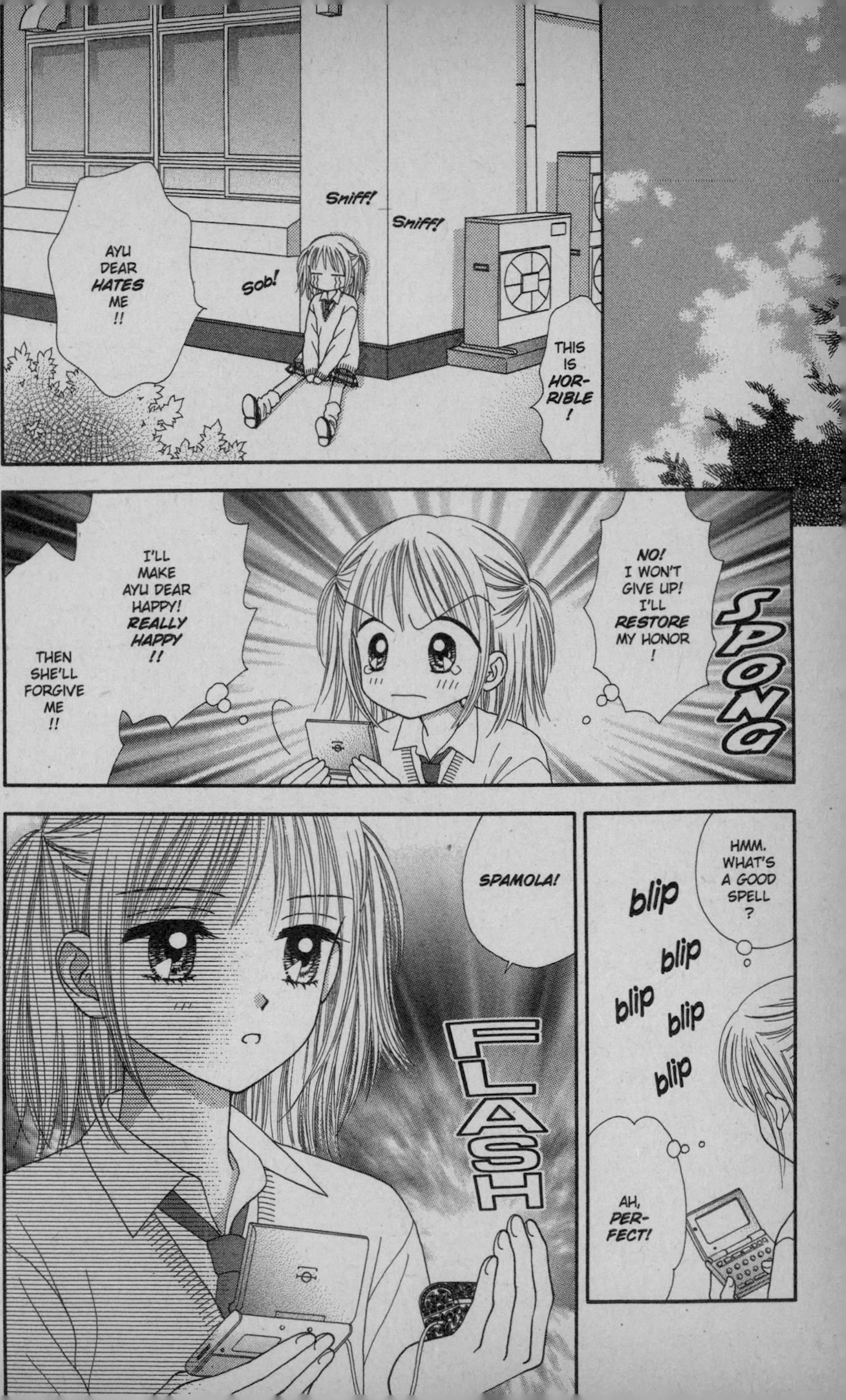
Sniff!
Sniff!
THIS IS HORRIBLE!
Sob!
AYU DEAR HATES ME !!
SPONG
NO! I WON'T GIVE UP! I'LL RESTORE MY HONOR !
I'LL MAKE AYU DEAR HAPPY! REALLY HAPPY !!
THEN SHE'LL FORGIVE ME !!
HMM. WHAT'S A GOOD SPELL ?
blip
blip
blip
blip
blip
AH, PERFECT!
SPAMOLA!
FLASH

HI, TET-SUSHI! ♡
GOOD LUCK AT PRACTICE! ♡
UH?
OKAY. THANKS.
BY THE WAY, TET-SUSHI...
COULD YOU HOLD YOUR HAND OUT... FOR A SECOND?

FREE TALK 8

But I have to say, making bead jewelry has become very popular. I know it was also popular once years ago, but it seems like it's much more serious and complex now.

If you go to bookstores, they're full of literature about how to make bead jewelry. Some of the books even come with jewelry-making kits. There's so much cute stuff—much more than there was years ago. I like to make jewelry. But I usually make it and don't wear it. The rare time I do wear it I lose it. (Ha! Ha!)

By the way, for the cover art of Chapter 3, I thought I would dress Nina up in Goth-Lolita fashion. Goth-Lolita, in my mind, is a fashion that "doesn't care about what anyone else thinks! It's the style that you want. Not the style that other people want for you."

I have no idea if that's what Goth-Lolita is like to other people. But that's my interpretation. . . and I thought it would look really good on Nina.

I really like it! ♡ Sometime I might dress Ayu in it too!

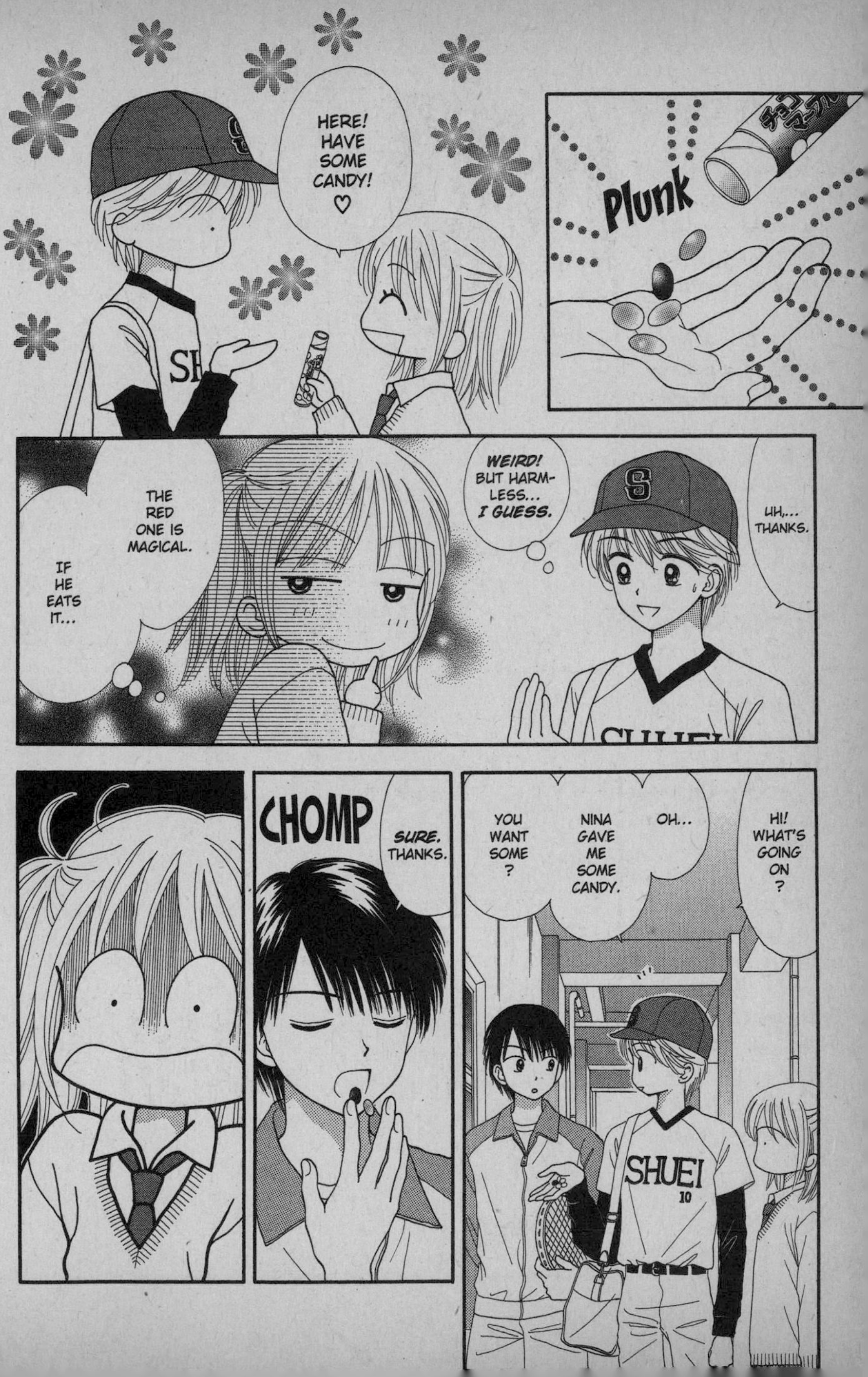
Plunk
HERE! HAVE SOME CANDY! ♡
UH,... THANKS.
WEIRD! BUT HARMLESS... I GUESS.
THE RED ONE IS MAGICAL.
IF HE EATS IT...
HI! WHAT'S GOING ON?
OH...
NINA GAVE ME SOME CANDY.
YOU WANT SOME?
SURE. THANKS.
CHOMP

FREE TALK 9

I'm writing this on July 4, 2002. The World Cup just ended. I couldn't get tickets, but I watched it on TV. It was really fun!

My feelings were even stronger four years ago. After the match with France, I wrote about this in the Free Talk of "We're in Mint Condition Vol. 2." I wrote, "I seriously love David Beckham!" ♡

Back then, Beckham was a beautiful, young man with flowing hair. These days Beckham is a father of one, with a soft Mohawk, facial hair, and mature looks. The change over four years is pretty amazing. . .

But I have to say, Beckham was the most popular player in this tournament.

Four years ago, there were a lot of other popular players, like Del Piero. Del Piero was here this time too, but it seems his fame wasn't as strong.

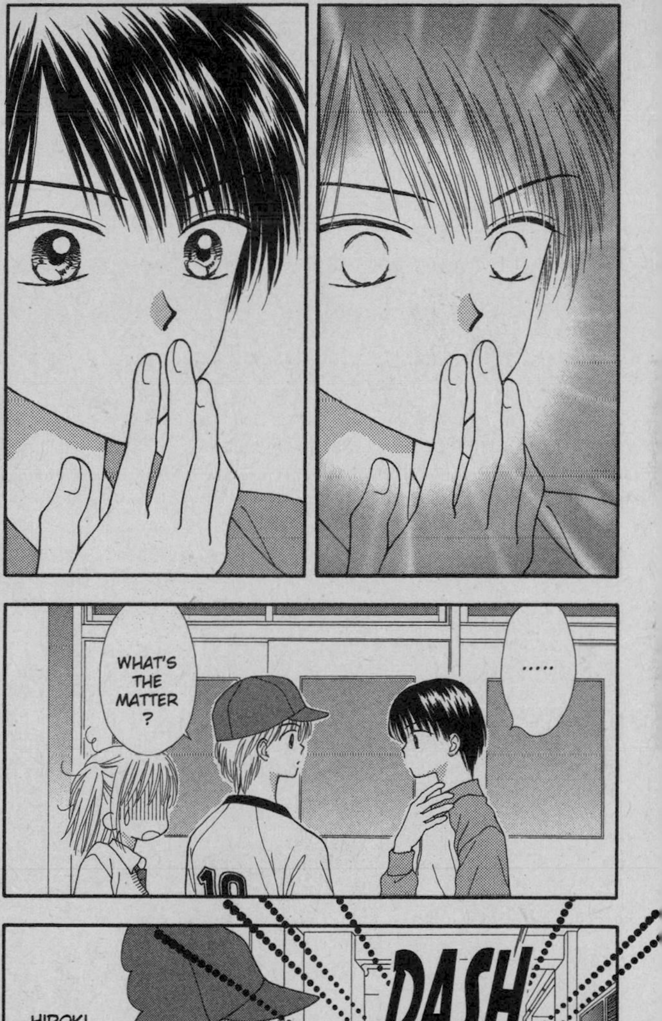
.....
WHAT'S THE MATTER ?
DASH
HIROKI ?!

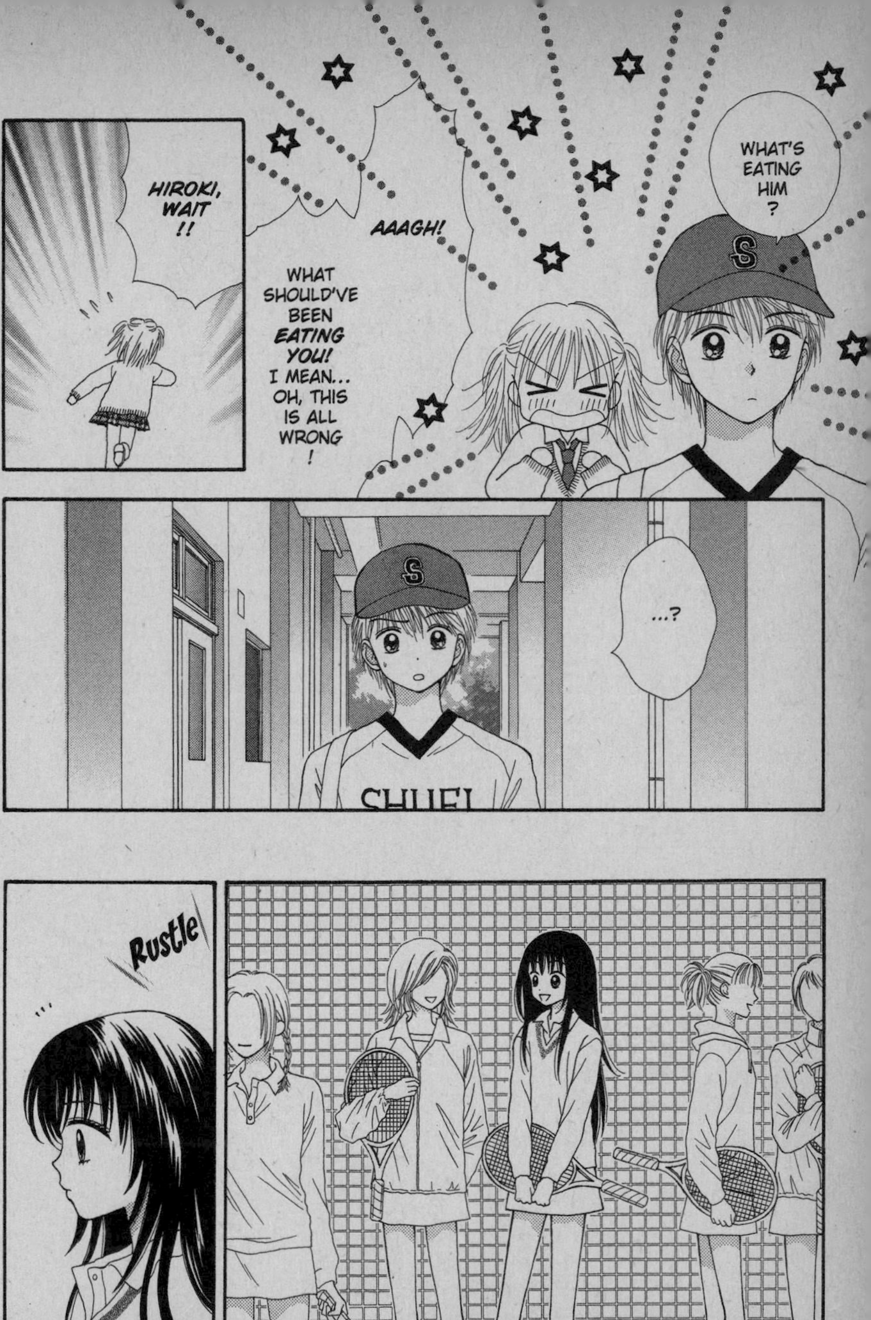
WHAT'S EATING HIM?
AAAGH!
WHAT SHOULD'VE BEEN EATING YOU! I MEAN... OH, THIS IS ALL WRONG!
HIROKI, WAIT!!
...?
SHUEI
Rustle
...

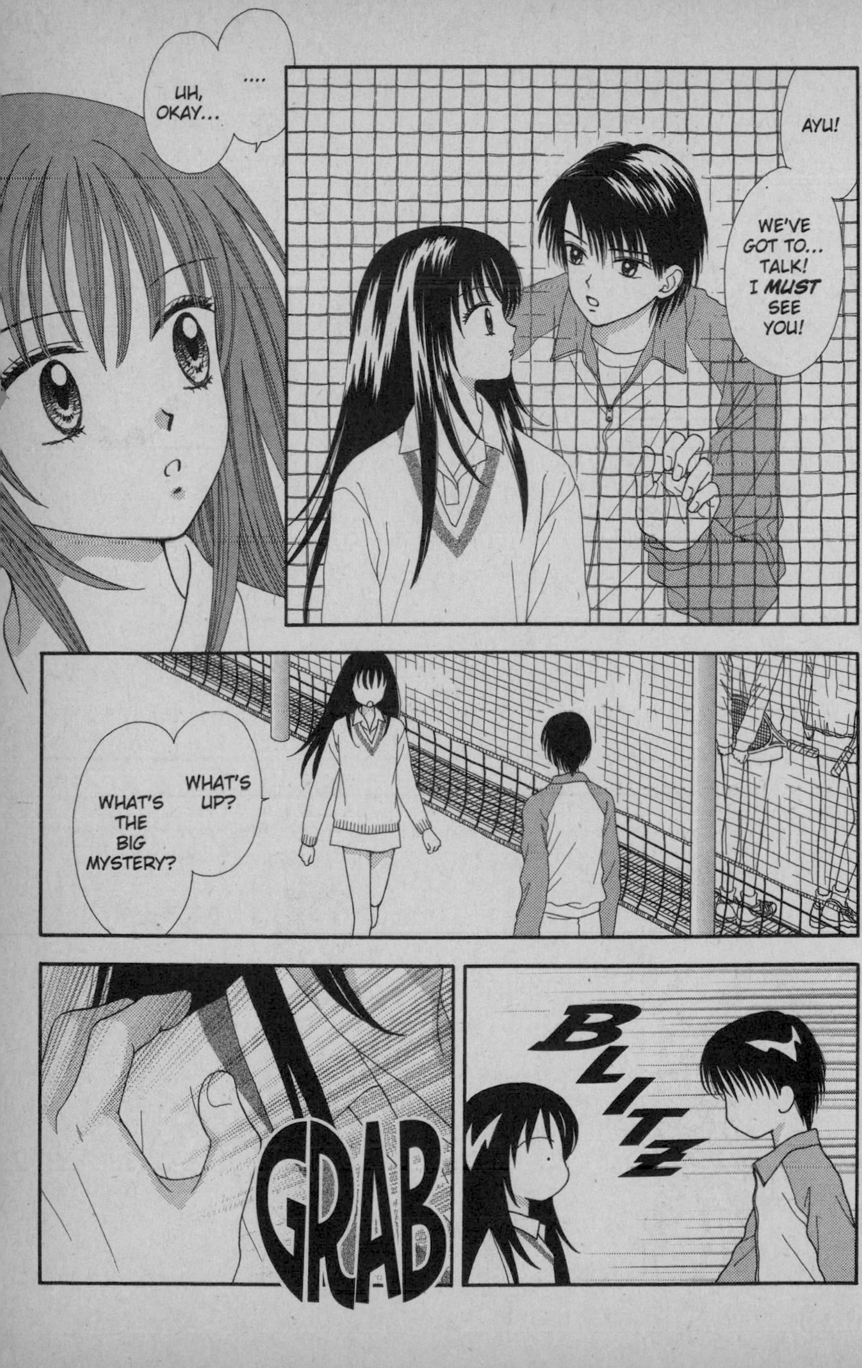
AYU!
WE'VE GOT TO... TALK! I **MUST** SEE YOU!
....
UH, OKAY...
WHAT'S UP?
WHAT'S THE BIG MYSTERY?
BLITZ
GRAB

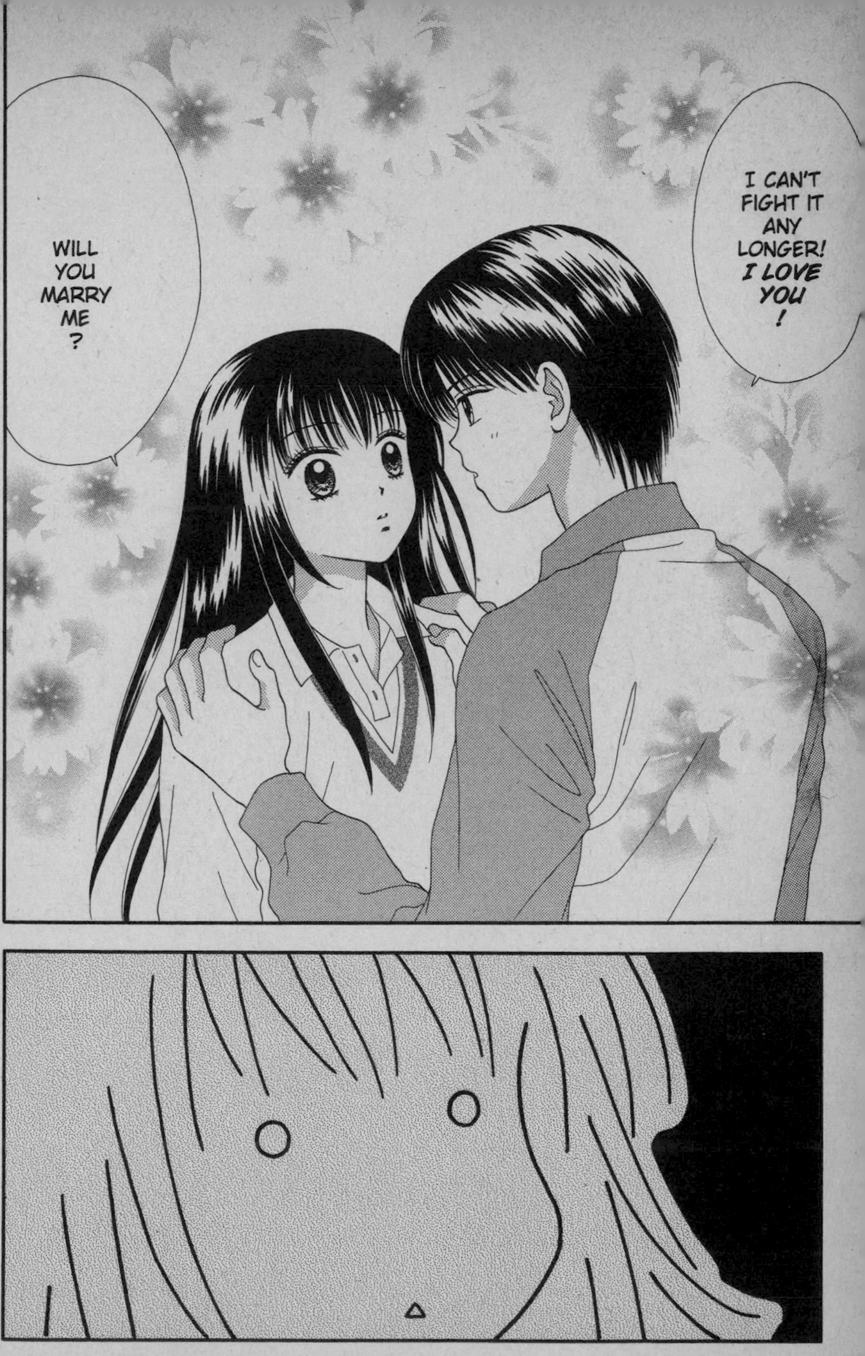
I CAN'T FIGHT IT ANY LONGER! I LOVE YOU!
WILL YOU MARRY ME?

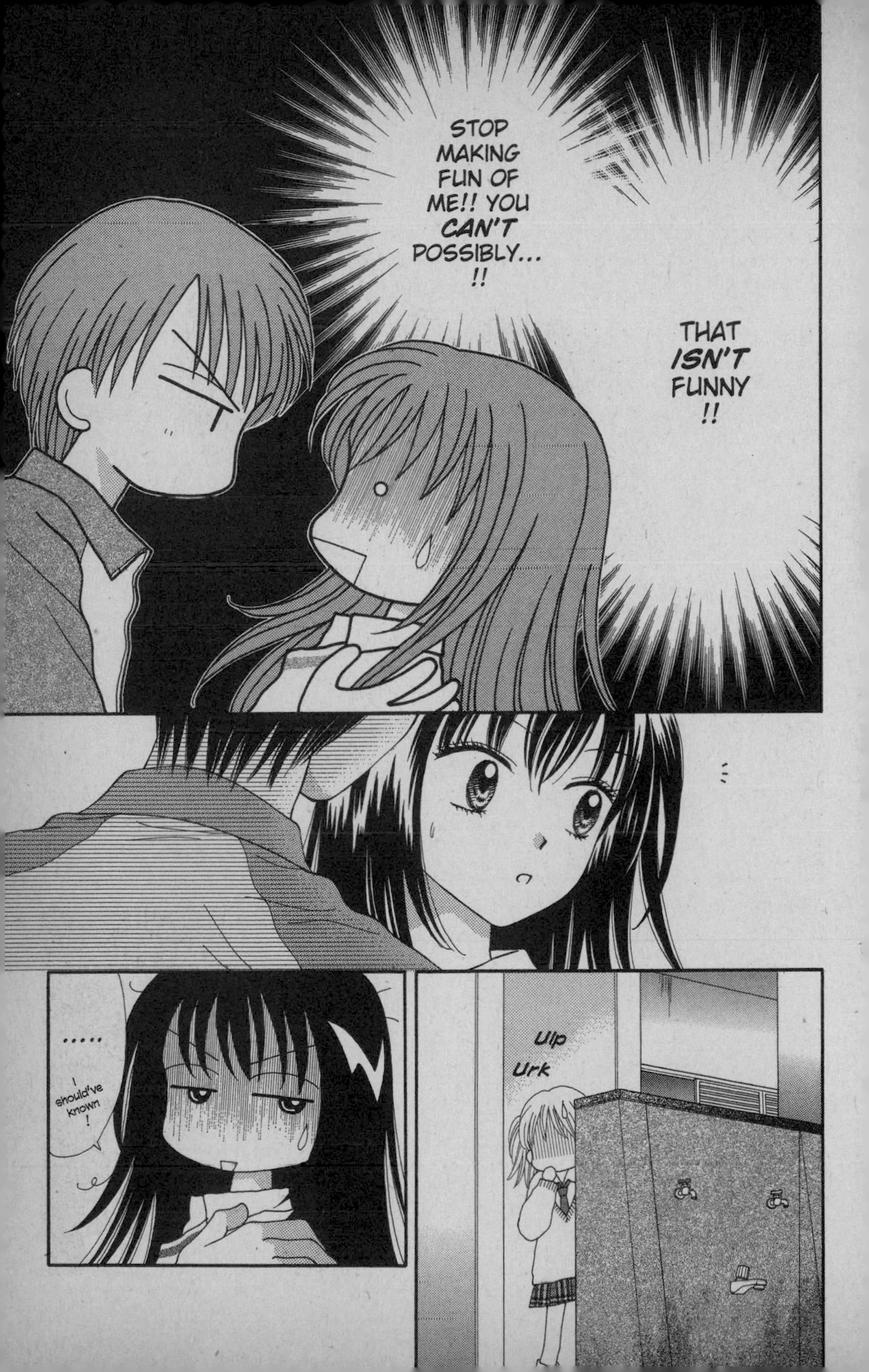

THAT ISN'T FUNNY !!
STOP MAKING FUN OF ME!! YOU CAN'T POSSIBLY... !!
Ulp
Urk
.....
I should've known !

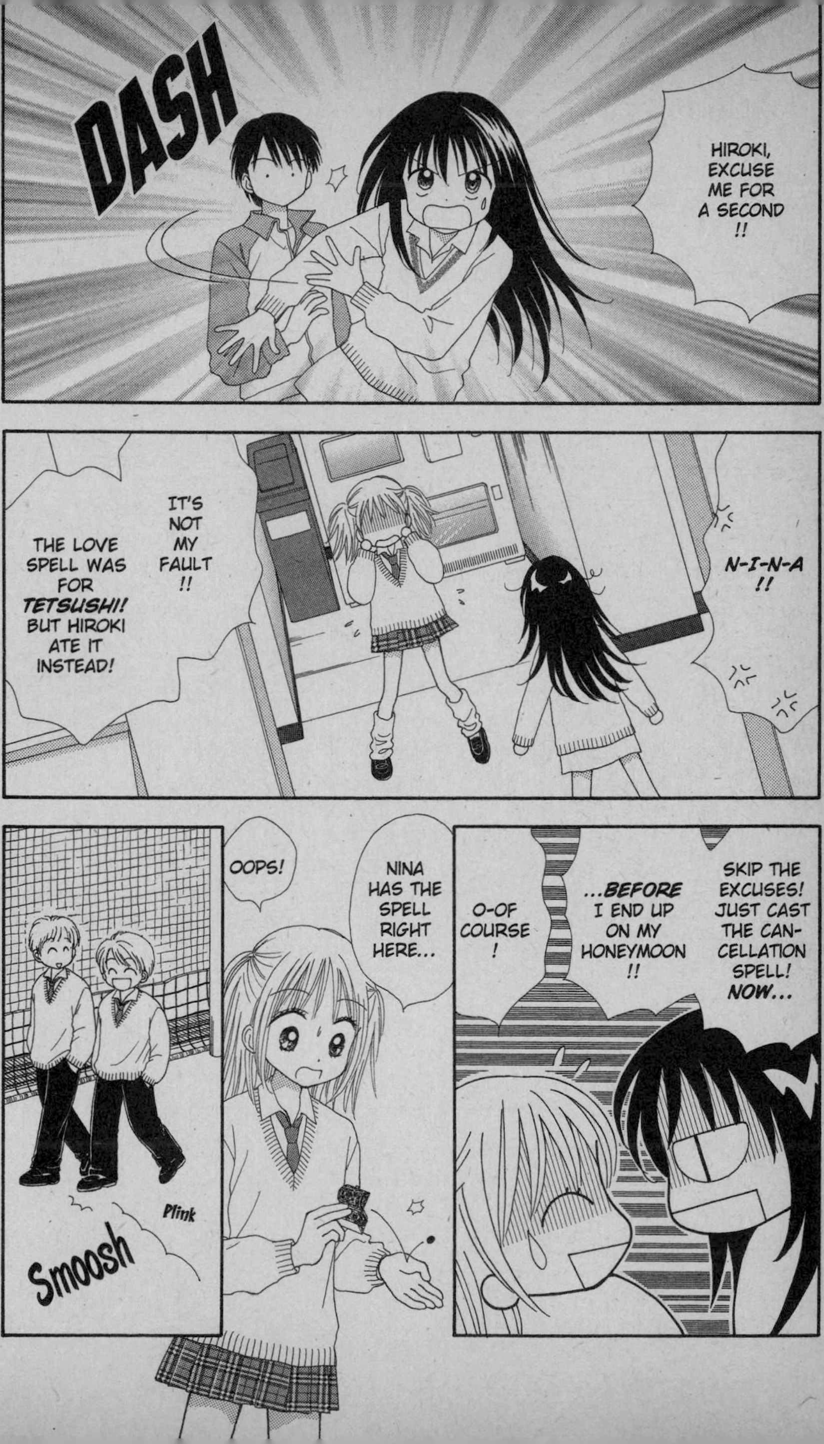
DASH
HIROKI, EXCUSE ME FOR A SECOND !!
N-I-N-A !!
IT'S NOT MY FAULT !!
THE LOVE SPELL WAS FOR *TETSUSHI!* BUT HIROKI ATE IT INSTEAD!
SKIP THE EXCUSES! JUST CAST THE CAN-CELLATION SPELL! *NOW...*
...*BEFORE* I END UP ON MY HONEYMOON !!
O-OF COURSE !
NINA HAS THE SPELL RIGHT HERE...
OOPS!
Plink
Smoosh

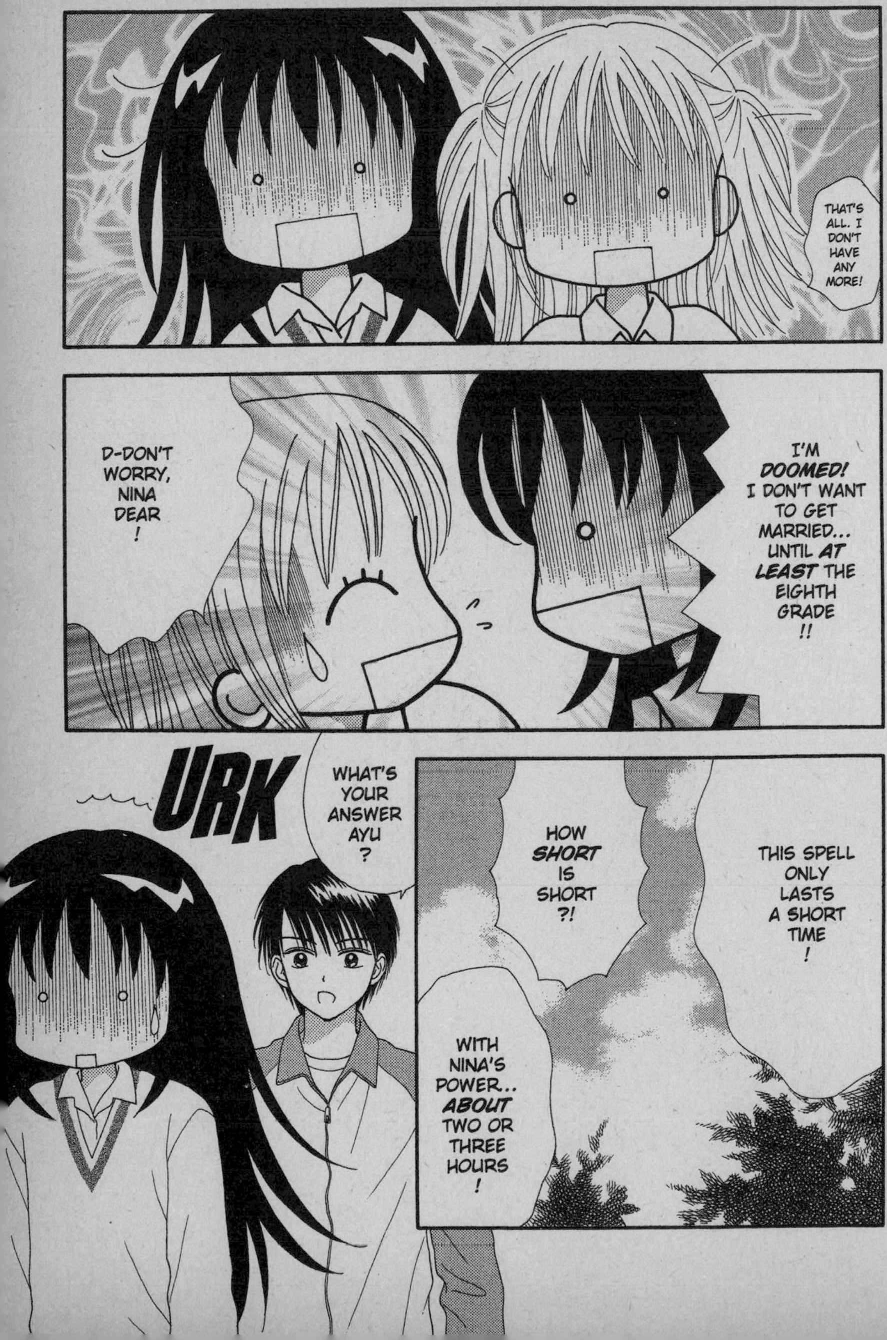
THAT'S ALL. I DON'T HAVE ANY MORE!
I'M DOOMED! I DON'T WANT TO GET MARRIED... UNTIL AT LEAST THE EIGHTH GRADE!!
D-DON'T WORRY, NINA DEAR!
THIS SPELL ONLY LASTS A SHORT TIME!
HOW SHORT IS SHORT?!
WITH NINA'S POWER... ABOUT TWO OR THREE HOURS!
WHAT'S YOUR ANSWER AYU?
URK

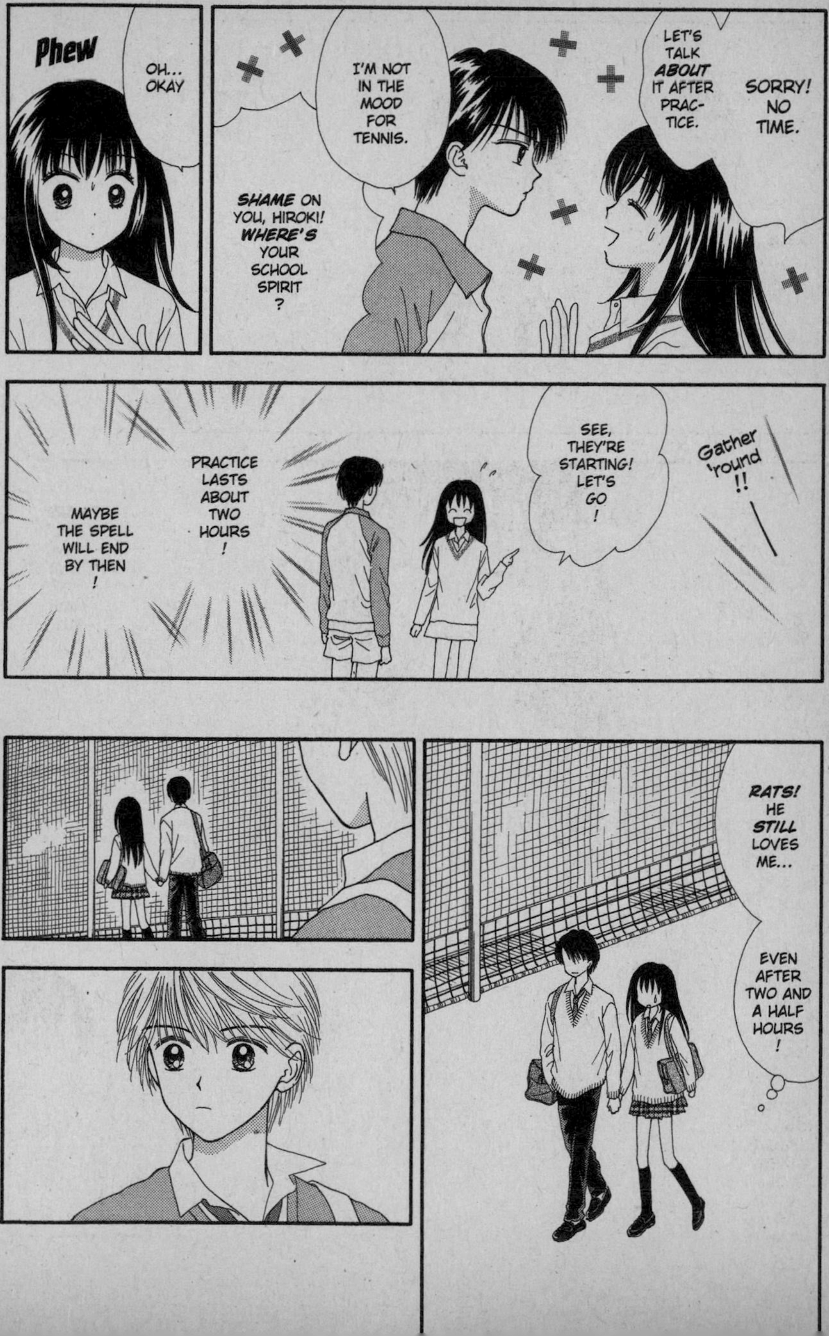
SORRY! NO TIME.
LET'S TALK ABOUT IT AFTER PRAC- TICE.
I'M NOT IN THE MOOD FOR TENNIS.
SHAME ON YOU, HIROKI! WHERE'S YOUR SCHOOL SPIRIT?
Phew
OH... OKAY
Gather 'round!!
SEE, THEY'RE STARTING! LET'S GO!
PRACTICE LASTS ABOUT TWO HOURS!
MAYBE THE SPELL WILL END BY THEN!
RATS! HE STILL LOVES ME...
EVEN AFTER TWO AND A HALF HOURS!

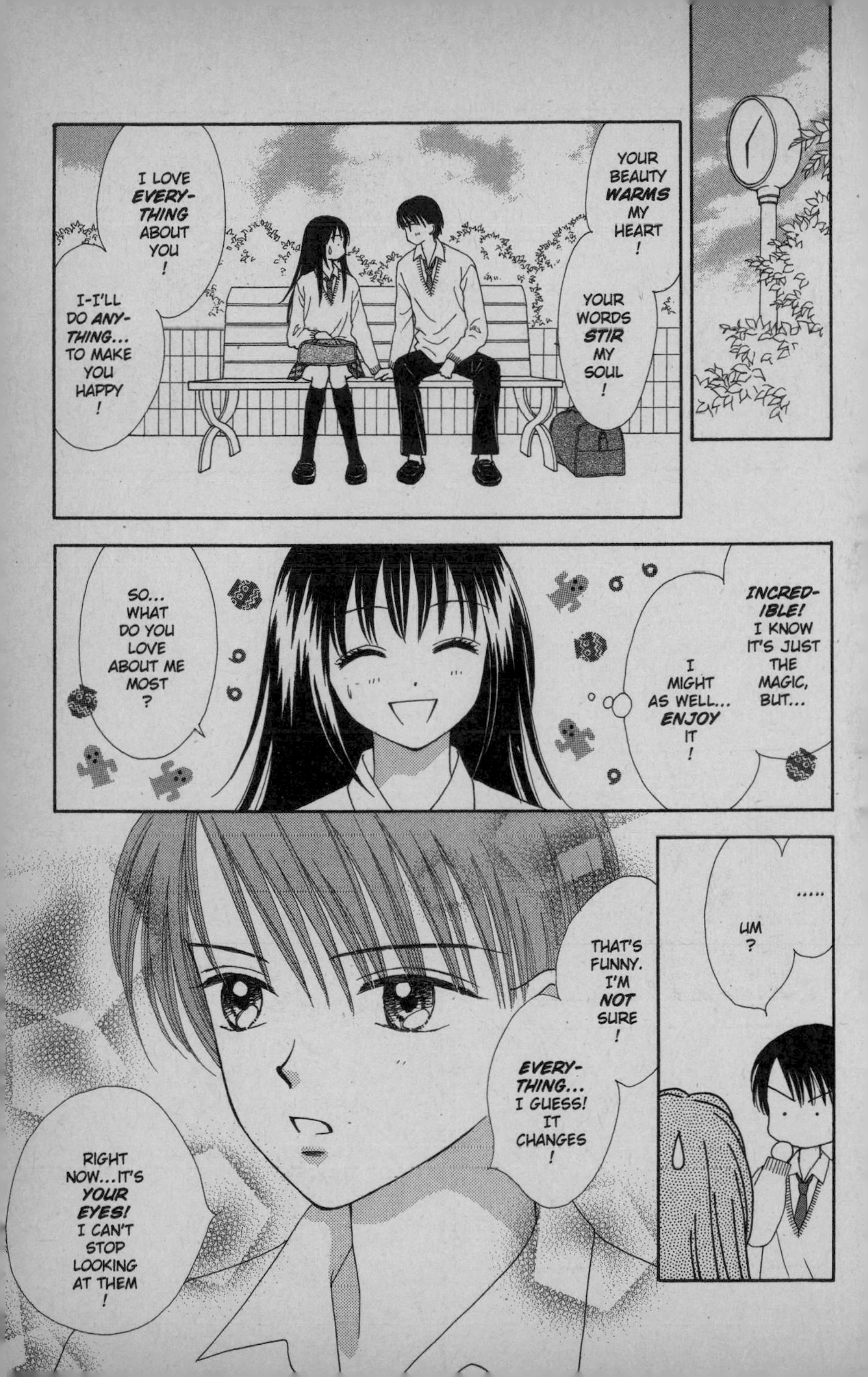
YOUR BEAUTY WARMS MY HEART!
YOUR WORDS STIR MY SOUL!
I LOVE EVERYTHING ABOUT YOU!
I-I'LL DO ANYTHING... TO MAKE YOU HAPPY!
INCREDIBLE! I KNOW IT'S JUST THE MAGIC, BUT...
I MIGHT AS WELL... ENJOY IT!
SO... WHAT DO YOU LOVE ABOUT ME MOST?
.....
UM?
THAT'S FUNNY. I'M NOT SURE!
EVERYTHING... I GUESS! IT CHANGES!
RIGHT NOW... IT'S YOUR EYES! I CAN'T STOP LOOKING AT THEM!

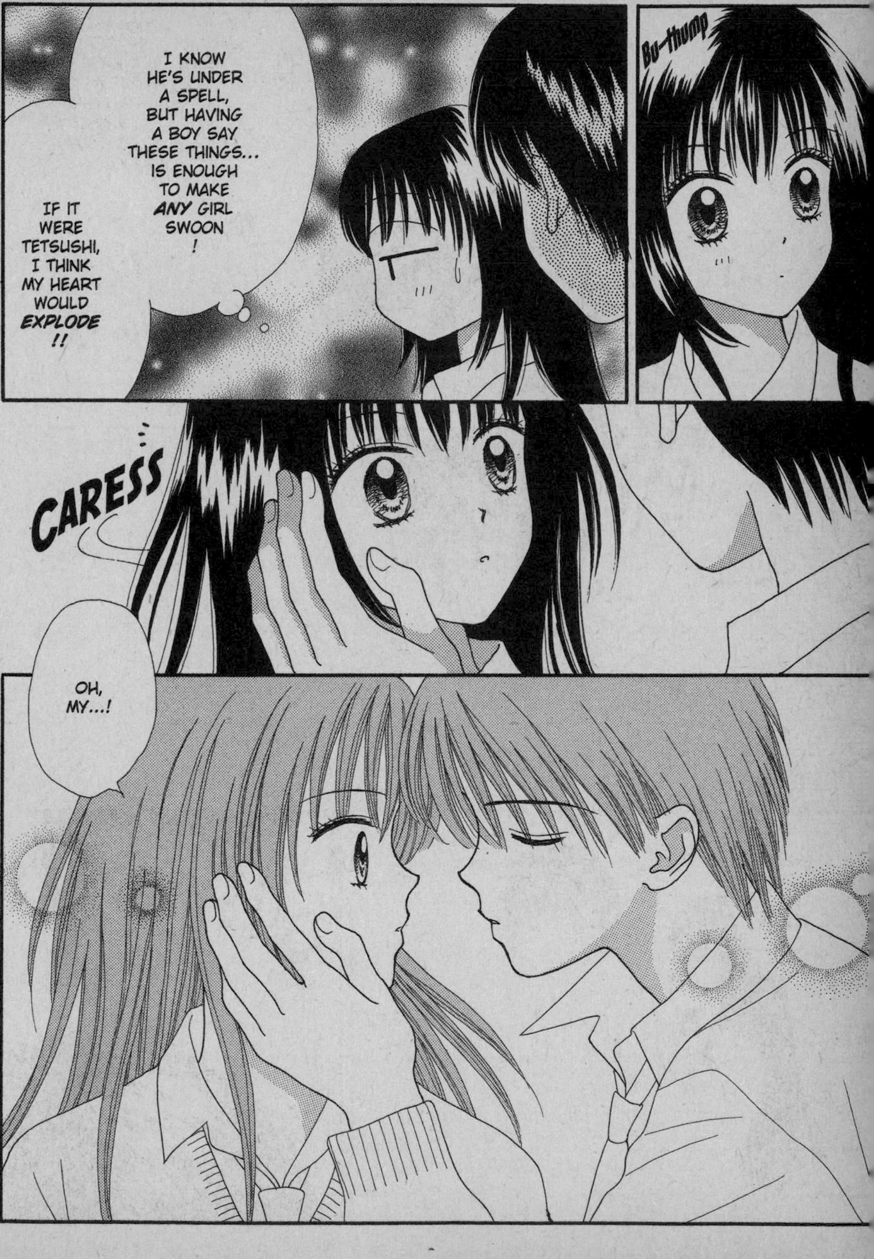
Bu-thump
I KNOW HE'S UNDER A SPELL, BUT HAVING A BOY SAY THESE THINGS... IS ENOUGH TO MAKE ANY GIRL SWOON!
IF IT WERE TETSUSHI, I THINK MY HEART WOULD EXPLODE!!
CARESS
OH, MY...!

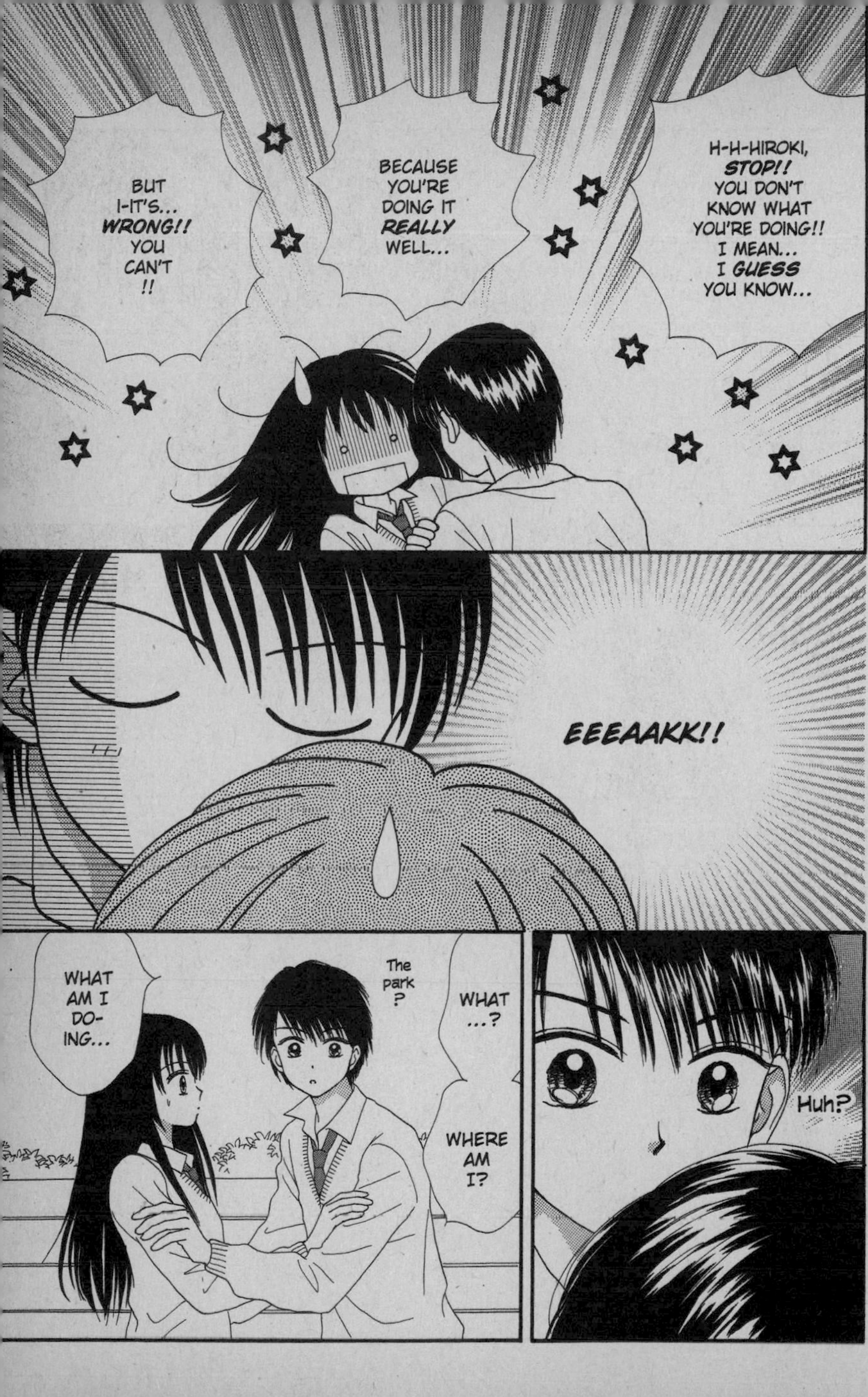
H-H-HIROKI, **STOP!!** YOU DON'T KNOW WHAT YOU'RE DOING!! I MEAN... I **GUESS** YOU KNOW...
BECAUSE YOU'RE DOING IT **REALLY** WELL...
BUT I-IT'S... **WRONG!!** YOU CAN'T !!
EEEAAKK!!
Huh?
WHAT ...?
WHERE AM I?
The park?
WHAT AM I DOING...

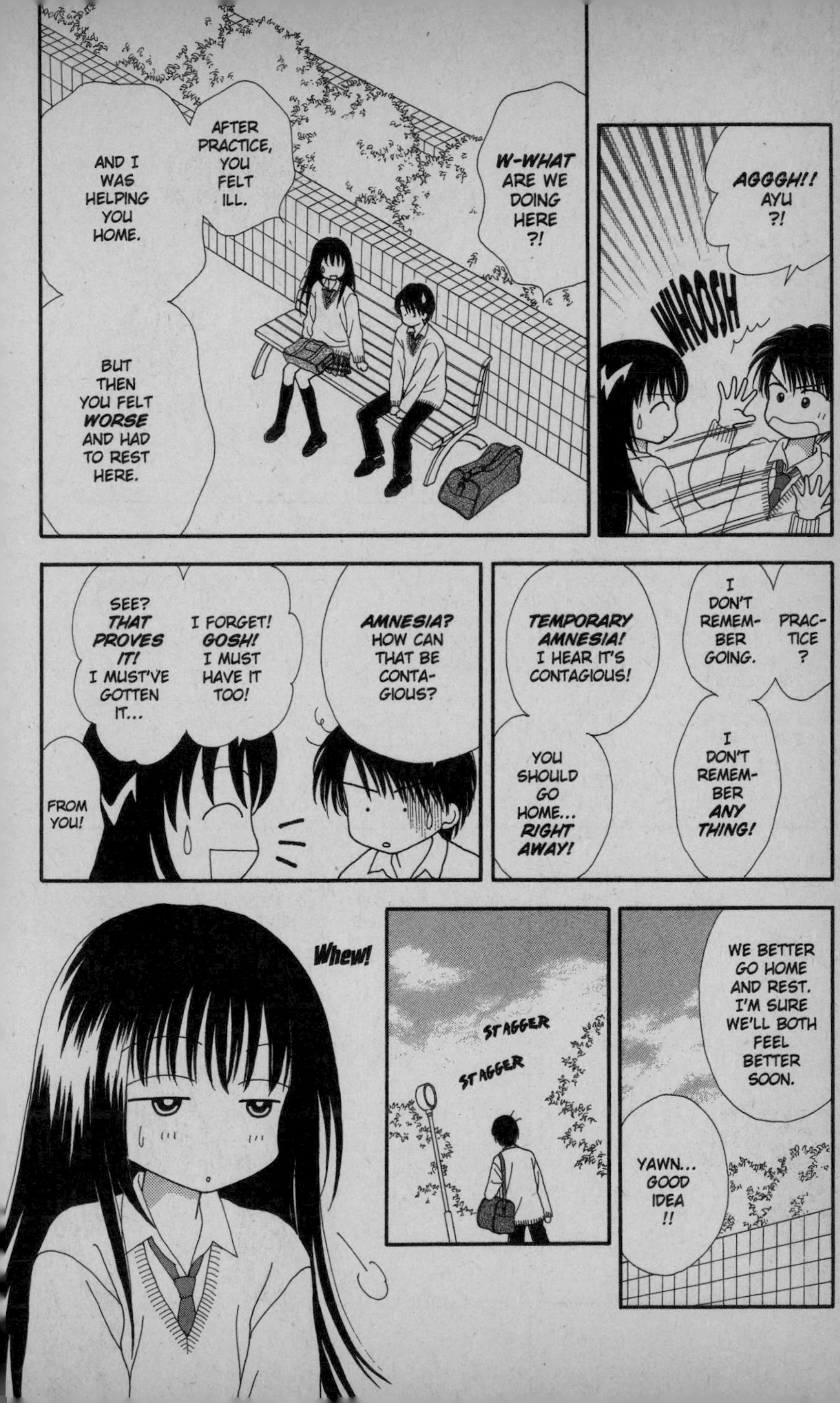

AGGGH!! AYU ?!
WHOOSH
W-WHAT ARE WE DOING HERE ?!
AFTER PRACTICE, YOU FELT ILL.
AND I WAS HELPING YOU HOME.
BUT THEN YOU FELT WORSE AND HAD TO REST HERE.
PRAC-TICE ?
I DON'T REMEM-BER GOING.
I DON'T REMEM-BER ANY THING!
TEMPORARY AMNESIA! I HEAR IT'S CONTAGIOUS!
YOU SHOULD GO HOME... RIGHT AWAY!
AMNESIA? HOW CAN THAT BE CONTA-GIOUS?
I FORGET! GOSH! I MUST HAVE IT TOO!
SEE? THAT PROVES IT! I MUST'VE GOTTEN IT...
FROM YOU!
WE BETTER GO HOME AND REST. I'M SURE WE'LL BOTH FEEL BETTER SOON.
YAWN... GOOD IDEA !!
STAGGER
STAGGER
Whew!

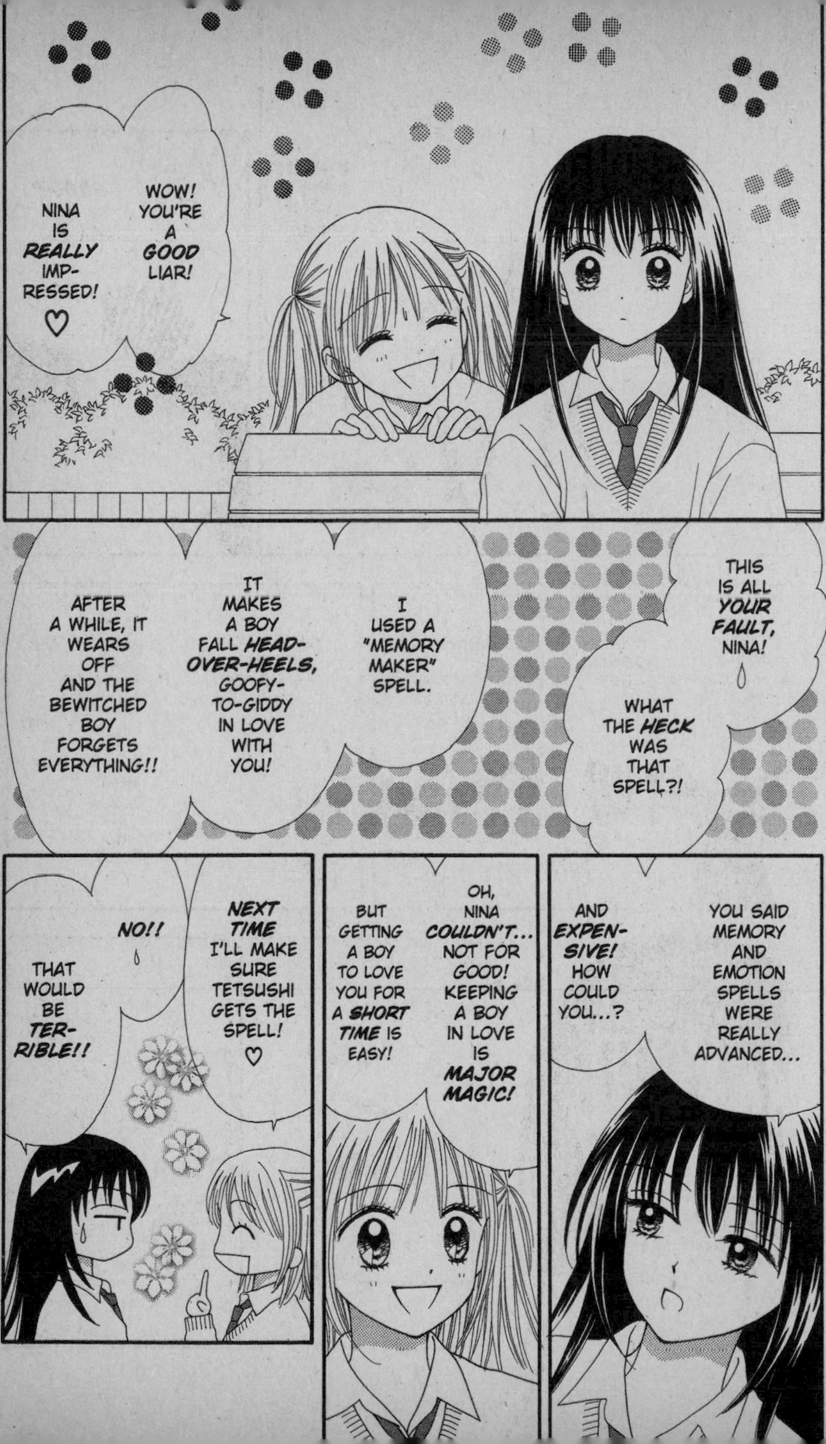
WOW! YOU'RE A GOOD LIAR!
NINA IS REALLY IMPRESSED! ♡
THIS IS ALL YOUR FAULT, NINA!
WHAT THE HECK WAS THAT SPELL?!
I USED A "MEMORY MAKER" SPELL.
IT MAKES A BOY FALL HEAD-OVER-HEELS, GOOFY-TO-GIDDY IN LOVE WITH YOU!
AFTER A WHILE, IT WEARS OFF AND THE BEWITCHED BOY FORGETS EVERYTHING!!
YOU SAID MEMORY AND EMOTION SPELLS WERE REALLY ADVANCED...
AND EXPENSIVE! HOW COULD YOU...?
OH, NINA COULDN'T... NOT FOR GOOD! KEEPING A BOY IN LOVE IS MAJOR MAGIC!
BUT GETTING A BOY TO LOVE YOU FOR A SHORT TIME IS EASY!
NEXT TIME I'LL MAKE SURE TETSUSHI GETS THE SPELL! ♡
NO!!
THAT WOULD BE TERRIBLE!!

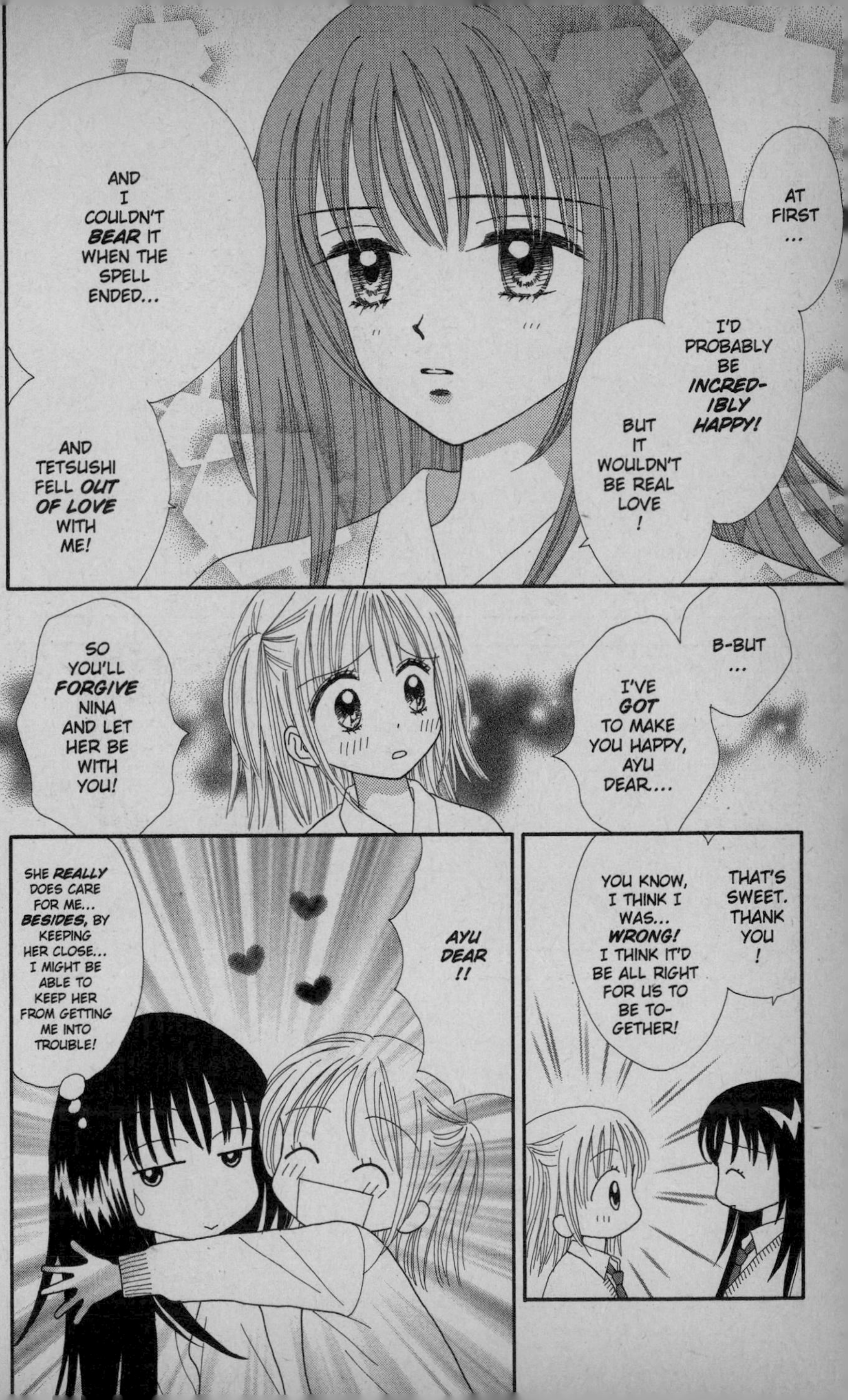
AT FIRST... I'D PROBABLY BE INCREDIBLY HAPPY!
BUT IT WOULDN'T BE REAL LOVE!
AND I COULDN'T BEAR IT WHEN THE SPELL ENDED...
AND TETSUSHI FELL OUT OF LOVE WITH ME!
B-BUT... I'VE GOT TO MAKE YOU HAPPY, AYU DEAR...
SO YOU'LL FORGIVE NINA AND LET HER BE WITH YOU!
THAT'S SWEET. THANK YOU!
YOU KNOW, I THINK I WAS... WRONG! I THINK IT'D BE ALL RIGHT FOR US TO BE TOGETHER!
AYU DEAR!!
SHE REALLY DOES CARE FOR ME... BESIDES, BY KEEPING HER CLOSE... I MIGHT BE ABLE TO KEEP HER FROM GETTING ME INTO TROUBLE!

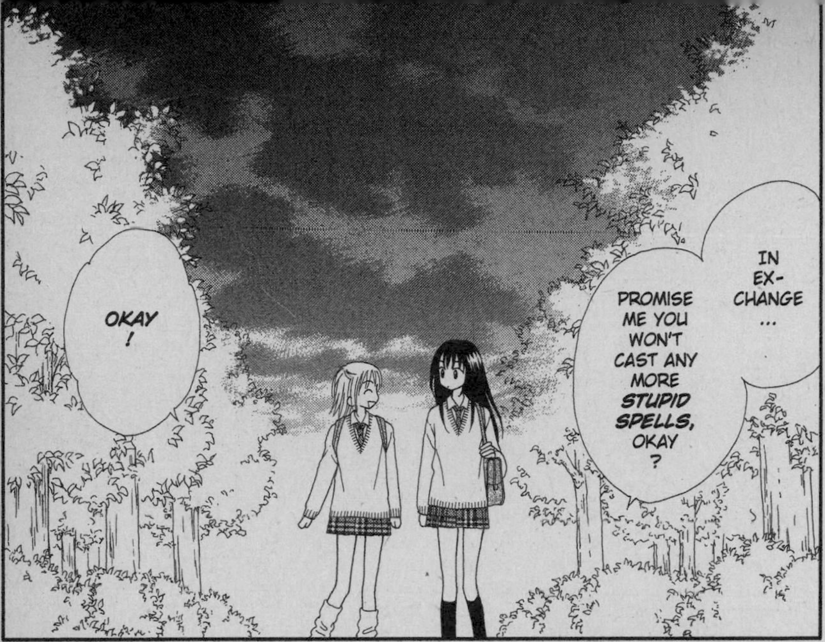
IN EX-CHANGE...
PROMISE ME YOU WON'T CAST ANY MORE STUPID SPELLS, OKAY?
OKAY!

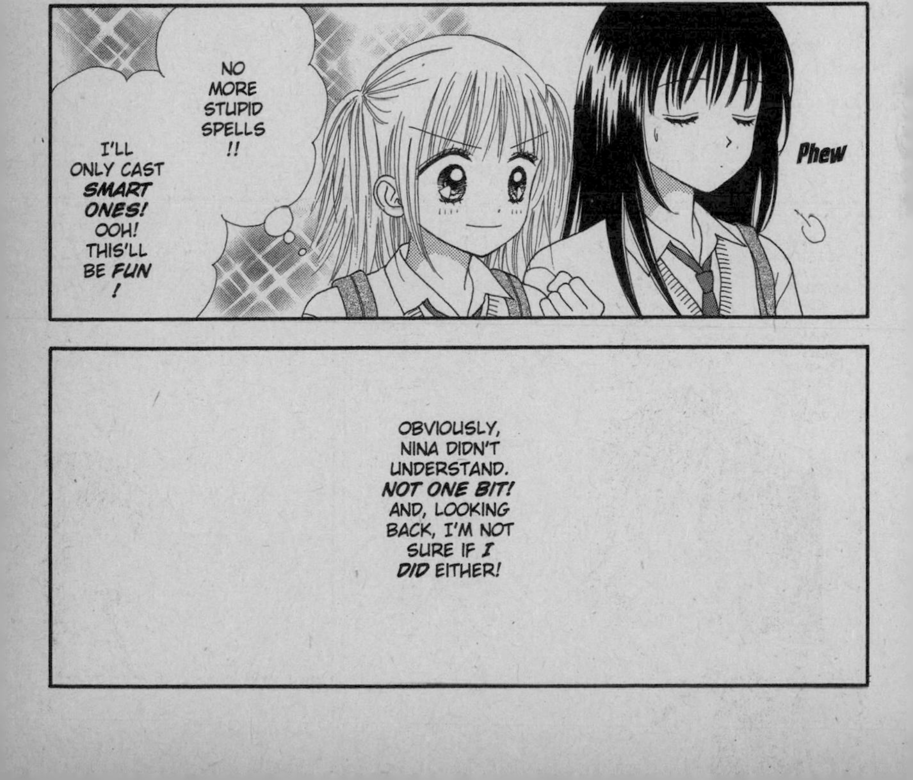
Phew
NO MORE STUPID SPELLS!!
I'LL ONLY CAST SMART ONES! OOH! THIS'LL BE FUN!

OBVIOUSLY, NINA DIDN'T UNDERSTAND. ***NOT ONE BIT!*** AND, LOOKING BACK, I'M NOT SURE IF ***I DID*** EITHER!

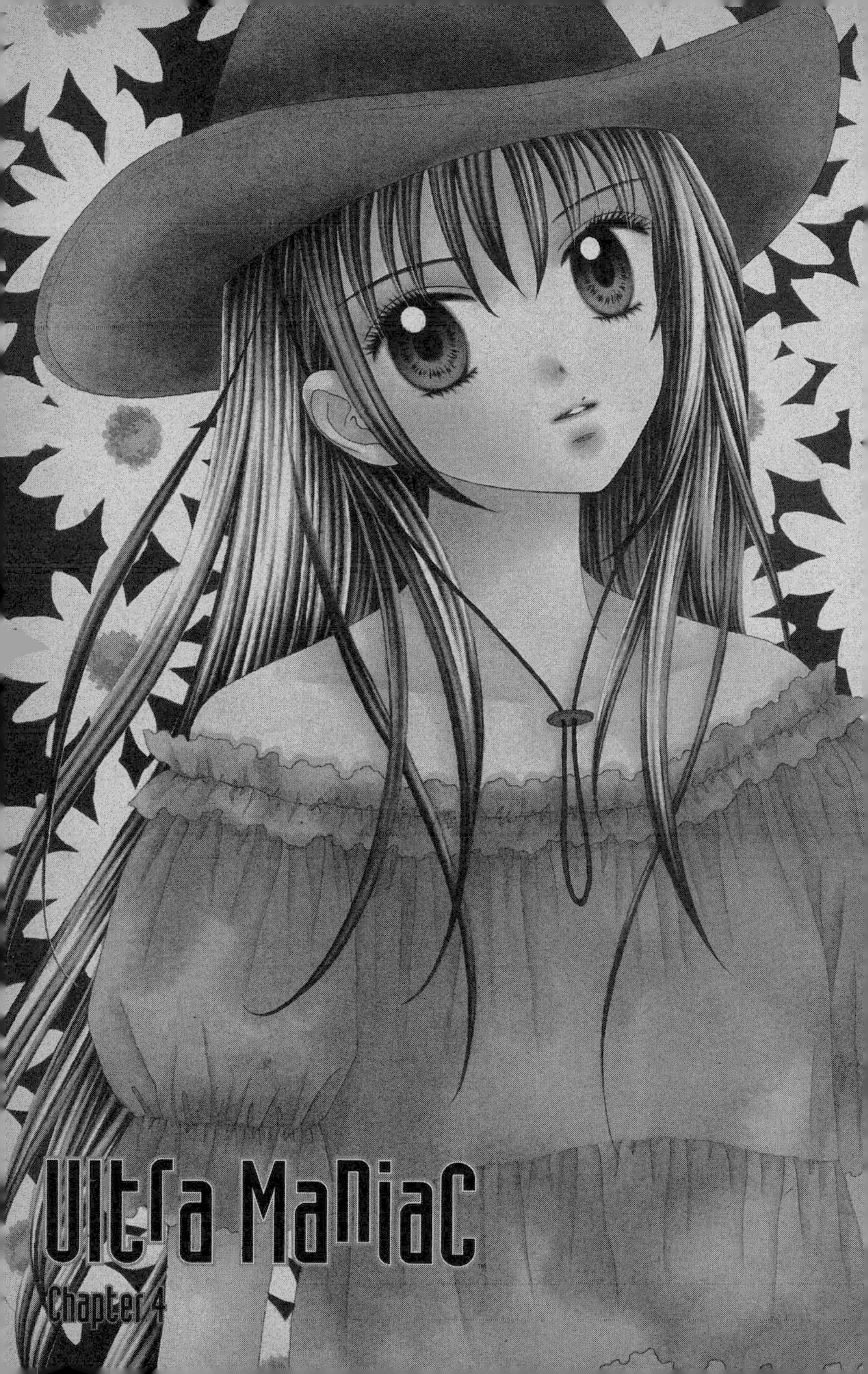
Ultra Maniac™
Chapter 4

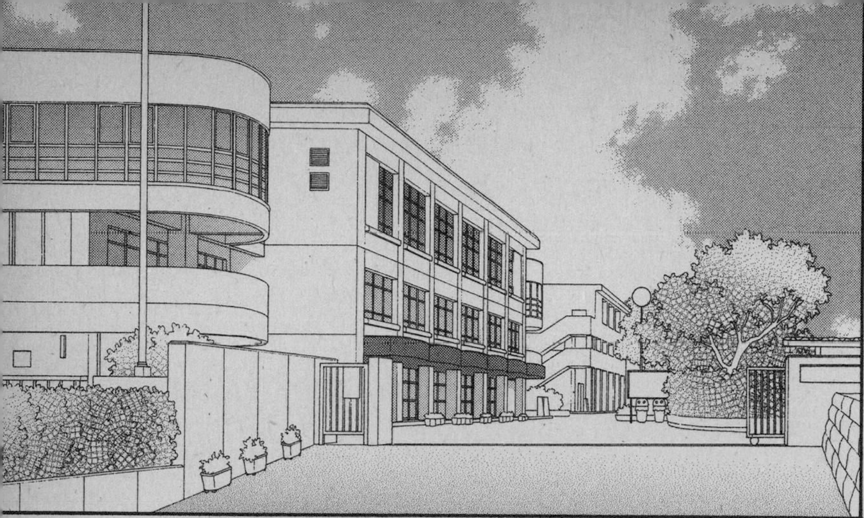

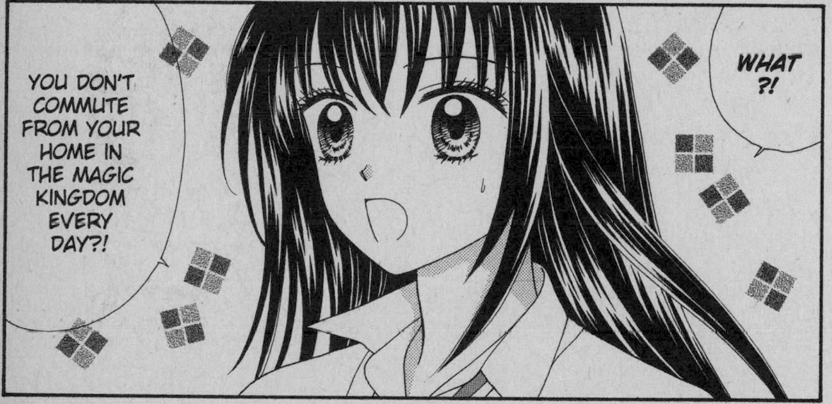
WHAT?!
YOU DON'T COMMUTE FROM YOUR HOME IN THE MAGIC KINGDOM EVERY DAY?!

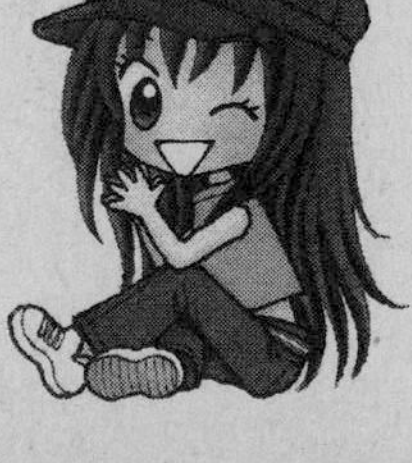

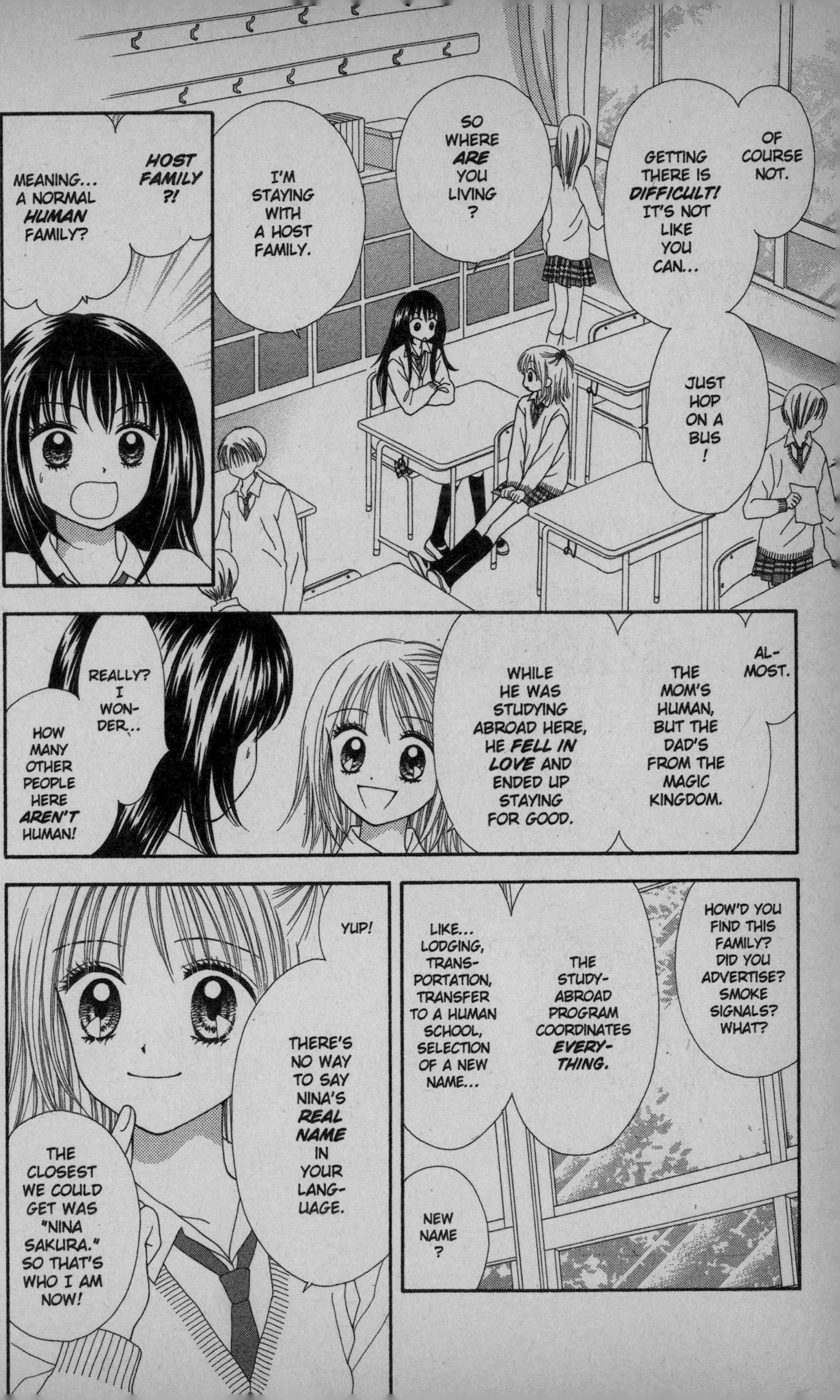
OF COURSE NOT.
GETTING THERE IS *DIFFICULT!* IT'S NOT LIKE YOU CAN...
JUST HOP ON A BUS!
SO WHERE *ARE* YOU LIVING?
I'M STAYING WITH A HOST FAMILY.
HOST FAMILY ?!
MEANING... A NORMAL *HUMAN* FAMILY?
AL-MOST.
THE MOM'S HUMAN, BUT THE DAD'S FROM THE MAGIC KINGDOM.
WHILE HE WAS STUDYING ABROAD HERE, HE *FELL IN LOVE* AND ENDED UP STAYING FOR GOOD.
REALLY? I WON-DER...
HOW MANY OTHER PEOPLE HERE *AREN'T* HUMAN!
HOW'D YOU FIND THIS FAMILY? DID YOU ADVERTISE? SMOKE SIGNALS? WHAT?
THE STUDY-ABROAD PROGRAM COORDINATES *EVERY-THING.*
LIKE... LODGING, TRANS-PORTATION, TRANSFER TO A HUMAN SCHOOL, SELECTION OF A NEW NAME...
NEW NAME ?
YUP!
THERE'S NO WAY TO SAY NINA'S *REAL NAME* IN YOUR LANG-UAGE.
THE CLOSEST WE COULD GET WAS "NINA SAKURA." SO THAT'S WHO I AM NOW!

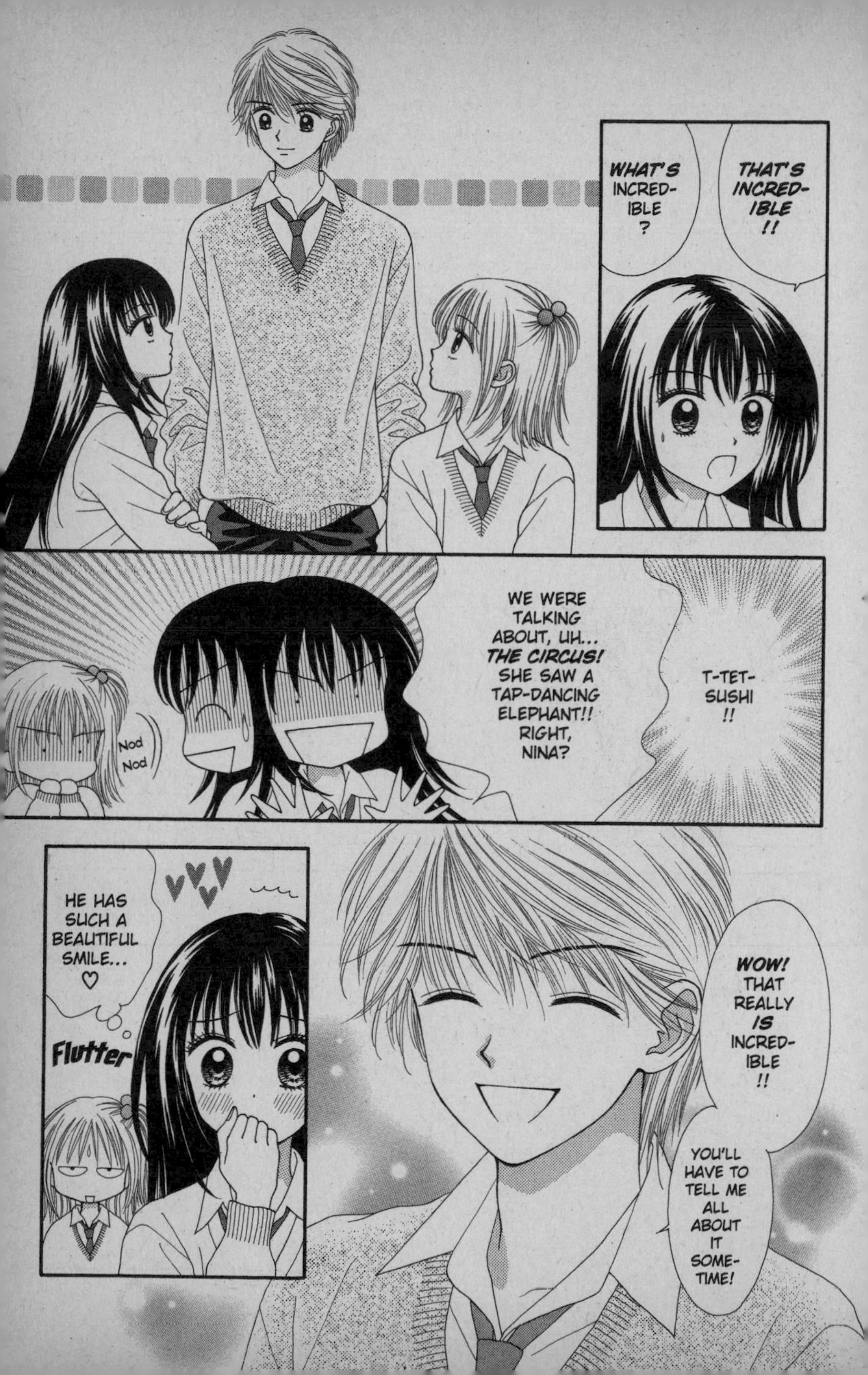
THAT'S INCREDIBLE!!
WHAT'S INCREDIBLE?
T-TETSUSHI!!
WE WERE TALKING ABOUT, UH... THE CIRCUS! SHE SAW A TAP-DANCING ELEPHANT!! RIGHT, NINA?
Nod Nod
WOW! THAT REALLY IS INCREDIBLE!!
YOU'LL HAVE TO TELL ME ALL ABOUT IT SOMETIME!
HE HAS SUCH A BEAUTIFUL SMILE... ♡
Flutter

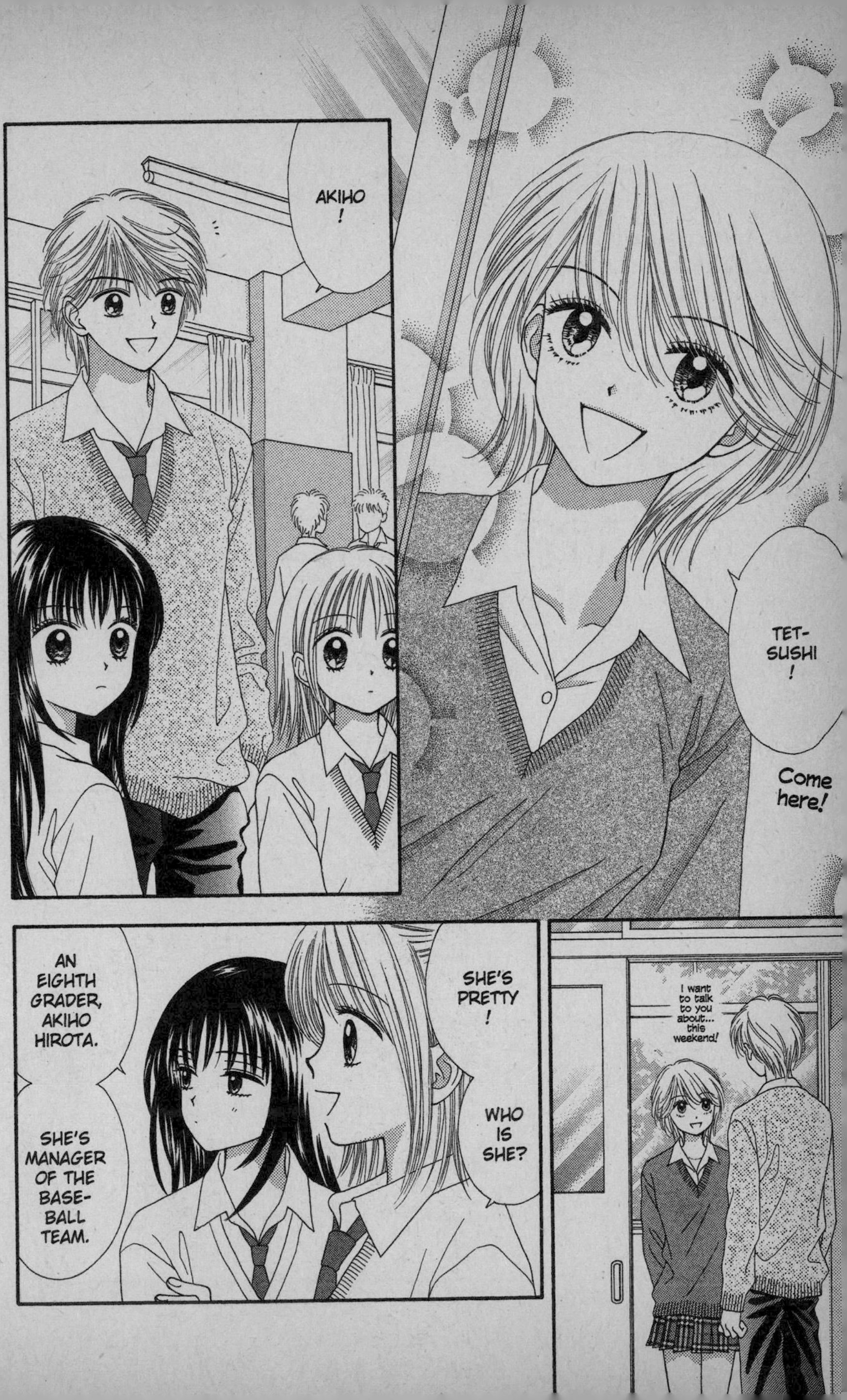
TET-SUSHI!
Come here!
AKIHO!
I want to talk to you about... this weekend!
SHE'S PRETTY!
WHO IS SHE?
AN EIGHTH GRADER, AKIHO HIROTA.
SHE'S MANAGER OF THE BASE-BALL TEAM.

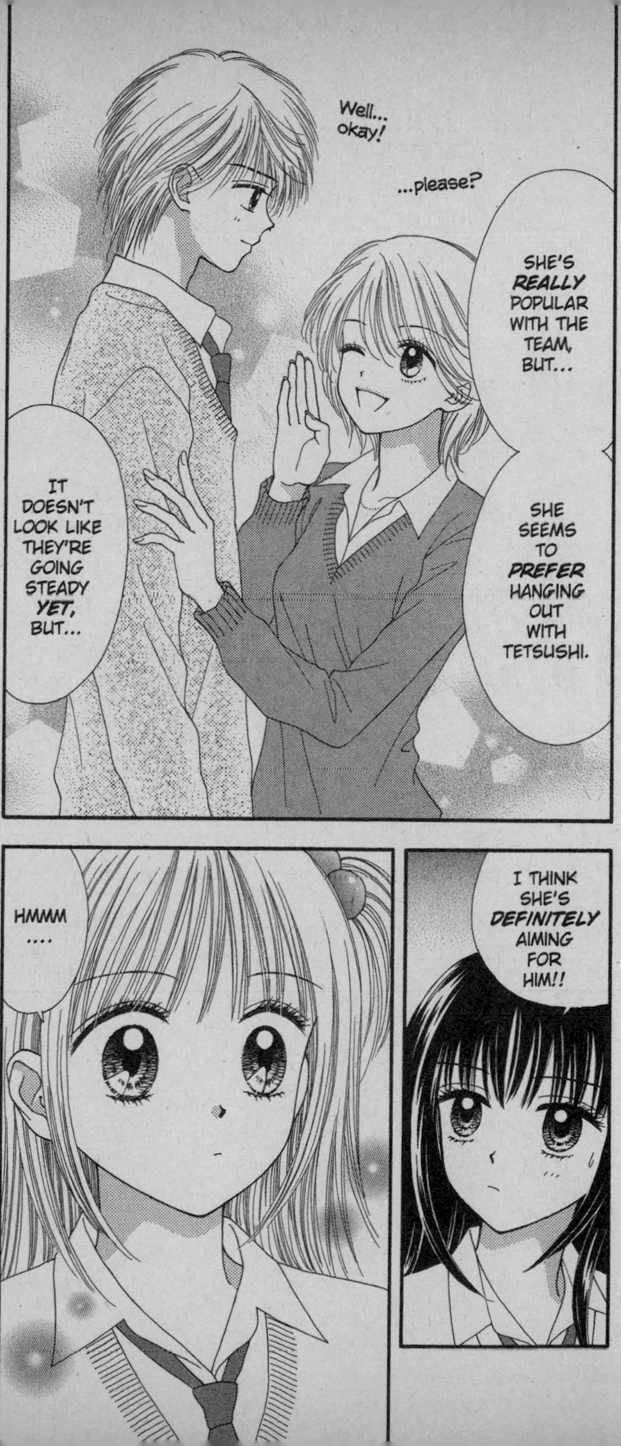
SHE'S REALLY POPULAR WITH THE TEAM, BUT...
SHE SEEMS TO PREFER HANGING OUT WITH TETSUSHI.
IT DOESN'T LOOK LIKE THEY'RE GOING STEADY YET, BUT...
...please?
Well... okay!
I THINK SHE'S DEFINITELY AIMING FOR HIM!!
HMMM ....

FREE TALK 10

Beckham was really popular, so there were features, articles and images about him all over the place.

Even the day after being beaten by Brazil, the sports newspapers still had a separate spread on Beckham.

To be honest, my "love" (Ha! Ha!) towards him cooled a little when he turned into a skinhead. (I missed his soft hair!) Plus, now that Beckham was bald and didn't really stand out on the field, he was harder to see during the games.

I stopped watching Premier League games. In the past, I'd been such a fan that I sometimes bought game tickets from a scalper!

I did, however, watch the match between Manchester United and England. During that match he had the worst actual Mohawk. I think his soft Mohawk is really cool though.

I apologize for being such a fashion snob.

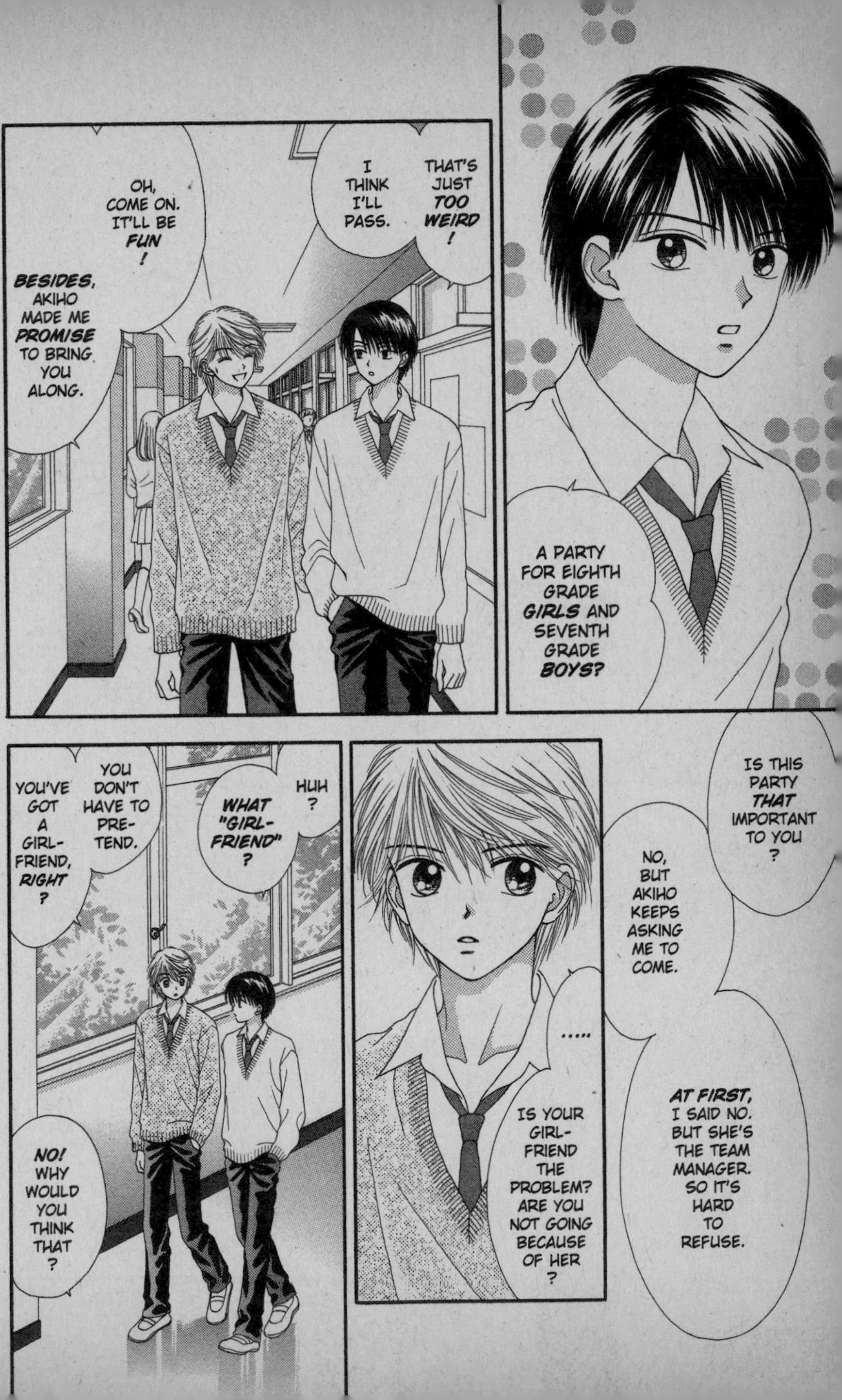

A PARTY FOR EIGHTH GRADE GIRLS AND SEVENTH GRADE BOYS?
THAT'S JUST TOO WEIRD!
I THINK I'LL PASS.
OH, COME ON. IT'LL BE FUN!
BESIDES, AKIHO MADE ME PROMISE TO BRING YOU ALONG.
IS THIS PARTY THAT IMPORTANT TO YOU?
NO, BUT AKIHO KEEPS ASKING ME TO COME.
AT FIRST, I SAID NO. BUT SHE'S THE TEAM MANAGER. SO IT'S HARD TO REFUSE.
.....
IS YOUR GIRL-FRIEND THE PROBLEM? ARE YOU NOT GOING BECAUSE OF HER?
HUH?
WHAT "GIRL-FRIEND"?
YOU DON'T HAVE TO PRE-TEND.
YOU'VE GOT A GIRL-FRIEND, RIGHT?
NO! WHY WOULD YOU THINK THAT?

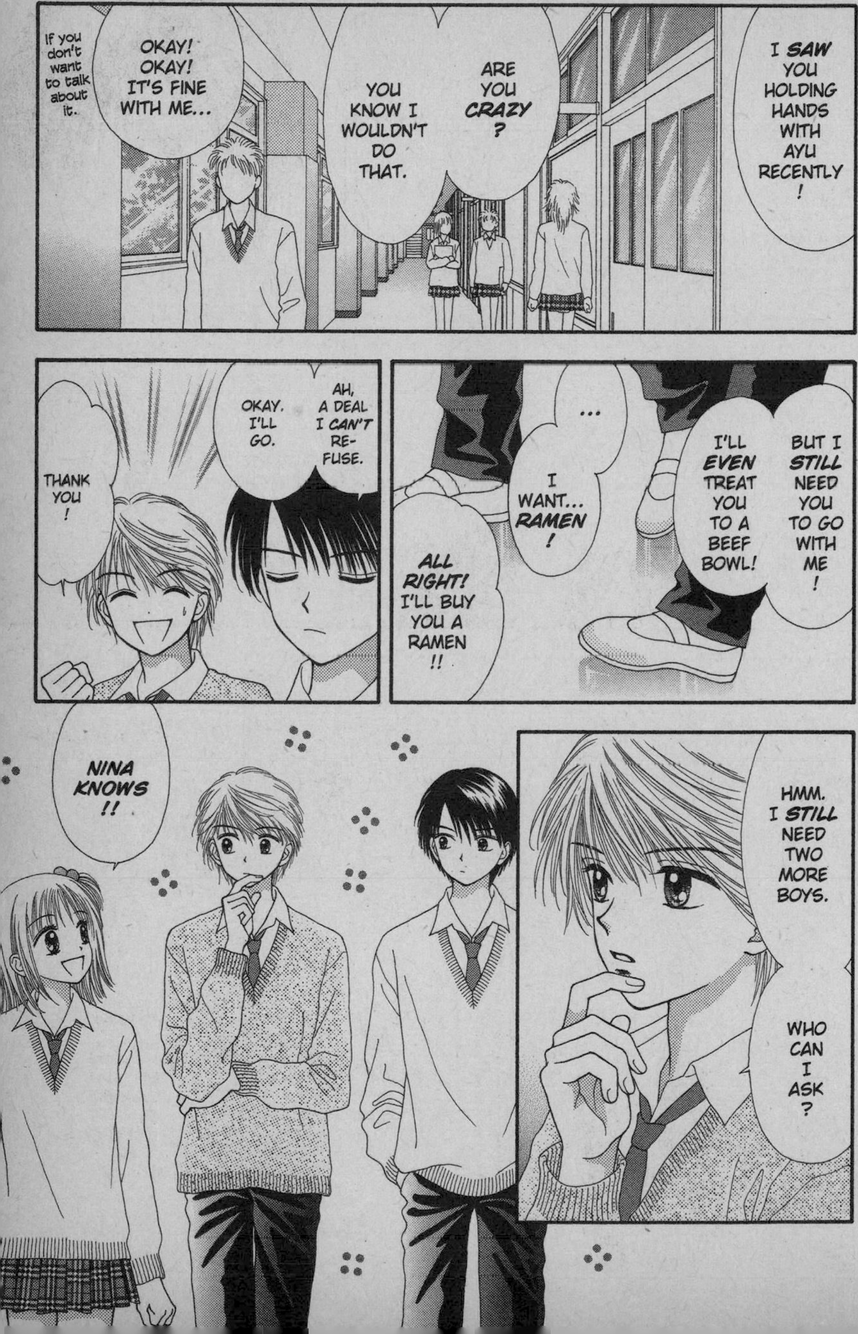
I SAW YOU HOLDING HANDS WITH AYU RECENTLY!
ARE YOU CRAZY?
YOU KNOW I WOULDN'T DO THAT.
OKAY! OKAY! IT'S FINE WITH ME...
If you don't want to talk about it.
BUT I STILL NEED YOU TO GO WITH ME!
I'LL EVEN TREAT YOU TO A BEEF BOWL!
...
I WANT... RAMEN!
ALL RIGHT! I'LL BUY YOU A RAMEN!!
AH, A DEAL I CAN'T REFUSE.
OKAY. I'LL GO.
THANK YOU!
HMM. I STILL NEED TWO MORE BOYS.
WHO CAN I ASK?
NINA KNOWS!!

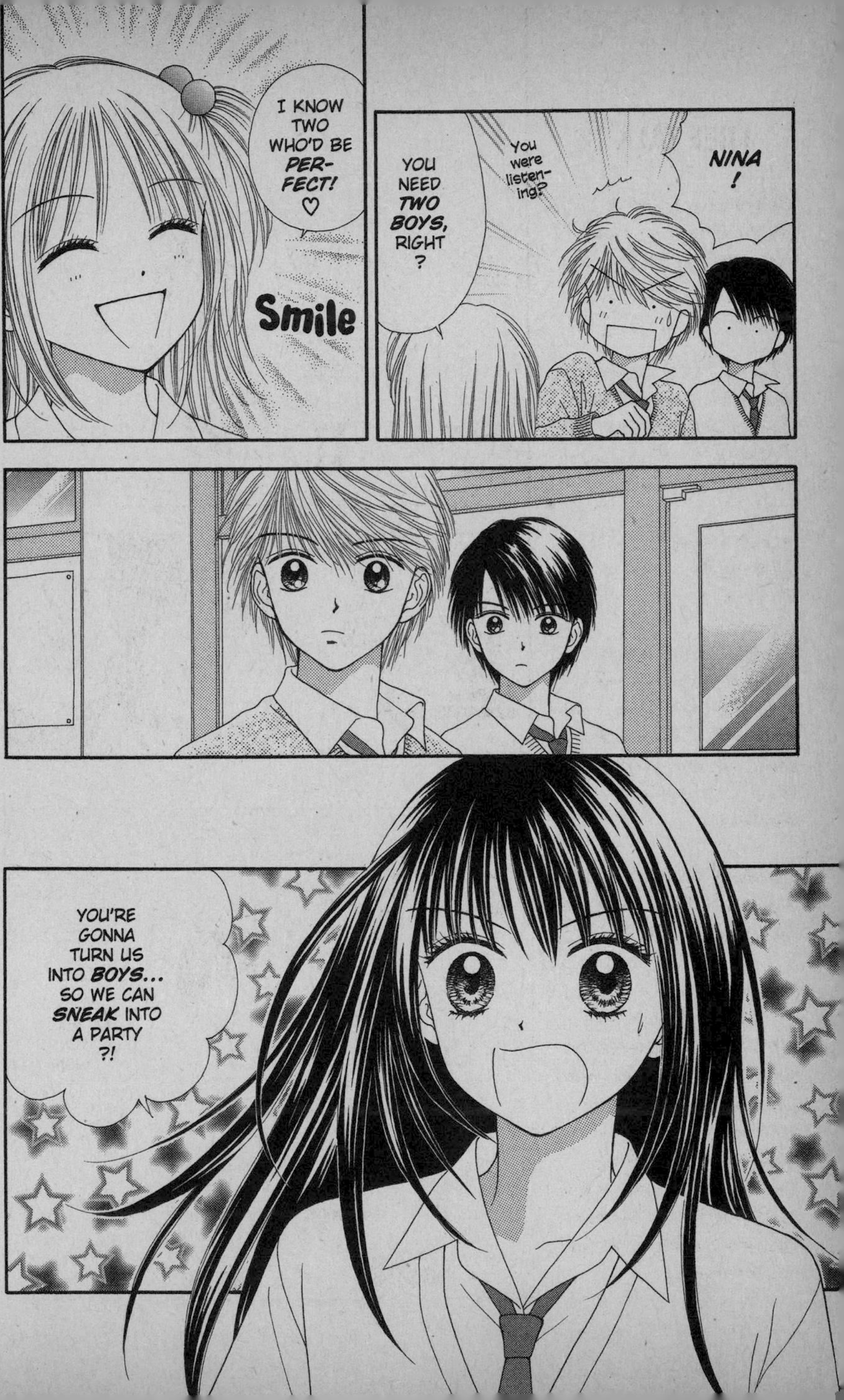
NINA!
You were listening?
YOU NEED TWO BOYS, RIGHT?
I KNOW TWO WHO'D BE PERFECT! ♡
Smile
YOU'RE GONNA TURN US INTO BOYS... SO WE CAN SNEAK INTO A PARTY?!

FREE TALK 11

Being a soccer fan can be a little stressful. Everyone has a team and players that they root for. If they win. . . great! If they don't. . . it's the pits.

There are a lot of different teams. And when they play each other there are lots of emotional conflicts for fans. A bad call from a referee can really stir up some hardcore fans.

If you're a soccer fan, I guess you just accept that as being part of the sport.

In tennis, a bad call made by a judge isn't very common. And it really doesn't have that much effect on the game. (Of course, there are players who let it get to them and lose their concentration. . . and their tempers.)

Speaking of tennis, I made yet another main character part of the tennis team.

I've done this a number of times. So I wanted to choose a different sport. But tennis seemed like the perfect choice. In the first chapter, a critical element of the story is a match in which suddenly becoming a boy would be a disadvantage. And, I was sure this would be true for tennis. If I knew more about other sports, I guess I could have used something else.

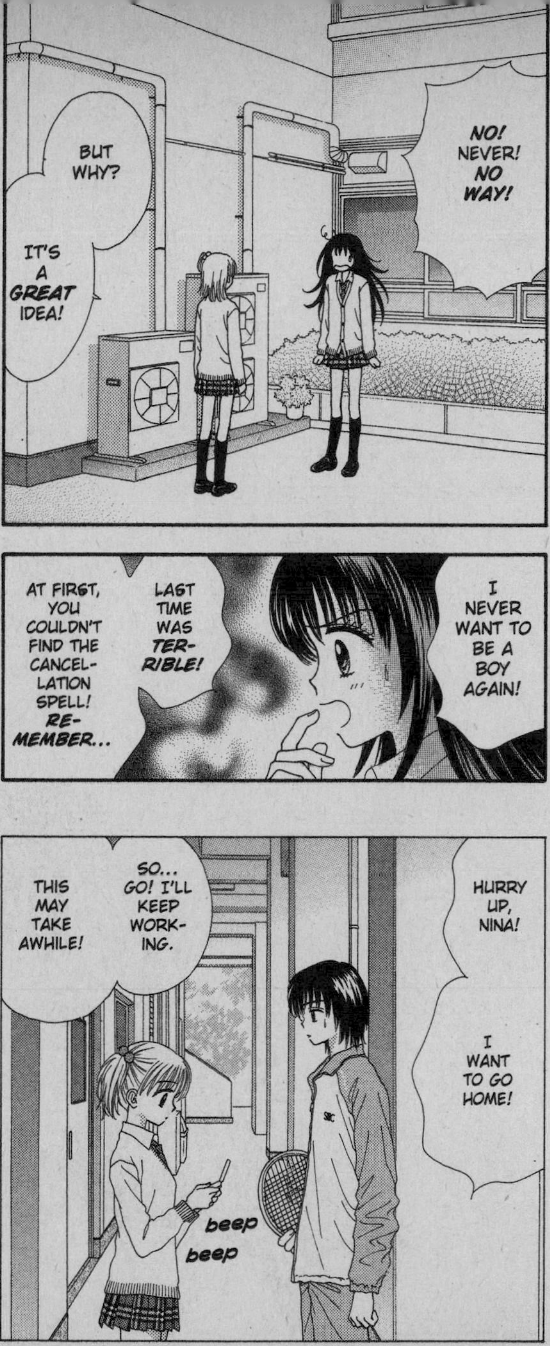
NO! NEVER! NO WAY!
BUT WHY?
IT'S A GREAT IDEA!
I NEVER WANT TO BE A BOY AGAIN!
LAST TIME WAS TERRIBLE!
AT FIRST, YOU COULDN'T FIND THE CANCELLATION SPELL! REMEMBER...
HURRY UP, NINA!
I WANT TO GO HOME!
SO... GO! I'LL KEEP WORKING.
THIS MAY TAKE AWHILE!
beep
beep

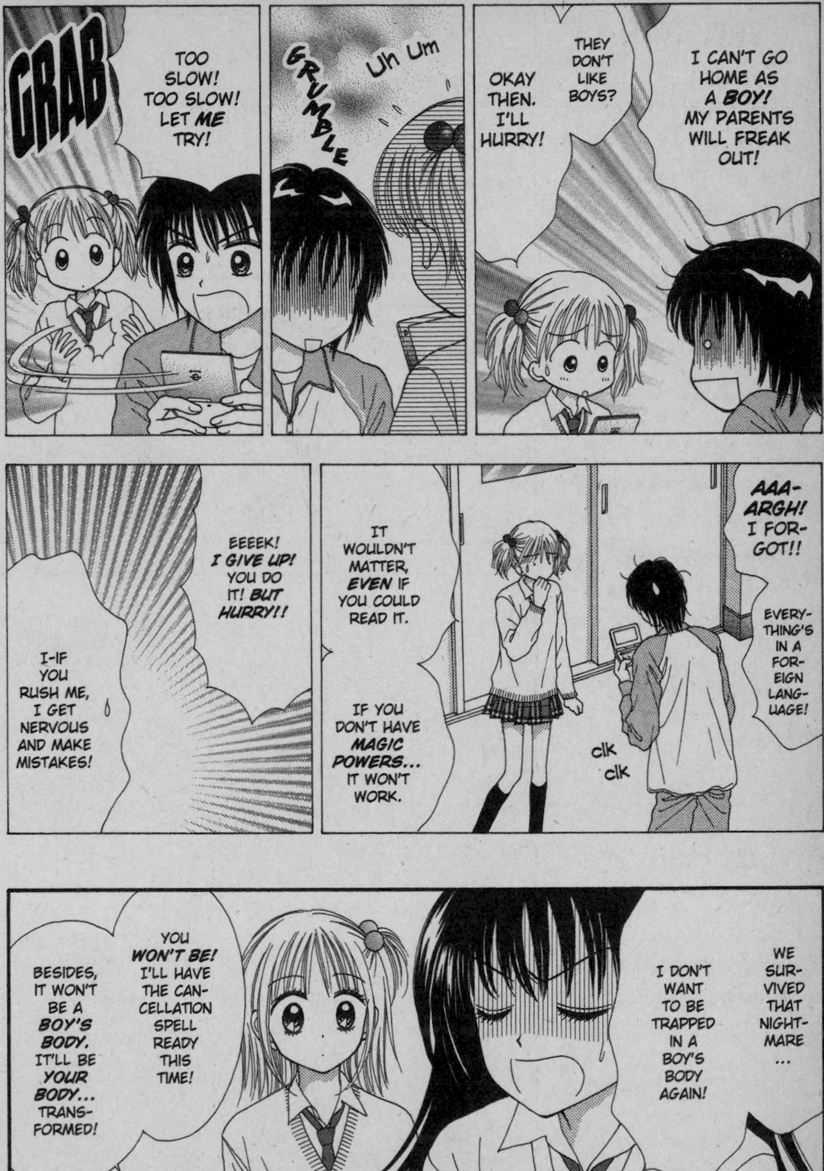
I CAN'T GO HOME AS A BOY! MY PARENTS WILL FREAK OUT!
THEY DON'T LIKE BOYS?
OKAY THEN. I'LL HURRY!
Uh Um
GRUMBLE
TOO SLOW! TOO SLOW! LET ME TRY!
GRAB
AAA-ARGH! I FOR-GOT!!
EVERY-THING'S IN A FOR-EIGN LANG-UAGE!
IT WOULDN'T MATTER, EVEN IF YOU COULD READ IT.
IF YOU DON'T HAVE MAGIC POWERS... IT WON'T WORK.
clk clk
EEEEK! I GIVE UP! YOU DO IT! BUT HURRY!!
I-IF YOU RUSH ME, I GET NERVOUS AND MAKE MISTAKES!
WE SURVIVED THAT NIGHT-MARE ...
I DON'T WANT TO BE TRAPPED IN A BOY'S BODY AGAIN!
YOU WON'T BE! I'LL HAVE THE CAN-CELLATION SPELL READY THIS TIME!
BESIDES, IT WON'T BE A BOY'S BODY. IT'LL BE YOUR BODY... TRANS-FORMED!

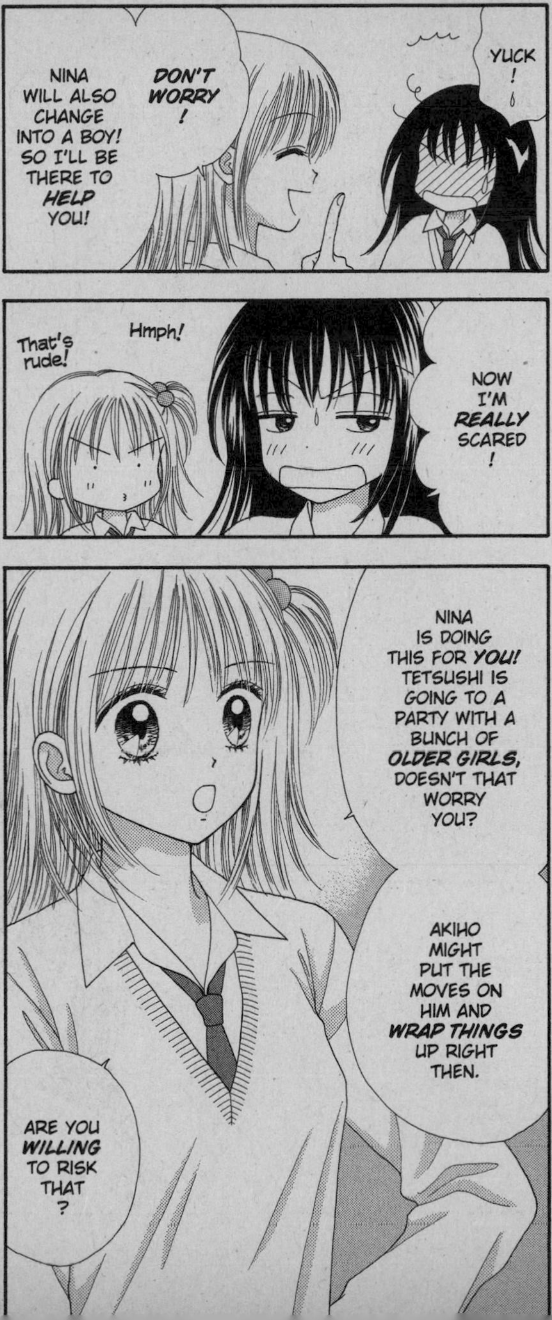
YUCK!
DON'T WORRY!
NINA WILL ALSO CHANGE INTO A BOY! SO I'LL BE THERE TO HELP YOU!
NOW I'M REALLY SCARED!
Hmph!
That's rude!
NINA IS DOING THIS FOR YOU! TETSUSHI IS GOING TO A PARTY WITH A BUNCH OF OLDER GIRLS, DOESN'T THAT WORRY YOU?
AKIHO MIGHT PUT THE MOVES ON HIM AND WRAP THINGS UP RIGHT THEN.
ARE YOU WILLING TO RISK THAT?

FREE TALK 12

What do you think of "Ultra Maniac" so far? We'd love to hear your thoughts. If you'd like to write, please send mail to the Shojo Beat team at:

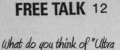

Ultra Maniac c/o Shojo Beat
Viz Media, LLC
P.O. Box 77010
San Francisco, CA 94107

When "Ultra Maniac" was first published in Japan, "Ribon" magazine gave away a snazzy teaspoon set illustrated with the images of Ayu and Nina.

They sort of looked like this:

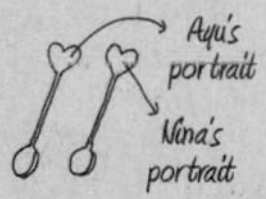
Ayu's portrait
Nina's portrait

Thanks for reading Volume 1. I hope to see you in Volume 2.

--Wataru Yoshizumi and the Shojo Beat team

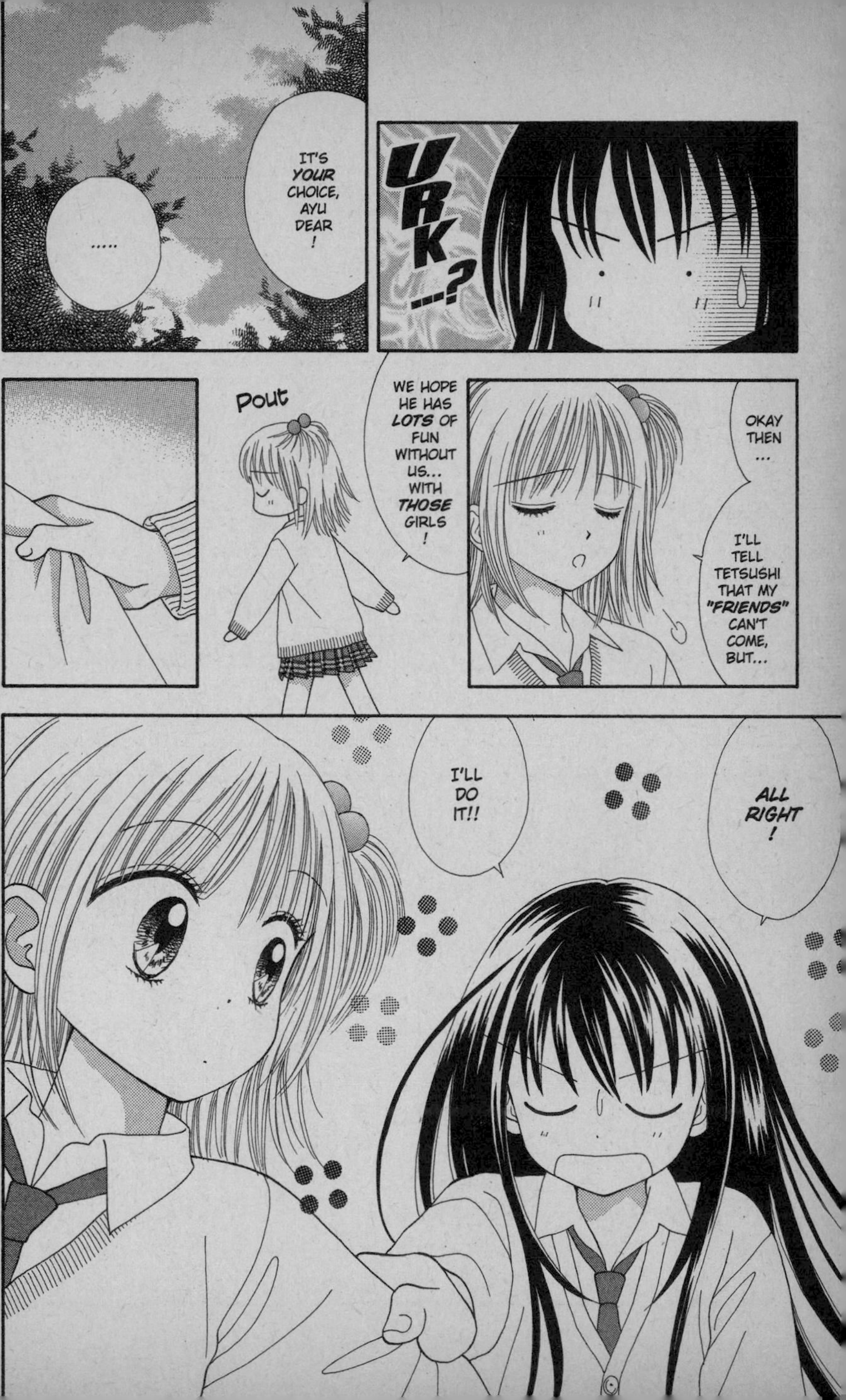
URK...?
IT'S YOUR CHOICE, AYU DEAR!
.....
OKAY THEN...
I'LL TELL TETSUSHI THAT MY "FRIENDS" CAN'T COME, BUT...
WE HOPE HE HAS LOTS OF FUN WITHOUT US... WITH THOSE GIRLS!
Pout
ALL RIGHT!
I'LL DO IT!!

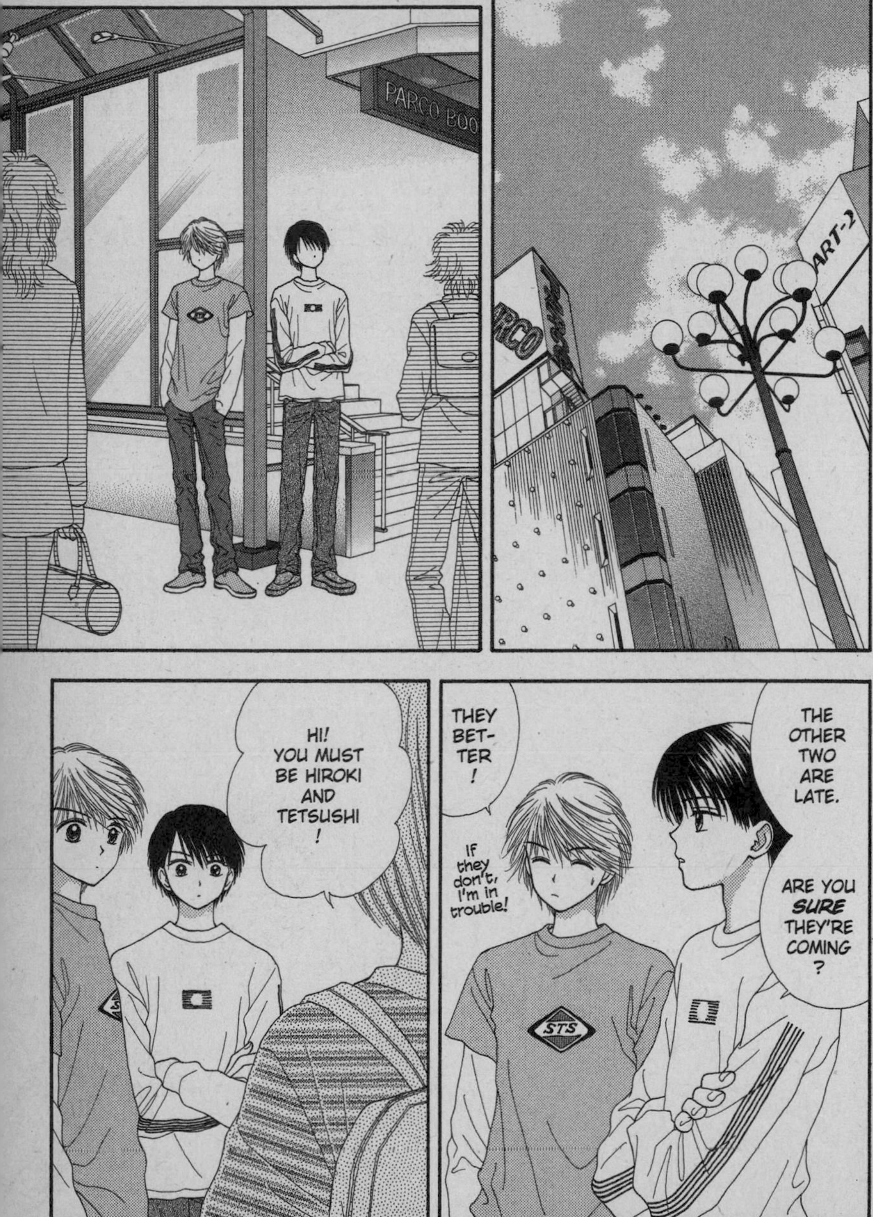
PARCO
THE OTHER TWO ARE LATE.
ARE YOU *SURE* THEY'RE COMING?
THEY BET-TER!
If they don't, I'm in trouble!
HI! YOU MUST BE HIROKI AND TETSUSHI!

NINA TOLD US ALL ABOUT YOU. WHAT A GREAT GIRL!
NINA
AYU
I'M JIN SATO.
I'M AYUOH TATEISHI.
YOU'RE THE GUY FROM THE TENNIS MATCH!
AYU'S RELATIVE... OR SOMETHING.
HER SECOND COUSIN.
YOU'RE AYU'S COUSIN? HOW COME YOU KNOW NINA?
WE, UH, MET AT AYU'S HOME.
ARE YOU TWO GOING OUT?
NO. THAT'S CRAZY! SHE WOULDN'T LEND HER BOYFRIEND OUT FOR A CO-ED PARTY!

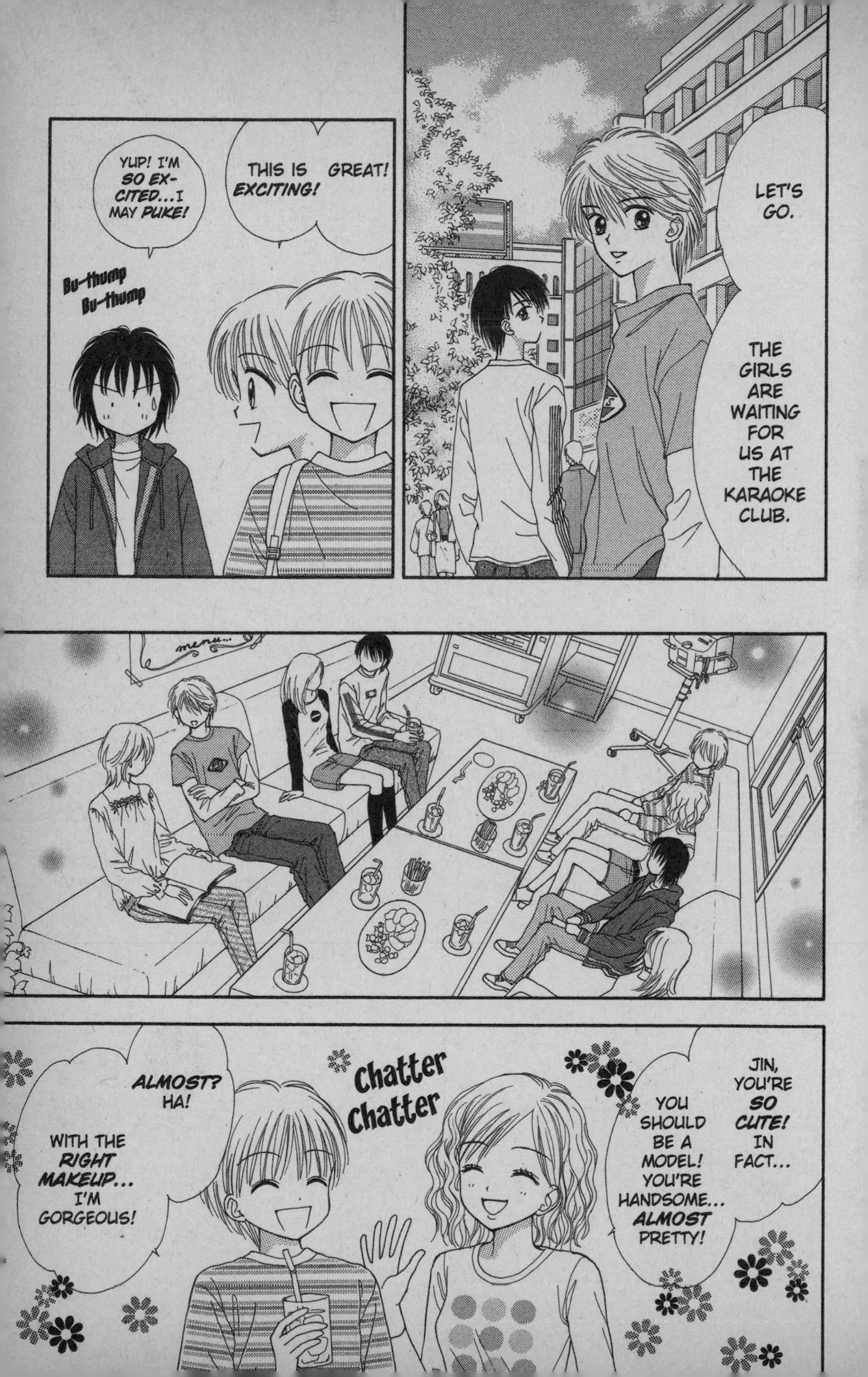
LET'S GO.
THE GIRLS ARE WAITING FOR US AT THE KARAOKE CLUB.
GREAT! THIS IS EXCITING!
YUP! I'M SO EXCITED...I MAY PUKE!
Bu-thump Bu-thump
menu...
JIN, YOU'RE SO CUTE! IN FACT...
YOU SHOULD BE A MODEL! YOU'RE HANDSOME... ALMOST PRETTY!
Chatter Chatter
ALMOST? HA!
WITH THE RIGHT MAKEUP... I'M GORGEOUS!

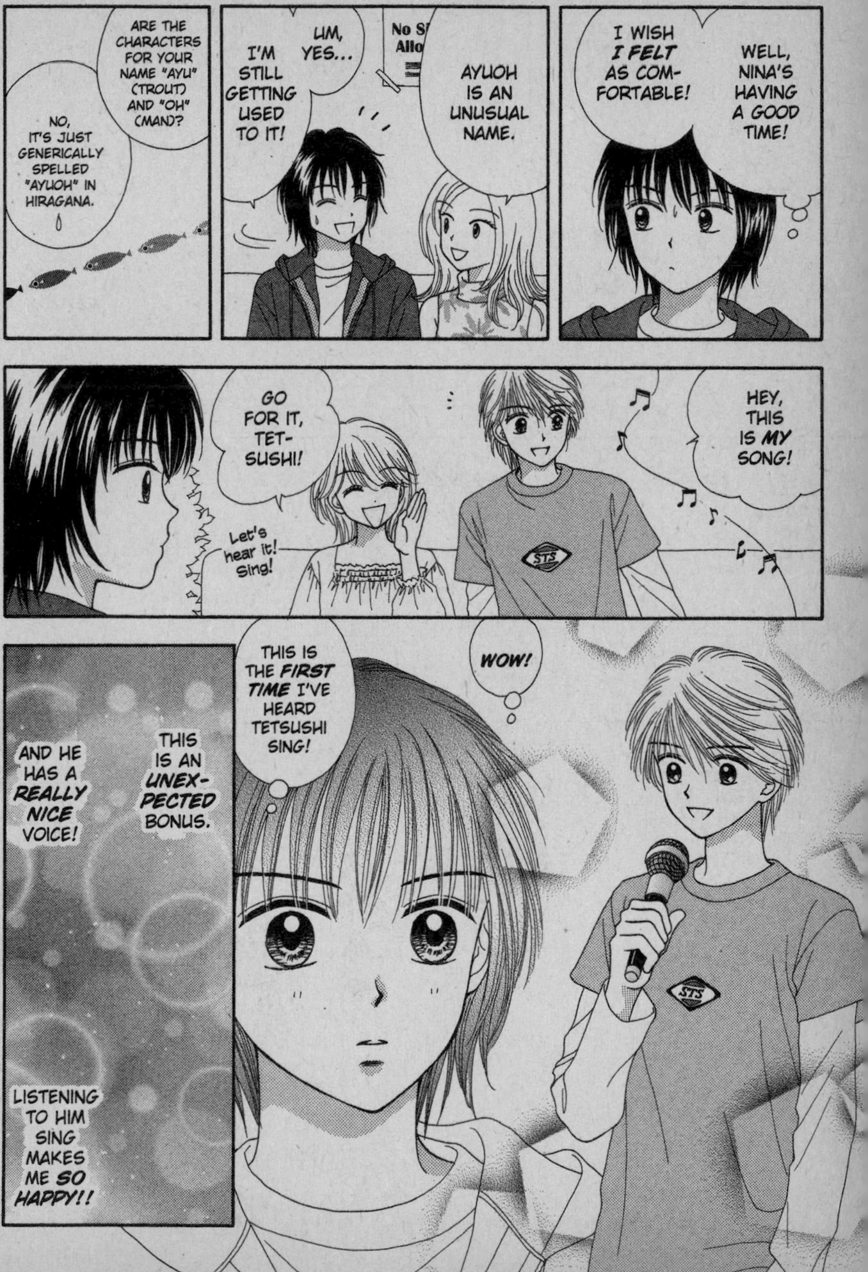
WELL, NINA'S HAVING A GOOD TIME!
I WISH I FELT AS COMFORTABLE!
AYUOH IS AN UNUSUAL NAME.
UM, YES... I'M STILL GETTING USED TO IT!
ARE THE CHARACTERS FOR YOUR NAME "AYU" (TROUT) AND "OH" (MAN)?
NO, IT'S JUST GENERICALLY SPELLED "AYUOH" IN HIRAGANA.
HEY, THIS IS MY SONG!
GO FOR IT, TETSUSHI!
Let's hear it! Sing!
WOW!
THIS IS THE FIRST TIME I'VE HEARD TETSUSHI SING!
THIS IS AN UNEXPECTED BONUS.
AND HE HAS A REALLY NICE VOICE!
LISTENING TO HIM SING MAKES ME SO HAPPY!!

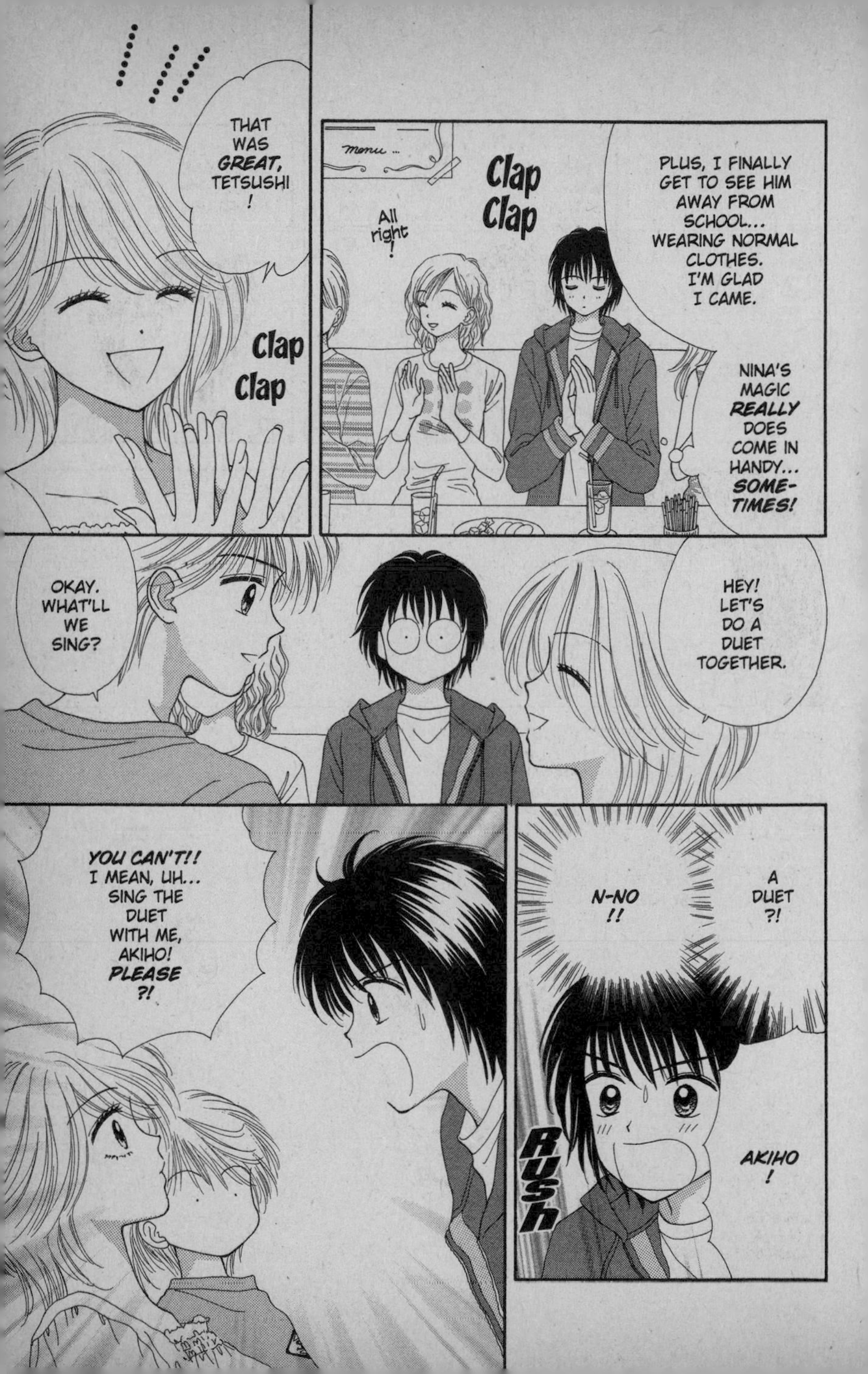
PLUS, I FINALLY GET TO SEE HIM AWAY FROM SCHOOL... WEARING NORMAL CLOTHES. I'M GLAD I CAME.
Clap Clap
All right!
NINA'S MAGIC REALLY DOES COME IN HANDY... SOME-TIMES!
THAT WAS GREAT, TETSUSHI!
Clap Clap
HEY! LET'S DO A DUET TOGETHER.
OKAY. WHAT'LL WE SING?
A DUET?!
N-NO!!
RUSH
AKIHO!
YOU CAN'T!! I MEAN, UH... SING THE DUET WITH ME, AKIHO! PLEASE?!

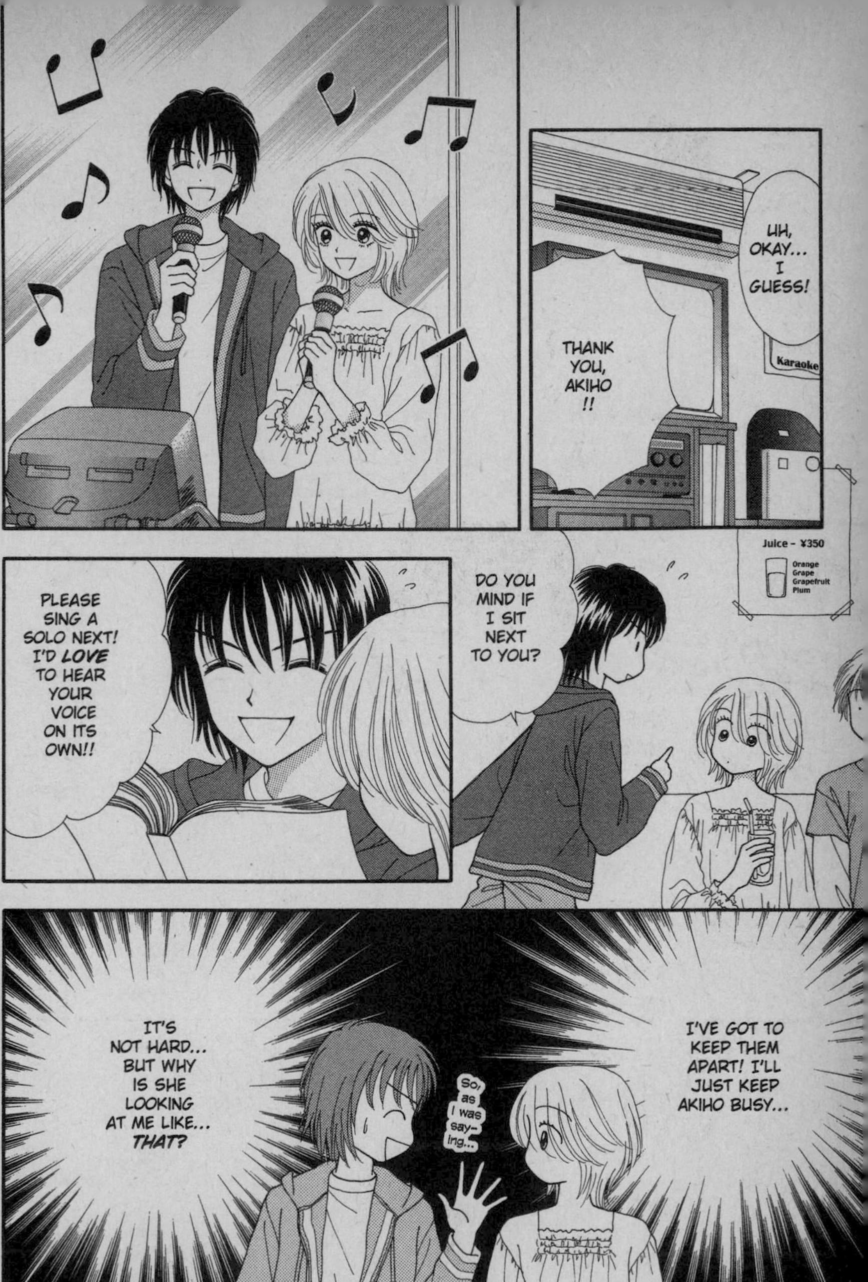
UH, OKAY... I GUESS!
Karaoke
THANK YOU, AKIHO!!
Juice - ¥350
Orange
Grape
Grapefruit
Plum
DO YOU MIND IF I SIT NEXT TO YOU?
PLEASE SING A SOLO NEXT! I'D *LOVE* TO HEAR YOUR VOICE ON ITS OWN!!
I'VE GOT TO KEEP THEM APART! I'LL JUST KEEP AKIHO BUSY...
So, as I was say-ing...
IT'S NOT HARD... BUT WHY IS SHE LOOKING AT ME LIKE... *THAT?*

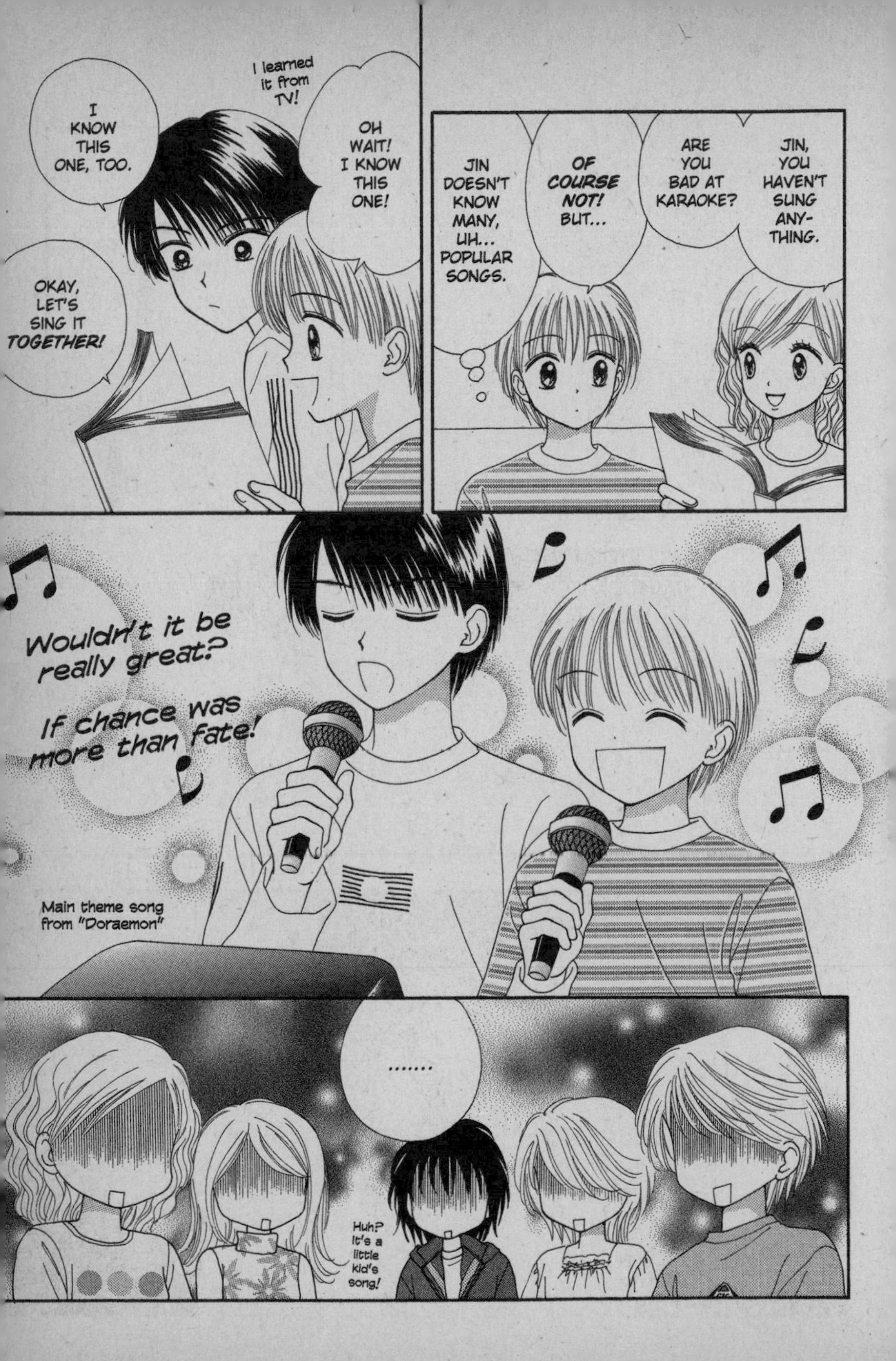
JIN, YOU HAVEN'T SUNG ANYTHING.
ARE YOU BAD AT KARAOKE?
OF COURSE NOT! BUT...
JIN DOESN'T KNOW MANY, UH... POPULAR SONGS.
I learned it from TV!
OH WAIT! I KNOW THIS ONE!
I KNOW THIS ONE, TOO.
OKAY, LET'S SING IT TOGETHER!
Wouldn't it be really great?
If chance was more than fate!
Main theme song from "Doraemon"
....
Huh? It's a little kid's song!

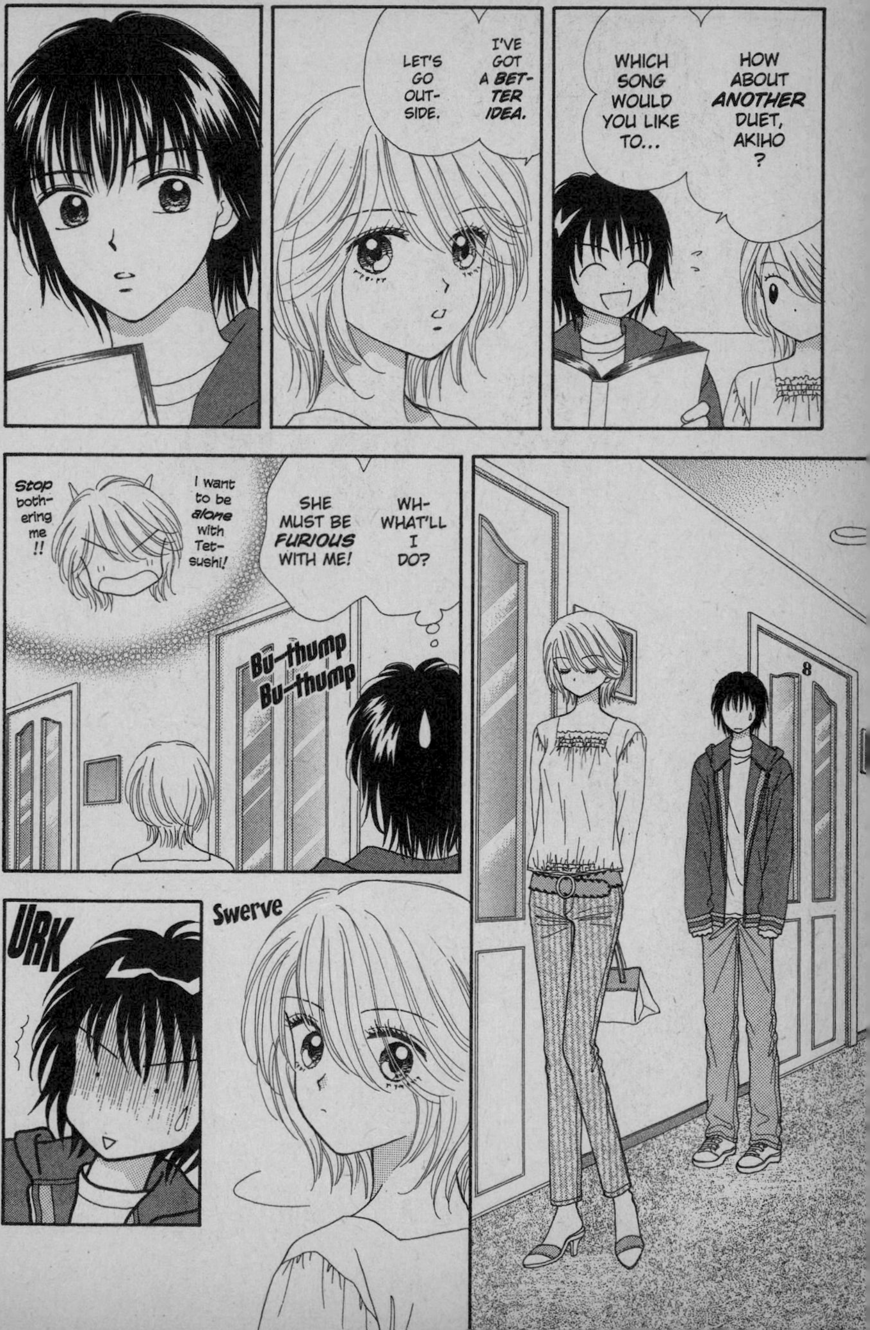
HOW ABOUT ANOTHER DUET, AKIHO?
WHICH SONG WOULD YOU LIKE TO...
I'VE GOT A BET-TER IDEA.
LET'S GO OUT-SIDE.
WH-WHAT'LL I DO?
SHE MUST BE FURIOUS WITH ME!
I want to be alone with Tet-sushi!
Stop both-ering me!!
Bu-thump Bu-thump
Swerve
URK

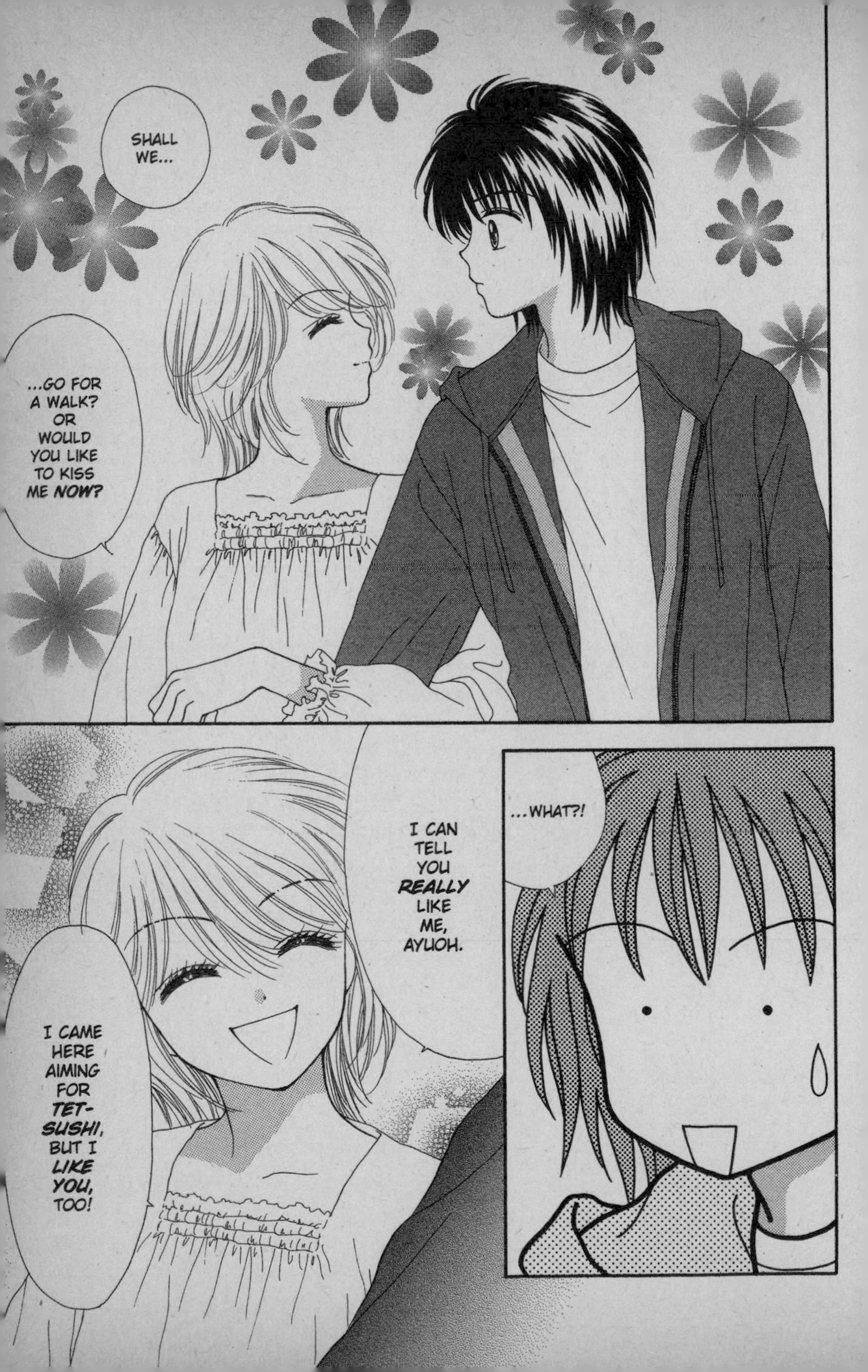
SHALL WE...
...GO FOR A WALK? OR WOULD YOU LIKE TO KISS ME *NOW?*
...WHAT?!
I CAN TELL YOU ***REALLY*** LIKE ME, AYUOH.
I CAME HERE AIMING FOR ***TET-SUSHI***, BUT I ***LIKE YOU***, TOO!

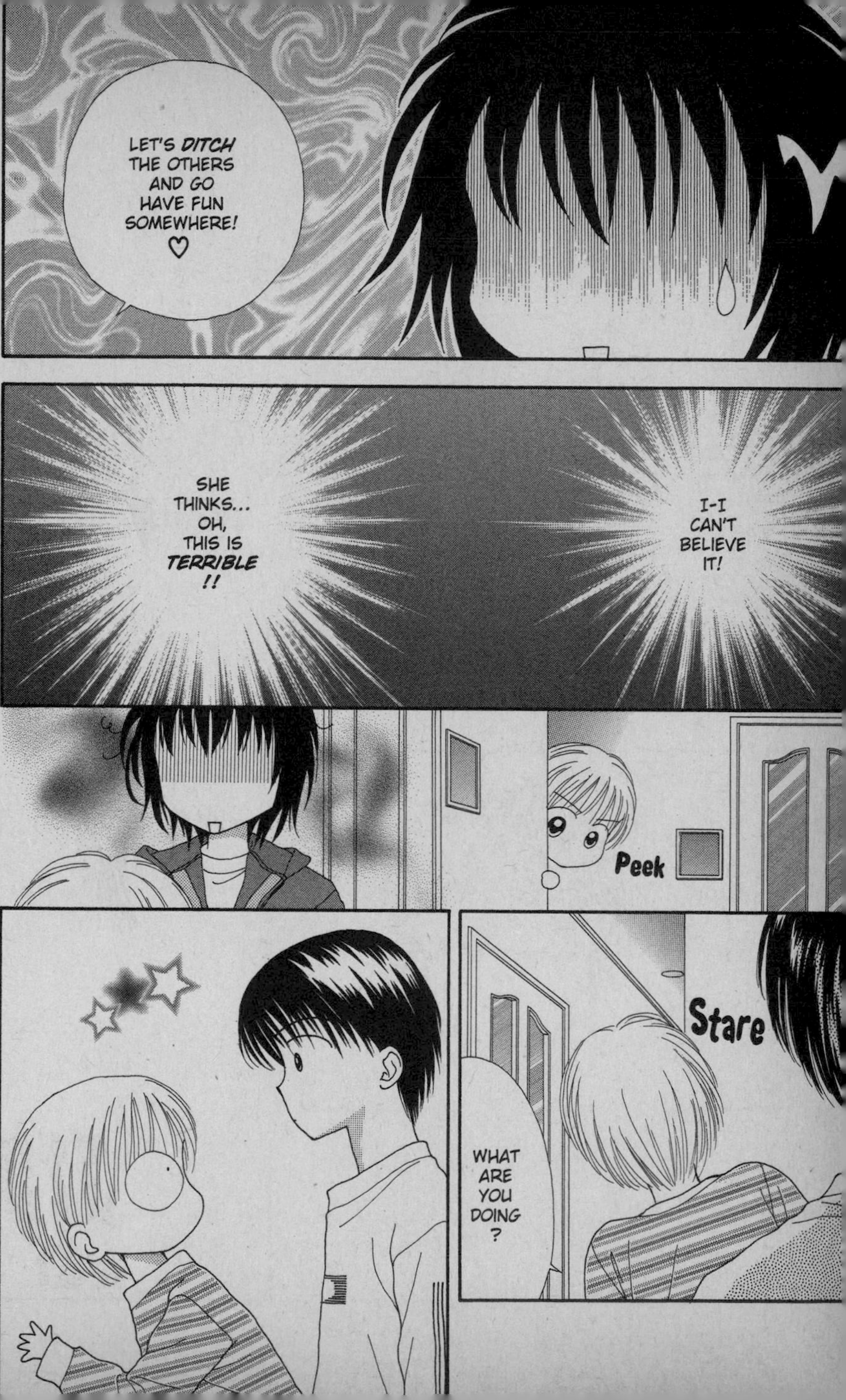
LET'S *DITCH* THE OTHERS AND GO HAVE FUN SOMEWHERE! ♡
I-I CAN'T BELIEVE IT!
SHE THINKS... OH, THIS IS *TERRIBLE* !!
Peek
Stare
WHAT ARE YOU DOING ?

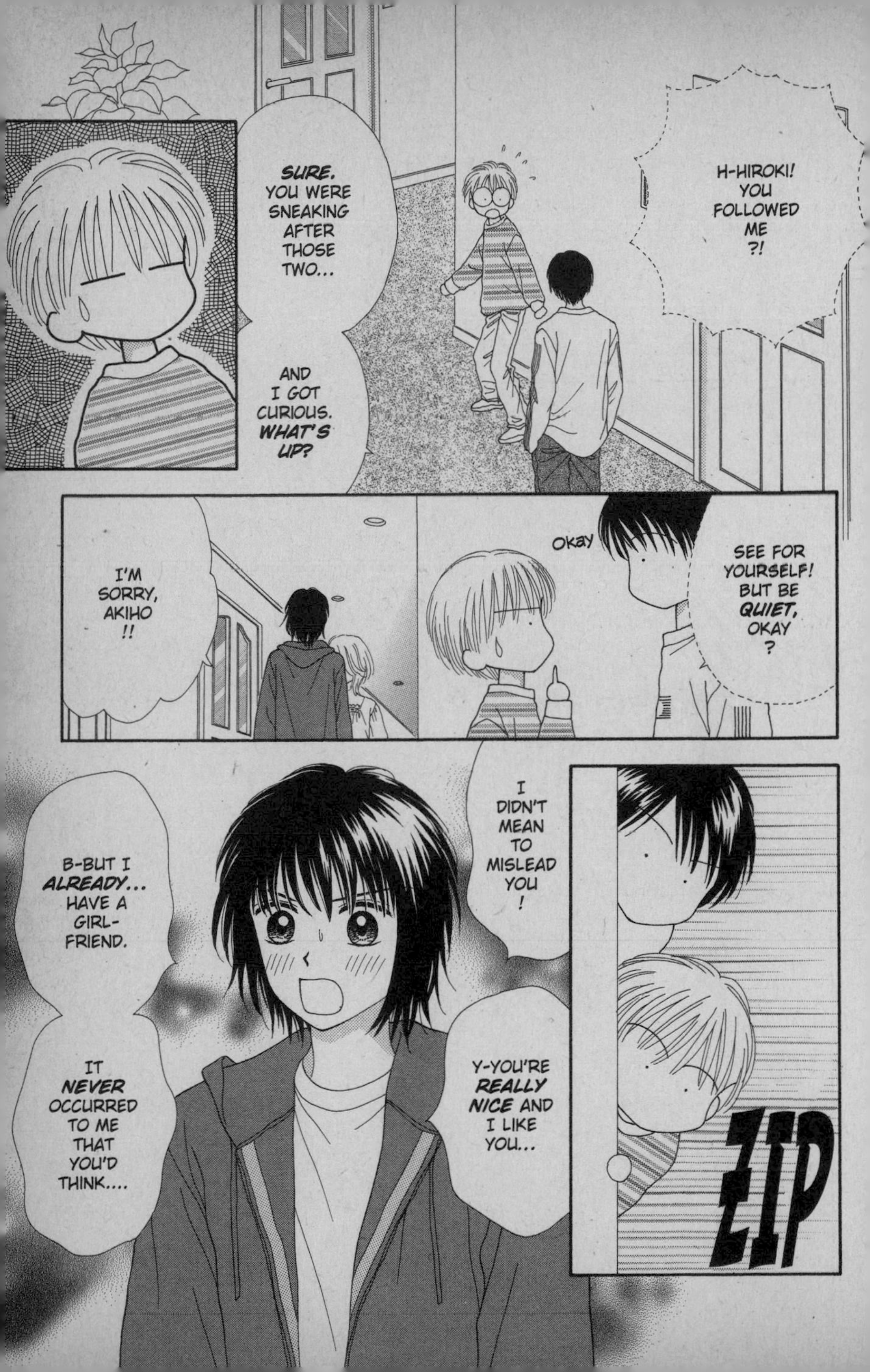
H-HIROKI! YOU FOLLOWED ME ?!
SURE. YOU WERE SNEAKING AFTER THOSE TWO...
AND I GOT CURIOUS. WHAT'S UP?
SEE FOR YOURSELF! BUT BE QUIET, OKAY ?
Okay
I'M SORRY, AKIHO !!
ZIP
I DIDN'T MEAN TO MISLEAD YOU !
Y-YOU'RE REALLY NICE AND I LIKE YOU...
B-BUT I ALREADY... HAVE A GIRL-FRIEND.
IT NEVER OCCURRED TO ME THAT YOU'D THINK....

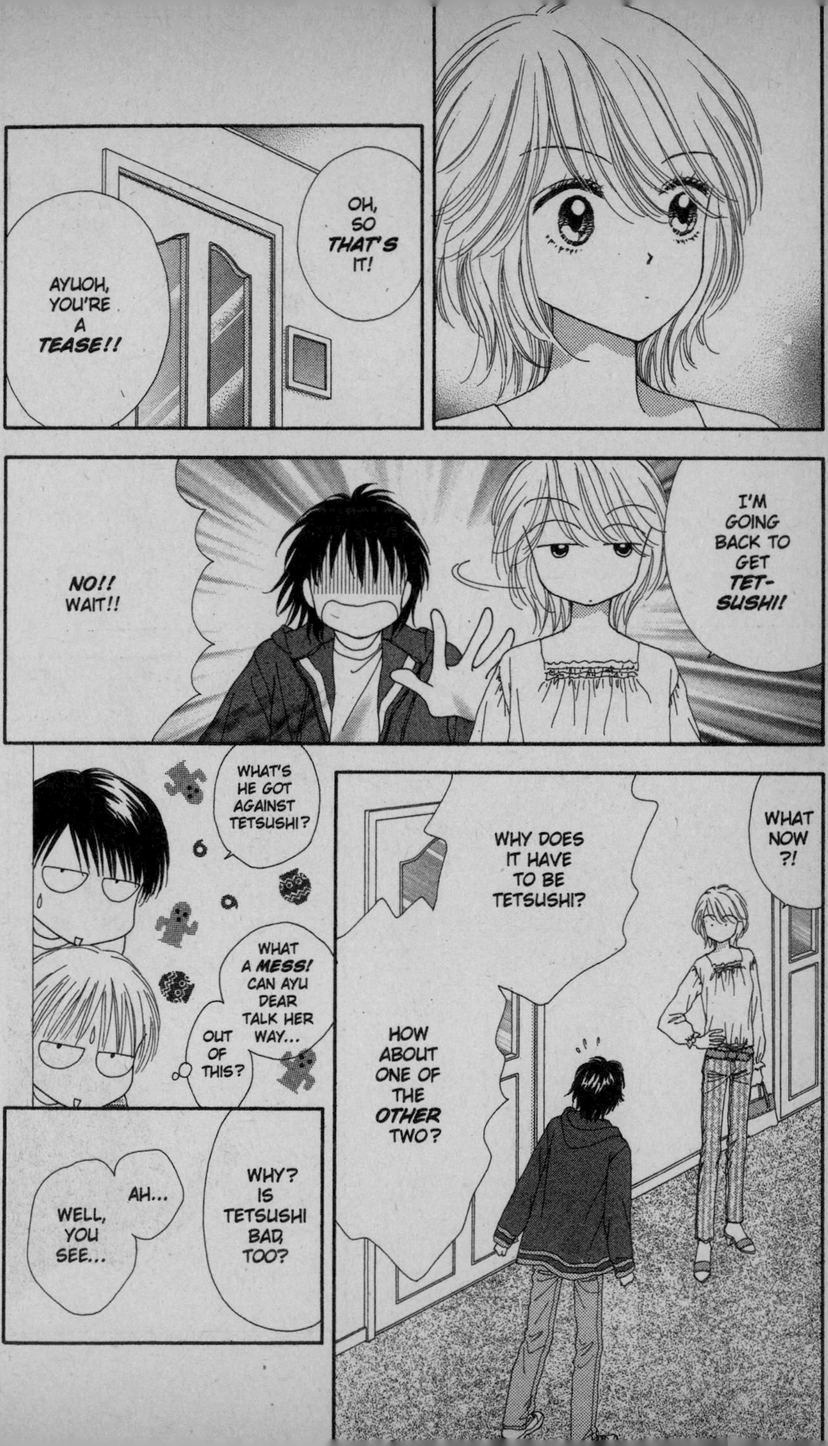
OH, SO THAT'S IT!
AYUOH, YOU'RE A TEASE!!
I'M GOING BACK TO GET TET-SUSHI!
NO!! WAIT!!
WHAT NOW?!
WHY DOES IT HAVE TO BE TETSUSHI?
HOW ABOUT ONE OF THE OTHER TWO?
WHAT'S HE GOT AGAINST TETSUSHI?
WHAT A MESS! CAN AYU DEAR TALK HER WAY...
OUT OF THIS?
WHY? IS TETSUSHI BAD, TOO?
AH... WELL, YOU SEE...

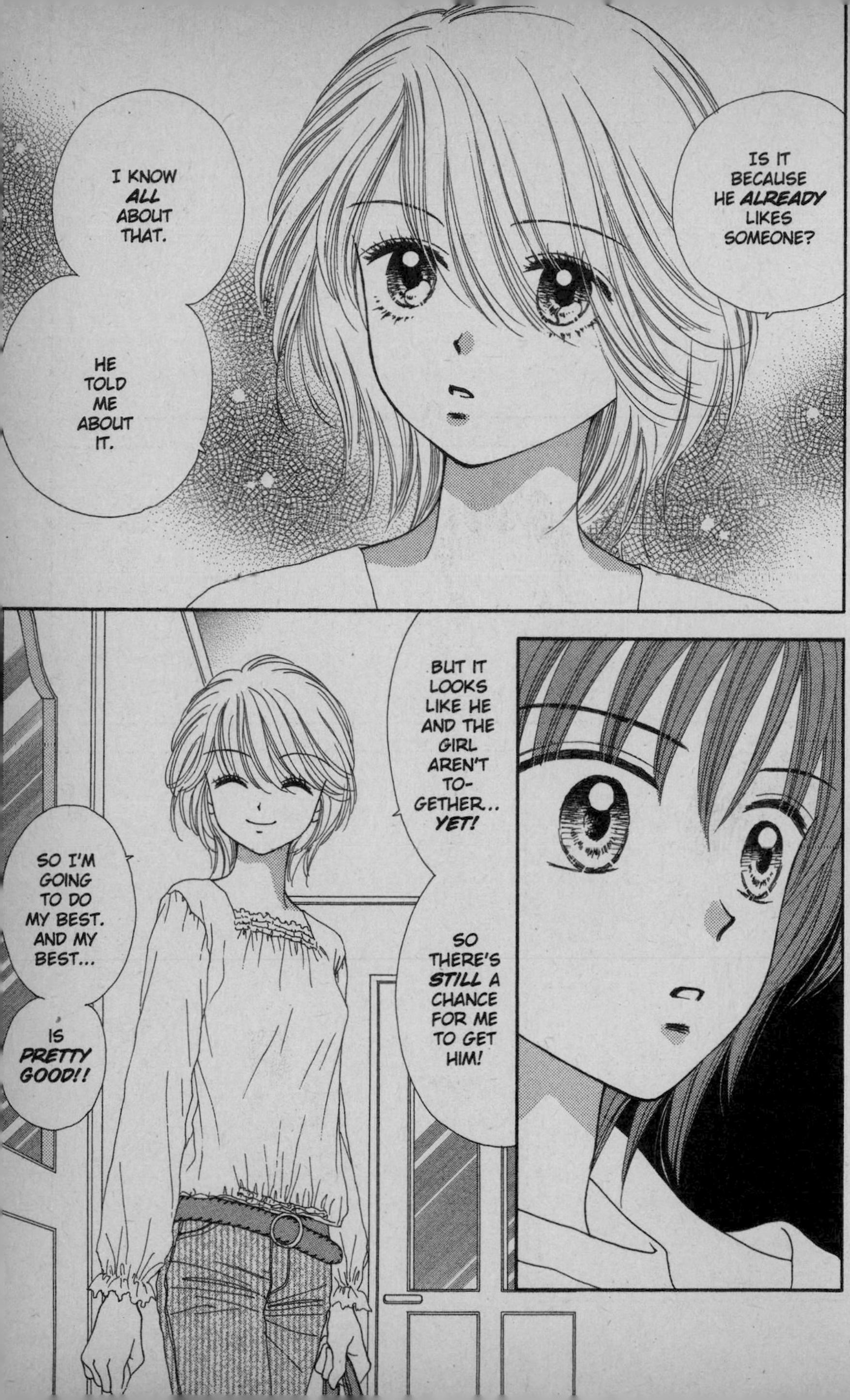
IS IT BECAUSE HE **ALREADY** LIKES SOMEONE?
I KNOW **ALL** ABOUT THAT.
HE TOLD ME ABOUT IT.
BUT IT LOOKS LIKE HE AND THE GIRL AREN'T TO-GETHER.. ***YET!***
SO THERE'S ***STILL*** A CHANCE FOR ME TO GET HIM!
SO I'M GOING TO DO MY BEST. AND MY BEST...
IS ***PRETTY GOOD!!***

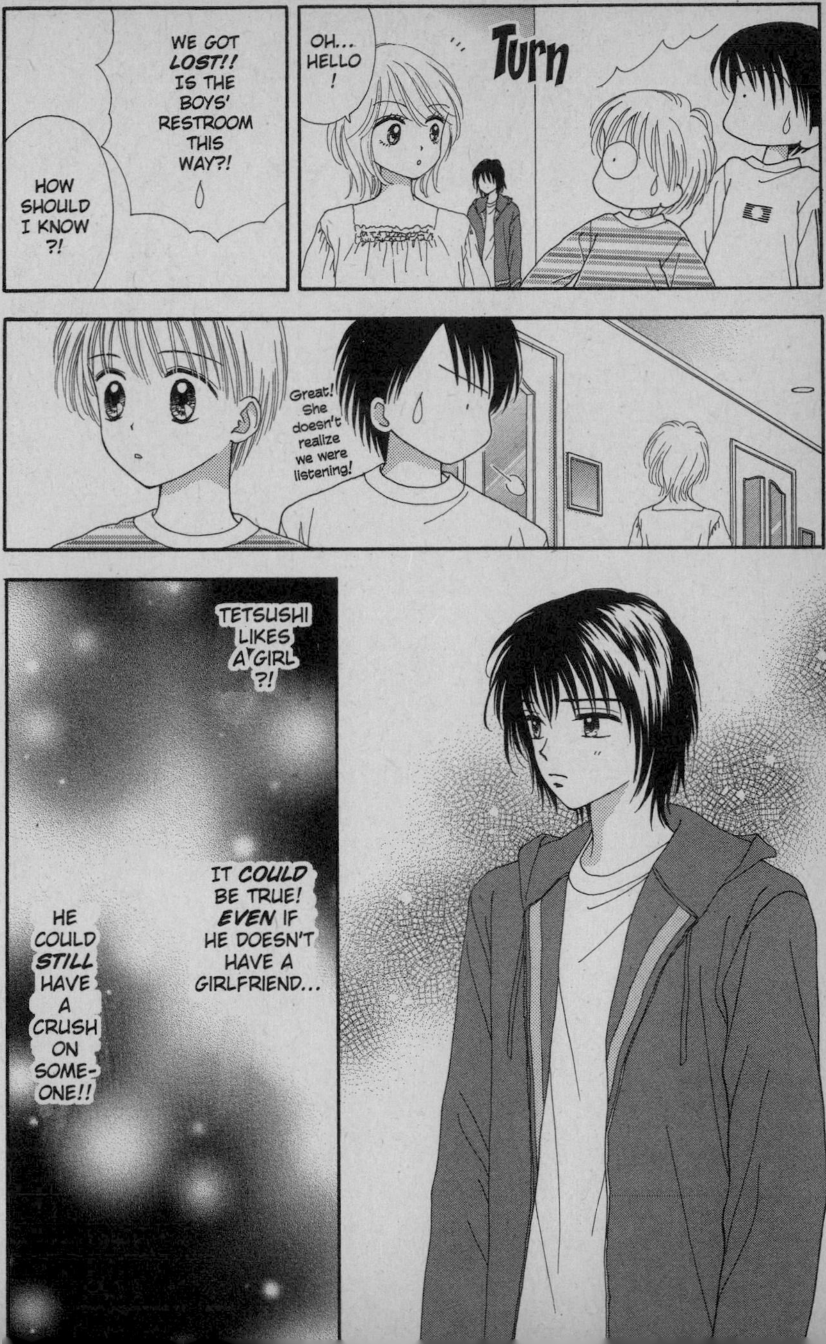
Turn
OH... HELLO!
WE GOT LOST!! IS THE BOYS' RESTROOM THIS WAY?!
HOW SHOULD I KNOW?!
Great! She doesn't realize we were listening!
TETSUSHI LIKES A GIRL?!
IT COULD BE TRUE! EVEN IF HE DOESN'T HAVE A GIRLFRIEND...
HE COULD STILL HAVE A CRUSH ON SOME-ONE!!

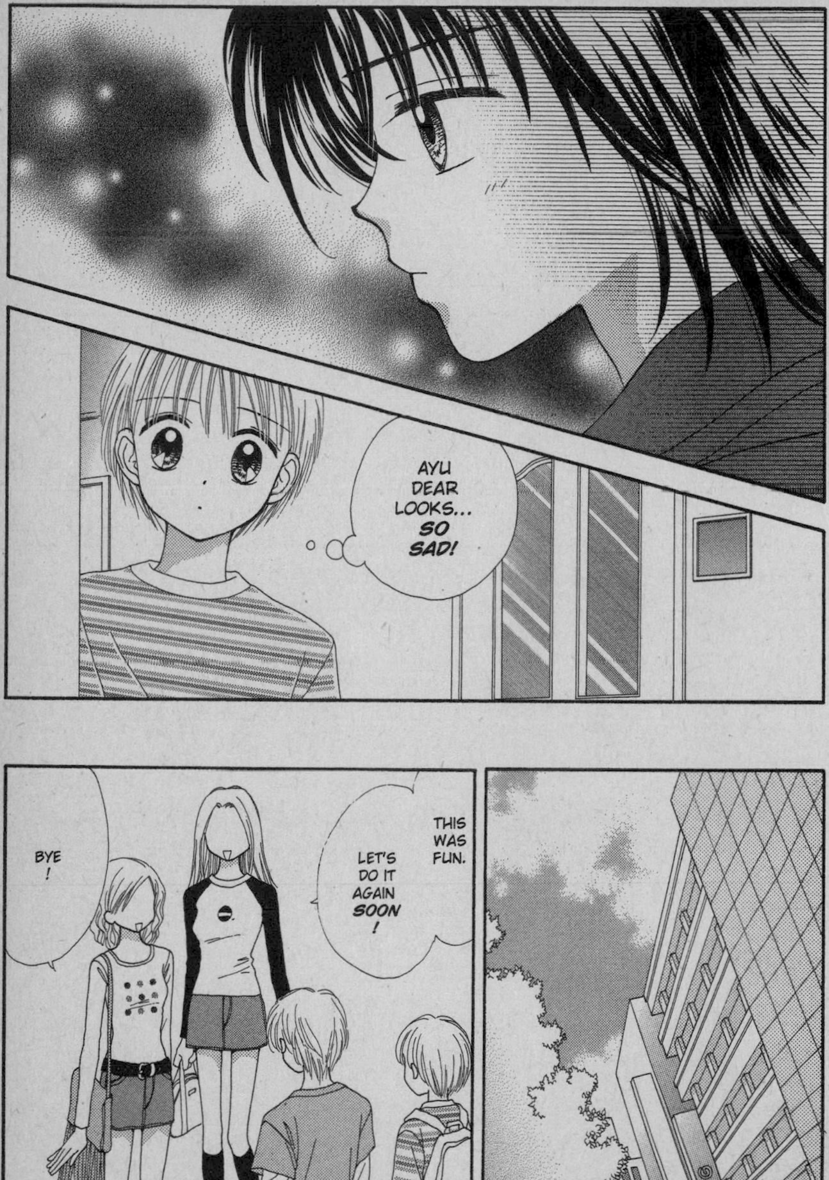
AYU DEAR LOOKS... SO SAD!
THIS WAS FUN.
LET'S DO IT AGAIN SOON!
BYE!

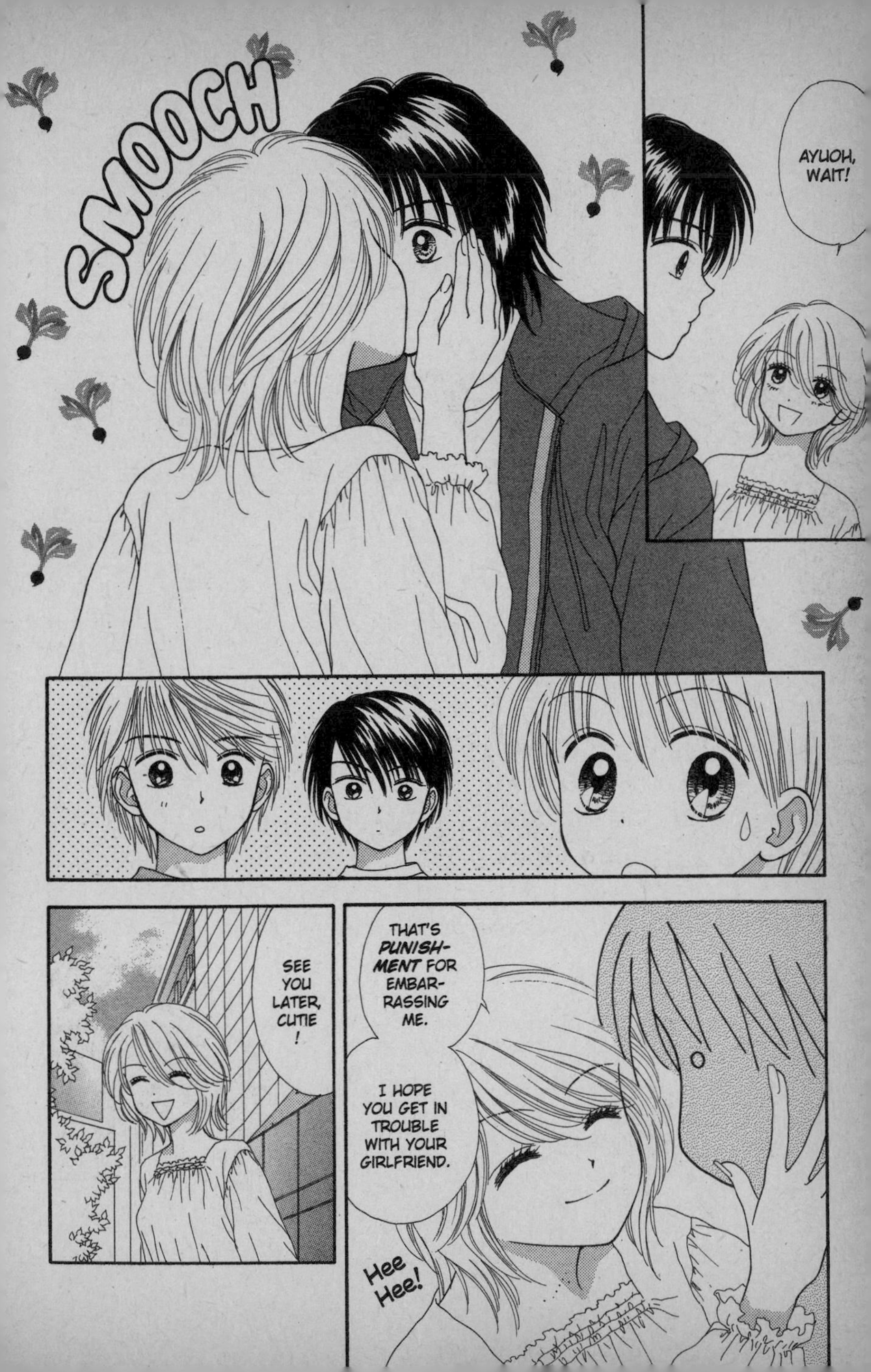
AYUOH, WAIT!
SMOOCH
THAT'S *PUNISHMENT* FOR EMBARRASSING ME.
I HOPE YOU GET IN TROUBLE WITH YOUR GIRLFRIEND.
Hee Hee!
SEE YOU LATER, CUTIE!

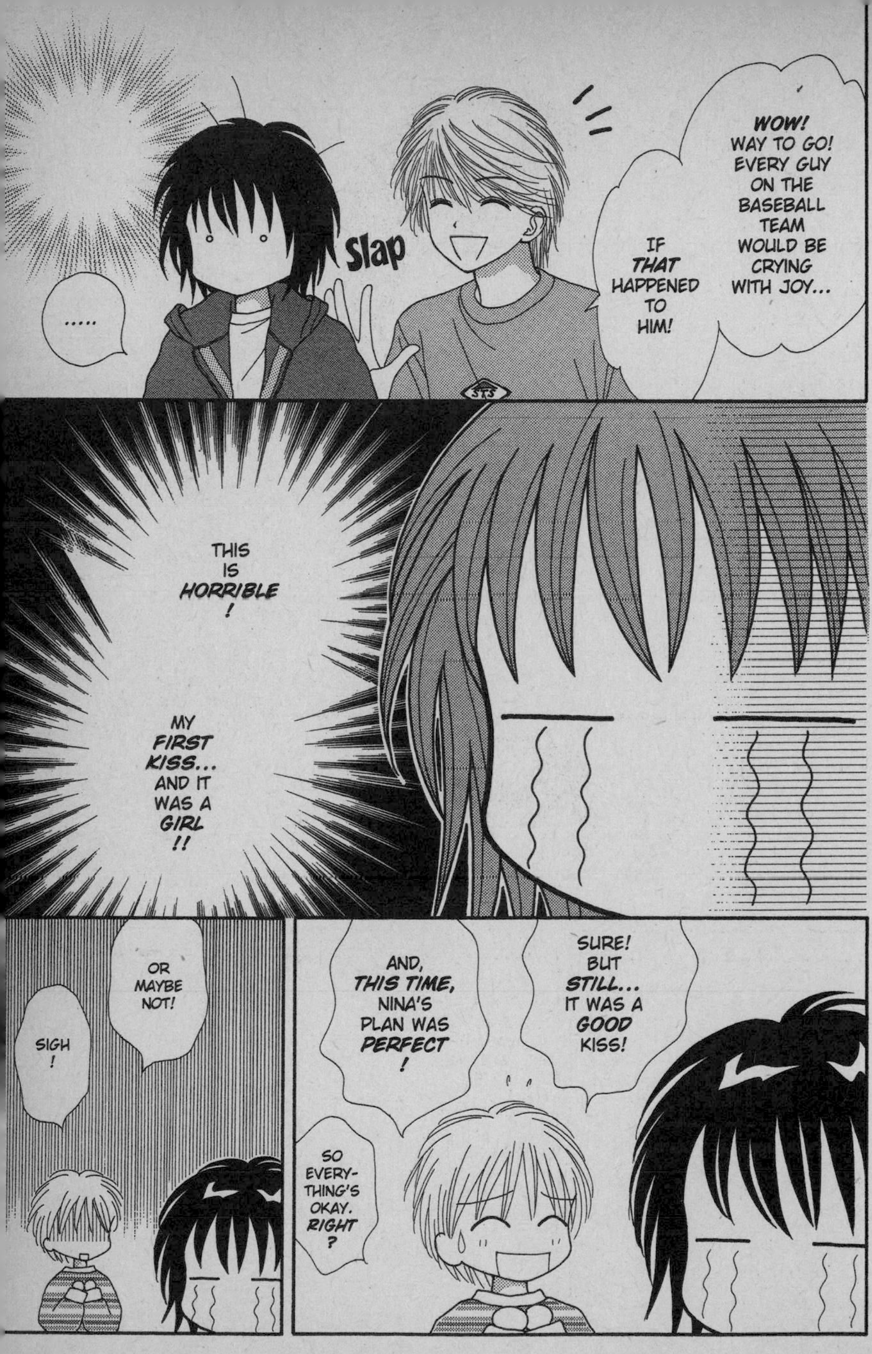

WOW! WAY TO GO! EVERY GUY ON THE BASEBALL TEAM WOULD BE CRYING WITH JOY...
IF THAT HAPPENED TO HIM!
Slap
.....
THIS IS HORRIBLE!
MY FIRST KISS... AND IT WAS A GIRL!!
SURE! BUT STILL... IT WAS A GOOD KISS!
AND, THIS TIME, NINA'S PLAN WAS PERFECT!
SO EVERYTHING'S OKAY. RIGHT?
OR MAYBE NOT!
SIGH!

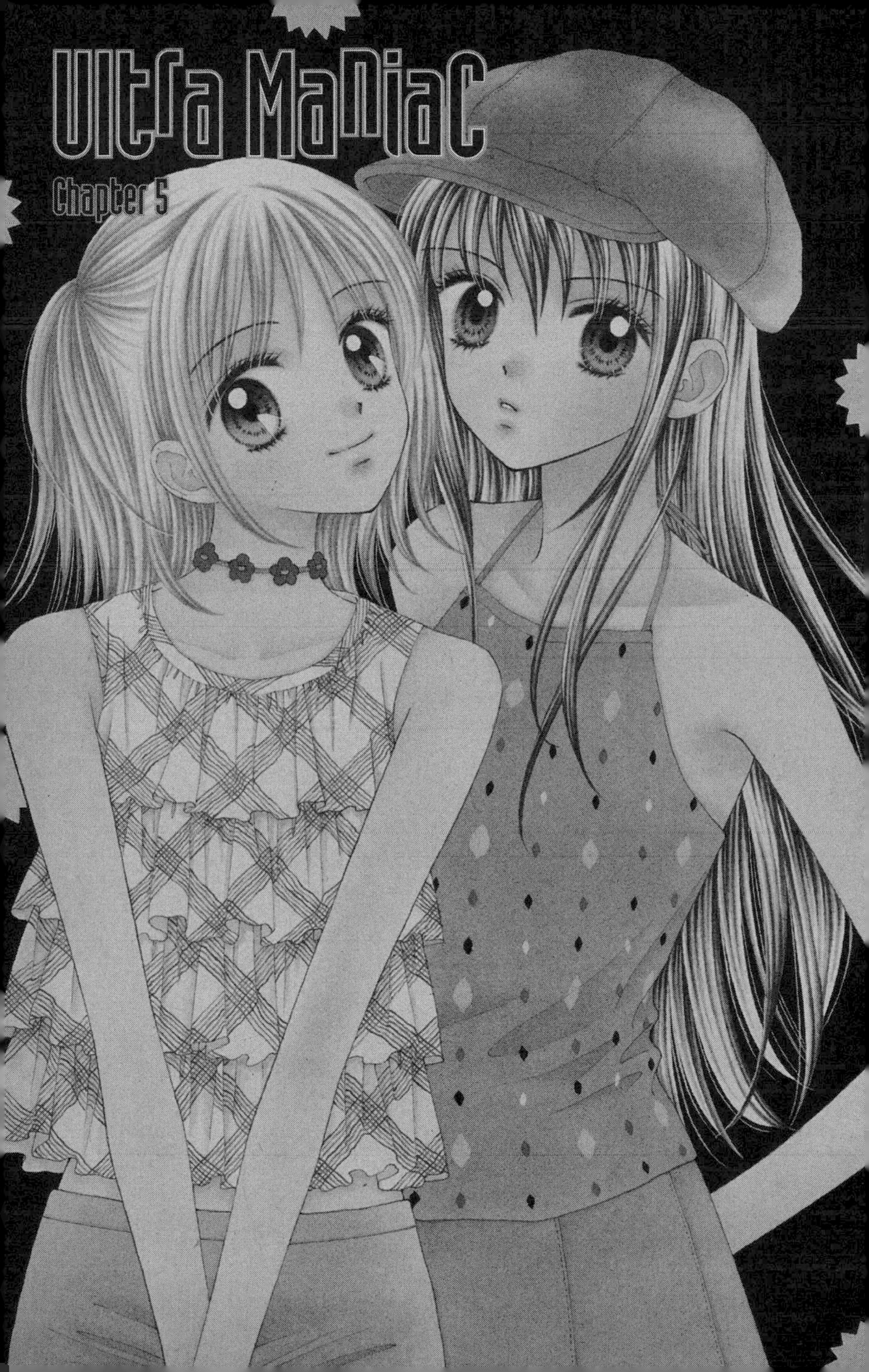
Ultra Maniac
Chapter 5

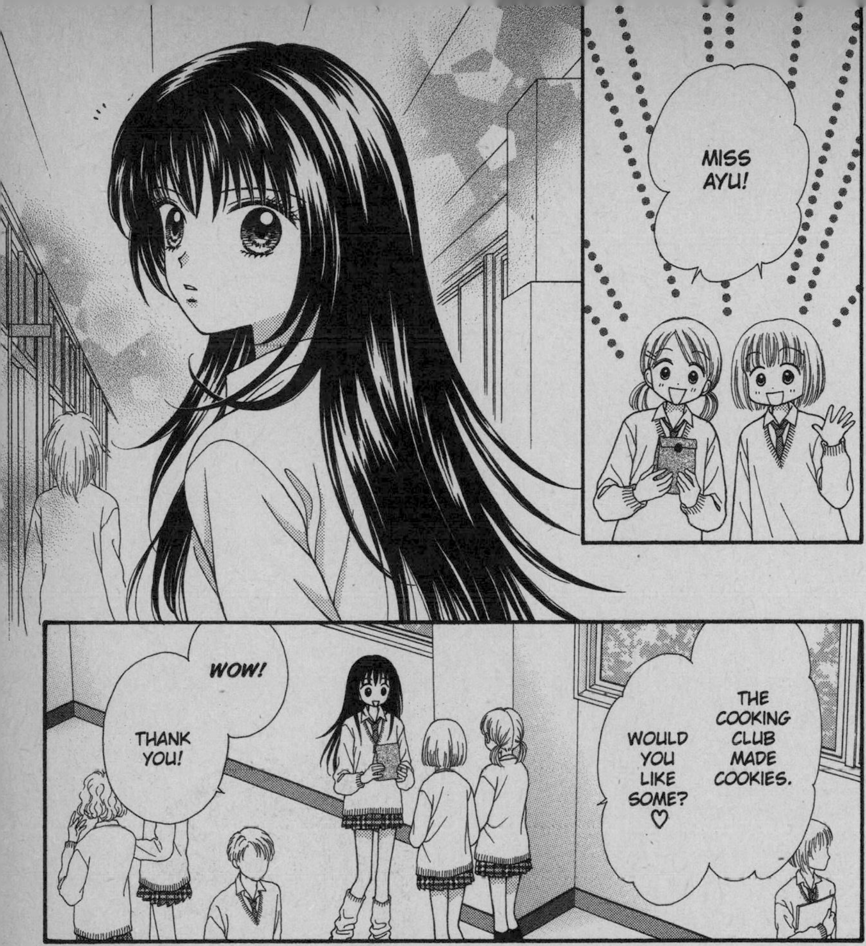
MISS AYU!
THE COOKING CLUB MADE COOKIES.
WOULD YOU LIKE SOME? ♡
WOW!
THANK YOU!

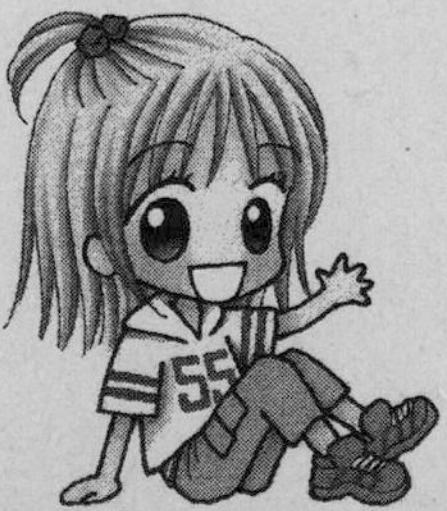

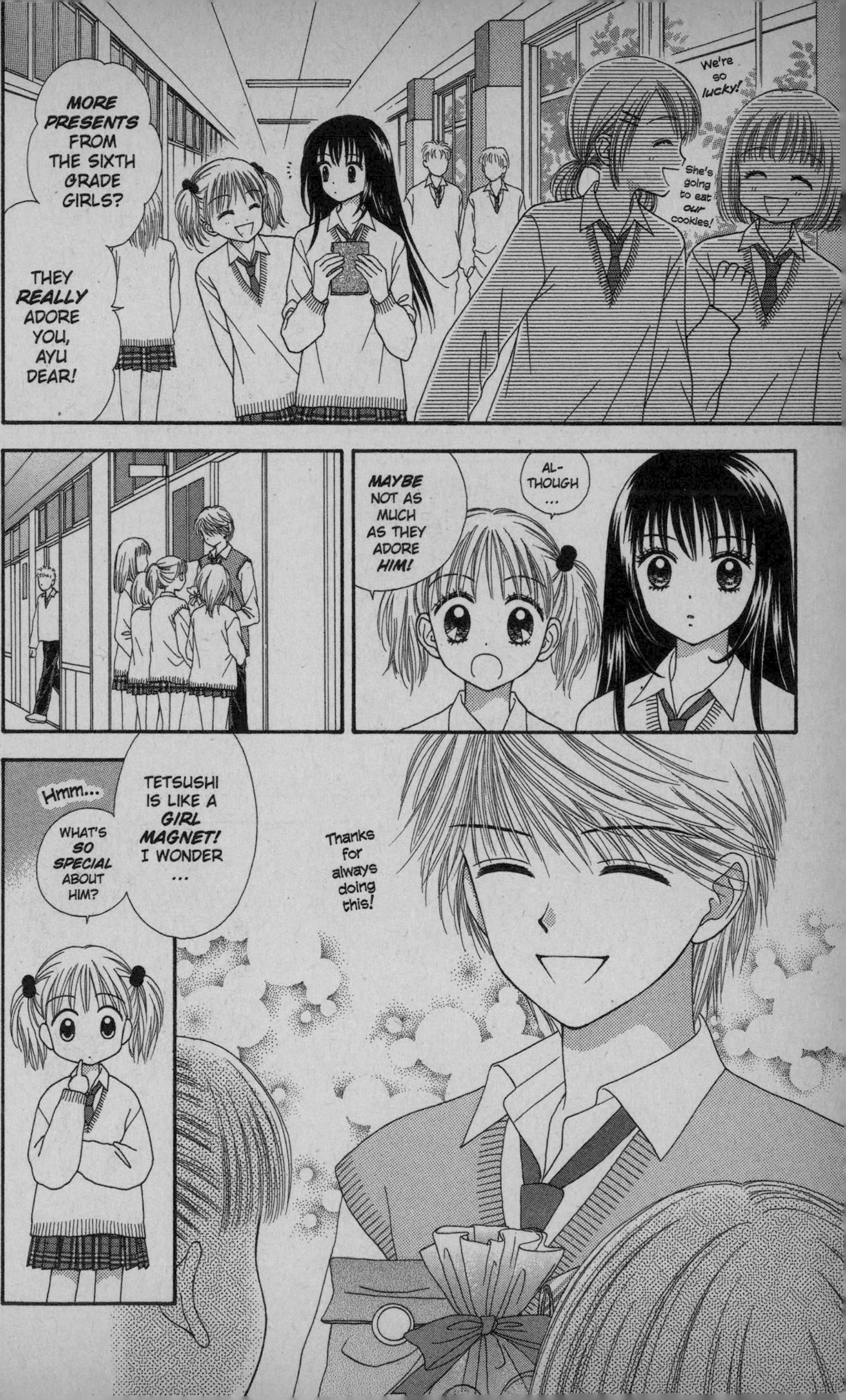
We're so *lucky!*
She's going to eat *our* cookies!
MORE PRESENTS FROM THE SIXTH GRADE GIRLS?
THEY ***REALLY*** ADORE YOU, AYU DEAR!
AL-THOUGH ...
MAYBE NOT AS MUCH AS THEY ADORE ***HIM!***
Thanks for always doing this!
TETSUSHI IS LIKE A ***GIRL MAGNET!*** I WONDER ...
Hmm...
WHAT'S ***SO SPECIAL*** ABOUT HIM?

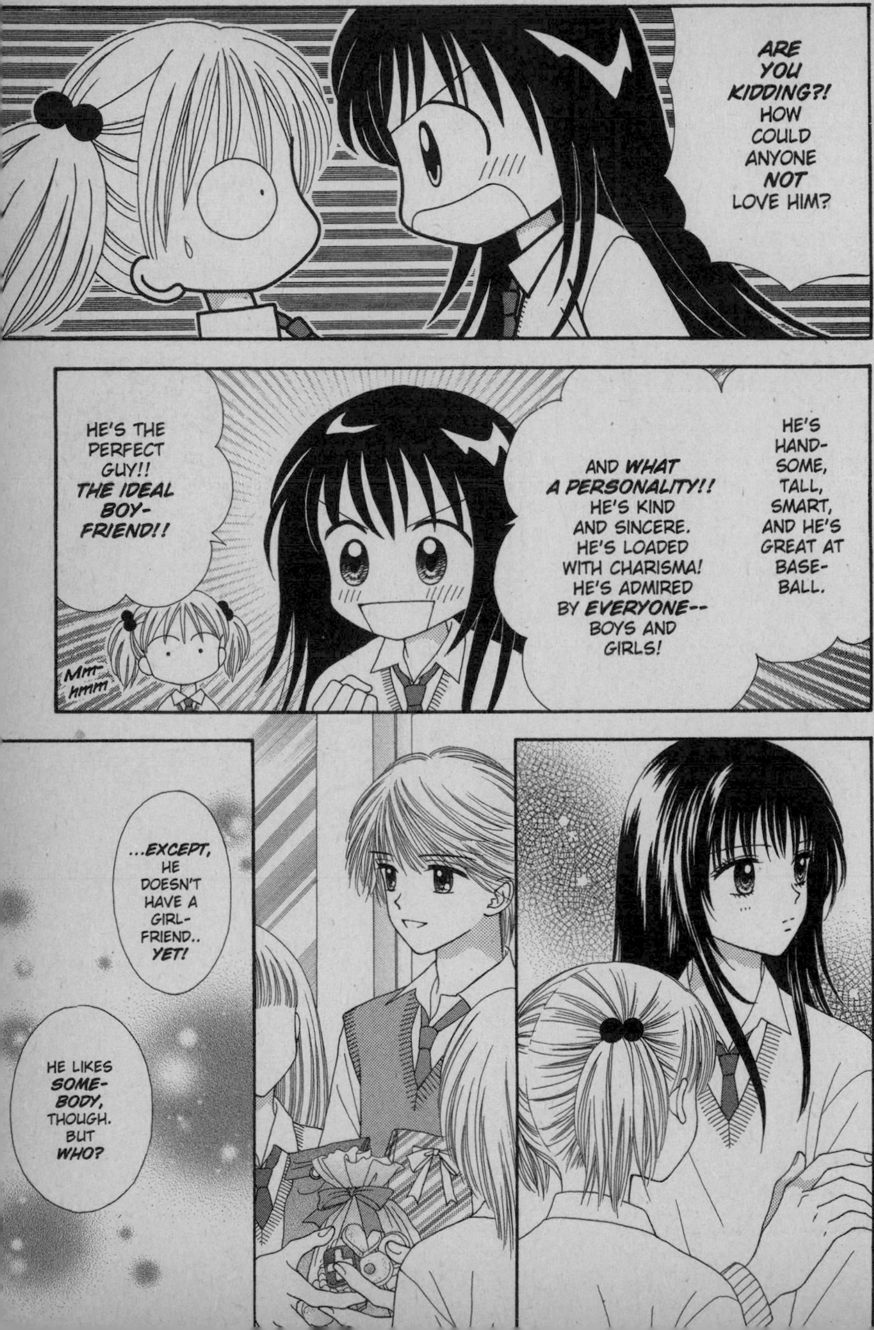
ARE YOU KIDDING?! HOW COULD ANYONE NOT LOVE HIM?
HE'S HANDSOME, TALL, SMART, AND HE'S GREAT AT BASEBALL.
AND WHAT A PERSONALITY!! HE'S KIND AND SINCERE. HE'S LOADED WITH CHARISMA! HE'S ADMIRED BY EVERYONE-- BOYS AND GIRLS!
HE'S THE PERFECT GUY!! THE IDEAL BOYFRIEND!!
Mm-hmm
...EXCEPT, HE DOESN'T HAVE A GIRLFRIEND.. YET!
HE LIKES SOMEBODY, THOUGH. BUT WHO?

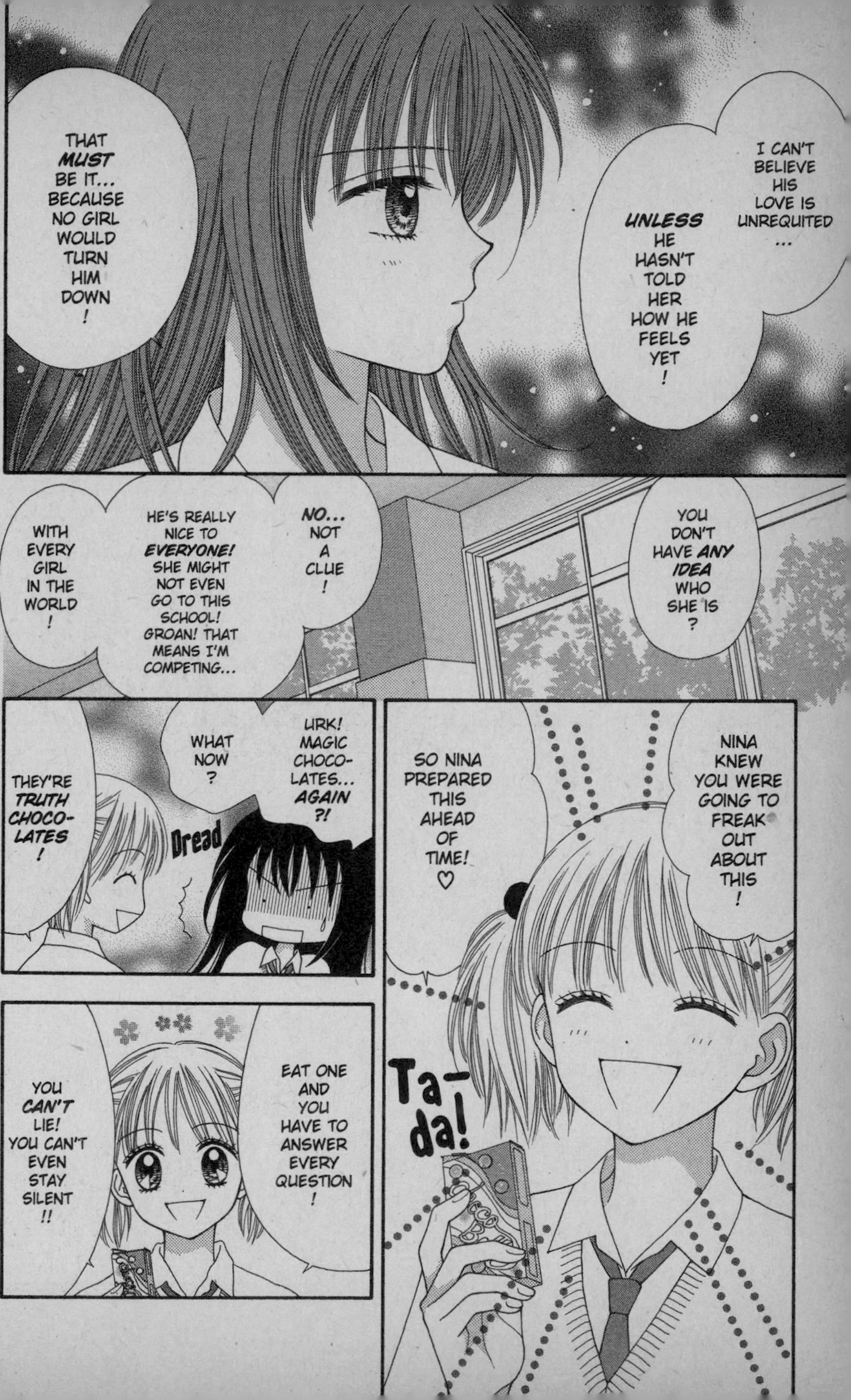
I CAN'T BELIEVE HIS LOVE IS UNREQUITED... UNLESS HE HASN'T TOLD HER HOW HE FEELS YET!
THAT MUST BE IT... BECAUSE NO GIRL WOULD TURN HIM DOWN!
YOU DON'T HAVE ANY IDEA WHO SHE IS?
NO... NOT A CLUE!
HE'S REALLY NICE TO EVERYONE! SHE MIGHT NOT EVEN GO TO THIS SCHOOL! GROAN! THAT MEANS I'M COMPETING...
WITH EVERY GIRL IN THE WORLD!
NINA KNEW YOU WERE GOING TO FREAK OUT ABOUT THIS!
SO NINA PREPARED THIS AHEAD OF TIME! ♡
Ta-da!
URK! MAGIC CHOCOLATES... AGAIN?!
WHAT NOW?
Dread
THEY'RE TRUTH CHOCOLATES!
EAT ONE AND YOU HAVE TO ANSWER EVERY QUESTION!
YOU CAN'T LIE! YOU CAN'T EVEN STAY SILENT!!

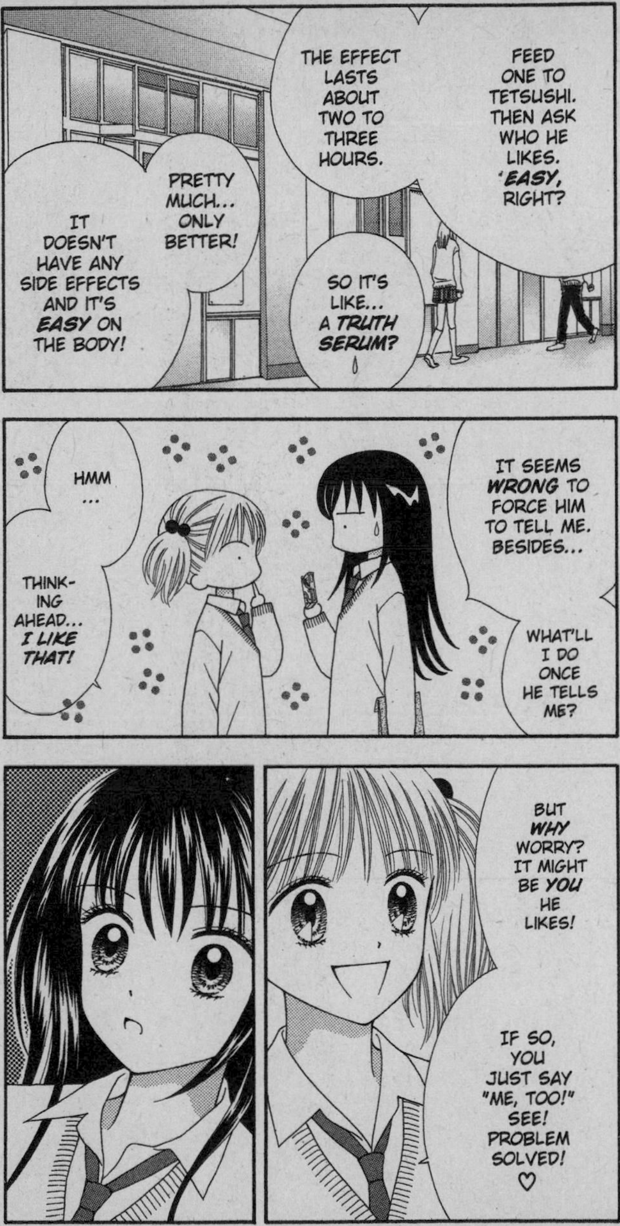
FEED ONE TO TETSUSHI. THEN ASK WHO HE LIKES. EASY, RIGHT?
THE EFFECT LASTS ABOUT TWO TO THREE HOURS.
SO IT'S LIKE... A TRUTH SERUM?
PRETTY MUCH... ONLY BETTER!
IT DOESN'T HAVE ANY SIDE EFFECTS AND IT'S EASY ON THE BODY!
IT SEEMS WRONG TO FORCE HIM TO TELL ME. BESIDES...
WHAT'LL I DO ONCE HE TELLS ME?
HMM...
THINKING AHEAD... I LIKE THAT!
BUT WHY WORRY? IT MIGHT BE YOU HE LIKES!
IF SO, YOU JUST SAY "ME, TOO!" SEE! PROBLEM SOLVED! ♡
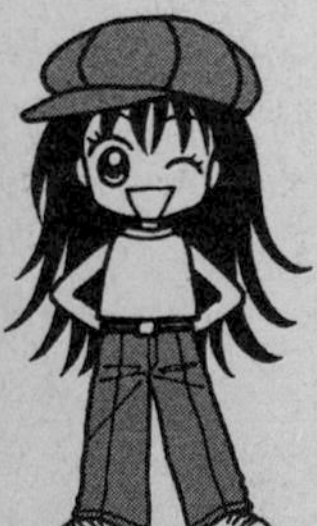

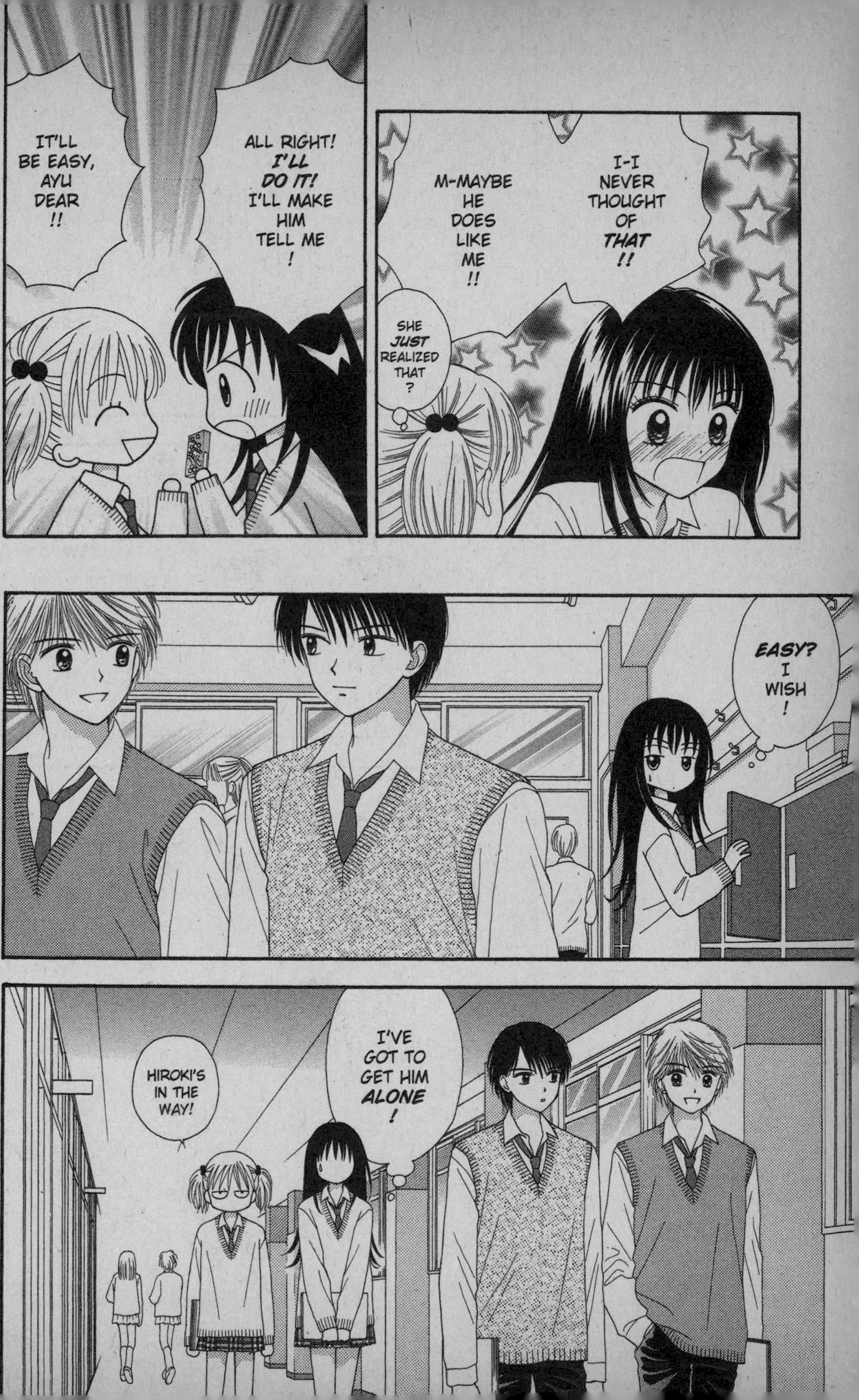
I-I NEVER THOUGHT OF THAT !!
M-MAYBE HE DOES LIKE ME !!
SHE JUST REALIZED THAT ?
ALL RIGHT! I'LL DO IT! I'LL MAKE HIM TELL ME !
IT'LL BE EASY, AYU DEAR !!
EASY? I WISH !
I'VE GOT TO GET HIM ALONE !
HIROKI'S IN THE WAY!

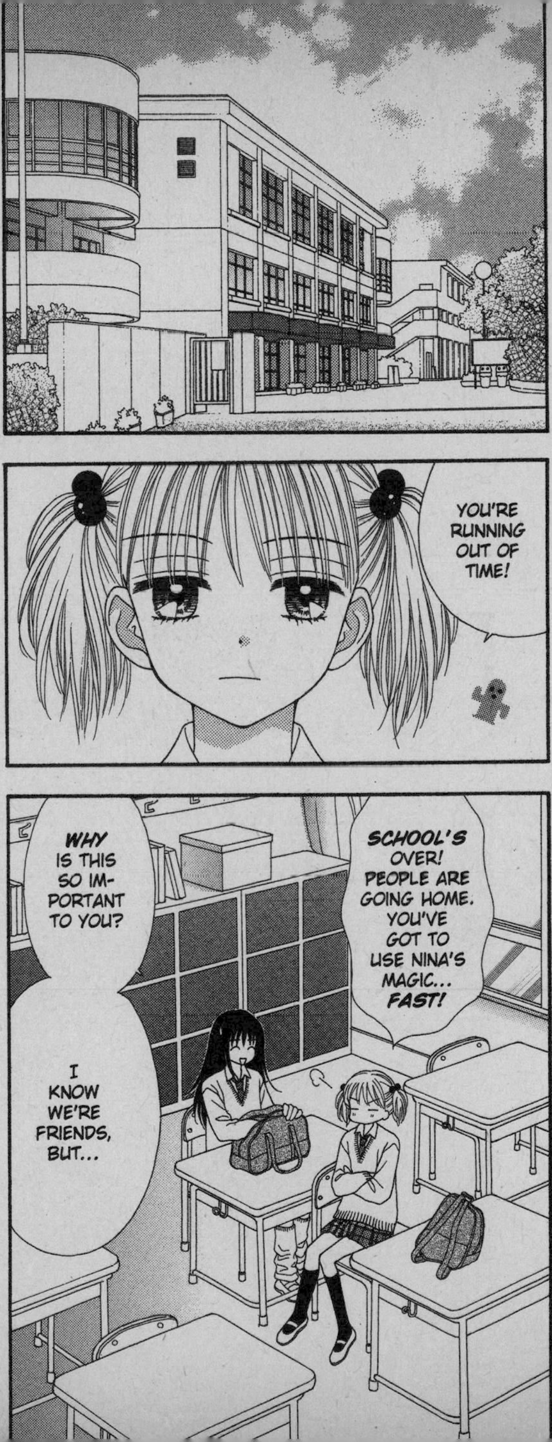
YOU'RE RUNNING OUT OF TIME!
SCHOOL'S OVER! PEOPLE ARE GOING HOME. YOU'VE GOT TO USE NINA'S MAGIC... ***FAST!***
WHY IS THIS SO IM-PORTANT TO YOU?
I KNOW WE'RE FRIENDS, BUT...
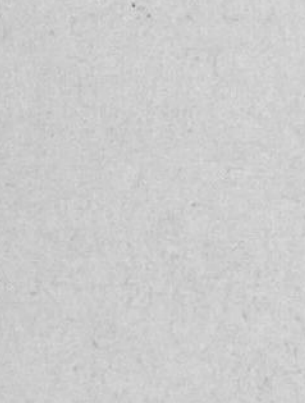
55

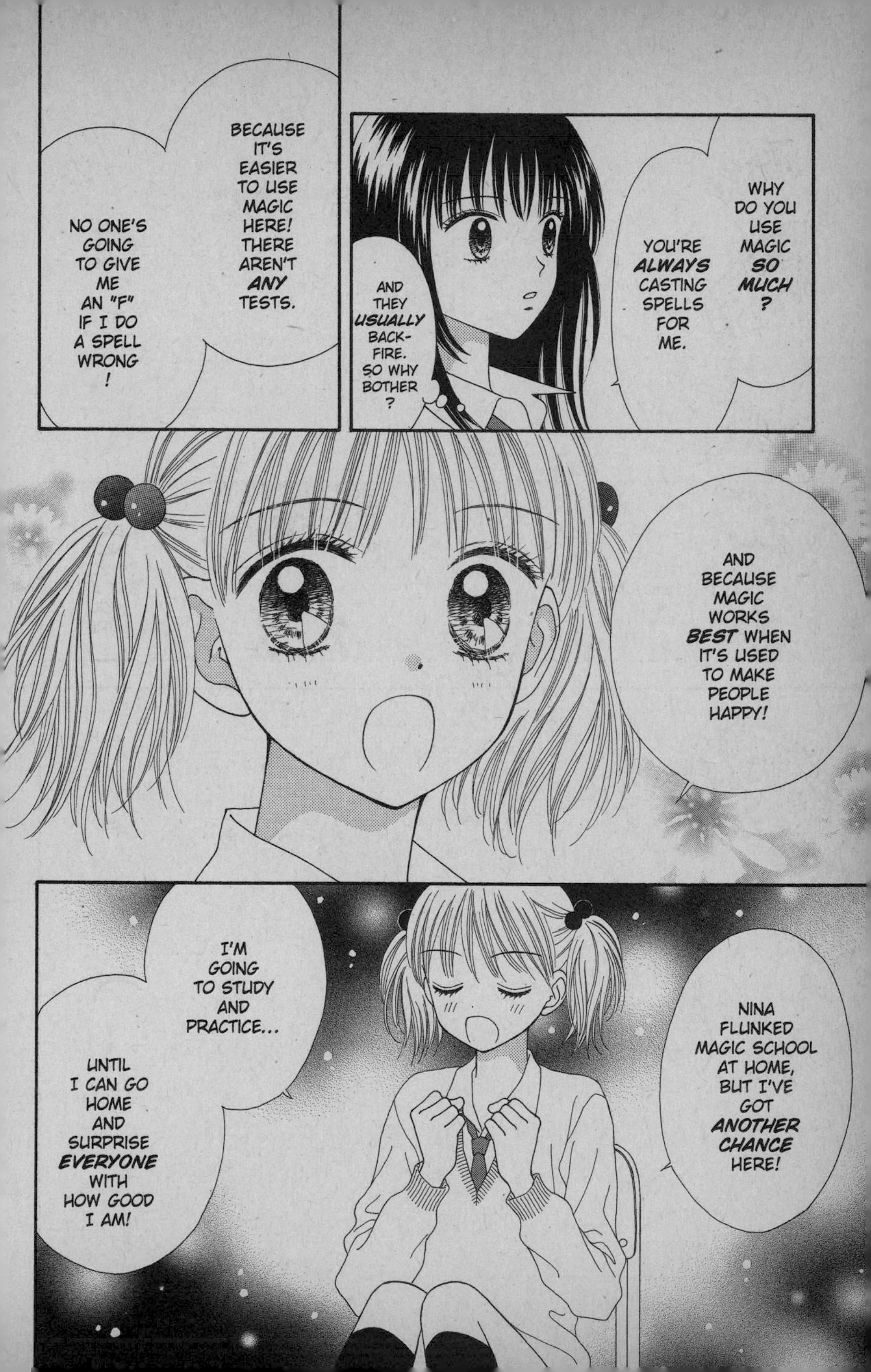
WHY DO YOU USE MAGIC SO MUCH?
YOU'RE ALWAYS CASTING SPELLS FOR ME.
AND THEY USUALLY BACK-FIRE. SO WHY BOTHER?
BECAUSE IT'S EASIER TO USE MAGIC HERE! THERE AREN'T ANY TESTS.
NO ONE'S GOING TO GIVE ME AN "F" IF I DO A SPELL WRONG!
AND BECAUSE MAGIC WORKS BEST WHEN IT'S USED TO MAKE PEOPLE HAPPY!
NINA FLUNKED MAGIC SCHOOL AT HOME, BUT I'VE GOT ANOTHER CHANCE HERE!
I'M GOING TO STUDY AND PRACTICE...
UNTIL I CAN GO HOME AND SURPRISE EVERYONE WITH HOW GOOD I AM!

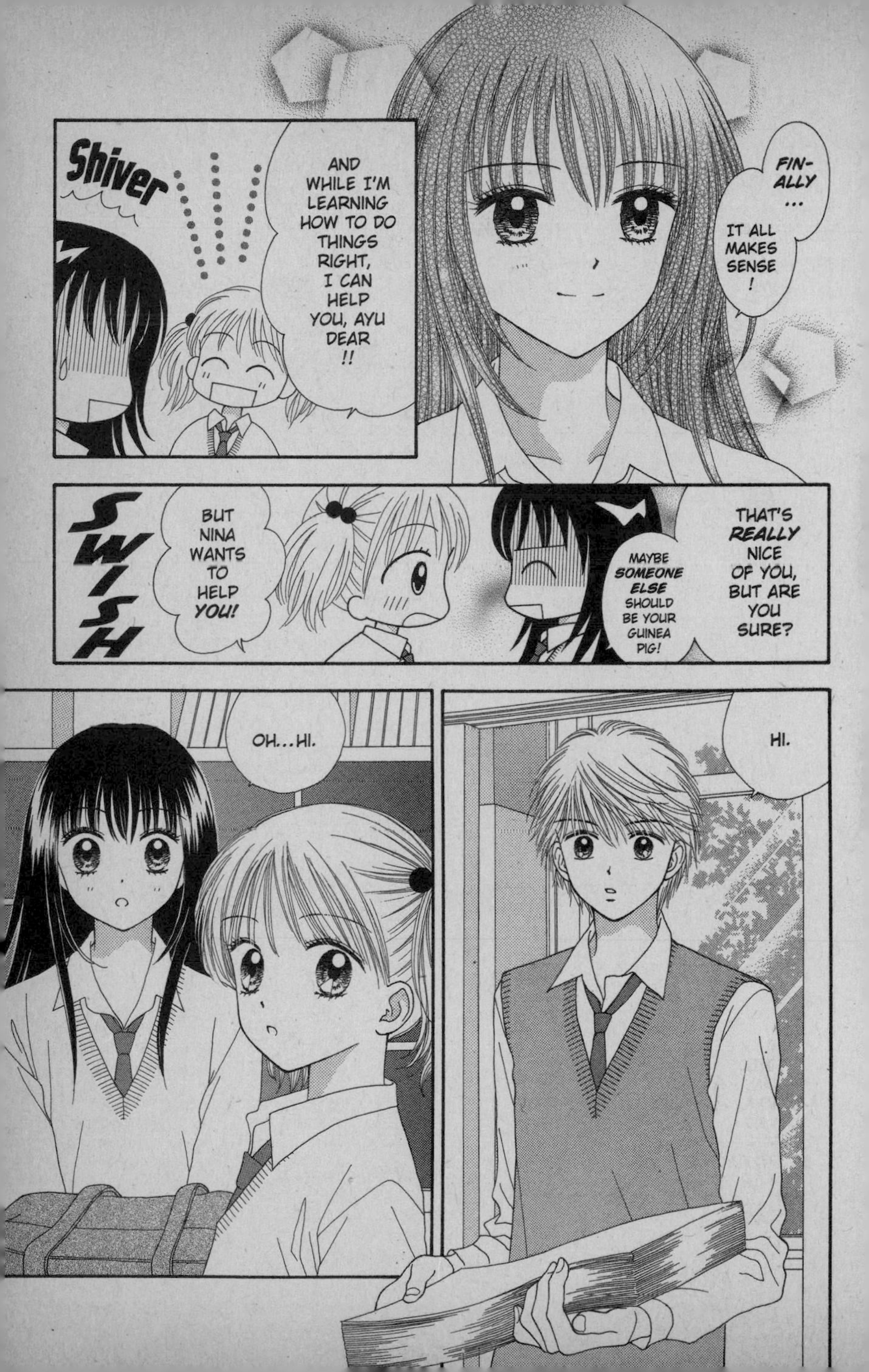
FIN-ALLY... IT ALL MAKES SENSE!
AND WHILE I'M LEARNING HOW TO DO THINGS RIGHT, I CAN HELP YOU, AYU DEAR!!
Shiver
THAT'S REALLY NICE OF YOU, BUT ARE YOU SURE?
MAYBE SOMEONE ELSE SHOULD BE YOUR GUINEA PIG!
BUT NINA WANTS TO HELP YOU!
SWISH
HI.
OH...HI.

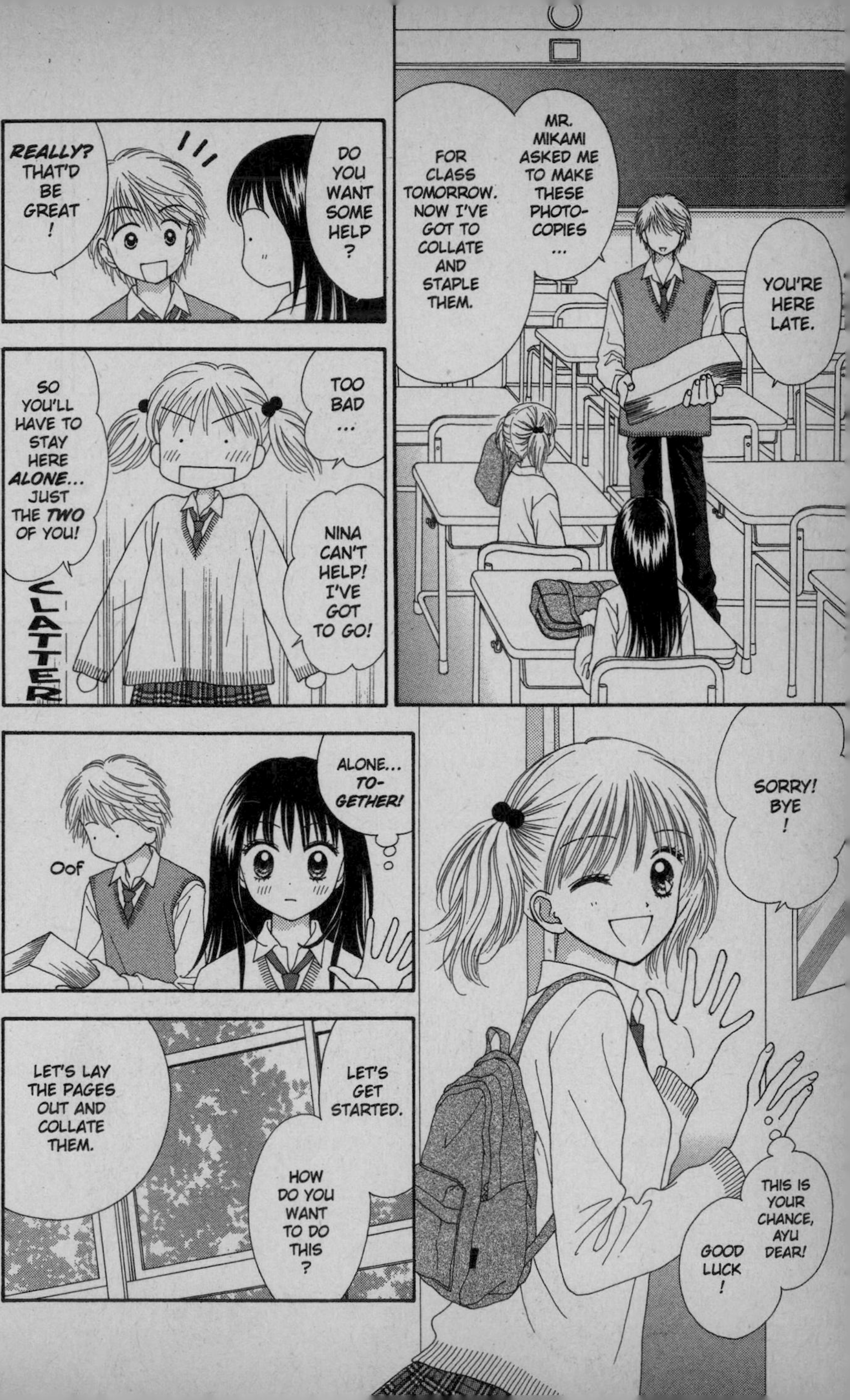
YOU'RE HERE LATE.
MR. MIKAMI ASKED ME TO MAKE THESE PHOTOCOPIES...
FOR CLASS TOMORROW. NOW I'VE GOT TO COLLATE AND STAPLE THEM.
DO YOU WANT SOME HELP?
REALLY? THAT'D BE GREAT!
TOO BAD...
NINA CAN'T HELP! I'VE GOT TO GO!
SO YOU'LL HAVE TO STAY HERE ALONE... JUST THE TWO OF YOU!
CLATTER
SORRY! BYE!
THIS IS YOUR CHANCE, AYU DEAR!
GOOD LUCK!
ALONE... TOGETHER!
Oof
LET'S GET STARTED.
HOW DO YOU WANT TO DO THIS?
LET'S LAY THE PAGES OUT AND COLLATE THEM.

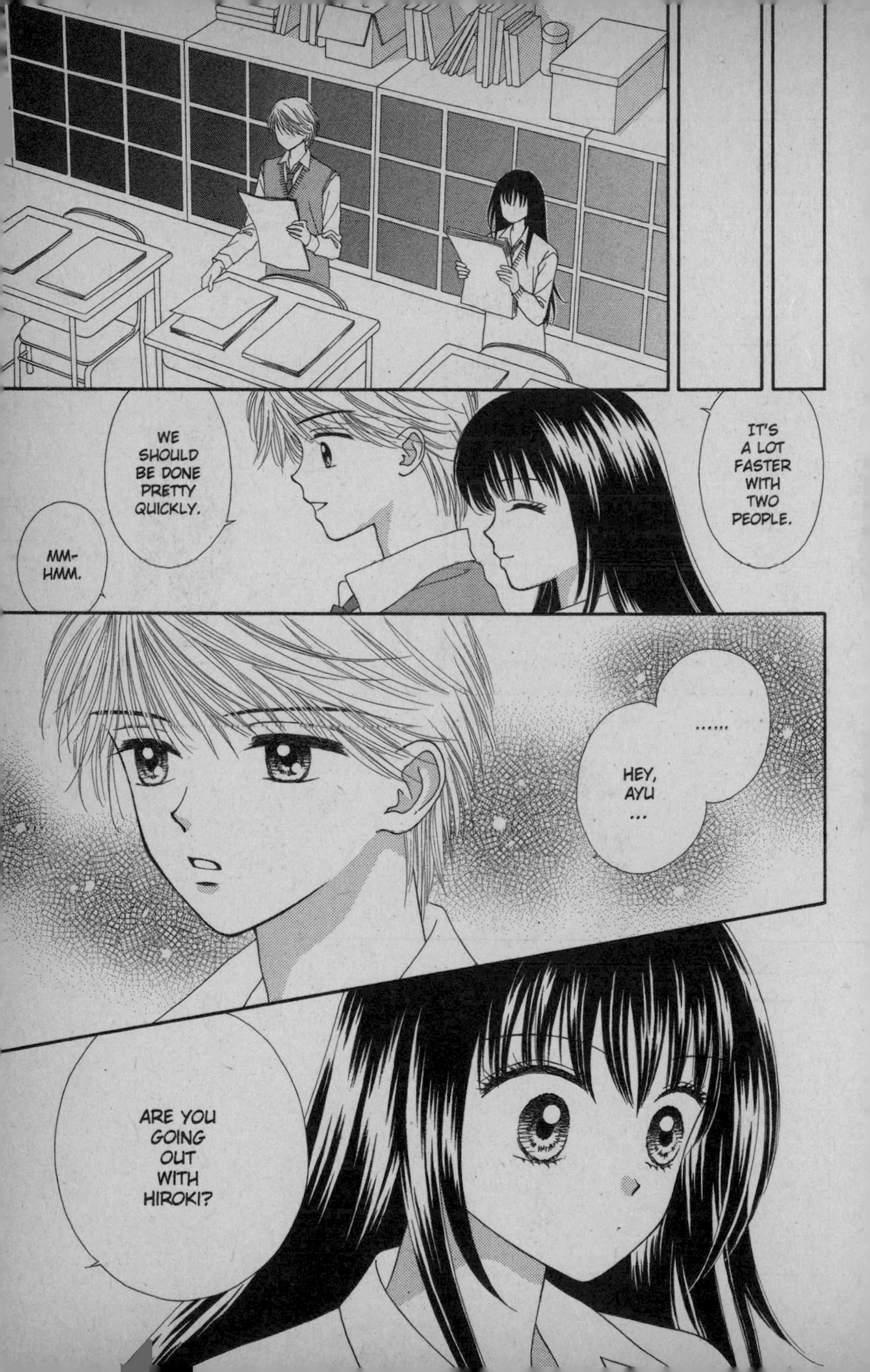
IT'S A LOT FASTER WITH TWO PEOPLE.
WE SHOULD BE DONE PRETTY QUICKLY.
MM-HMM.
......
HEY, AYU ...
ARE YOU GOING OUT WITH HIROKI?

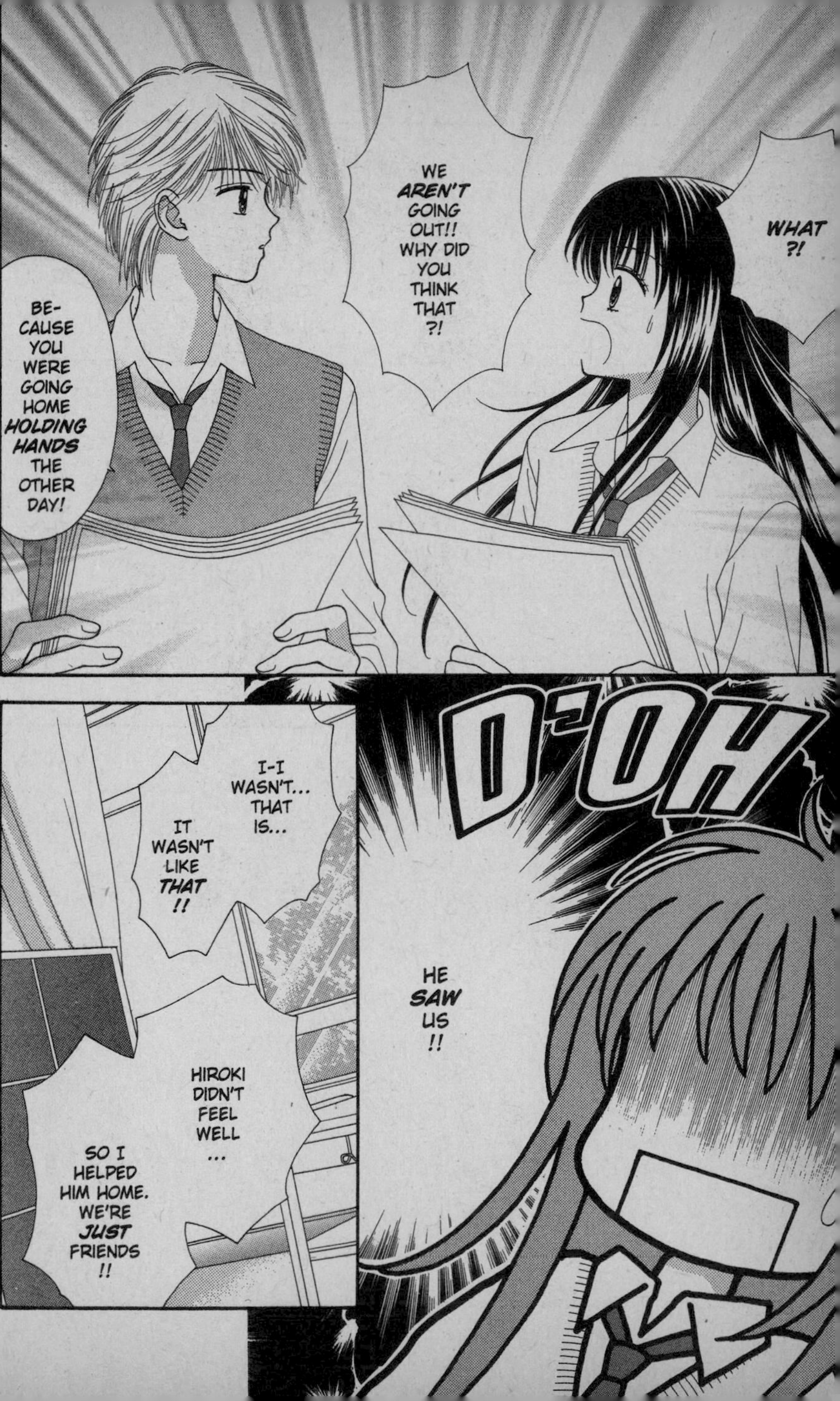
WHAT?!
WE AREN'T GOING OUT!! WHY DID YOU THINK THAT?!
BE-CAUSE YOU WERE GOING HOME HOLDING HANDS THE OTHER DAY!
D'OH
HE SAW US!!
I-I WASN'T... THAT IS...
IT WASN'T LIKE THAT!!
HIROKI DIDN'T FEEL WELL...
SO I HELPED HIM HOME. WE'RE JUST FRIENDS!!

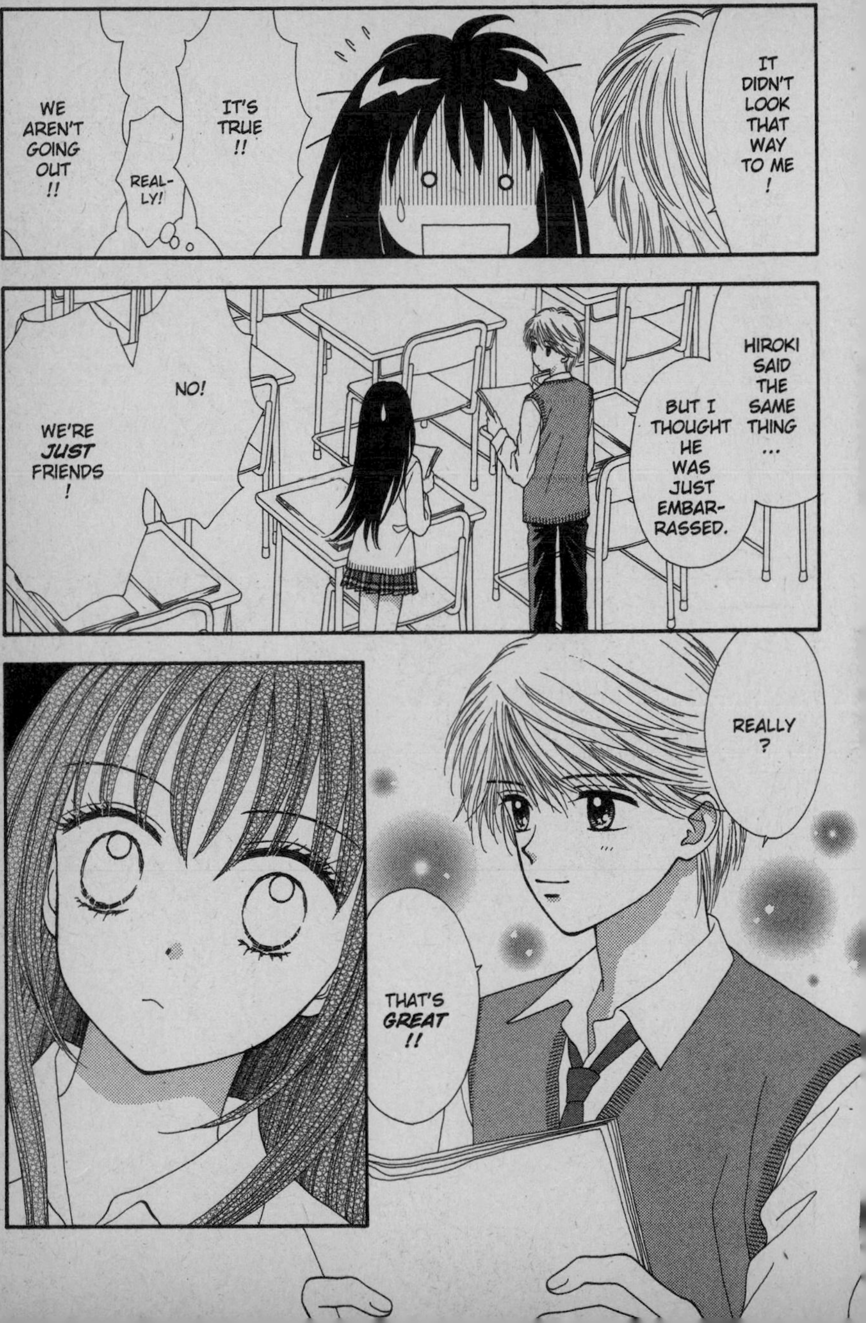
IT DIDN'T LOOK THAT WAY TO ME!
IT'S TRUE!!
REALLY!
WE AREN'T GOING OUT!!
HIROKI SAID THE SAME THING...
BUT I THOUGHT HE WAS JUST EMBARRASSED.
NO!
WE'RE *JUST* FRIENDS!
REALLY?
...
THAT'S *GREAT*!!

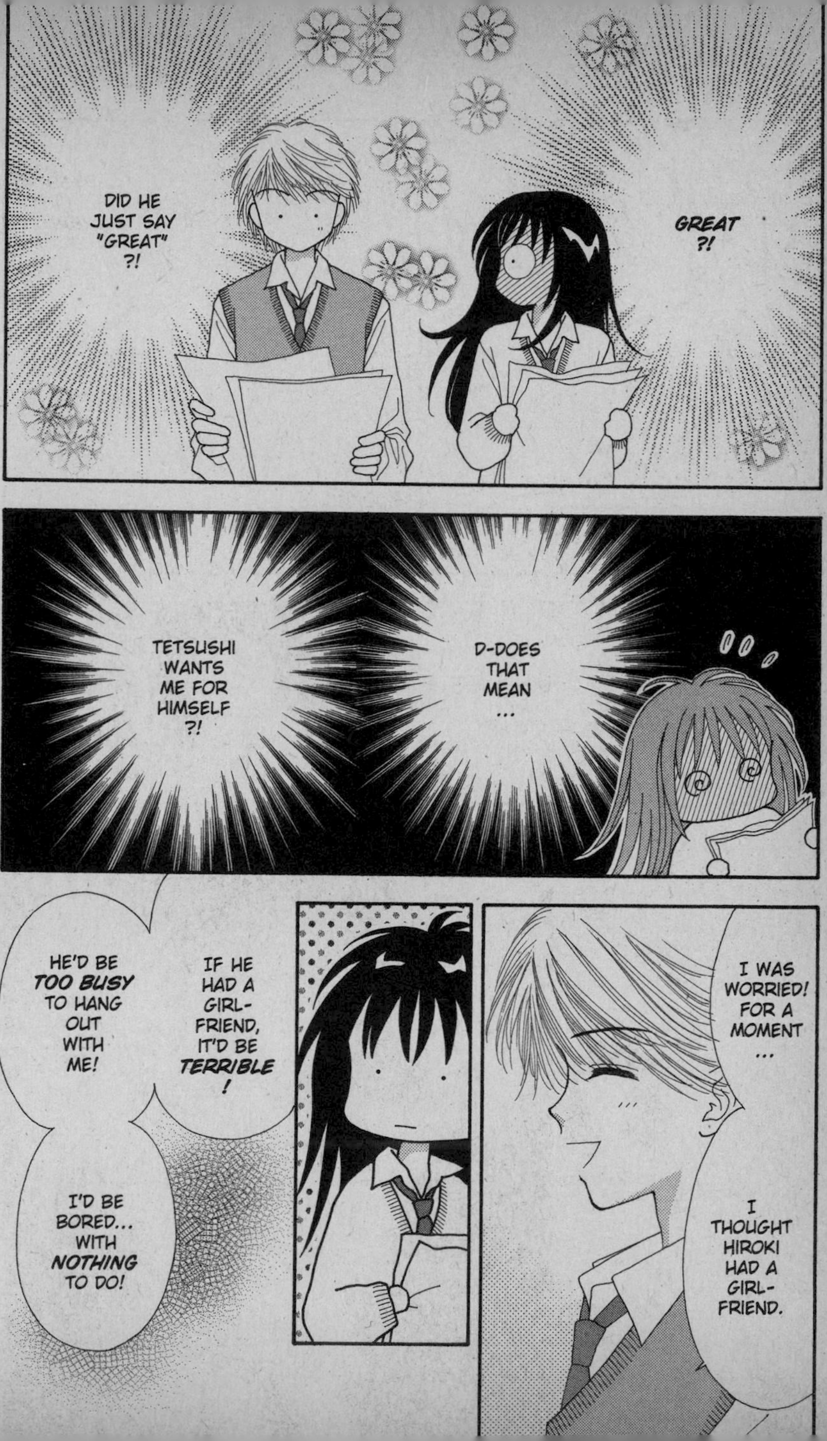
GREAT ?!
DID HE JUST SAY "GREAT" ?!
D-DOES THAT MEAN ...
TETSUSHI WANTS ME FOR HIMSELF ?!
I WAS WORRIED! FOR A MOMENT ...
I THOUGHT HIROKI HAD A GIRL-FRIEND.
IF HE HAD A GIRL-FRIEND, IT'D BE *TERRIBLE* !
HE'D BE *TOO BUSY* TO HANG OUT WITH ME!
I'D BE BORED... WITH *NOTHING* TO DO!

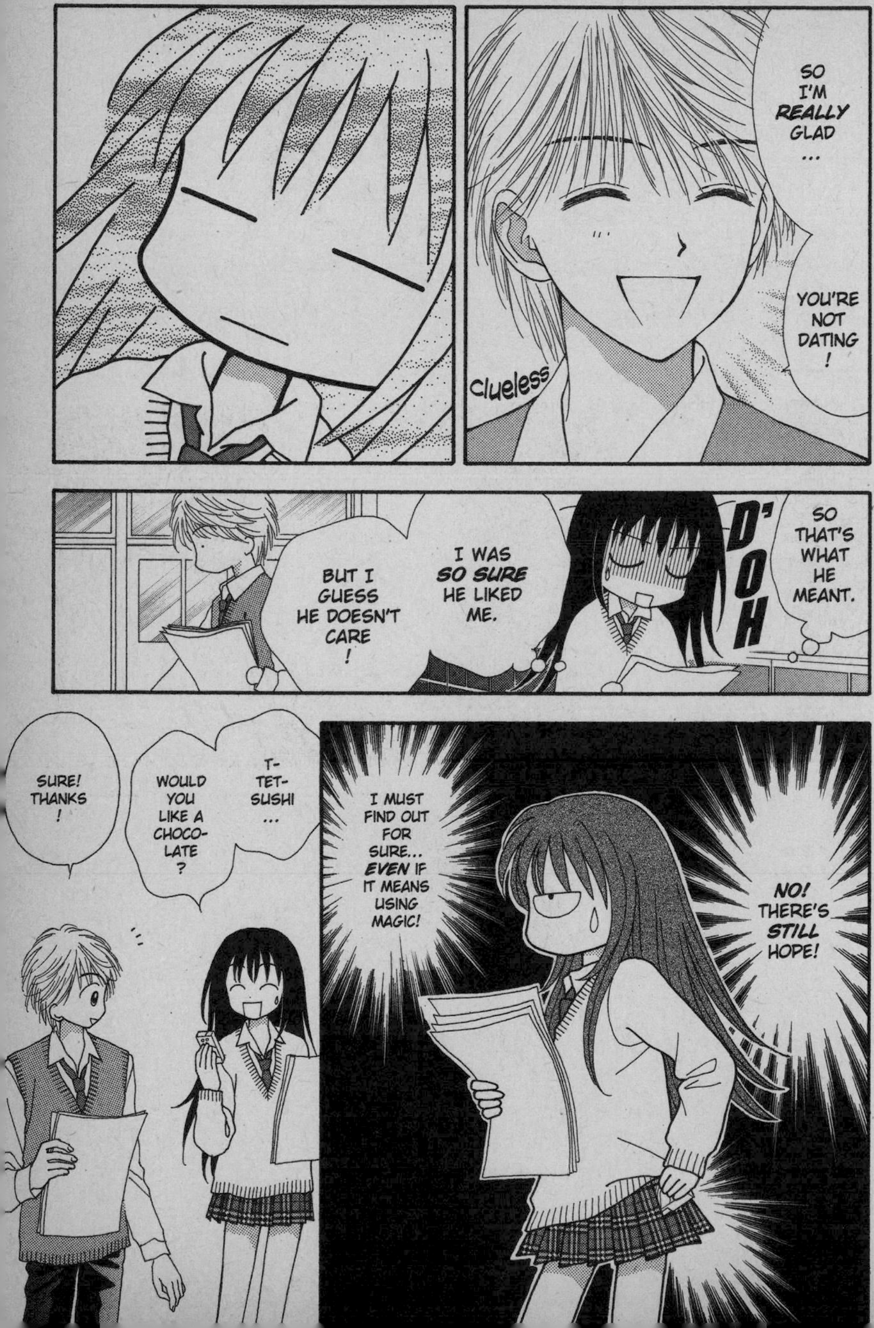
SO I'M REALLY GLAD...
YOU'RE NOT DATING!
Clueless
SO THAT'S WHAT HE MEANT.
D'OH
I WAS SO SURE HE LIKED ME.
BUT I GUESS HE DOESN'T CARE!
NO! THERE'S STILL HOPE!
I MUST FIND OUT FOR SURE... EVEN IF IT MEANS USING MAGIC!
T-TET-SUSHI...
WOULD YOU LIKE A CHOCOLATE?
SURE! THANKS!

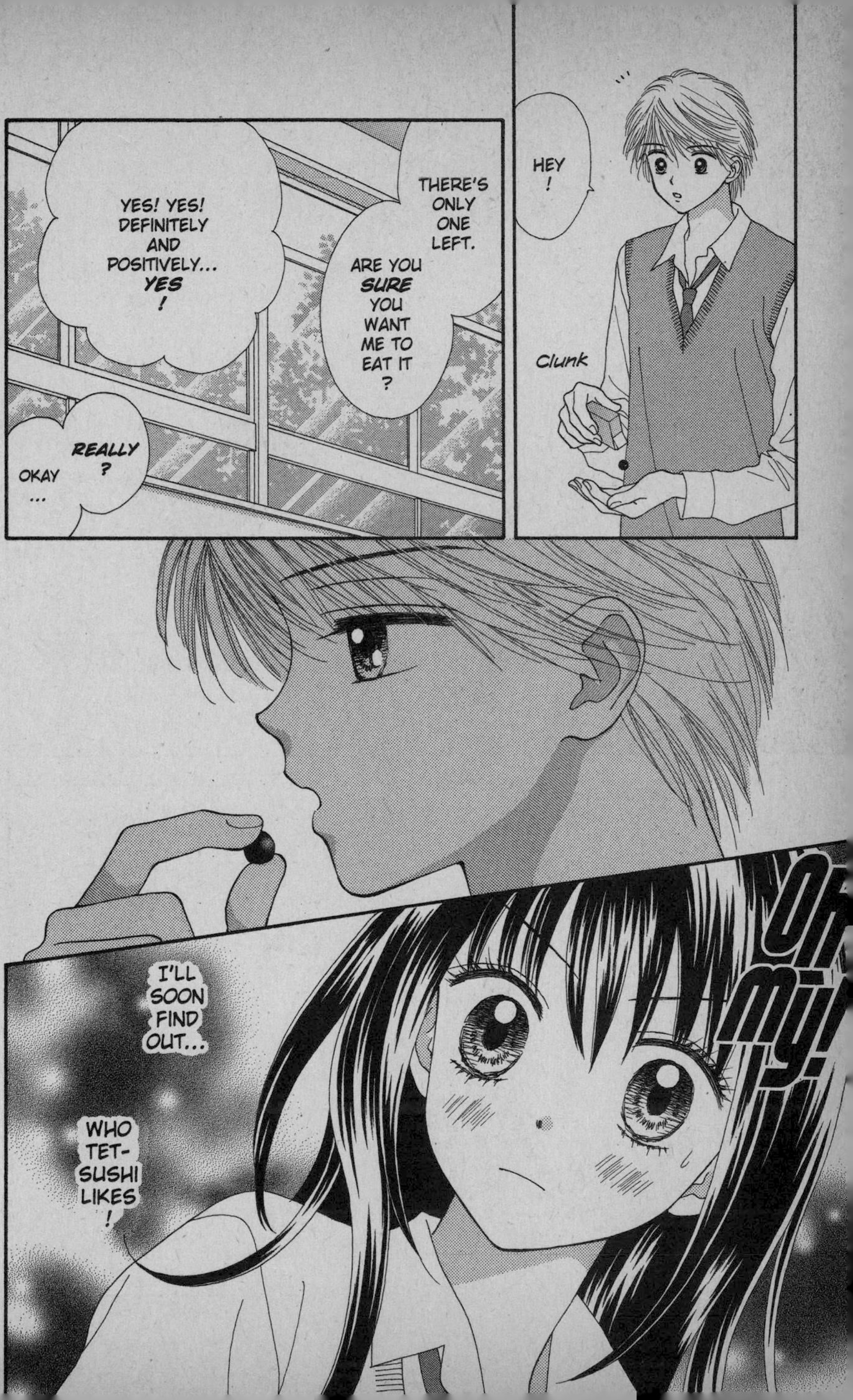
HEY!
Clunk
THERE'S ONLY ONE LEFT.
ARE YOU *SURE* YOU WANT ME TO EAT IT?
YES! YES! DEFINITELY AND POSITIVELY... *YES*!
REALLY?
OKAY...
Oh my!
I'LL SOON FIND OUT...
WHO TET-SUSHI LIKES!

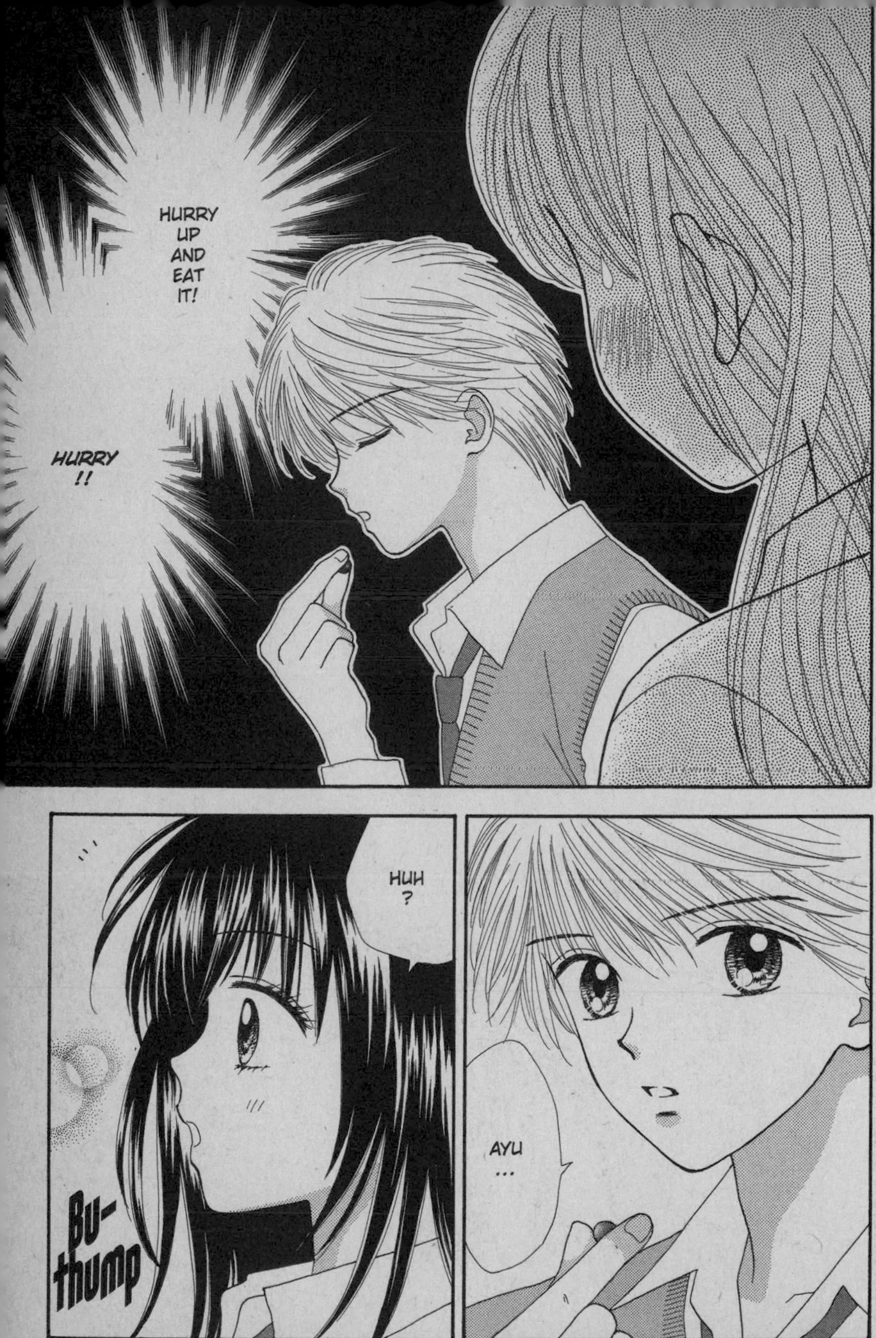
HURRY UP AND EAT IT!
HURRY !!
AYU ...
HUH ?
Bu-thump

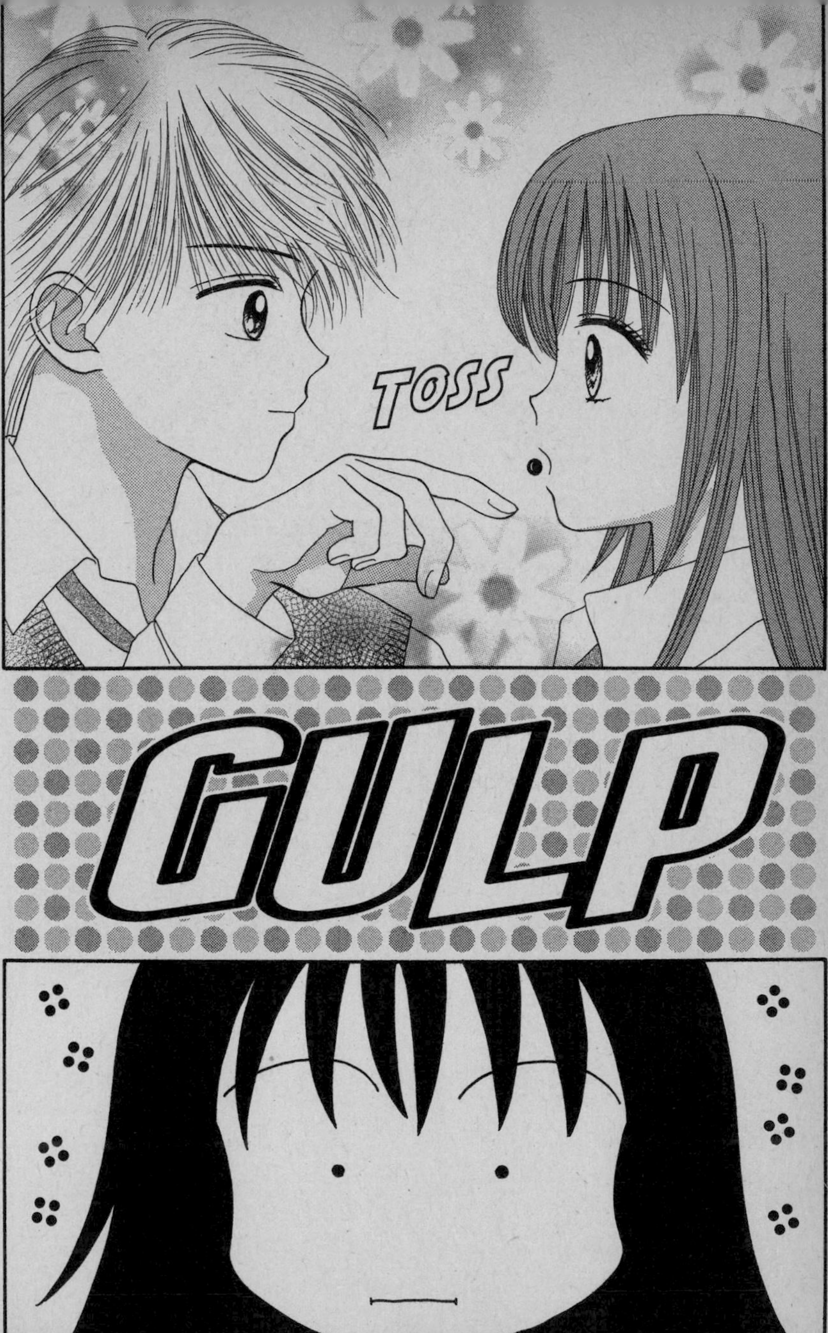
TOSS
GULP

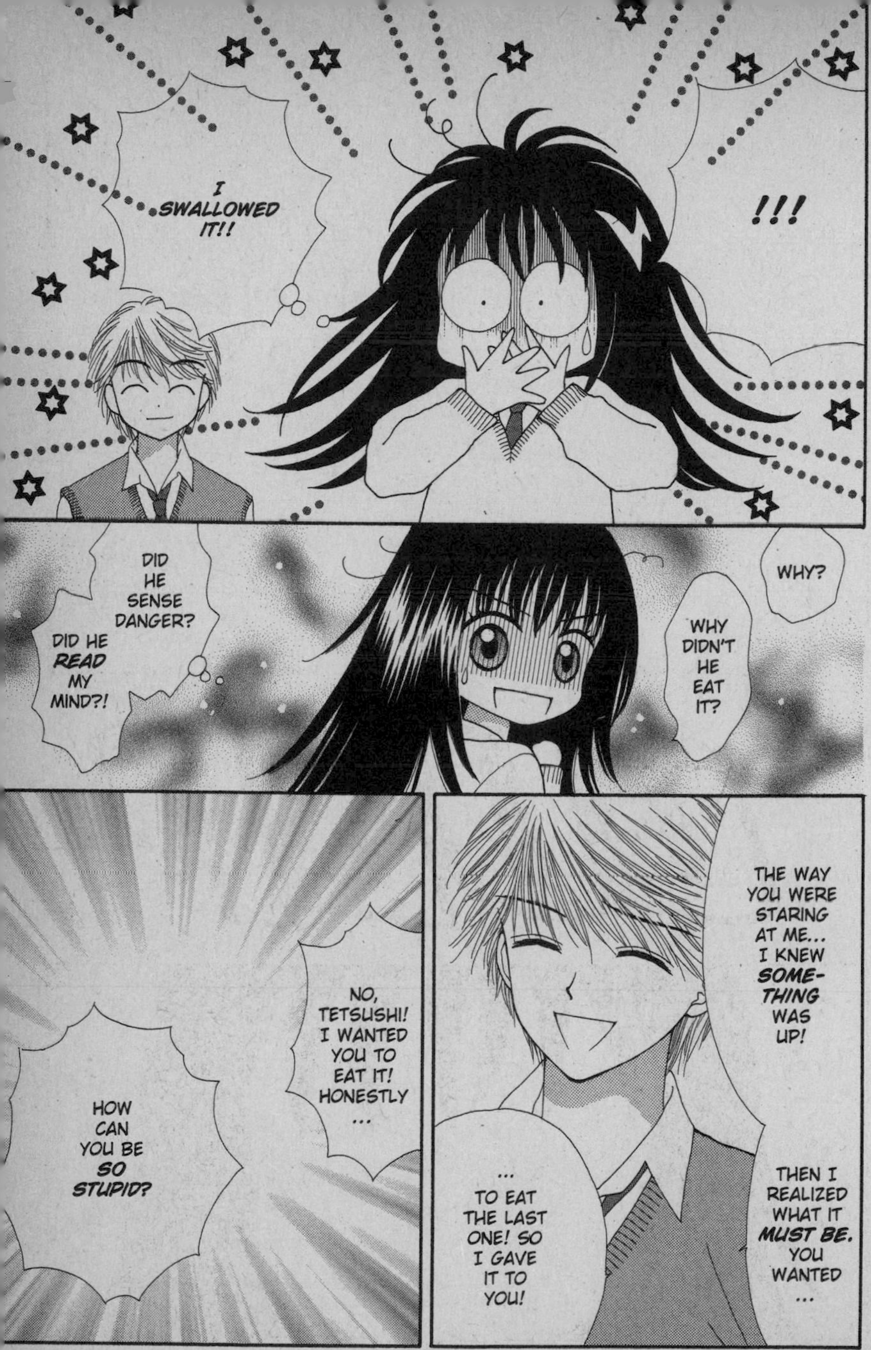
!!!
I SWALLOWED IT!!
WHY?
WHY DIDN'T HE EAT IT?
DID HE SENSE DANGER?
DID HE READ MY MIND?!
THE WAY YOU WERE STARING AT ME... I KNEW SOME-THING WAS UP!
THEN I REALIZED WHAT IT MUST BE. YOU WANTED...
...TO EAT THE LAST ONE! SO I GAVE IT TO YOU!
NO, TETSUSHI! I WANTED YOU TO EAT IT! HONESTLY...
HOW CAN YOU BE SO STUPID?

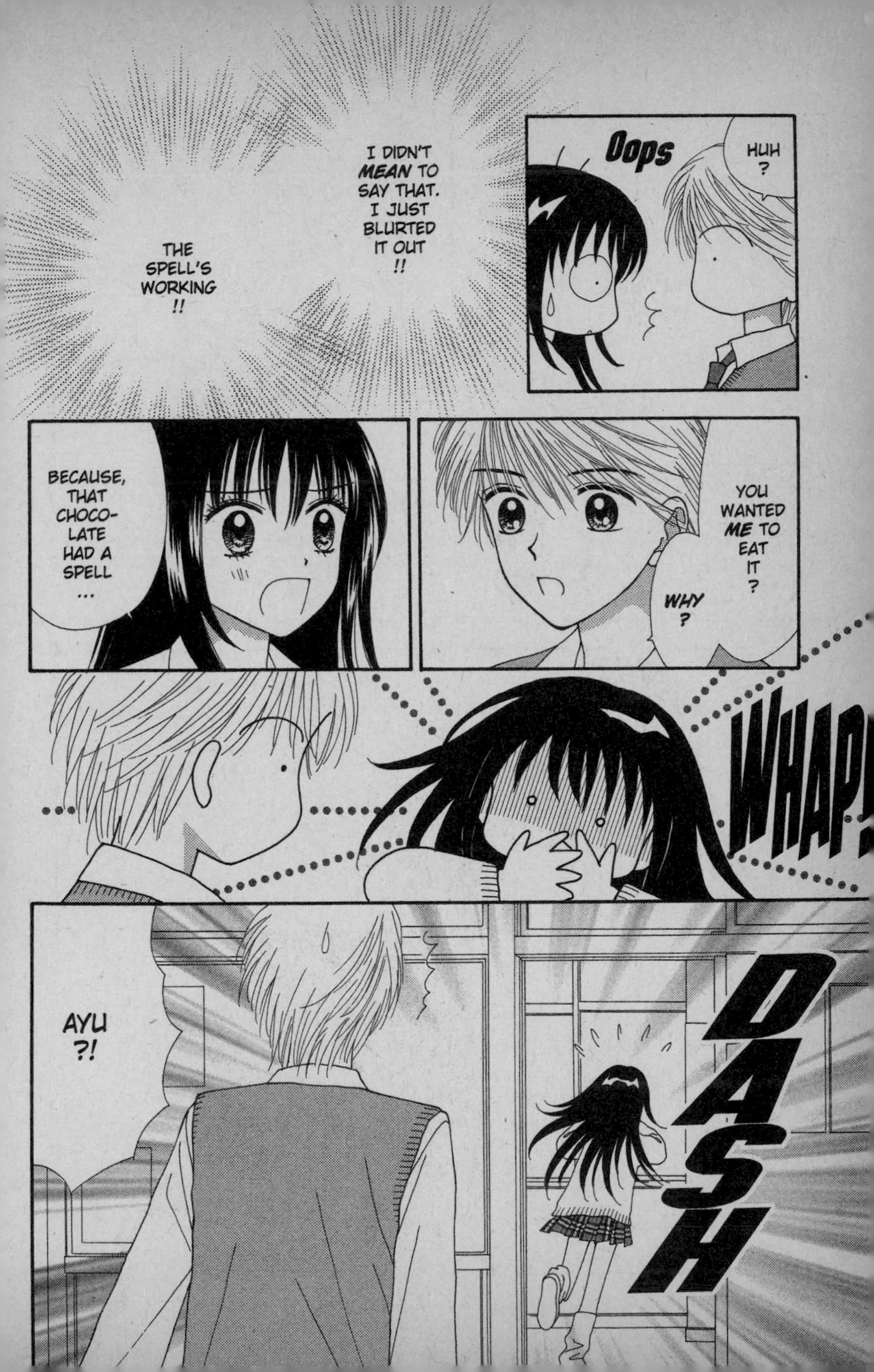
HUH?
Oops
I DIDN'T MEAN TO SAY THAT. I JUST BLURTED IT OUT!!
THE SPELL'S WORKING!!
YOU WANTED ME TO EAT IT?
WHY?
BECAUSE, THAT CHOCO-LATE HAD A SPELL...
WHAP!
DASH
AYU?!

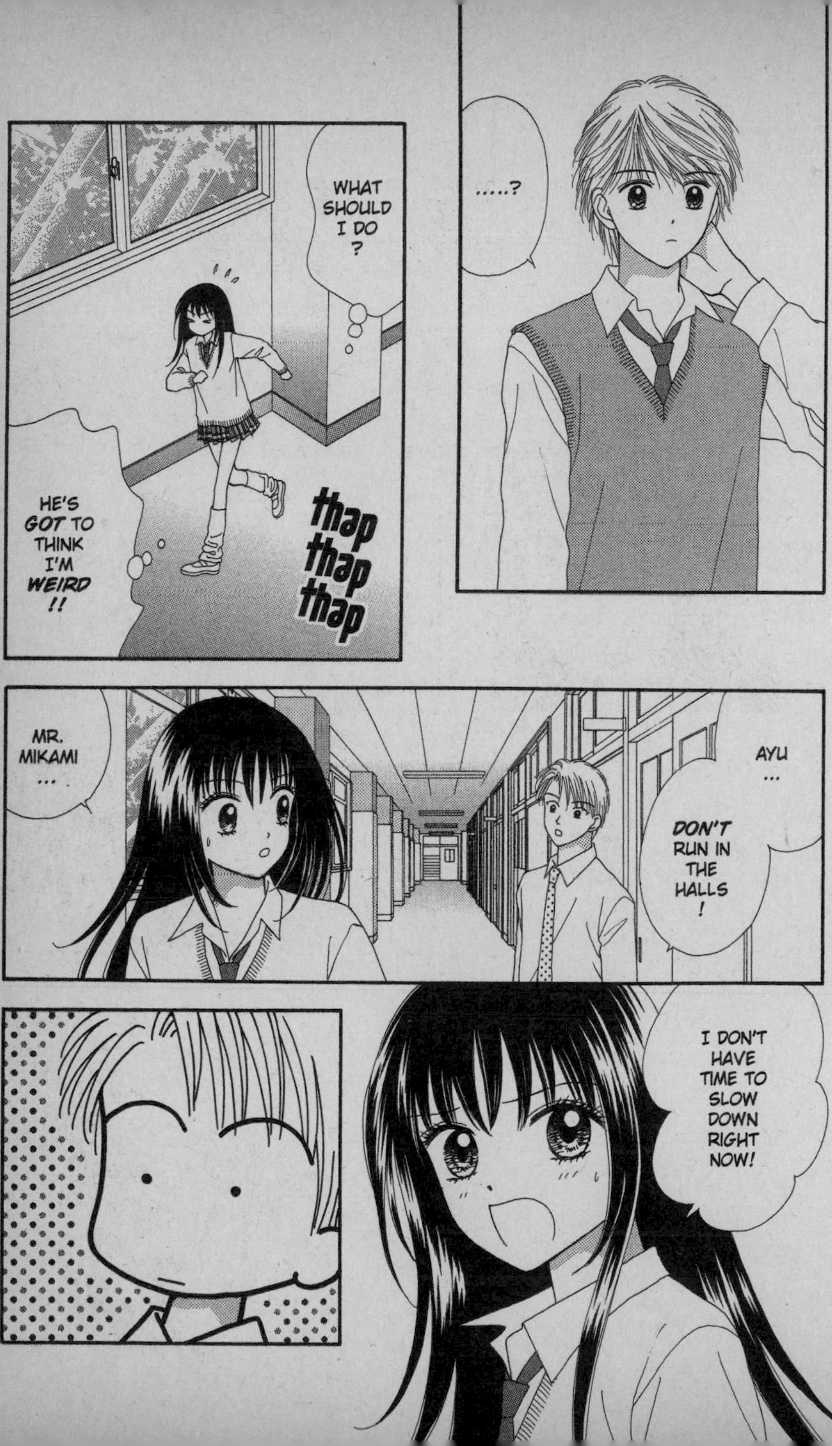
.....?
WHAT SHOULD I DO ?
HE'S GOT TO THINK I'M WEIRD !!
thap thap thap
AYU ... DON'T RUN IN THE HALLS !
MR. MIKAMI ...
I DON'T HAVE TIME TO SLOW DOWN RIGHT NOW!

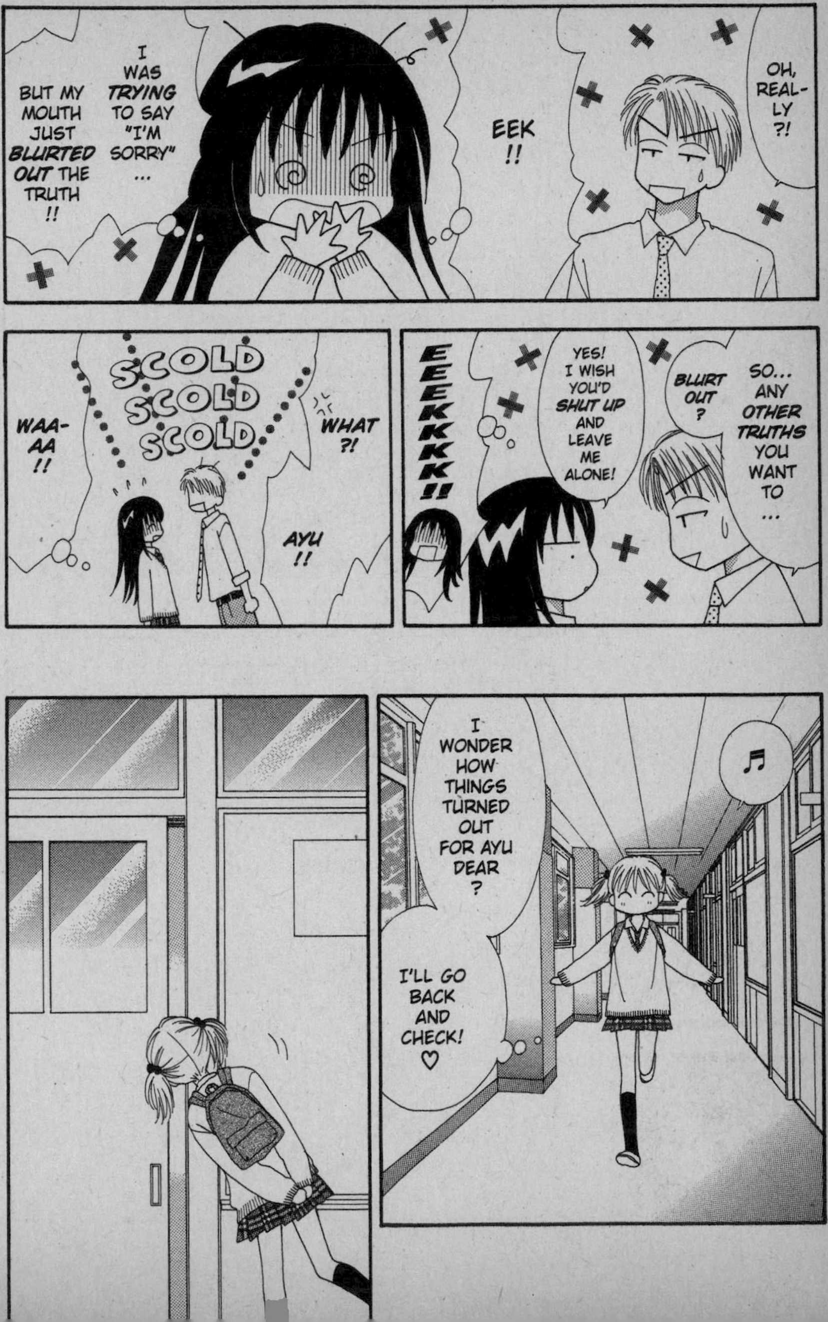
OH, REAL-LY ?!
EEK !!
I WAS TRYING TO SAY "I'M SORRY" ...
BUT MY MOUTH JUST BLURTED OUT THE TRUTH !!
SO... ANY OTHER TRUTHS YOU WANT TO ...
BLURT OUT ?
YES! I WISH YOU'D SHUT UP AND LEAVE ME ALONE!
EEEKKKK!!
WHAT ?!
SCOLD SCOLD SCOLD
WAA-AA !!
AYU !!
♪
I WONDER HOW THINGS TURNED OUT FOR AYU DEAR ?
I'LL GO BACK AND CHECK! ♡

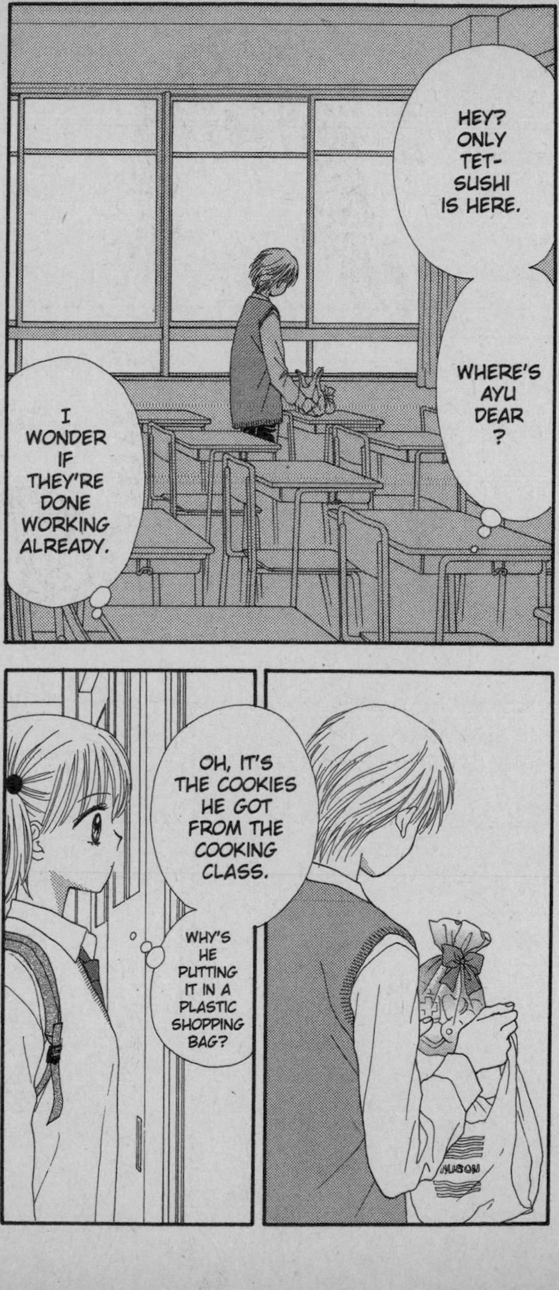
HEY? ONLY TET-SUSHI IS HERE.
WHERE'S AYU DEAR ?
I WONDER IF THEY'RE DONE WORKING ALREADY.
OH, IT'S THE COOKIES HE GOT FROM THE COOKING CLASS.
WHY'S HE PUTTING IT IN A PLASTIC SHOPPING BAG?
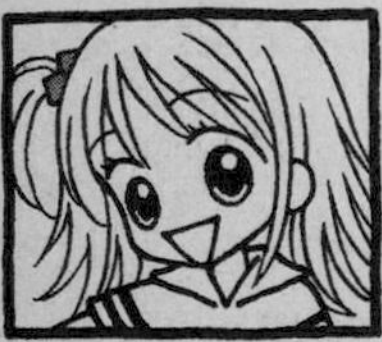
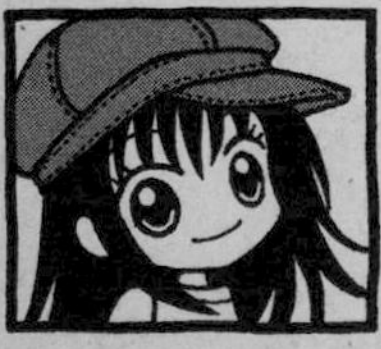

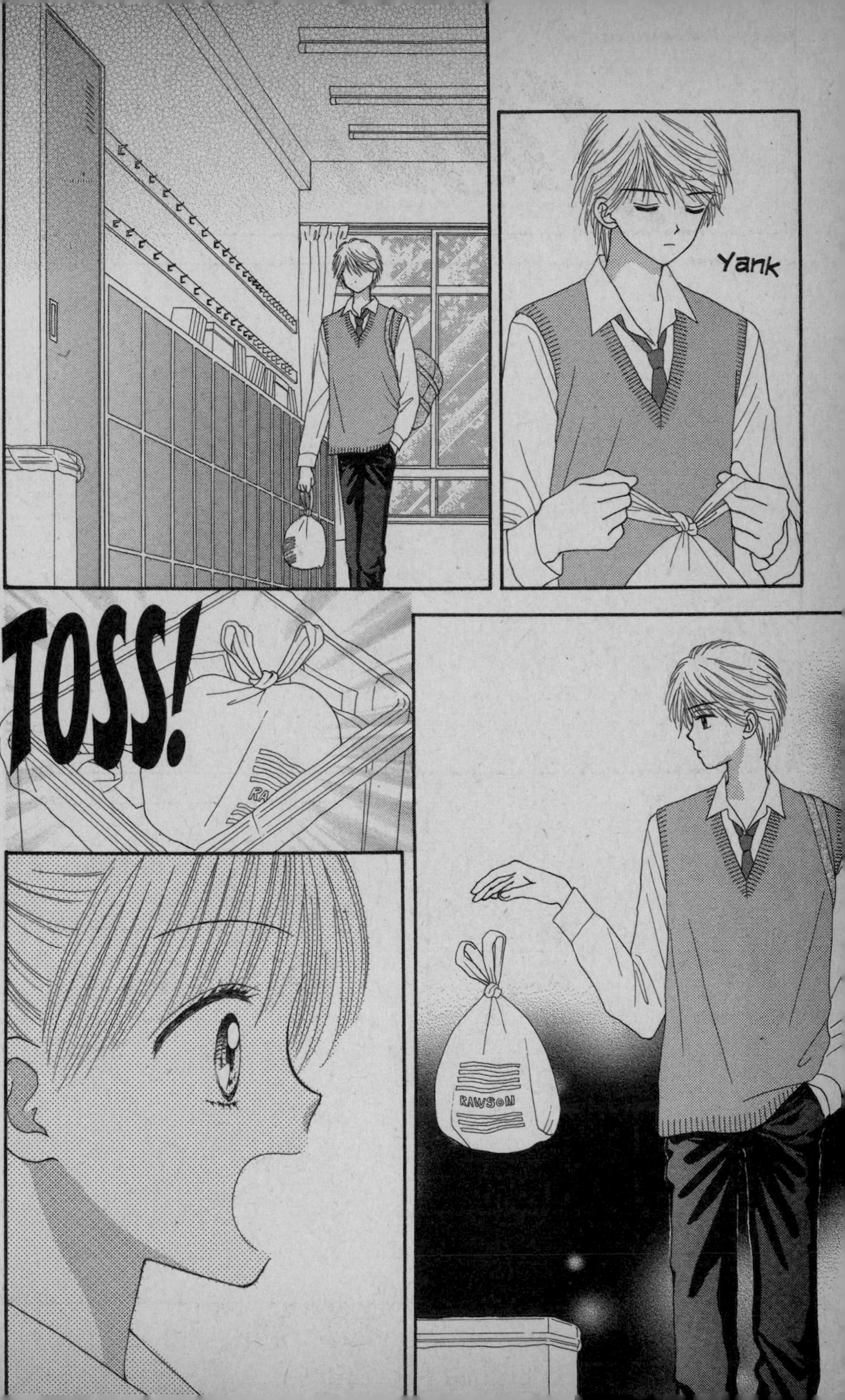
Yank
RAWSON
TOSS!

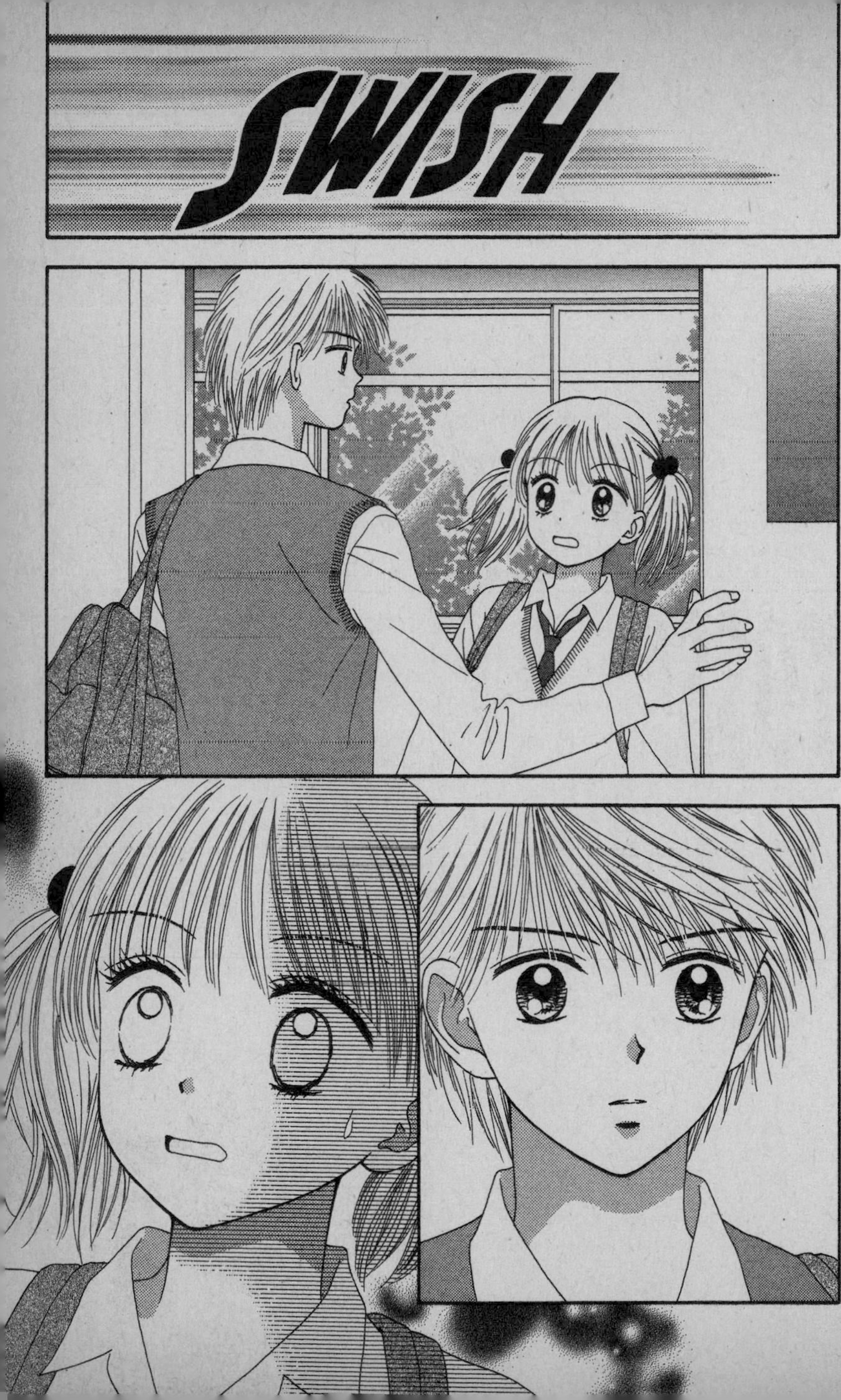
SWISH

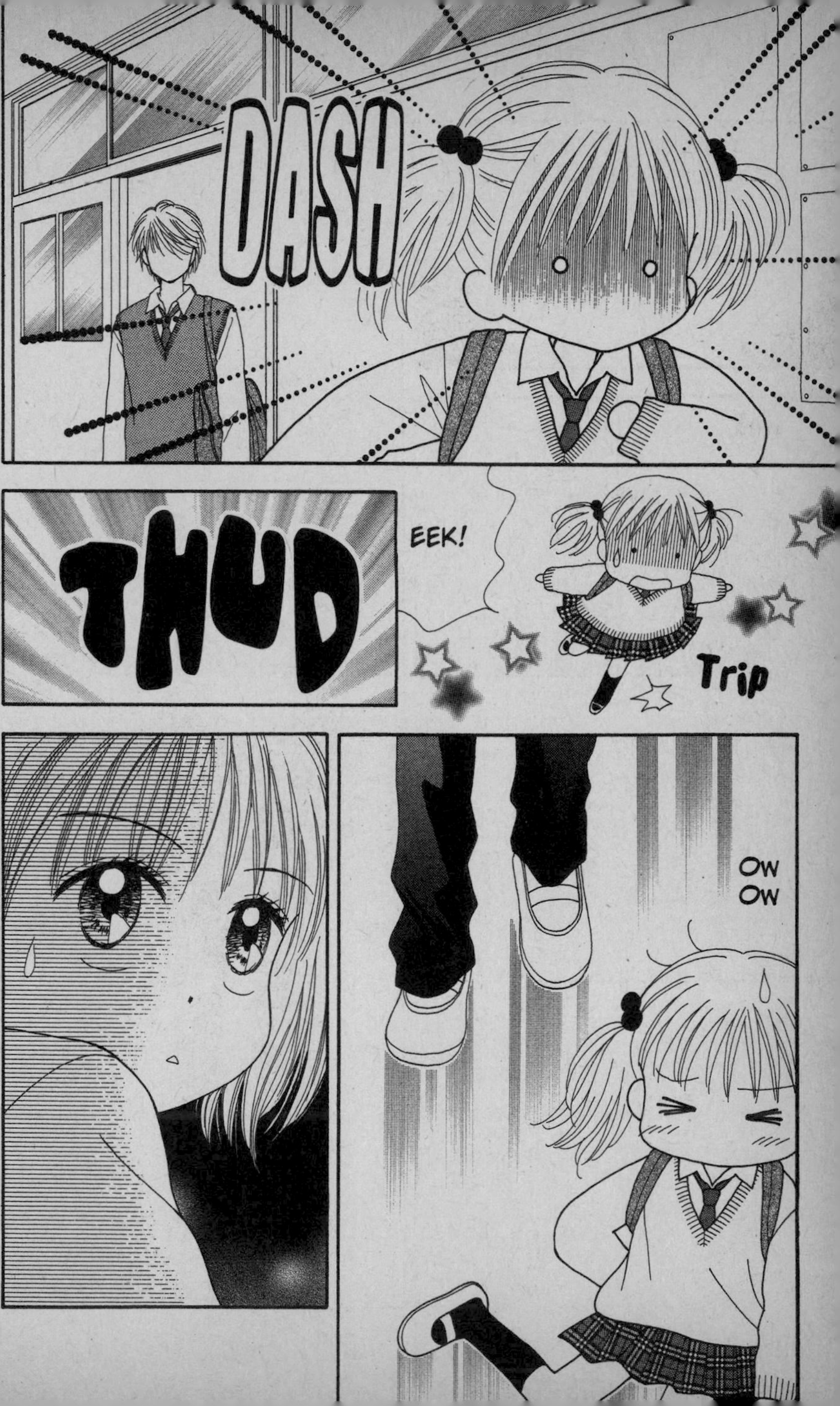
DASH
EEK!
Trip
THUD
OW
OW

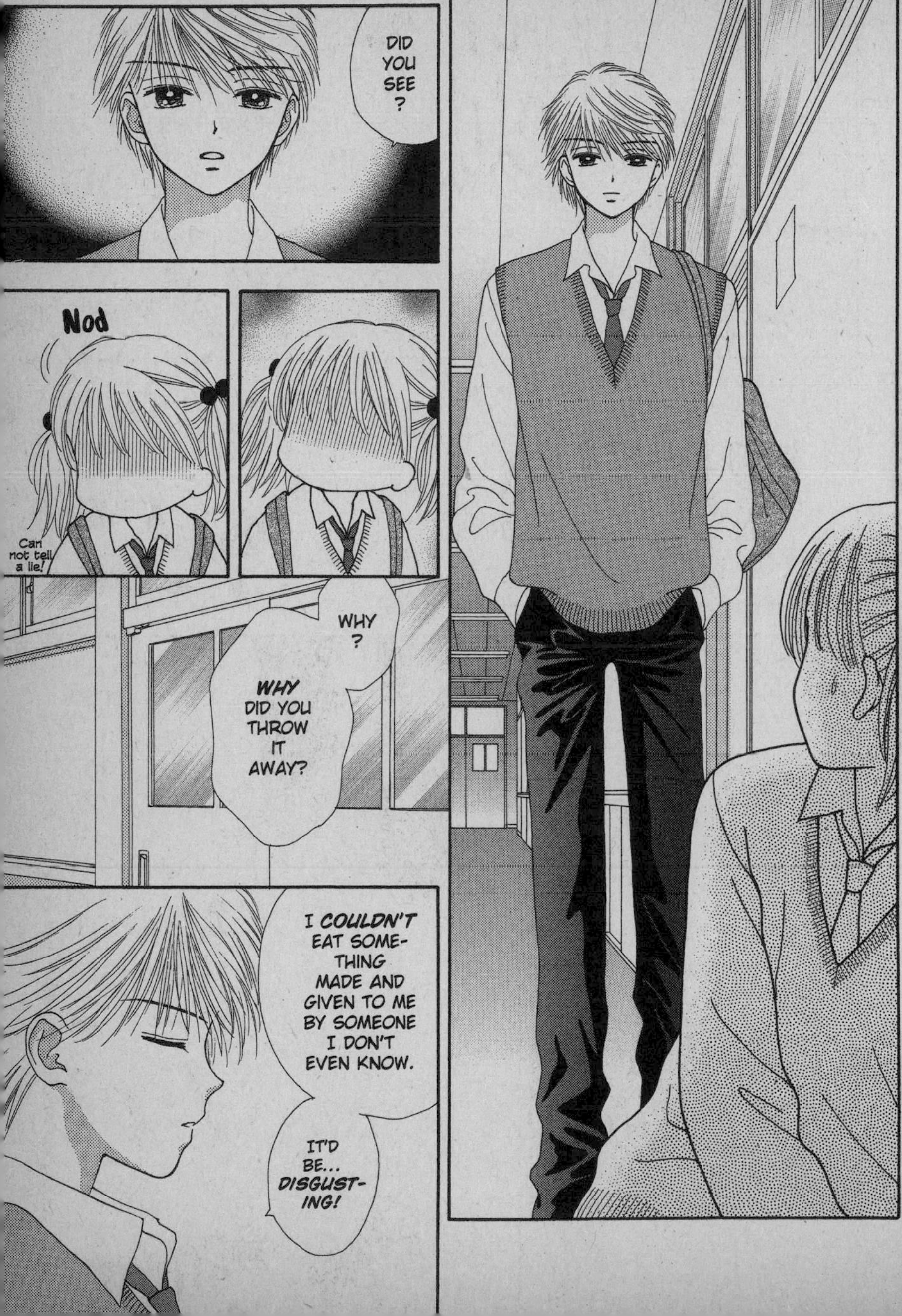
DID YOU SEE?
Nod
Can not tell a lie!
WHY?
WHY DID YOU THROW IT AWAY?
I *COULDN'T* EAT SOMETHING MADE AND GIVEN TO ME BY SOMEONE I DON'T EVEN KNOW.
IT'D BE... *DISGUSTING!*

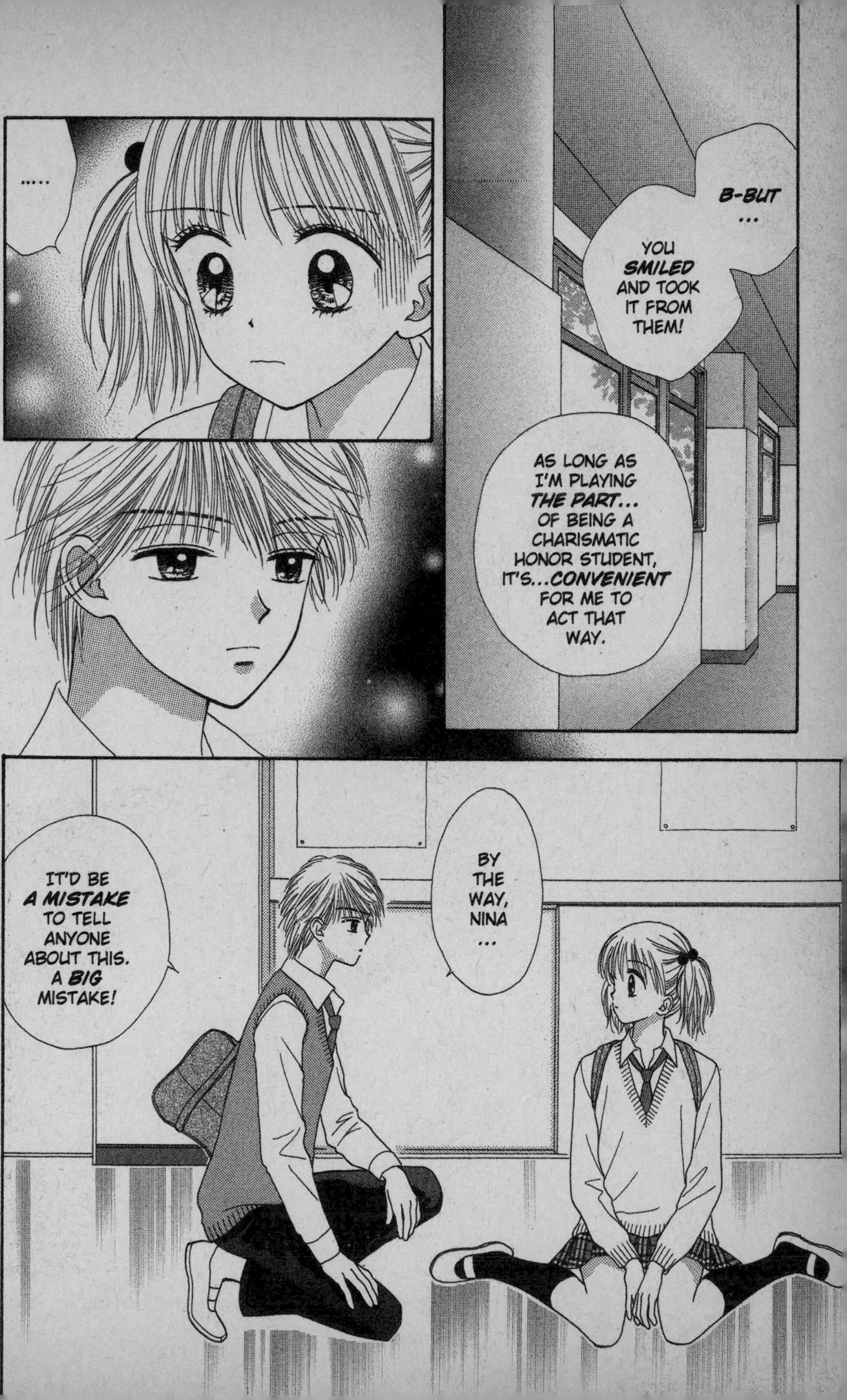
B-BUT ...
YOU **SMILED** AND TOOK IT FROM THEM!
AS LONG AS I'M PLAYING **THE PART...** OF BEING A CHARISMATIC HONOR STUDENT, IT'S...**CONVENIENT** FOR ME TO ACT THAT WAY.
.....
BY THE WAY, NINA ...
IT'D BE ***A MISTAKE*** TO TELL ANYONE ABOUT THIS. A ***BIG*** MISTAKE!

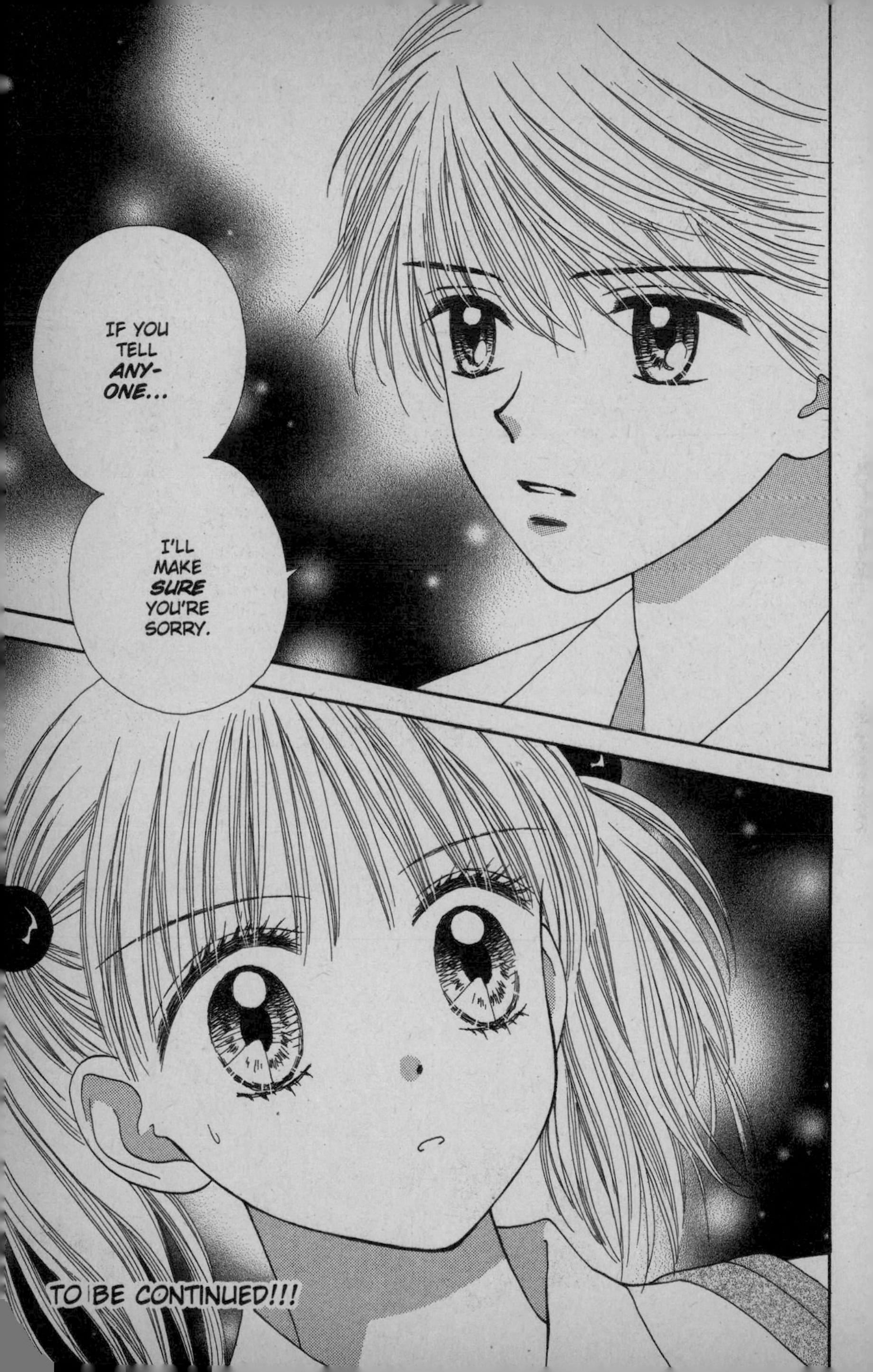
IF YOU TELL ANY-ONE...
I'LL MAKE SURE YOU'RE SORRY.
TO BE CONTINUED!!!

Wataru Yoshizumi

Comments

"A new genre that I attacked with half-anticipation and half-trepidation. I'm doing my best creating this with a lot of trial and error. I hope you'll enjoy it." So writes the creator Wataru Yoshizumi in her heart-to-heart *Diary of Wonders*.

Bio

Wataru Yoshizumi hails from Tokyo and made her manga debut in 1984 with *Radical Romance* in *Ribon Original* magazine. The artist has since produced a string of fan-favorite titles, including *Quartet Game, Handsome na Kanojo* (*Handsome Girl*), *Marmalade Boy*, and *Random Walk. Ultra Maniac,* a magical screwball comedy, is only the second time her work has been available in the U.S. Many of her titles, however, are available throughout Asia and Europe. Yoshizumi loves to travel and is keen on making original accessories out of beads.

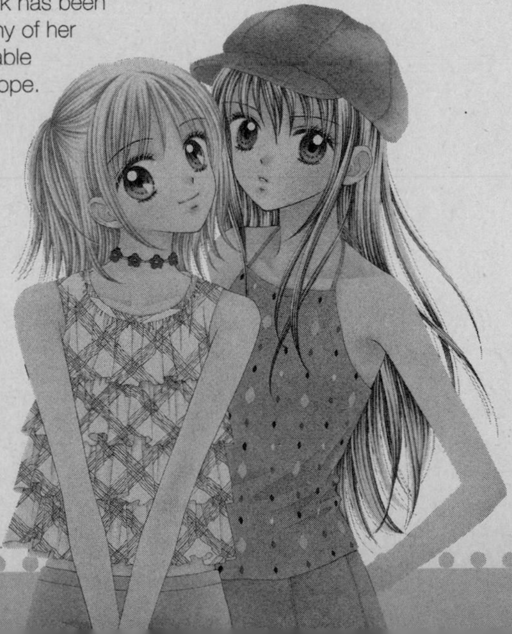

ULTRA MANIAC VOL. 1

The Shojo Beat Manga Edition

**STORY AND ART BY
WATARU YOSHIZUMI**

English Adaptation/John Lustig
Translation/Koji Goto
Touch-up Art & Lettering/Elizabeth Watasin
Cover & Graphic Design/Izumi Evers
Editor/Eric Searleman

Managing Editor/Megan Bates
Director of Production/Noboru Watanabe
Vice President of Publishing/Alvin Lu
Vice President & Editor in Chief/Yumi Hoashi
Sr. Director of Acquisitions/Rika Inouye
Vice President of Sales & Marketing/Liza Coppola
Publisher/Hyoe Narita

Printed in the U.S.A.

Published by VIZ Media, LLC
P.O. Box 77010
San Francisco, CA 94107

Shojo Beat Manga
10 9 8 7 6 5 4 3 2 1
First printing, June 2005

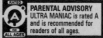

store.viz.com

PARENTAL ADVISORY
ULTRA MANIAC is rated A and is recommended for readers of all ages.

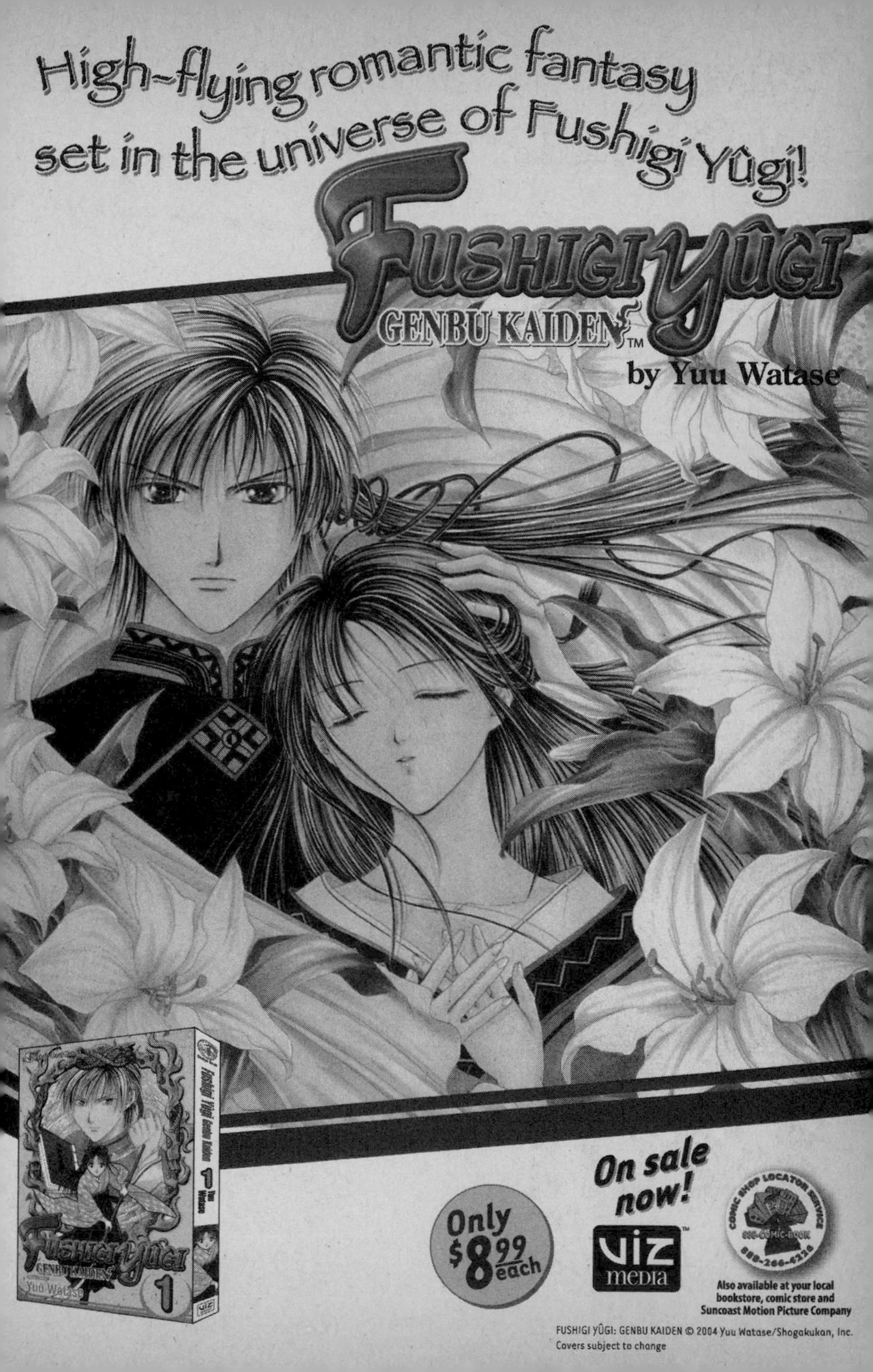
High-flying romantic fantasy
set in the universe of Fushigi Yûgi!
FUSHIGI YÛGI
GENBU KAIDEN™
by Yuu Watase
On sale now!
Only $8.99 each
VIZ media™
COMIC SHOP LOCATOR SERVICE
888-266-4226
Also available at your local bookstore, comic store and Suncoast Motion Picture Company
FUSHIGI YÛGI: GENBU KAIDEN © 2004 Yuu Watase/Shogakukan, Inc.
Covers subject to change

Find the Beat online!
Check us out at

www.shojobeat.com!